A SHORT HISTORY OF

WARFARE

OTHER WORKS BY THE SAME AUTHORS

DAVID H. ZOOK, JR.:

The Evolution of the Chaco Dispute (1959)
The Conduct of the Chaco War (1960)
(revised, enlarged Spanish edition, 1962)
Zarumilla-Marañón; The Ecuador-Peru Dispute (1964)
José de San Martín (1967)

ROBIN HIGHAM:

Britain's Imperial Air Routes, 1918-1939 (1960)
The British Rigid Airship, 1908-1931; a study in weapons policy (1961)
Armed Forces in Peacetime: Britain 1918-1940 (1963)
The Military Intellectuals (1965)
"Official Histories" (1966)

A SHORT HISTORY OF
WARFARE

by

DAVID H. ZOOK, JR.

and

ROBIN HIGHAM

Foreword by

SIR BASIL LIDDELL HART

TWAYNE PUBLISHERS

New York 10003

Second Edition, 1967.

Library of Congress Catalog Card No.: 65-28533

MANUFACTURED IN THE UNITED STATES OF AMERICA

TYPOGRAPHY BY ELECTRA COMPOSITION, NEW YORK 1

Foreword

This "short history of warfare" by Captain David Zook and Dr. Robin Higham admirably fulfils the purpose for which it is designed—as set forth and defined by the joint authors in their Preface. It should be very useful to students, and to the wider reading public that has become increasingly interested in the story of wars and warfare throughout the ages. It is well balanced as well as remarkably free from the basic errors and misinterpretations, arising from prevalent historical myths, that have all too commonly occurred in previous books of this kind that have tried to summarise the course of events and military trends over such a long span of time. There are some points on which I differ from the authors' judgments, but I agree with most of them. Naturally, too, there are places where a fuller exposition of changes in technique, their origin and development, could be desired. Working within the limits of space, however, the authors have succeeded in achieving a summary that distils and provides a remarkable amount of valuable information for students.

For such a compact volume it is also remarkably comprehensive in its scope. It covers all the more significant wars in Europe, from ancient Greece and Rome down through the Middle Ages to early modern times, and then through the seventeenth, eighteenth and nineteenth centuries to the First and Second World Wars. Moreover, it deals with a wide range of wars that are not covered in most historical outlines of this kind. Besides chapters on the American Revolution, the War of 1812, and the Civil War, it has a fairly extensive one on "The Liberation of Spanish South America," as well as shorter sections on the lesser wars of the nineteenth century in various parts of the world.

There is a good outline of military ideas in the various countries between the two World Wars, and the volume ends with a study of the limited wars since 1945 and their bearing on the development of armed forces in a "transitional age." The descriptive outline of wars, large and small, is illuminated by many passages of analytical comment, running throughout the book. It is one that should have a very wide welcome.

Sir Basil Liddell Hart
December 1965

Preface

THE FIELD of military history has never been accorded the academic importance which war, as a major facet of human endeavor, indicates that it merits. Although this situation has improved greatly since World War II, an era when the survival of the Western World has been so clearly dependent upon armed forces in being, there has nevertheless been insufficient offering of military history survey courses in colleges and universities to justify competitive lines of general textbooks. Consequently, each professor of military history has followed his own bent as to emphasis and usually has selected several textbooks for student use.

During the four years that Captain Zook had a major role in shaping the military history program at the United States Air Force Academy, it became clear that no single text was suited to the Academy's survey course; therefore many were used, each for the area of its greatest strength. Some texts neglect the pre-modern period, others focus only on U.S. national military history, others stress Europe, some dwell on technology, and others suffer from serious imperfections of method and scholarship. Professor Higham's experience has confirmed that a resulting and common problem for the military history student is lack of continuity in his textual materials.

This modest volume was conceived as a partial solution and is intended to provide a brief, unified outline history of Western warfare from Marathon to the present. As such, it is designed to accompany more detailed studies and not to stand alone. Where a U.S.-oriented text is used, this book may furnish a minimum background in European military history or vice versa. If a course stresses examination in depth of certain conflicts or periods, it may provide convenient bridging. For the military affairs course, it can give a strategic and tactical background, and even for the Western Civilization program this book can prove useful as a military history supplement. For nearly 200,000 ROTC students, it should be helpful as a study guide.

The ruling principles in the development of *A Short History of Warfare* have been brevity, clarity, and simplicity. Some readers may feel that it is imbalanced, that some wars are accorded more space than others of greater global significance, that naval warfare is neglected, that air war should have more emphasis, or that one or another aspect of strategy could be traced more fully. Some may feel that battles are neglected, and others that they are overly detailed. In keeping with the intended purpose, however, compromises have been necessary at every turn, and the authors hope that their decisions will prove an acceptable least common denominator.

Parts of the manuscript were read critically by distinguished scholars and experts. Of the portion of the book for which Captain Zook assumes responsibility, Dr. Donald Kagan, Cornell University, read Chapters II and III; Dr. Warner F. Woodring, The Ohio State University, Chapters IV-VIII; Dr. Eugene Roseboom, also of Ohio State, IX and X; Dr. Jay Luvaas, Allegheny College, XII-XIII and XIX-XX; Colonel Edward M. Collins, USAF, Chapter XIV; Dr. Otis A. Singletary, University of North Carolina, Greensboro, Chapter XV; and Colonel Mark M. Boatner, III, USA, Chapters XVI-XVIII. Professor Higham's Chapters XXIII-XXXVI were read by Dr. Theodore Ropp, Duke University; Dr. Forrest Pogue, The George C. Marshall Foundation; and Colonel Thomas A. Badger, USA, Kansas State University. The authors are most grateful for the advice that these colleagues have given, and wish to absolve them from responsibility for any errors which may remain.

Finally, the opinions and judgments in this book are those of the authors and do not necessarily reflect the official views of any institution or service with which they have been, or are, associated. Each author is responsible for evaluations and opinions in his portion of the volume.

David H. Zook, Jr.
University of Maryland

Robin Higham
Kansas State University

Contents

List of Maps

CHAPTER I

Introduction to War

I. INTRODUCTION

FROM THE TIME man first settled in the fertile valleys of the Tigris and Euphrates and the Nile, and defended his sedentary agricultural society from the challenge of nomadic herdsmen who coveted his plains, war has been closely related to existence and survival. Conflict has not been an aberration of the historical process, but rather an intimate facet of it. Warfare has both shaped and been influenced by the development of civilization. It has never been far removed from human life. Generations of historians have erred in neglecting its study in favor of other aspects—political, economic, social, and cultural—of human experience. Professional military men have erred by confining their writing to a narrow tactical orientation for the appreciation and edification of other professionals. Separating the study of war from the study of society has been an error that has led to terrible consequences in many ages. Certainly it is not history that repeats itself, but the errors that result from ignorance of history. In this nuclear age, when technology has virtually annihilated time (i.e., the application of firepower over space that once required years is now a matter of minutes), Western man can no longer afford the luxury of ignorance. Knowledge has replaced the club as the instrument of survival.

The specialized study of military operations has not ceased to have value, but the Age of the Atom has placed a greater premium upon the general appreciation of war and its broad environment, than upon the movement of forces in the field. Furthermore, any real understanding of the causes and effects of field action must be acquired within the general context of human experience. For example, to recognize that military technology today is the cornerstone of United States existence requires only an examination of the last budget. Military history, to be meaningful, must consequently be considered as part of a cosmic whole.

II. DETERMINANTS

"The history of mankind has been profoundly influenced by war," wrote Falls. War has affected the course of civilization. All the economic considerations extant in 331 B.C. were rendered meaningless when Alexander the Great applied his unshod, cheaply equipped, saddleless cavalry in a decisive charge against the wealthy army of Darius III. By this victory the course of world history was changed. The resultant Hellenistic society owed its being to a *tactical* stroke in a single battle. The Crusades stimulated the rebirth of Western commerce, not vice versa. The *technological* advantage of firearms helped Cortez and Pizarro to conquer the Aztec and Inca states and liberate treasures which decisively influenced the emergence of modern economy. The *leadership* of Bonaparte spread the ideas of revolutionary France over Europe and revolutionized society. The faulty *doctrine* of twentieth century France facilitated the destruction of the old European system and ushered in an era of groping; the solution of its problems cannot presently be foreseen. Military tactics, technology, doctrine, and leadership have conditioned the course of the world. Most important, they promise to continue to do so.

III. ACTIVITY LEVELS

There are three levels of activity within which the military operates. The highest, *grand strategy,* is concerned with the utilization of all instruments of the state—political, economic, psychosocial, technological, and military—in pursuance of a national goal. The basic or minimal goal is always the preservation of the country, within its own frontiers, and of its political and social system. Wars occur when minimal goals come into conflict, or when one party has a greater aspiration. The second level, *military strategy,* deals with campaigns during which military means are directed toward attainment of the national goal. The lowest level, *tactics,* concerns the conduct of forces in battle in search of the fulfillment of military strategy.

IV. PRINCIPLES OF WAR

Employment of armed force is an art, not an exact science. It may be assessed and contemplated in terms of the principles of war. Widely misunderstood, these premises—ten of which are currently recognized by the United States Air Force and the United States Army—were suggested after World War I by the great English military thinker and historian, Major General J. F. C. Fuller. They were intended as guides to assist the commander and planner in avoiding errors. Although of greatest interest, therefore, to the professional, laymen also should be acquainted with these principles. Succinctly, they are: the *objective,* which must be realizable, clearly understood, and pursued by the commander; the *offensive,* which must be undertaken at the proper time and place if victory is to be achieved; *security,* which must be preserved so that the other principles may be applied unimpeded; *concentration* or *mass,* the commitment of means at the decisive time and place; *economy of force,* the best use of available means; *maneuver,* the positioning of forces through mobility for maximum advantage; *simplicity,* especially in planning; *unity of command,* the concentration of authority and responsibility; *surprise,* striking the enemy in areas least expected. The USAF substitutes *flexibility* for mobility, stressing the ready adjustment of intentions in response to changing circumstances. These principles are not infallible, nor did Fuller intend them to be. They are merely aids to valid judgment. For the student, they provide a synthesis to assist him in understanding military history and its unity. Recognition of this fact is essential if past experience is to be related to present problems.

V. DIMENSIONS OF CONFLICT

Until the twentieth century, war had two dimensions, land and sea. The appearance in World War I of the third dimension, air, added to the complexity of conflict and revolutionized the application of firepower in time and space. Just as increased economic resources and gunpowder enabled early modern rulers strategically to extend the length and breadth of war, and tactically to direct a missile (ball) toward a target more distant than ever before, so the aircraft geographically extended war and made it possible to apply firepower faster and at a greater distance from the base of operations. The space age extends still further the potential scope of operations, but since the aerospace is a single, indivisible medium, no completely new dimension is added.

VI. TERMINOLOGY

Certain basic terms associated primarily with land war are historically paralleled in each of the other dimensions. Consequently, an understanding of them is necessary to any study of the history of war. Fundamental to each is the *base of operations,* or seat of military power from which action is initiated. If the enemy has converged upon the base, then the defender has the advantage of *operations on interior lines*—an advantage which lies in the greater ease of shifting forces to meet the external threat, in maintaining communications, and in the distance to be covered to reach the opponent. In the same situation, the foe is operating on *convergent lines,* i.e., he is converging on the base from different directions.

Concentration, necessary before opening battle, occurs *on the field* when forces are assembled immediately in front of the enemy, or *off the field* when troops are brought together before advancing toward the foe.

After concentrating, offensive action may be undertaken. Several forms of attack exist. A *coordinated attack* finds all forces employed deliberately and in unity. A *piecemeal attack* develops when successive units are thrown into action, often as they arrive from a rear area. This, of course, has grave disadvantages and is seldom successful. A *frontal attack* is an assault directly upon the enemy, and is not generally desirable. A *secondary attack* seeks to fix him in position, often to cover maneuver at another point. A *penetration* involves driving through the enemy's front.

The more advantageous forms of offensive action involve maneuver. An *envelopment* consists of striking the flank or rear of the opponent, a *double envelopment* occurs on both his flanks and seeks to surround and destroy him. Envelopments attempt to defeat him in position. A *turning movement,* which is broader than an envelopment and does not anticipate direct contact, aims at lines of communications or vitals well to the enemy rear and endeavors to render his position untenable, obliging him to retreat. A *strategic envelopment,* the highest goal of the strategist, is a very broad maneuver in space aimed at sealing off the entire zone of operations from its home base.

There are several forms of defense. An *offensive-defense* lures the foe into weakening himself by attacking under unfavorable circumstances that are conducive to successful counterattack. A *cordon defense* is a line of equal strength at all points, usually lacking in depth, and with few forces in reserve. A *mobile defense* relies upon depth and strong reserve forces to meet enemy thrusts. It may employ a series of strong points and exploits flexibility. A variant is the *position defense,* in which a given line is to be held, not necessarily with equal strength at all points, and with reserves available.

If defense fails, retrograde movements will ensue. A *withdrawal* (voluntarily) endeavors to break contact with the enemy in order to retain freedom of action. A *retirement* (under pressure) seeks to avoid decisive action or defeat by marching away. A *retreat* is really the same thing, but is the term used for psychological reasons when the opponent retires. A *rout* is a retreat in which the commander loses control and his force disintegrates. A *delaying* or Fabian *action* is a fighting retirement over successive positions. It endeavors to gain time without accepting a decisive engagement.

There are two forms of following a retreating enemy. In reality, pursuit is a new attack, and should be pressed to the last resource to complete the destruction of the foe. A *direct pursuit* advances along the same lines the opponent has chosen for retreat, and maintains continuing direct contact with him. An *encircling pursuit* is a type of envelopment aimed at getting behind the enemy and forcing him to accept surrender or a last-ditch engagement under unfavorable conditions after he has already been defeated.

CHAPTER II

Greek Warfare

I. INTRODUCTION

THE GREEKS of the Homeric Age filtered out of the Balkans and formed communities fragmented in fertile valleys among the mountains of Greece. There they preserved their original tribal structure around an acropolis, or fortified stronghold. In time, on this nucleus developed the city-state or *polis* to which each citizen, descendant of the original conquerors, owed fervent allegiance. Particularism reigned and unity could be imposed only by force of arms.

A favorable climate, naturally defensive terrain, and an initial lack of population pressure permitted the development of stable societies. When population grew beyond the limited agricultural capacity of the valleys, the Greeks emigrated and colonized coastal areas by the seas, but each new city was independent rather than part of an empire. The new settlements along the Black Sea and in Sicily provided vital food exports to the homeland and maritime commerce became a vital part of Greek life.

II. CHARACTER OF GREEK WAR

Greek warfare was peculiarly unsuited to aggression. The standard formation, the phalanx, emulated earlier Asiatic practice. Infantry probably never enjoyed such an elite status. Every free citizen was obligated to serve as a heavily armored soldier, or *hoplite*. Slaves and aliens performed menial tasks; free men made war. Improved smelting made possible a relatively large, cheaper armor production. When a war call was issued, the citizen gathered his equipment and took his place in the phalanx. The position of greatest honor was in the front rank; the least desirable in the eighth, or last. The hoplite held an elliptical shield on his left arm, and carried a nine-foot spear in his right hand. Typically, a battle saw two such cumbersome formations advance until they met, whereupon war became a contest of brute force against brute force. The discipline of free men and great physical stamina were necessary to retain the formation.

Given limited domestic food production, the usual objective was the enemy's crops. Consequently, the autumn harvest season was favored for war, and standing armies were unnecessary. Since the soldier was a citizen militiaman who had his own crops and affairs which demanded attention, armies could not long remain in the field. War usually was decided in a single battle with victory going to the heaviest, most rugged files. Battles occurred on the few level areas near the fields. The phalanx was prone to break up and lose its natural defensive character when crossing broken ground. Increased mobility was impossible because speed meant loss of dress. Generalship had no place, for control vanished when battle began. There was no contending cavalry tradition because Greece was not geographically suited to horses; neither was siege warfare well developed. Consequently, organization, terrain, state of the military art, and society were not conducive to fielding aggressor forces for extended periods. Military imperialism was limited, and no state was able to dominate all of Greece.

III. PERSIAN WAR

A. Background

Greece faced her first foreign foe in the fifth century, the Persian Empire, the greatest military power of the age. Its imperial army consisted of levies of the great landholders, who constituted the Persian ruling class, and their retainers. Cavalry and archers were the main components, while infantry consisted of hill tribes and serfs acting as skirmishers. Decimally organized into divisions of 10,000, the Persian Army was a formidable instrument.

Emperor Darius (521-483 B.C.) had consolidated his domain and organized it into twenty great satrapies ruled by efficient governors and united by fleet runners on royal roads. After securing his Northern and Indus River frontiers, Darius was left with only the problem of the West. The natural limit of the empire was the Aegean, but there were Greeks on each shore. The only viable solution, an ethnic frontier, necessitated the conquest of Greece. This was the first struggle between East and West.

B. *Marathon (21 September 490 B.C.)*

The immediate excuse was Athenian aid to Miletus—one of the Greek cities on the Asia Minor coast—which rebelled against Persia. Within Athens the democratic party was pro-Persian, while Miltiades, the recently returned tyrant of Gallipoli, assumed the leadership of conservatives bent on resistance. Darius believed that if the Athenian Army could be enticed from the city, his "fifth column" could seize power and betray the polis, the Peloponnesus could be cut off, and the backbone of Greece could be broken. Obviously, perennial Greek internal discord was borne in his mind.

Miltiades persuaded the Athenians to march out to meet the enemy force that had landed at the Bay of Marathon. Sparta, the other most powerful polis, agreed to participate in the expedition after a religious festival on the night of 19 September. Athens' army of about 10,000 therefore marched with only 1,000 Plataean allies. After the armies had confronted one another for several days, Miltiades, as *strategos* or commander of one of the ten Athenian tribes among whom the position of Chief of Staff rotated, won consent for an attack. On 21 September it became his turn to draw up a plan of action. He weakened the center of the Greek line to four ranks for the half-mile downhill charge. Since Persian archery had a range of 200 yards, the attack had to be rapid beyond that point. Whether by accident or design, the heavier flanks advanced faster; when the Persians pushed back the weak center, they found themselves taken in the first recorded double envelopment. Morale collapsed and a slaughter of the numerically superior Persians ensued; they lost 6,400 but Greek casualties were only 192.

Rapidly returning to Athens, the army prevented Persian seizure of the city. That evening the Spartan van arrived and marched on to Marathon to view the enemy dead. Marathon was not a decisive battle; it marked only the beginning of the Persian wars, but it elevated Greek morale and, says Fuller, "was the birth cry of Europe."

C. *Salamis (23 September 480 B.C.)*

Darius was diverted from further action by a revolt in Egypt and died before it was suppressed. In 484 B.C. his son Xerxes (485-465 B.C.) began preparing a huge expedition against Greece, crossed the Hellespont in 481 B.C. on two bridges of 674 ships lashed together, and descended into Greece. His land and sea forces were mutually supporting. Under Spartan leadership, the Greeks held a Panhellenic Conference at Corinth and resolved to use their numerically inferior forces to strategic advantage by delaying the enemy land advance at the pass of Thermopylae long enough to lure him to attempt to outflank them by sea through the strait of Salamis. There, crowded quarters would benefit the small Greek fleet. An army under Leonidas, the Spartan king, was divided at Thermopylae, where the commander and his 300-man royal guard were killed. Xerxes poured through and the Peloponnesians began abandoning Northern Greece and fortifying the Isthmus of Corinth. Although Athens came under siege, her leader, Themistocles, went ahead with the naval strategy.

To deceive Xerxes, Themistocles sent him a message that the other Greeks were withdrawing into the Peloponnesus, that Themistocles opposed this, and that if Xerxes made haste he could prevent their evacuation and win the war. The Persian fell into the trap and left the Greek allies no alternative but to fight. Greek naval war was similar to land warfare; a general commanded the fleet of triremes, or three bank galleys. Ramming and boarding were the usual modes of fighting. The Persian fleet, which was largely Egyptian and Phoenician, entered the narrow Salamis Straits and was defeated in a tactically uninteresting action. Strategically, Salamis was the decisive action of the war, for it denied Xerxes command of the sea and rendered his land position untenable.

IV. PELOPONNESIAN WAR

A. *Delian League*

In the face of a continuing Persian threat, Greek survival came to depend upon naval power organized under Athenian leadership into the Delian League. In the quest for security, sea power became the strategic deterrent of the day. Athens gradually extended her power. In 454 B.C. she removed the League treasury from the island of Delos, denied her allies the right of secession, urged democracy upon them, and converted the League into the first naval empire. She flourished and became a splendid imperial capital and cultural center. Commerce progressed rapidly as an export olive oil and wine economy replaced subsistence agriculture, and grain was imported from the Black Sea to feed the citizens. Prosperity and leisure—and the attempt to preserve them—led to the construction of the Long Walls connecting Athens with her port. Relatively secure from attack, Athens could for the first time pursue a policy of offensive action. The lower classes came to share the burden of expanded war, the manning of the fleet, and in return citizenship was extended to them. The sum of these effects of Salamis was the undermining of the moral fibre of old agrarian Athens.

B. *Peloponnesian Confederation*

Sparta, meanwhile, remained the great land power. To solve her food problems she had conquered neighboring lands. The original inhabitants, called *helots,* were kept in servitude to till the soil. Every Spartan male was born to a heritage of landed aristocracy with military responsibility. His life of service lasted from seven years of age, when he was taken from his mother, until he was sixty. This vigorous system produced the best infantry of the age, but it subordinated all other aspects of life to defense and preservation of internal order; i.e., the master-serf relationship of ruling class and helot.

C. *The Conflict (431-404 B.C.)*

The inevitable clash between Sparta's Confederation and Athens' League produced the Peloponnesian War. Athens attempted to intervene in internal matters in the island of Corcyra, which lay astride the coastal shipping lanes to Sicily. This provoked hostilities between the two contending systems. Ultimately, Sparta secured financial aid from Persia, created her own fleet, and in 405 B.C., at Aegospotami in the Dardanelles defeated Athens which had become undermined financially by the lengthy conflict. The Long Walls were destroyed and Athens lost predominance. The war saw the emergence of class struggle throughout the Greek community, which rent it asunder. Many hoplites, when peace came, turned professional and hired out as mercenaries because they knew no other occupation, and because many citizens no longer wished to assume military obligations.

In a preponderant position, Sparta attempted to enforce her oligarchical political system in place of the democracy which Athens had pressed upon her allies. Unfortunately the defeat of Athens destroyed the balance of power with Persia. To suppress revolts, Sparta in 386 B.C. accepted the King's Peace by which the emperor became the arbiter of Greece, guaranteeing Spartan hegemony in exchange for abandonment of the Asiatic Greek states.

V. THEBAN POWER

Thebes replaced Spartan domination in 371 B.C. when Epaminondas, in the tradition of Theban innovation, defeated the Spartans at Leuctra by means of an oblique order, or refused flank. His left was well in advance and deepened, while his right was drawn back. Thebes' ascent depended upon the life of her field commander, who was killed in 362 B.C. Thus, three great city-states, Athens, Sparta, and Thebes had successively sought to solve the problem of Greek unity and all had failed. The particularism of the polis was too strong an obstacle, and Greek unification awaited the impositions of an outside conqueror.

VI. ALEXANDER OF MACEDON

A. Philip

This conqueror, as a boy hostage in the household of Epaminondas, had been grounded in the Theban art of war, the only breath of tactical innovation in all Greek military history. A skilled diplomatist, practical, and unscrupulous, Philip II in 359 B.C. became King of Macedonia. The Greeks considered his country barbaric, but it was well suited to its task because it had preserved unity under a personal monarchy. Furthermore, Philip's great ambition was to unify Greece with himself as Captain General and then to wage war against Persia. In September 338 B.C. he defeated Thebes and Athens at Chaeronea and "sounded the death-knell of the independent polis." At the Congress of Corinth he imposed unity, universal peace, and a perpetual alliance with Macedonia upon all Greece except for Sparta, which held out until 331 B.C.

The following year he presented to the Federal Council his project for war on Persia. Proposed as a holy war to avenge Persian outrages, he realized it would unite Greece in a common cause. Such a crusade had been preached by the Athenian Isocrates (436-338 B.C.) who commended it to Philip in his *Philippus*. When the council voted for war and appointed Philip supreme commander, he initiated action by pushing a force across the Hellespont in 336 B.C. Philip was assassinated and succeeded by his twenty-one year old son, Alexander.

B. The Army

The military instrument Alexander inherited was the finest of classical times, the first balanced army in history. The King's personal force consisted of the Companion Cavalry of eight 200-man squadrons, and the Hypaspists or *agema,* three 1,000-man foot battalions. There was also the standing army of six 1,536-man regiments derived from the old Macedonian tribal levies. The hoplites carried a longer, fourteen-foot spear and formed a sixteen-rank phalanx. Contingents of allied and subject peoples rounded out the infantry and cavalry. The latter rode bareback on unshod horses. Nevertheless, it was the decisive arm. There were archers, javelin men and slingers, a siege train or artillery, engineering corps, and probably a medical service. The first efficient supply service supported the army.

C. *The Idea*

According to Tarn, Alexander invaded Persia because he had never thought of doing otherwise. He had doubtless read Xenophon's *Anabasis,* which detailed the fighting exit from Persia of a force of stranded Greek mercenaries. Certainly, he understood clearly the vulnerability of the polyglot Persian Empire to a moral attack and to the defection of satraps. Tutored by Aristotle, he loved Greek culture and hated Persia. His knowledge of contemporary geography enabled him to view the world as comprising little more than Greece, Egypt, and Persia. Yet his war theatre was immense, with an estimated population of some fifty millions. This was an auspicious time, for the enemy was not the Persia of Xerxes but of Darius III, a weakling with unreliable satraps. The Persians had abandoned reliance on archers, but still had plenty of good cavalry from the great landholders. The road system, however, which held the empire together, could be converted to a liability by a bold enemy. Such a one was Alexander.

D. *The Invasion of Persia*

1. ASIA MINOR

After securing Greece and Macedonia, Alexander, bankrupt, set out in 334 B.C. with about 40,000 men, to capture Persian financial resources as the initial objective. In June on the river Granicus he defeated 20,000 enemy cavalry who were supported by Greek mercenaries. Proclaiming himself the champion of Greek democracy against Persian tyranny, he subverted most of the Asiatic Greek towns, but they did not join the League of Corinth. Finding his communications threatened by the Persian fleet, he adopted the strategy of defeating it on land by taking its ports. In October 333 B.C. he overcame Darius in person at Issus. Asia Minor had been conquered, but Alexander held to his strategy and moved south along the coast. Thus he first passed beyond what was probably his original intention, the conquest only of Asia Minor. He had set up financial control of the conquered areas. Occupying Damascus, he captured Darius' war chest and thus ended his own financial problems.

2. TYRE

When the Phoenician port of Tyre refused to welcome him, Alexander conducted one of the most famous sieges of all times. The great fortress city stood on an island half a mile from shore. Alexander began a mole toward it, but the besieged came out in boats after a fire ship attack and tore down the mole. He formed a fleet and sealed off the city by sea, placed war machines on barges, and attempted to bring the walls down. The Tyrians sank great rocks which Alexander swept away and finally breached the wall to end the seven-month siege in July 332 B.C. This gave him Syria, uncovered Egypt, and enabled him to achieve his aim of dominating the Eastern Mediterranean. Nullification of the enemy fleet, securing his communications, and occupation of Egypt cleared the way for Alexander's movement into the heart of the Persian Empire.

3. ARBELA (1 OCTOBER 331 B.C.)

Darius had made a tremendous effort to assemble a new army capable of defeating Alexander, although, as Tarn says, the most necessary step was the removal of Darius himself from command. The imperial cavalry levies were rearmed with short spears, but Greek mercenaries could no longer be had and there was no other source of quality infantry. Avoiding pitched battle and wearing Alexander down would have been the best course, but

Darius' dignity demanded otherwise. Therefore, to counter the phalanx, the Persians began forming a force of 200 scythed chariots, but there was not adequate time to train the drivers to act in unison.

In the summer of 331 B.C. Alexander crossed the Euphrates and Tigris and advanced toward the village of Gaugamela where occurred the Battle of Arbela, one of the most decisive of all time. Alexander had 7,000 cavalry and 40,000 infantry. Darius' army was vastly superior in numbers, and he carefully drew it up with cavalry and chariots in front of the infantry line. Alexander characteristically positioned his crack cavalry on the right with the agema on its left as an anchor point. His remaining foot was in the center, while his left consisted of allied cavalry. The Persians stood at arms all night, but Alexander gave his men a good meal and sleep.

As the battle developed, the javelin men broke the charge of the Persian chariots. Alexander advanced in an oblique order from the right, withstood enemy charges, and when a gap appeared in the Persian front, he himself led the Companion cavalry in a charge against the decisive point, Darius himself. The emperor fled the field, covered by his foot guard who fought to the death. When these facts became known, a rout took place and Alexander pursued the enemy until darkness, rested until midnight, and resumed the advance, determined that Darius should never be able to re-create an army. The vitals of the empire had been exposed. Alexander occupied Babylon, but continued operations until the murder of Darius in 330 B.C. left him unopposed as King of Kings.

4. RESULTS

Although Alexander conducted consolidation campaigns within the empire and fought one of his most brilliant battles in India on the Hydaspes, Arbela was his decisive action. By force of arms he profoundly altered the character of the world. Behind his army advanced a wave of Hellenistic civilization to unify his empire and carry into execution Alexander's great idea, the brotherhood and unity of mankind. The city he founded in Egypt, Alexandria, became the center of an intellectual movement of inquiry. By establishing common coinage and increasing the amount of precious metals in circulation, Alexander provided the lubrication for a quickening world commerce. When he died in 323 B.C. at the age of thirty-three, he had remade the world with the military instrument bequeathed by his father. The societal developments of the feuding Greeks had paradoxically become the norm for a unified mankind.

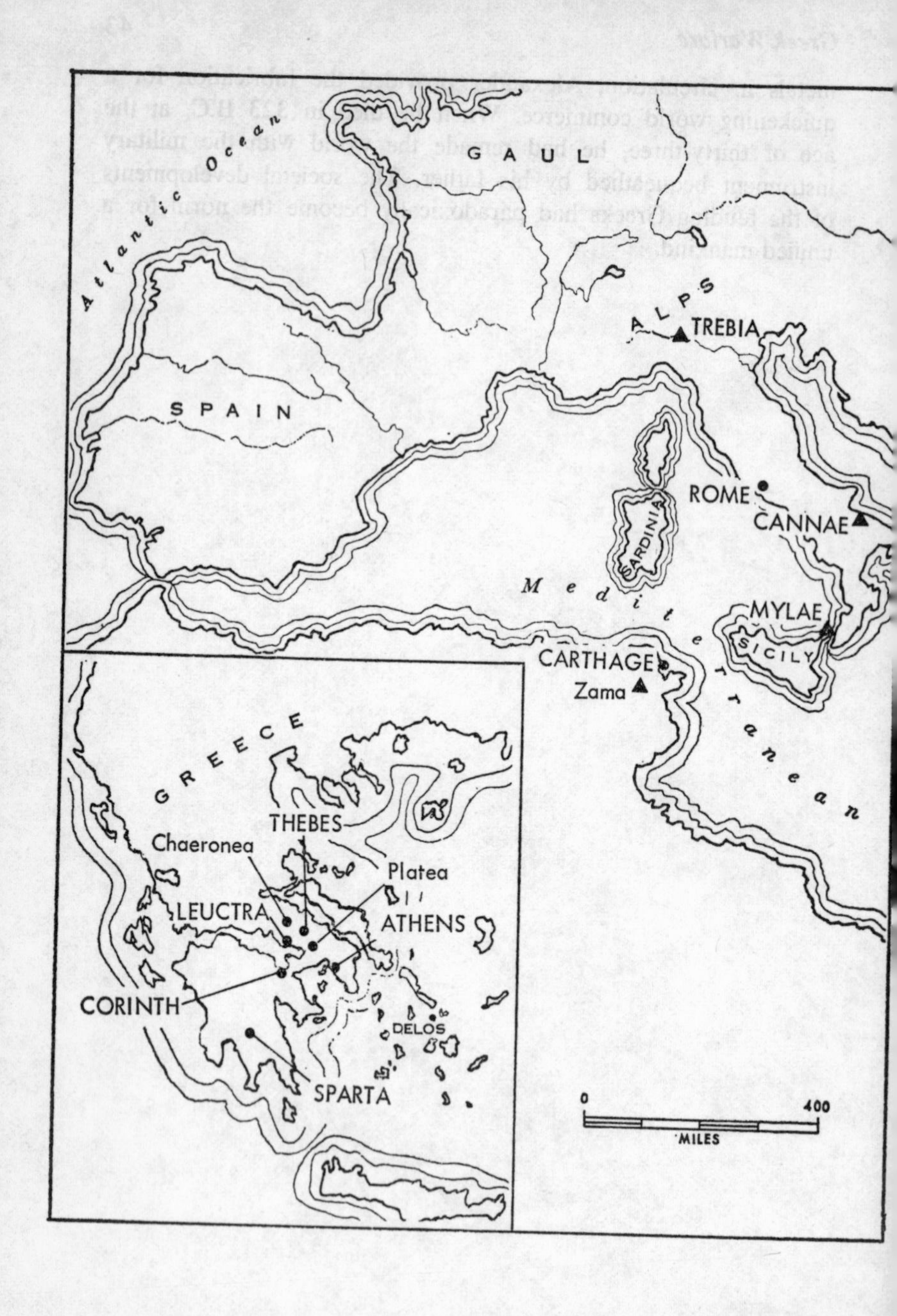
GAUL
Atlantic Ocean
ALPS
TREBIA
SPAIN
ROME
CANNAE
SARDINIA
Mediterranean
MYLAE
SICILY
CARTHAGE
Zama
GREECE
THEBES
Chaeronea
Platea
LEUCTRA
ATHENS
CORINTH
DELOS
SPARTA
0
400
MILES

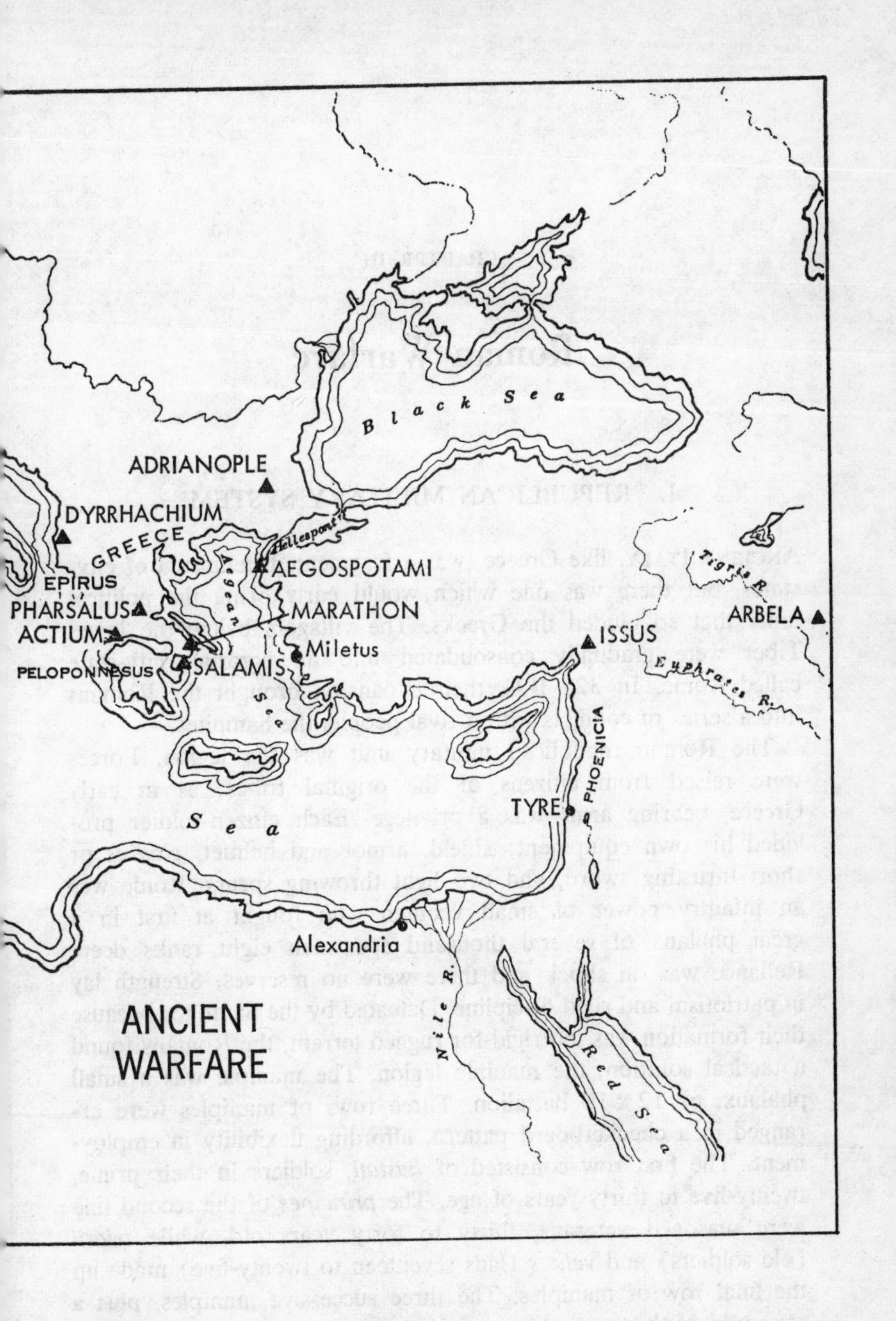

Black Sea
ADRIANOPLE
DYRRHACHIUM
GREECE
Hellespont
AEGOSPOTAMI
EPIRUS
Aegean Sea
PHARSALUS
MARATHON
ACTIUM
Miletus
PELOPONNESUS
SALAMIS
ISSUS
ARBELA
Tigris R.
Euphrates R.
PHOENICIA
TYRE
Sea
Alexandria
Nile R.
Red Sea
ANCIENT WARFARE

CHAPTER III

Roman Warfare

I. REPUBLICAN MILITARY SYSTEM

ANCIENT ITALY, like Greece, was a fragmented peninsula of city-states, but there was one which would early bring the political unity that so eluded the Greeks. The villagers below the lower Tiber were gradually consolidated into an agrarian city-state called Rome. In 325 B.C. their expansion brought the Romans into a series of conflicts with a rival people, the Samnites.

The Roman republican military unit was the legion. Forces were raised from citizens of the original tribes; as in early Greece, bearing arms was a privilege. Each citizen-soldier provided his own equipment: shield, armor and helmet, *gladius* or short thrusting sword, and two light throwing spears. Rome was an infantry power of small yeomen who fought at first in a great phalanx of several thousand spearmen eight ranks deep. Reliance was on shock and there were no reserves. Strength lay in patriotism and rigid discipline. Defeated by the Samnites because their formation was too rigid for rugged terrain, the Romans found a tactical solution, the maniple legion. The maniple was a small phalanx, or 12 x 10 battalion. Three rows of maniples were arranged in a checkerboard pattern, affording flexibility in employment. The first row consisted of *hastati,* soldiers in their prime, twenty-five to thirty years of age. The *principes* of the second line were seasoned veterans, thirty to forty years old, while *triarii* (old soldiers) and *velites* (lads seventeen to twenty-five) made up the final row of maniples. The three successive maniples, plus a squadron of thirty cavalry, constituted a loose *cohort* of 450 men.

A legion consisted of ten such cohorts. Each maniple individually was engaged for shock effect. This military system evolved gradually in response to geography and early defeats inflicted by the Samnites.

Roman government reflected society and rested upon the family unit headed by the tribal citizen. The soundly conservative, patrician Senate was the chief political entity. Two consuls or executives were elected annually and alternated daily in command of the army. While this reduced the danger of military tyranny, it also prevented unity of command and constituted a grave military weakness. Conquered peoples in Italy were treated as allies and allowed to preserve their local autonomy. Eventually, Roman citizenship was extended to all of them. The peninsula was united by splendid roads.

Having conquered the Samnites, the Romans faced the colonial Greek city-states of southern Italy. The latter appealed for aid to Pyrrhus, King of Epirus, a leading soldier of the day. He landed in Italy in 280 B.C. and won several battles at such high cost that the term "Pyrrhic victory," denoting a costly success, entered the language. The Roman maniples proved their mastery over the Greek phalanx and forced the Epirote from Italy with the comment, "What a battlefield I am leaving for Carthage and Rome."

II. THE PUNIC WARS

A. *First Punic War (265-241 B.C.)*

Carthage, a powerful African sea power, was certain to clash with rising Rome. Rome's initial problem was how to combat the enemy navy which dominated the western Mediterranean. A beached Carthaginian trireme provided a ship model. Ignorant of naval practice and always indifferent sailors, the Romans sought to place sea war on a man-to-man basis in order to exploit the advantage of their legionaries. The solution was the *corvi,* an 18-foot plank pivoted from the mast and tipped by a hook for grappling. It enabled infantry to charge across to the vessels to wage a land battle on the decks. At Mylae in 260 B.C., Rome won her first naval victory, gaining control of the waters about Sicily. On the island itself and on Sardinia, the legions also were victorious and acquired Rome's first overseas possessions, marking her embarkation upon the road to empire.

B. Second Punic War (219-202 B.C.)

To compensate for her losses in the central Mediterranean, Carthage extended her sphere of influence into Spain. An uneasy truce with Rome, then occupied by a frontier war against the Gauls of northern Italy, divided Spain along the Ebro. In 219 B.C. war again broke out.

1. HANNIBAL

Carthage had produced a brilliant leader in Hannibal, who understood the revolution in the art of war born of Alexander's use of cavalry. He was able to motivate men of many nationalities to fight for him alone. Rapidly he conquered all of Spain. In 218 B.C. after securing his Spanish base, Hannibal began a strategically indirect approach to Italy by land. His objective was not to conquer, but to break up Rome's confederation of subject peoples. By moving through southern Gaul, he hoped to acquire allies for the destruction of Roman power.

Hannibal's crossing of the Alps in October's snows was a tremendous feat. It was a reflection of careful planning, intelligence collection, skill, and energy. With a balanced army of 20,000 foot and 6,000 horse, Hannibal debouched into the Po Valley and crushed a Roman army at Trebia in December 218 B.C. by the use of his splendid cavalry. In April he left winter quarters and placed his forces between the armies of the two Roman consuls. On the shores of Lake Trasimene he concealed his troops along the high ground to the east of the lake, trapped the marching Romans front and rear in a defile, and annihilated an army of 40,000. "By the simple effectiveness of his plan of battle," wrote Dupuy, "Hannibal destroyed the morale of his enemy and nullified his powers of resistance. The intellect of the great Carthaginian was the deciding factor."

2. CANNAE (2 AUGUST 216 B.C.)

Rome responded to military disaster by temporarily surrendering the republic to a capable military dictator, Fabius. The Roman contested Hannibal with a series of small actions, avoiding pitched battle and falling back over successive positions. He kept to the hills, where Carthaginian cavalry was neutralized. While this highly effective conception won a breathing spell and weakened enemy morale, pressure from the populace against *Fabian tactics* led to the consul's replacement by Paulus and the aggressive, but stupid, Terentius Varro. Hannibal knew the temper of Varro and that most of his army had been raised hastily and poorly trained. He therefore provoked the enemy by seizing a depot at Cannae and dominating the surrounding wheat country.

Hannibal drew up his army for battle with his infantry in the center, his heavy cavalry on the left opposite the Roman horse and 2,000 light cavalry on the right. Varro, whose day it was to command, sacrificed flexibility for weight, abandoned the maniple and massed his troops. The legionaries pushed Hannibal's center backward into a crescent. This well suited his purpose. Cavalry and the elite Carthaginian infantry phalanx enclosed Varro's men in a double envelopment. Panic struck the hapless Romans; 70,000 perished. Carthaginian shock and mobility had readily bested maniple infantry. Once again Hannibal, the superior tactician, had inflicted a crushing defeat upon the efficient but poorly generaled enemy. The elected citizen-generals were no match for the skilled, professional commander who appreciated that war is an art.

Rome did not collapse—a credit to her resiliency—and Cannae passed into history as a tactically brilliant but strategically indecisive battle. Fabius returned to power, mustered new forces, and maintained the allegiance of the Italian peoples. Hannibal, unassisted by Carthage, was left the nuisance role of devastating the countryside. His great shortcoming was inability to wage successful siege operations against walled cities. After thirteen years, an army of reinforcement was defeated in 207 B.C. at the Metaurus in northern Italy. With it failed Hannibal's invasion of Rome.

3. SCIPIO

In desperation, Rome elected twenty-four-year-old P. Cornelius Scipio as consul and gave him command in Spain. Scipio realized that Hannibal could best be defeated there and in Africa. Consequently he seized Cartagena (New Carthage) and embarked upon an unbroken record of successes. While other generals profited little from Rome's defeats, Scipio learned more from them and from the great Hannibal, than he did from his own victories. He quickly proved himself expert at *gaining* and *retaining* the strategic initiative. With Spain conquered, Scipio in 205 B.C. received Sicily as a province. There he formed a small veteran army of 25,000, with which a year later he invaded Africa itself. By diplomacy he secured the support of Numidian allies, who brought him invaluable cavalry contingents. Carrying the war to the Carthaginian homeland secured the objective of Hannibal's recall from Italy. The Carthaginians, their food supplies threatened, pressed the Great Captain for immediate action, thus further acceding to Scipio's wishes.

4. ZAMA (202 B.C.)

Scipio fell back from the gates of the city, luring Hannibal—by the reciprocal attraction of forces—to an arena of his own choosing. On an open field, where the Carthaginians were short of water and he could apply superiority in newly arrived Numidian cavalry, Scipio met the master. There was no fortress at hand in which Hannibal could seek refuge if defeated. When Scipio in a parley refused to treat, Hannibal had no choice but to accept battle. His elephant charge was neutralized by a clever troop disposition, his cavalry was driven from the field, his infantry was defeated and, finally, returning Roman and allied cavalry administered the coup de grâce. More than 20,000 fell in battle and with them died Carthaginian power.

5. RESULTS

Zama decided the rule of the western Mediterranean and turned Rome onto "the high-road of world domination." She modified her citizen-based military system, creating a long-term imperial professional force. Rome's democratic development was arrested. Devastation of Italy had ruined small freeholders; war profits plowed into cheap land created a class of great landed aristocrats who operated their *latifundia* with slave labor procured by conquests. The displaced farmers swelled the unemployed Roman city herd existing on doles; worse, their destruction as a class eliminated the traditional source of citizen soldiers. The solid virtues of old rural Rome were undermined by the fruits of conquest. War had indeed altered the character of Roman society and now came to dominate it.

Rome next turned eastward where the empire of Alexander had disintegrated into the three states of Macedonia, Syria, and Egypt. At Pydna in 168 B.C. the degenerate phalanx collapsed before the legion; Macedonia went with it. Eastern victories brought Rome great stores of precious metals which affected her economy; more important, they introduced as slaves cultured, learned Greeks who transmitted Hellenistic culture. As a result, Rome not only stood politically astride the Mediterranean world, but she became the melting pot into which all the progress of classical man was stirred into a unique brew: Western Civilization.

C. *Third Punic War (146 B.C.)*

Rome had conquered an empire, but her senatorial government structure had fashioned no viable system of imperial organization. Proconsuls, sent to rule provinces, had virtually unlimited powers which could be employed against the state. The attempt to govern the classical world with the instrumentalities of a small agrarian democracy led to civil disorder and a century of conflicts of consolidation. Perhaps the most brutal of these ventures was the annihilation of Carthage. By sound administration, the African city had resumed a position of harmless prosperity which excited Roman greed. Cato preached the doctrine that Rome would never be safe as long as Carthage existed. Despite Carthaginian efforts to appease the rapacious enemy at her gates, the city was starved out and obliterated.

III. EMERGENCE OF IMPERIAL ROME

Altered social conditions provoked by wars of conquest created a hotbed of class struggle which invited the appearance of ambitious men who could mold politics and the army for their own purposes. The first of these, Marius, secured repeated illegal election as consul through demagoguery; he exploited his authority to reshape the armed forces. By eliminating property qualifications for service, he opened the ranks to the proletariat and made the legion mercenary rather than patriotic. Given the decline in virtue of the soldiers, the maniple, predicated upon the initiative of men of quality, was replaced by a new organization: the cohort. Ten 360-man cohorts made up the new formation. They were trained with most severe discipline by gladiators for less flexible mass tactics. In the field men slept each night in a palisaded camp the layout of which was precise and always the same. The legion became essentially the property of its commander, owing its allegiance to him, rather than to the state. It afforded him a military instrument of personal political power.

A. *Caesar*

The greatest of the Roman political generals was Julius Caesar. Entering a military career late in life, Caesar took command in Gaul. There he taught himself the art of war, profiting from experience. He was a man of great personal courage, an inspiring leader who fully understood the moral factor, an able organizer and an adept practitioner of mobility. He recognized the importance of intelligence. Primarily, he was a great general because he appreciated time in war. Decisiveness and speed, both intellectual and tactical, distinguished him. In his Gallic campaigns, Caesar added present-day France and the area west of the Rhine to the Roman Empire and invaded primitive Britain. Ever ambitious for political power, he wrote his classic *Conquest of Gaul* as propaganda for home consumption. The primitive, ill-organized Gauls were no fair match in quality for trained legionaries, but the conquest of Gaul required eight years and was a grand adventure in empire.

Threatened with removal from command because of his growing popularity and power, Caesar crossed the Rubicon into Italy 16 December 50 B.C. and, despite numerically inferior forces, mastered the country within two months. This brought him into conflict with Pompey, a powerful general who had returned victorious from campaigns in the East. Opening operations against Pompeian generals in Spain, Caesar defeated them through maneuver without battle and then turned rapidly to Pompey himself in

Greece. Wintering in Albania, Caesar was repulsed; he lost his fleet at Dyrrhachium, but marched into Greece seeking ultimate victory. Pompey followed.

B. *Pharsalus (9 August 48 B.C.)*

By maneuver, Caesar lured Pompey into a plain where each rested a flank upon a river. Caesar stationed six cohorts behind his right in a position to support his inferior cavalry force. Pompey's superior legions awaited the attack in position. As Caesar's cavalry was driven back, his reserve cohorts struck the flank of the enemy horse and disrupted its advance. Pompey thereupon fled the field. Caesar committed his reserves at the tactical culminating point in a flank attack which led to overwhelming victory. His pursuit was exceptionally vigorous. He followed Pompey to Egypt, became involved with its Queen Cleopatra, and wasted time, which enabled the Pompeian forces to rally in Spain and Africa. Not until 45 B.C. did he eliminate all military opposition. Superior generalship briefly established Julius Caesar as "perpetual dictator" of Rome. This emasculated the constitution and paved the way for the political conversion of the Republic into the Empire.

C. *Actium (2 September 31 B.C.)*

After Julius Caesar's assassination, intermittent civil conflict broke out between his lieutenant, Mark Anthony, and his designated heir and grand-nephew, Octavian. In the popular mind the contest was between East and West, for Anthony ruled in Egypt with Cleopatra, while Octavian's seat was in Rome. Anthony advanced from Egypt and, although Rome was always primarily a land power, the decisive battle took shape on the eastern Ionian. The legionaries were the principal factor on sea, as well as on land.

Octavian's ships severed Anthony's supply lines and left him little choice but battle. The latter knew that the wind blew strongly seaward in the afternoon. He planned to turn Octavian's left, drive his fleet downwind, and thus isolate his land forces. Each employed over 200 galleys with about 40,000 men on board. Anthony's heavier craft hurled stones and arrows in showers and cast the *harpago,* a flying grappling hook attached to a winch, used to reel in snagged vessels. The lighter, speedier, two-bank

Italian ships relied upon maneuver, flaming arrows, and ramming to disable the Egyptians. Defeated and betrayed by subordinates, Anthony and Cleopatra fled. Their land and sea forces were lost. Octavian reached Alexandria in July 30 B.C. The suicide of Anthony and Cleopatra ended both Egyptian independence and the Roman civil wars.

D. Pax Romana

Octavian took the title of Caesar Augustus and founded the Roman Empire. Although he outwardly restored the Republic, in reality power reposed after 27 B.C. in his own hands. He abolished professional armies whose allegiance was to their commanders. His new standing imperial army of twenty-eight legions swore allegiance to him alone. Enlistments were voluntary for twenty years and the retired soldier received a grant of land. Augustus' state policy was peace and consolidation, not further conquest. The army also preserved internal order. The longest peace in history was born at Actium. The legions garrisoned the 10,000 mile boundary within which Western Europe was Latinized and Christianized. From these developments emerged the most vital portion of the Western heritage.

The imperial army was constructed upon cohorts of 500 to 600 employing sword and spear. Increased emphasis was eventually placed upon war machines and cavalry. Catapult and *ballista* were integral in each legion for defense of the *castella,* or fortified camp. As the purpose of the constabulary-type military became prevention rather than waging of war, valor and spirit gradually declined. Apathy of citizens, who rejected military duty in favor of material pleasure, invited barbarian infiltration of the ranks. Augustus organized a private army, the Praetorian Guard of nine reinforced cohorts. These troops maintained the imperial authority, but after years of conflict the people became too drunk on the wine of peace to be disturbed by the ebbing of their republican rights. Since the succession to the imperial crown had never been regulated, the Praetorian Guard and the provincial legions, which eventually handled locally their own recruiting, became the arbiters. Emperors were made and deposed by the will of the military. To civilians was left only the burden of oppressive taxes; ancient agrarian virtues responsible for Rome's rise faded beyond recall.

IV. ADRIANOPLE (9 AUGUST 378)

By the mid-fourth century the old agile, flexible legion had been weakened by incorporation of increasing numbers of light foot and cavalry. This reflected pressure and raids by Germanic tribes on border areas. The speed of barbarians bent on plunder rendered the old heavy legion ineffective. Cavalry and light foot were the only answer. Heavy infantry, recruited now wherever men might be had, was qualitatively unworthy of comparison with its legionary namesake of the Second Punic War. It is an error, however, to assign Roman collapse to military decline. The decline was a reflection of the moral decadence which sapped the Empire's internal strength and left it a hollow facade.

Pressure by Asiatic Huns drove the Goths southward across the Danube and into the eastern portion of the Roman Empire. Thousands of them had served as Roman mercenaries; they were well equipped and no mere crude barbarians. They fought from wagon forts formed in circles, preferably on a hilltop, as a fixed point upon which to maneuver their superb cavalry. The irresolute Emperor Valens rejected Gothic demands for lands in Thrace. He marched out of Adrianople on a hot, dusty day and in the afternoon, with his men already exhausted and thirsty, he attacked a wagon fort. Heavy Gothic cavalry returned from foraging in time to drive the Roman horse from the field, whereupon the deserted, tightly massed foot was annihilated. Valens and 40,000 were left on the field.

Adrianople stands as a great watershed in military history. It indicated the exhaustion of the classical tactics of phalanx and legion. The defensive cohesion of the ancient infantry formation had gradually been weakened by specialist troops who destroyed the solid shield front. Heavy cavalry became the ruling power in war. Adrianople further reasserted valor as the primary requisite of shock operations. The tactical problem became how to combine missile power with security against cavalry shock. A new cycle of war, the cavalry age, was dawning. The Roman military system vanished and was replaced by mercenary cavalry. Vegetius, the greatest military theoretician of the classical world, prepared a plea for a belated return to the virtues of ancient Rome, but he was ignored. Societal decay had progressed too far to be arrested.

CHAPTER IV

The Cavalry Age

WHEN HEAVY CAVALRY demonstrated its superiority over heavy infantry at Adrianople, it indicated exhaustion of the aged tactics of phalanx and legion and signaled the advent of a new age in which cavalry was to become for a thousand years the ruling instrument of war. The problem now was how to combine fire-power with security against the offensive shock power of cavalry. Like all historical phenomena the change was gradual and a close reflection of its societal framework, but cavalry warfare, in turn, had profound influence upon the societies within which it was dominant.

I. WESTERN WARFARE

A. The Franks

At Châlons in 451 the Huns of Attila—light Asiatic cavalry—went down to defeat before the Gothic heavy cavalry. Infantry had no recorded role in the action, but if it participated, there is little reason to believe it could have held the field. Despite the early vigor of the Goths, contact with the easy materialistic life of decadent Rome sapped their vitality in a few generations. In Western Europe there was for a time a rebirth of infantry tactics among the West Germanic forest peoples—especially the Franks—who lacked a cavalry tradition.

At Tours in 732, Charles Martel, with a Frankish host arrayed in solid formation, withstood a party of raiding Moorish light cavalry. Raised in the tradition of the Teutonic tribal levy and armed with battle-axe and javelin, the Franks possessed a nascent shock and missile combination. With the decay of cities, stagnation of commerce and scarcity of money, Western Europe was unprepared to establish professional cavalry; kings lacked revenue to maintain such forces. Charles Martel found a solution in an agrarian age. He rewarded distinguished soldiers with land grants, in return for which they assumed military obligations. Retaining the principle of universal military obligations for every free man, Martel's grandson, Charlemagne, organized his subjects into small groups, each of which would provide one well-armed soldier. Thus service was connected to land, and its holders had sufficient income to present themselves for war properly equipped. The resultant increase in available cavalry in place of tribal foot had much to do with Charlemagne's military successes. Although he established a great state and the Pope recognized him as emperor in 800, his domain was partitioned by his sons. Their strife, together with invasions of Western Europe by Norsemen and Magyars, brought about the solidification of feudalism.

B. *The Norse*

Seeking plunder, the Norse came in small, seaworthy ships light enough to move up rivers. With their two-handed pole axes, they were superior, man for man, to continental soldiers. Surprise and speed, for they customarily seized horses, served them as psychological weapons. The old Frankish levy was too slow in mustering to provide effective defense. Only standing cavalry could keep pace with the increased peril. For protection, people surrendered their land to local lords who had fortifications. Small lords sought the protection of greater ones, conceding their allegiance as vassals. Thus feudalism was born.

A great feudal ladder was formed reaching from man to monarch. A vassal received in perpetuity, a *fief*, or grant of land, in exchange for fulfilling a contractual relationship to his overlord. The purpose of the contract was military in essence, the lord pledging to protect his vassals and they to serve him in war. There was little place for the small freeholder; either he became a petty vassal or sank into serfdom. Perhaps never before or since has the professional officer commanded such a high price for his services. Feudal warfare signified the supremacy of cavalry over infantry and replacement of foot by the castle as the base for cavalry operations. The Magyar invasions of tenth century Europe proved the system and stimulated its spread and consolidation. War had passed full cycle from the democratic basis of Greece to an aristocratic footing.

C. *Hastings (14 October 1066)*

Although feudal cavalry became dominant on the Continent, England retained the older military system founded upon the Anglo-Saxon tribal levy or *fyrd*. In harmony with a mode traceable to Greece, each freeman (citizen) had the duty of performing militia-type service in perilous times. In the face of Norse (Danish) invasions of the ninth century, Alfred the Great divided the host into two parts, so that he could field a year-round force and still afford the people time for agricultural pursuits. Stockaded frontier fortresses called *burghs* were created as local strongholds and in time these formed the nuclei of many English towns. Alfred, who is also popularly credited with founding the English navy, raised a body of standing retainers; in the next century a small class of professionals called *thegns* also appeared.

In 1066, to press a weak claim to the throne of England, William the Conqueror, Duke of Normandy, the bastard son of a tanner's daughter and Duke Robert, mounted a mighty force to cross the Channel. William was an able soldier and a great administrator, a masterful man with tremendous will and sense of purpose. He had fought many wars around his duchy and was a skilled field general. Since no feudal lord had the right to call his vassals for duty beyond the sea, William attracted adventurers and younger sons of the nobility to the conquest of large and wealthy England. His army, the only one ever successfully to invade England, was primarily a magnificent continental cavalry force probably approaching 5,000 men.

King Harold of England had at his disposal the fyrd and his retainers, the housecarles. Though the latter rode to war, all fought on foot with spear, sword, and long-handled Danish axe. The carles wore steel caps, and chain mail and carried stout shields.

In classical infantry fashion, they relied upon the defensive solidity of the formation to stand off cavalry. Having defeated a Norse invasion of his kingdom 24 September 1066, Harold marched south in haste, and accepted action when his forces were not fresh; he had suffered battle losses and the fyrd had not fully assembled. This he partially compensated by taking up a strong stockaded hill position with the available 4,000-5,000 men.

William opened the action at 0900 in the morning. He formed three forces, or "battles," while Harold presented a single massed line. Following an opening barrage of arrows, William's foot charged and were repulsed. This lured the English right to a counterattack which opened Harold's close formation. William personally led his cavalry forward but in several hours of hard fighting failed to pierce the English line. He directed his archers to employ high angle fire to overcome the English shields. The Norman then feigned retreat, whereupon the encouraged English levies descended the hill to administer the coup de grâce, only to be pounced upon by the wheeling cavalrymen who cut them down. Toward twilight Harold was killed by a bolt in the eye. The charges of the continental cavalry, the disintegration of the English formation, and the loss of the king brought collapse of the army in the evening, allowing William to carry the day. Throughout the action, he had maintained close personal command and the victory was rightly his own.

The real lesson of the day, the power of infantry and cavalry in combination and the continuing vitality of properly massed foot, was not recognized. Instead, Hastings was erroneously regarded as proving beyond question the superiority of cavalry. The social and political ruling class of mounted lords readily accepted and disseminated this appraisal of their superiority over the commoner foot soldier. Balanced armies were in fact incompatible with the feudal social order.

William proceeded to feudalize England, although he grafted the continental system onto English practices. He preserved the fyrd as an important balance to check the power of his vassals; by this means and by requiring each vassal to take his oath directly to the King rather than through the feudal ladder, he made the English monarchy much stronger than its continental counterparts and contributed to the evolution of England's unique political institutions.

D. The Church

The military-based feudal system assured the stability of European society and its ally was the Church. The ideal knight was the very embodiment of Christian principles; chivalrous, honest, loyal, and pious. His warfare was a test in battle of moral principle. A large landholder, the medieval church inculcated esthetic emphasis on the next life and was little concerned with this world. As such it strengthened and supported knight warfare by attempting to ban from Christian conflict the crossbow, a powerful anticavalry weapon. This was no more effective than other arms-limitation measures in Western history, for when a weapon exists, it demands its own use. Nevertheless, the sole authority higher than arms was the Church and vigorous popes wielded tremendous moral influence. At its peak of power in the twelfth century, the Church frequently intervened in diplomacy and war.

II. BYZANTINE WARFARE

While feudalism and its military expression, heavy cavalry, reigned in Western Europe, the Eastern Roman or Byzantine Empire existed as a Greco-Roman survival of the extinguished classical world. Although the West lived by subsistence agriculture with little trade and a few miserable large towns, the East flourished with commerce radiating from the great metropolis of Constantinople. Byzantine merchants commercially dominated the Mediterranean world and the empire's cities. A small freeholder class met urban food needs. The East was far more modern than the West.

In the sixth century, Emperor Justinian undertook the reconquest of the Western Roman Empire and was successful in Africa and Italy. This success he owed to the mobility, fire-power, and shock of his horse archers and to the brilliant generalship of Belisarius and Narses, the one a handsome youth in his twenties, the other a septuagenarian Armenian eunuch. Although their armies were small, numerically inferior elites, they bested heavy Gothic cavalry. The political result was short-lived, however, for the overextension of the empire exaggerated defense requirements and gradually the conquests were lost. Thereafter, a stable defense system evolved.

A. The Defense System

In preserving its affluent society, Byzantium employed a highly developed civil service, diplomatic corps, and military establishment. An aged merchant people, the Byzantines generally were interested in buying security. A large defense budget maintained well-equipped forces and fortifications by deceitful diplomacy and bribery of potential opponents and by maintenance of a powerful fleet to protect maritime trade. The Eastern Roman Empire fashioned a highly polished system predicated upon defense. War was accepted as a normal condition; it was studied as an art, not as an application of brute force as it was in the West. Two notable works, Maurice's *Artis Militaris* (c. 595) and Leo's *Tactica* (c. 900), had economy of means as their prevailing theme. Combat was a last resort when other defensive measures failed. Neither daring nor chivalry was esteemed, for each could lead to useless sacrifice.

The methods of probable opponents were carefully studied. For example, in the event of war with the Franks, as Byzantines called all Westerners, advantage should be taken of knightly courage and daring, lack of discipline and organization and negligible logistics. Maneuver and the indirect approach were used against the mature Persians; extermination against Balkan peoples. To cope with the Arabs, who fought in a single line, three successive waves of horse archers were employed.

By the tenth century "the urban populace was idle and vicious, subsisting on the grain dole and exhibiting its fighting qualities only in street riots";* the frontiers were guarded by mercenaries and the sons of the sturdy peasantry. In the eighth century the empire was divided into military districts or *themes*. Each had a permanent

* Lynn Montross, *War Through the Ages* (New York: Harper & Bros., 1960), 106.

corps and organized militia. The commander served also as civil governor; political institutions reflected military necessity. In the event of attack, the theme fought a Fabian action until armies of neighboring themes could rally to its aid. The defense system utilized border fortifications but preserved elasticity through highly developed communications.

B. The Navy

On the sea, naval themes provided five great fleets. The vitals of the empire were in Constantinople and geography made it formidable. By sea, the Dardanelles and Bosporus were readily defensible; by land, the narrow approaches to the city could easily be held.

Naval decline set in when Venice and other Italian cities entered competition for the carrying trade. Luxury destroyed the vitality of the Byzantines when they devoted their time to dissipation and debauchery. Control of trade passed to foreign hands. Since a strong merchant marine goes hand in glove with a powerful navy, especially in providing experienced seamen, the decline in maritime trade undermined the fleet. By the late eleventh century, wealth shifted from commerce to land; the freeholders were bought out and in Asia Minor was created a class of great landed aristocracy. The peasantry, which had produced the core of the army, was ruined. Decline in shipping and the navy, change in landholding systems, and military declivity were intimately interwoven. The resulting debilitation was aggravated by civil war encouraged by social dislocation traceable to the land problem. The dispossessed farmers expanded the mob of urban unemployed. Their civil wars led rival imperial claimants to foreign adventures as external diversion; this meant ruinous taxes, costly military campaigns and, when they failed, palace coups. All the while, unspeakable corruption and vice—fruits of luxury, comfort, and greed—gnawed out the moral and spiritual core of the Empire. Defense funds were squandered in the dissipation of government officials.

C. Manzikert (4 July 1071)

In this condition, the Byzantine Empire was challenged by the Seljuk Turks, one of the nomadic peoples who periodically poured out of Central Asia. Using lance, sword, and horse-archer tactics typical of Asiatic light cavalry, they would have been no match for the Empire in its day of vigor. As it was, undue expansion to the east and in the Balkans had increased the defense burden at this inopportune time. At Manzikert, the Emperor's pursuit carried him far beyond drinking water. When he retreated, a jealous subordinate deserted, opening the formation to Turkish cavalry. The defeat permitted the Turks speedily to occupy and devastate fertile Anatolia. The result of Manzikert was fatal for the Empire. Its breadbasket was lost, but worse, the provinces which had been for 500 years the recruiting ground of the best peasant soldiers passed from Byzantium.

III. THE CRUSADES

The Byzantine crisis which followed Manzikert led the Eastern Roman emperor to appeal for assistance to the Pope, the supreme head of Western Christendom. The Pope saw the opportunity to reunite Christendom and to initiate a holy war against Islam. Consequently, he proclaimed the First Crusade in 1095 aiming strategically to relieve Byzantium and conquer the Holy Land. Counterattacks on Islam had been under way in the West for generations, with successes in Sicily, Sardinia, and Spain. Psychological preparation had been initiated with tales of Turkish atrocities and the wealth of the East offered economic appeal. A population explosion in Europe provided human impetus.

At the end of the eleventh century, the supremacy of heavy cavalry in Europe was firmly established. The problem of the Crusades was whether such a force would be capable of achieving a permanent foothold in the East. The propitious political disintegration of the Seljuk Turks into small principalities made the contest entirely one of contending military systems and religions.

A. The Crusaders

Opening operations in 1097, the crusaders advanced successfully to storm Jerusalem 15 July 1099. They then established feudal states along the Mediterranean littoral, endeavoring to project their politico-military system into the East. Sea power was strategically vital; the fleets of the Italian commercial cities assisted in conquering the coast of the Holy Land and thereafter gave the crusaders a secure maritime rear and supply line. Inland, a defense perimeter of powerful feudal fortresses was constructed. Between this line and the sea the crusaders endeavored to maintain a feudal army as a mobile reserve. The states depended upon the simultaneous existence of castles and army.

The crusaders manifested all the weaknesses of feudal warfare, notably lack of discipline and unity of command. They were accustomed to a single tactic, heavy cavalry shock. Nevertheless, against the Turk they were generally successful when they combined cavalry with a solid body of infantry, preferably bowmen, and chose terrain where the enemy could not surround and harass them or exploit breaks in their formation. Infantry was imperative as a fixed point upon which the cavalry could operate.

The manpower yielded by the feudal levy in the principalities was never really adequate for continuing defense needs and since the lands were quickly allotted, newcomers were not prone to stay in the East. Such poor and untrained foot as went to the Holy Land did so from religious fervor and stayed for a campaign season. This reinforcement was vital. Mercenaries and native Syrian Christians were also used.

B. The Turks

As with the crusaders, the Turks' principal component was cavalry. The greater mobility of their light eastern horse archers was employed (1) to maintain distance until a favorable moment to strike, (2) to feign retreat to lure the pursuer into ambush, (3) to attack the rear and flanks, and (4) to attack and force action on crusaders on the march, usually from the rear. Their fire was at high volume, but lacked killing velocity against crusader armor. Primarily, it served to disrupt cohesion and to wound horses. The Turk could not stand against a heavy cavalry charge, but due to his evasive tactics and speed he could avoid damage and convert a precipitous retreat into an ambush. When opportunity occurred, the Turk closed with lance, sword, and club.

Summarily, Turkish fire and movement were no match for crusader shock when supported by steadfast infantry, but given time and space they could best the heavy European horseman. The one great lesson of the Crusades for the West was that a proper combination of cavalry and foot in line of battle was successful and vice versa. This fact was neither uniformly recognized nor transported back to the battlefields of Europe.

C. *Results*

A 4 July 1187 defeat at Hattin was the decisive action of the Crusades. The greatest crusader army was lost and Saladin became lord of the Moslem world. The great castles ceased resistance. On 2 October, Saladin entered Jerusalem, imposing moderate terms. Since the True Cross had been lost at Hattin, it was a victory for Allah and undermined the crusaders' spiritual zeal. The nadir was reached in 1204 when the Fourth Crusade stormed Constantinople, fatally weakening the power base of the Byzantine Empire. Left a feeble shell, it collapsed in 1453 before the Ottoman Turks. Considered thus, the Crusades ultimately debilitated the position of Christendom against Islam by paving the way for loss of the greatest barrier to its advance.

On the positive side, the Crusades provided a spiritual unifying and revitalizing force to Western Europe. They introduced new products and new tastes. The commercial stimulus of the eastern trade they opened revolutionized European commerce, banking, and the money economy, and provided impetus to urbanization, and freer communication of peoples, goods and ideas. Greater prosperity once more made for profitable leisure and interacted with the opening of communication with Eastern centers of learning to touch off the age of inquiry. These economic, social, and intellectual currents produced the Renaissance, but the touchstone was the military conquests of the Crusades.

IV. THE MONGOLS

Medieval Christendom was subjected to three great waves of Asiatic invaders. In the tenth century the Magyars carved out a kingdom in the Danube Basin and were absorbed into Europe; in the eleventh, the Seljuk Turks entered Asia Minor at the expense of Byzantium, but their central monarchy disintegrated into several small princedoms harassed by the Crusaders. In the thirteenth century the Mongols erupted from deep Asia, thrust into the heart of Europe, and established a two-century domination of Christian peoples; the Golden Horde devastated Russia and profoundly affected its later history, giving it a semi-Asiatic national character.

Starting as a Mongol subchief, Genghis Khan spent forty years subduing other chieftains. In his old age he embarked upon the conquest of Asia. He passed through Manchuria and by treachery breached the Great Wall in 1211 to pour into China. Herdsmen have always been more warlike than agricultural peoples. In their early youth the Mongols learned to ride, use the bow, steal, and ambush, for their individual survival depended upon it. Men hunted and fought; women saw to other matters. They were individualistic, undisciplined, and addicted to plunder, but the occupation of ancient, civilized China modified their military character.

The Chinese study of war has come down to us in the maxims of Sun Tze, written c. 500 B.C., which advocated tactics of the indirect approach. Avoidance of pitched battle unless on very favorable terms, constant harassment, surprise attack and what we would now consider guerrilla operations, were characteristic of the Chinese. Fortification and siege-craft were highly developed arts as was psychological warfare, the indirect attack on the will. But when the Khan invaded China, he found it wealthy and indolent, seeking security behind the Wall in place of opportunity. Through formalism the art of war had stagnated.

A. Mongol Tactical System

The brutal, vigorous Mongols melded their methods to those of the more schooled and deliberate Chinese and the result was world conquering. The Mongol army was a cavalry host of vassals and allies from all Asia in which the ethnic Mongol was a minority. It never exceeded 230,000. Starting with the *touman,* a division of 10,000, the army was organized decimally. Several toumans made up an army under a single commander who had considerable initiative. Discipline was brutal; if part of a unit of ten fled, all were executed. Each trooper wore leather body armor and

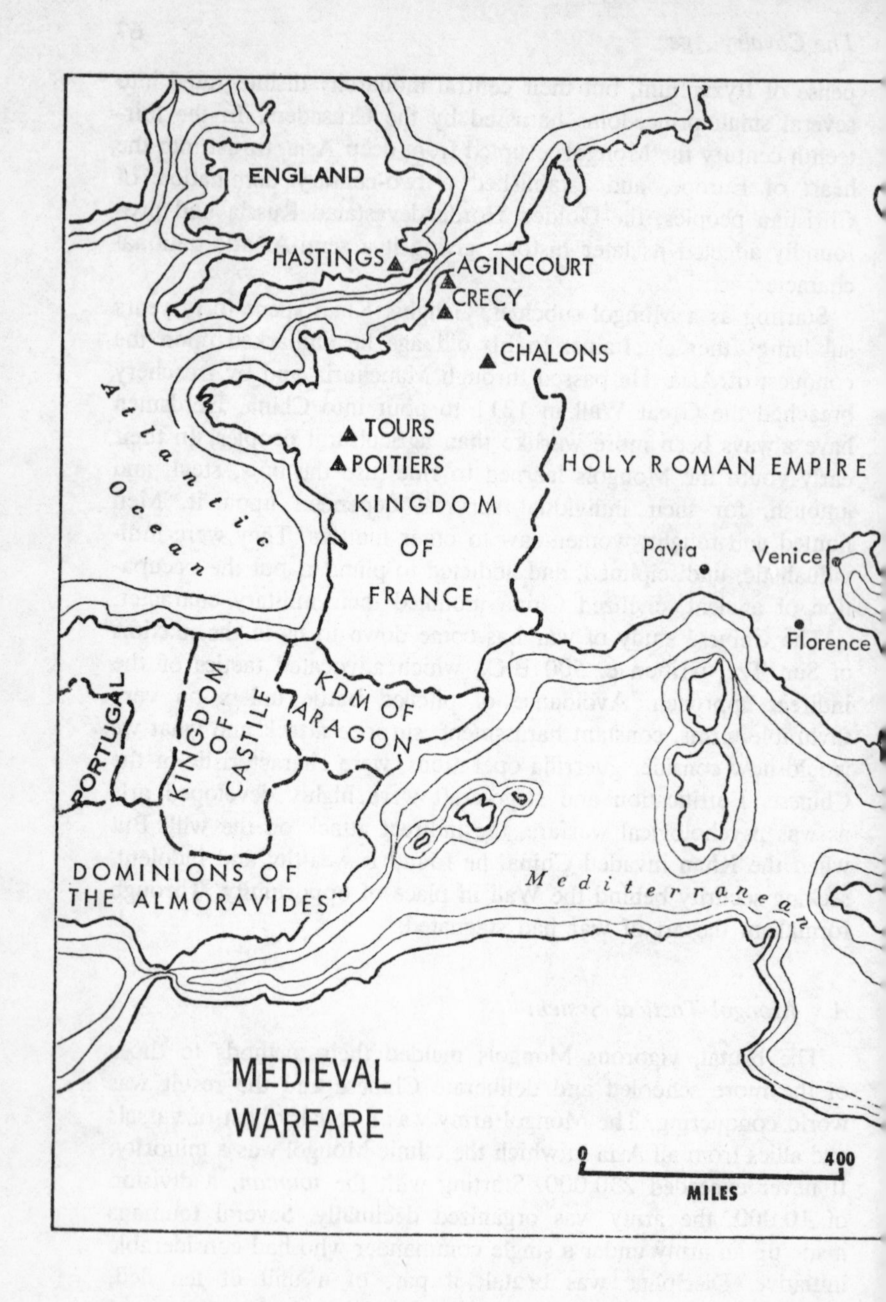
ENGLAND
HASTINGS
AGINCOURT
CRECY
CHALONS
Atlantic Ocean
TOURS
POITIERS
HOLY ROMAN EMPIRE
KINGDOM OF FRANCE
Pavia
Venice
Florence
PORTUGAL
KINGDOM OF CASTILE
KDM OF ARAGON
DOMINIONS OF THE ALMORAVIDES
Mediterranean
MEDIEVAL WARFARE
0
400
MILES

Sarai
Black Sea
Caspian Sea
KINGDOM OF POLAND
iegnitz
Kiev
KINGDOM OF HUNGARY
KDM. OF BULGARIA
SERBIA
Black Sea
Constaninople
NORMAN KINGDOM OF SICILY
LEPANTO
BYZANTINE EMPIRE
MANZIKERT
COUNTY OF EDESSA
PRIN. OF ANTIOCH
Sea
CO. OF TRIPOLI
HATTIN(TIBERIUS)
KINGDOM OF JERUSALEM
Jerusalem

carried several bows of varying weights; some had a scimitar and a lance.

In operation, the first wave of attackers was a fifth column of agents who spied out the land, endeavored to bribe or to intimidate by murdering viciously and at random, and attempted to undermine morale while the main body was many miles away. The Mongols advanced as much as fifty miles per day and concentrated against their objective gaining local superiority at the decisive point. They pillaged, massacred, and ravaged the countryside. Their advance was a model of mobility with well-laid plans based on complete prior intelligence. Thus they supported the warnings of their advance agents and terrorized all men. Each conquest made easier the destruction of the next victim's will.

In battle, the commander remained well to the rear with the women and disabled, all of whom were mounted and posted on high ground to give the impression of a reserve. Movements were controlled by signal flags. The center of the line consisted of prisoners and vassals attacking in waves, while the crack troops were on the wings to strike the enemy's flanks. If the enemy fought well, the Mongols permitted him to break through, only later to fall upon him by surprise. If he was contained, they harassed him with arrow and javelin until his line was broken and then charged with lance and scimitar. Their combination of missile and shock tactics was the most effective known during the Middle Ages.

If faced with a siege, the Mongols sealed the city and subjected it to day and night bombardment with bow and war machines by alternate toumans. If this did not wear down the besieged, they employed fire missiles, even using the bodies of prisoners. Mining was utilized. Once inside the city pillage occurred (after the commanding general gave permission) whether the place surrendered to guileful promises or was taken by storm. The Mongols took what they wanted and destroyed the rest, not knowing what else to do with it.

B. Campaigns

In five months the Mongols conquered the 400,000-man army of the great Persian Empire which included Afghanistan and Turkestan. Four columns totaling about 150,000 thrust through the latter, converging upon the fabled cities of Bokhara and Samarkand. Deliberate excesses were wreaked upon them, including the destruction of priceless art and devastation of agricultural resources. So great was the terror thus spread that a single Mongol supposedly might enter a city and without resistance could kill hundreds.

The monk, Carpin, who was sent to the Mongols as a papal envoy, left one of the few source accounts of them. He advised the princes of Europe to emulate their methods. He suggested that princes remain in the rear instead of leading the action, that they form a single powerful Christian league, create a permanent field organization to control innumerable lords and vassals, maintain rigid discipline, employ scouts and flank guards, arm infantry with the crossbow which could pierce Mongol armor, and avoid pursuit which could lead only to ambush. A flat plain would be the best battlefield for the Christians. The country should be burned off to deny the enemy fodder for his mounts. Carpin failed to mention that forest, marsh, and rough country were naturally unsuited to the steppe warfare of the Mongol.

Unfortunately for Europe, in neither Russia nor Poland was there a central power capable of concerting such effective resistance. The Russians had a large feudal foot levy of axemen while the Poles had only lancers. Neither had many fortified cities.

In 1224 Sabutai swept below the Caspian, through the Caucasus, and debouched into the Russian steppes on a reconnaissance in force. The South Russian princes charged recklessly to defeat along the river Kalka. Few escaped alive. After a few years' respite, Genghis' son Oktai, who had completed the conquest of China, resumed the attack upon Christendom in December 1237. With Sabutai as Chief of Staff, Batu Khan came from due East directly upon the rear of the North Russian states, swept them in a winter campaign, and turned south from the swamps near Novgorod to sack Kiev in December 1240. After gathering intelligence, he sent a fourth of his troops to protect his flank against Poland, crossed the Carpathians in 1241, and descended upon Hungary using mobility and a deliberate reign of terror. In March the Poles were defeated; the Mongols entered Silesia, and in April 20,000 Germans and Polish light cavalry were hopelessly crushed at Liegnitz. The flank secured, the Mongols were free to join their brethren across the Carpathians. Liegnitz sent a shock through all Europe.

Meanwhile, in Hungary, King Bela and a feudal levy of 100,000 faced Batu on a too short front along the River Sajo. Morale and leadership were poor. Batu probably studied the enemy's position 26 April 1241 and observed to his generals: "They are crowded together like a herd of cattle in narrow stalls, with no room to move about." By night he pushed a strong force across upstream, attacked frontally with arrow and catapult at dawn to fix the Magyars until the flank attack developed, and then he pursued the vanquished. At leisure, the Mongols spread over the Hungarian plain pillaging and looting.

The King of Bohemia was massing a great force of survivors and neighboring princes for war in 1242. This posed a threat to the Mongol flank. In this condition Batu learned of the death of Oktai, the Great Khan. The problem of a successor was raised and Batu had ambitions. He was over a thousand miles from his base in Turkestan and doubtless his force had been depleted by four years of fighting. Moreover, his advance agents had met great obstacles in the Alps; many themselves had been ambushed and Batu no doubt recognized the unfavorability of further operations in the forests and mountains. The great fortresses of western Europe may have posed a barrier. In any event, the Mongols suddenly evacuated Europe east to the Vistula. The Western nobility returned to its internecine strife with scarcely a lesson learned.

C. *Russia*

Russia was not so fortunate. Batu returned from Mongolia to pitch his tent toward the Volga at Sarai, which became the capital of the Khans of the Golden Horde. In 1260 this state became independent and ruled Russia for two centuries, interbreeding, and leaving indelibly stamped upon the Russian character the traits of the Mongol.

CHAPTER V

The Transition from Feudal to Modern War

I. FEUDAL WARFARE

FEUDALISM militarily preserved the European social and political order, but conditions changed. By the fourteenth century new influences were altering the character of war. The feudal military system had inherent weaknesses; the term of an army was short because a knight was usually obligated to give only forty days' annual service and would then return to agricultural affairs on his manor; English vassals were not required to serve overseas; on the Continent unity of command was impossible because service was owed only to the immediate lord from whom the vassal held his land; the feudal host was undisciplined and battle disintegrated into multiple individual contests. Strategy was weak; swift decision rare. Lacking infantry as a mobile strong point upon which to maneuver, cavalry was strategically bound to castles. Within these a noble could stave off attack, even if he were in rebellion against his king. Feudal warfare, strategically defensive, was therefore dependent upon fortification keeping ahead of siegecraft.

Feudalism limited the power of continental monarchs, for they could directly command only the service of their vassals-in-chief. A few rebellious great lords could disrupt the martial capacity of a kingdom. The Crusades, marking perhaps the highest achievement of feudal forces, also signaled their demise by stimulating a money economy. Because they were commoners, merchants were free from war service but they were not free from taxation. If the king could find sources of revenue, he could hire professionals who would remain in the field for pay, in complete obedience, for as long as desired. Since his financial resources were greater than any lord's, he had the means to eliminate private war. Indeed, the word "soldier" comes from *solidus,* Latin for a piece of money. The English system of *scutage* inaugurated service for pay. To maintain year-round armies against the Welsh, Edward I utilized a twelfth-century method and levied contributions upon knights who remained at home. Agriculture, increasingly prosperous because of the demands of expanding cities and towns, drew the attention of many knights away from war. Their scutage was used to pay others. In Europe mercenary specialist forces became available for hire. The effect was to broaden the scope and add to the duration of wars and to give kings power apart from the feudal system. The foundation was laid militarily for the emergence of unified modern states.

II. THE HUNDRED YEARS WAR

Feudal warfare was discredited and rendered obsolete in the field during the Hundred Years War. By a series of marriages, the kings of England had become the vassals-in-chief of large territories held from the kings of France. In 1346 Edward III finally claimed the inheritance of the entire kingdom and invaded France to enforce his rights. "The English people stood at this time possessed of a commanding weapon, the qualities of which were utterly unsuspected abroad," according to Churchill.

Edward's paid army included the most formidable foot of the day, longbowmen, who rode to war but fought on foot. These sturdy troops were schooled from boyhood in the use of the six-foot bow and the cloth-yard arrow. The accuracy and power of the weapon is legendary. A well shot arrow pierced a mail shirt, the thigh beneath, and embedded itself deep in the flank of the victim's horse. An inch oak timber could be penetrated. The shire levy, descendant of the fyrd, enabled English kings to augment heavy cavalry by calling such yeomen out for pay. Thus the English army contributed to an increasing democratization of society because it was raised on the basis of popular service obligation rather than merely on social and economic status or privilege.

A. Crécy (26 August 1346)

After landing in France during July, Edward advanced on Paris but found it too strongly defended. He retreated toward the coast. Deciding to fight, he positioned his combined infantry and cavalry force along a ridge behind a small stream to await the onslaught of the host of Philip of France. The French king, in addition to his feudal levy, had the army of the King of Bohemia and 6,000 mercenary Genoese crossbowmen. His numerical superiority was about three to one. Late in the day when his van came upon the English, his lords would have nothing but immediate battle. Edward's knights were dismounted with longbowmen on their flanks. For defense against enemy riders each bowman may have had a metal-tipped stake planted before him on an angle.

Philip sent forward his Genoese, who ran down hill, shouted for courage, and fired. The missiles fell short, but not so those of the longbowmen whose bolts, fired from the head, decimated the Genoese, pinning helmet to head, brigandine to breast. As the mercenaries fled back up the hill, the French knights reportedly assumed treason and charged through them shouting: "Away with these faint-hearted rabble! They do but block our advance." As the French rode down their own infantry, confusion destroyed their front. The accuracy of the longbowmen littered the field with dead and dying men and horses. Hearing the action, approaching waves of French horsemen, motivated by chivalric honor to participate, charged recklessly. Few reached the English line. Well into the night the French cavalry came on; in the morning the little valley was filled with the dead and Philip's army was gone.

B. Results

The reaction to Crécy was explosive. The victory of the ignored, numerically inferior English suddenly made them a great military power. They had won by skillful combination of archery and dismounted men-at-arms, but the French did not learn the lesson. They were afraid to arm the peasantry to create reliable foot. Their military caste system was the most rigid in Europe. Their response was, therefore, typical of the history of war when missile power suddenly moves beyond defense: a strengthening of the defense. Occasioned by improved metalworking, the French replaced the traditional chain mail with heavier plate armor. This sixty-pound suit rendered the venerable shield superfluous. Even the chargers were armored. Lances grew longer and heavier. And, again, typically, this addition of weight to the defensive "fortification" sacrificed the mobility which alone could answer increased fire or missile power.

C. *Poitiers and Agincourt*

At Poitiers 19 September 1356, the French incorrectly copied English tactics and, after their cavalry charge failed, dismounted and plodded forward. At the decisive moment, a wisely withheld English reserve launched a then rare flank attack. The burdened French men-at-arms, slow and unwieldy, were massacred. France fell into despair, for she had now been defeated both on horse and on foot. At Agincourt, 25 October 1415, the errors were repeated with like results as knights slogged through ankle-deep mud. But the slaughter was greater because the added armor weight made withdrawal impossible.

D. *Why France Won*

Despite her great victories—and although Henry V succeeded in temporarily merging the English and French crowns—England did not win the Hundred Years War. She failed to advance tactically beyond the fourteenth century. Aside from her vast demographic and economic inferiority and strategic inability to capitalize tactical successes, her failure resulted from French nationalism and the creation of a professional standing army. Joan of Arc, as an inspirational figure, served to restore French national will to fight. In 1445 France organized a standing army of 6,000 men who rode to war but fought on foot. These moral and physical advances enabled the king to defeat his foreign enemies; with increased personal means, he also defeated his internal foes and laid the beginnings of the consolidation of France into a modern monarchy. In exchange for the protection of trade, merchant classes supported monarchy with money against the feudal class. Trade shifted the economic center of gravity from country to city, undermining the feudal social order.

III. ADVENT OF GUNPOWDER

A. Western Europe

Feudal warfare, characterized by localization of military power, reflected equally limited political and economic life. Technologically, the defense remained superior to the offense. The advent of gunpowder reversed that relationship, however slowly, and sounded the death knell of feudalism. Reputedly, Roger Bacon invented gunpowder in 1249; a few crude guns were present at Crécy. In 1418, Henry V had artillery at the siege of Rouen, but the extreme immobility of early pieces limited their employment. By 1453 French guns had mastered English tactics by increasing the range and power of the missile.

B. The Fall of Constantinople

As barrel-casting and shot improved and gunners became more expert, the stone castle, pillar of feudalism, was rendered obsolete. In 1453 the Ottoman Turks, an Anatolian remnant of earlier Turkish invaders, took forty days to knock down the previously impregnable walls of Constantinople and end the thousand-year survival of Byzantium and thereby, incidentally, signalled a new onslaught of Islam on Christendom.

C. Implications of Gunpowder

The cost of the weapons limited their acquisition to free cities and monarchs with great revenue power. Artillery was made by the urban middle class of merchants and manufacturers, and used to destroy their class of social betters, the feudal rural aristocracy. Centralization of political power was therefore hastened and the technological basis laid for the modern state.

The money economy which grew from both manufacturing and the expansion of international trade touched off by the Crusades and the tactical aspects of the Hundred Years War together gave warning of the end of the cavalry age. The increased trade disrupted medieval society by interposing a middle class which controlled wealth.

The displaced feudal nobility resented gunpowder because it gave all men equality—the equality of thugs in the street. Rabble with handguns were the betters of unarmed gentlemen. Class vanished as a basis for monopoly of the means of war and the trend toward social quantity rather than quality was set in motion. The gentleman made the transition from feudal to modern war by becoming an officer—a commander—in place of an elite warrior. Control of standing forces replaced possession of lands as his economic base, or sinecure.

IV. THE SWISS

The English combination of horse and foot, missile and shock, posed a tactical revolution; the money economy led to a new financial basis of war focused on greater length and breadth through well-equipped standing forces; gunpowder technologically destroyed the old military order. It was left to the Swiss, however, to complete the revolution by turning warfare full cycle. The Swiss confederation, formed in 1291 by liberty-loving citizens, was successful because of military innovation in making good national independence from Austria. With naturally defensive terrain, high morale of free men fighting for liberty, and universal service (the democratization of war), the Swiss resurrected the forgotten art of disciplined infantry warfare.

The phalanx was their standard formation. Soldiers were armed with an eighteen-foot pike having a long iron shank which could not be chopped off by cavalry swords. Trained and disciplined, they were more than a match for charging feudal cavalry. Defensively, the Swiss phalanx presented the lowered pikes of the first four ranks. With no armor except a steel cap and breastplate, they were fast and agile. For offense, the rear ranks used the eight-foot halberd, which had a spear point, an armor-cutting axe blade, and a hook below to pull men-at-arms from the saddle.

The Swiss had a serious weakness in their election of officers. Their tactical formula mastered the knight. Due to population expansion, Switzerland was able to export her men as mercenaries to much of Europe and with them her system. Their invincibility, which was basically defensive against feudal methods of war, was eventually destroyed by firearms and Swiss inability to adjust tactically to modern war.

V. THE ITALIAN WARS

A. The Italian States

Feudal warfare was dying and with it passed medieval society. The facets of the new military age were present when Charles VIII of France invaded Italy in 1494. Italy was in the Renaissance, that great age of revival of learning, science, and art, which was motivated by the profits of the Eastern trade opened by the Crusades. She was, however, politically fragmented into many small states which, comfortable and prosperous, were dominated by merchants. It is axiomatic that men of commerce have no taste for war. The Italian merchants therefore preferred to hire their protection. The cavalry armies of Italian mercenary captains, or *condottieri,* waged neat little campaigns for their paymasters; not always seriously, however, because soldiers were valuable and a long "war" was more profitable than a short, decisive one. Charles shocked Italy by fighting in earnest to attain complete victory and not merely to take prisoners for ransom.

B. The French

The French Army was a balanced force. It was modern because it was a political instrument, armed at least in part with firearms, and formed around professional infantry. All the troops were trained, disciplined, and paid. Besides well-drilled French foot, the army had Scottish archers, Swiss pikemen, French men-at-arms, arquebusiers, and a varied artillery on horsedrawn carts. This gave greater mobility in firepower.

The arquebus was a shoulder weapon, the first important infantry firearm. It was aimed after the match had been inserted, and was fired by triggering the match into the flash powder. The weapon weighed twelve pounds or more and had a range of 100 yards. In action, arquebusiers fought alongside pikemen who provided them protection during the slow loading process.

C. *Machiavelli*

The military lessons left by the French invasion were clear to the Italian statesman Machiavelli (1469-1527). In his works *The Prince* and *The Art of War,* this brilliant Florentine diplomat synthesized changes in politics and contemplated the advent of modern war. He argued for conscripted native militia in place of hirelings. Although he was impressed with firearms, the times were not conducive to a clear prognostication of their future. Perhaps most important, Machiavelli signaled a rebirth of the study of war which had lapsed in the West since Vegetius and in all Europe since Leo. He hoped to see a united Italy restored to power and prominence under a great prince. He recognized clearly that the existence of the modern state rested upon war and not upon the unrealistic, Church-dominated political morality of the Middle Ages. Consequently he scorned limited war in favor of all-out war. He endeavored to reconcile politics to modern states and conflict, because he understood the new age of armed diplomacy. He had learned from Charles.

D. *The Spanish*

1. TACTICS AND WEAPONS

Charles's invasion touched off the first modern dynastic war by upsetting the balance of power in Italy where Spain also had interests. The Spanish military tradition had grown in the long *reconquista* of the Iberian Peninsula from Islam, completed 2 January 1492 with the fall of Moorish Granada. At the same time, central power was established under Ferdinand and Isabella and a standing army was created. Pikemen, swordsmen, crossbowmen, and arquebusiers, trained and drilled into a superb infantry force, were the principal components. Agile with sword and dagger, Spanish infantry mastered the Swiss by getting under their unwieldy pikes and stabbing them.

The army which Ferdinand poured into Italy felled charging Swiss and French at Cerignola in 1503 with a hail of arquebus bullets. In later action, the French used their guns to blast out the Spanish, but at Pavia in 1525 the Spanish overcame the artillery. Arquebusiers dispersed behind available cover annihilated the enemy. Gonzalo de Córdoba, called "the Great Captain," had solved the tactical riddle from sword methods to infantry firepower. Pikes protected volley-firing arquebusiers from cavalry attack. The later two-man musket with forked rest could disable a horse at 300 yards, or smash armor at close range. The musketeers, usually in eight ranks, fired, went to the rear to reload and then came forward in successive waves. Continuous fire was therefore possible provided the men were well drilled. Artillery and cavalry supported foot.

The Spanish formula for the integration of handguns into the infantry formation enabled the armies of Ferdinand's grandson, Charles I (V of the Holy Roman Empire), to become the greatest force in Europe. They were partially propelled economically by the conquered treasure of the Aztecs and Incas. Tactical, organizational, technological, and command superiority enabled the tiny Spanish forces of Cortez and Pizarro to subdue entire New World empires. Spain was to enjoy her turn as the world's greatest power, but it traced from tactical innovation.

2. ORGANIZATION

Spanish organization after 1534 consisted of the *tercio* (or regiment) of twelve 250-man companies. Four companies made up a *coronelia,* or battalion headed by a *coronel* or, in English, colonel. Divided with two-thirds pikes and one-third arquebusiers, there were attached 300 light and 300 heavy cavalry. Tercios massed into great "battles," the gun age phalanx. Spanish tactics were methodical. The army moved slowly with great bands of camp followers. Keen professional spirit derived from vigorous training made for high morale that would not admit defeat.

VI. SUMMARY

In the two centuries after 1346, warfare underwent a complete transition from the Age of Cavalry to the Age of Gunpowder. Professional infantry replaced cavalry as the queen of battles. Missile power replaced shock power. Economically, urban commerce displaced the dominance of manorial agriculture. Money replaced barter. Dynastic monarchy replaced feudally decentralized political power. Armed diplomacy replaced armed anarchy. The way was opened to the modern era. And, while the causes and effects within their societal context were mutually supporting, the basis for these profound changes was to be found in military tactics and technology. War was the key to the evolutionary process.

CHAPTER VI

Transitions in Naval Warfare

I. INTRODUCTION

SINCE ACTIUM, the only naval innovation the Western world had seen was the Viking "sea cavalry." These light craft afforded speed and surprise for raids and reconnaissance. Nevertheless, naval war in the North evolved from armed merchantmen. England raised her early fleet by a feudal levy system on the Cinque Ports of the Channel. When called, the ports armed their trading ships to meet the King's demands. Medieval naval gunnery paralleled the land form, arrows. Boarding, ramming, and hand-to-hand combat decided engagements. Command was by "land" officers, but the crews were professional seamen. Naval war is always closely bound to maritime commerce, both in quantity and quality of forces. England, engaged in a vital wool trade with Flanders, consequently was well armed at sea. Vessels were actually floating castles and used with the techniques of land warfare.

In the Mediterranean, the tactics of Salamis and Actium survived. The galley had changed little. Propelled by sail or oar, she was single decked, 130-180 feet in length, and always rowed into action. A new craft, the all-sail galleon, was introduced into Mediterranean fleets by the sixteenth century.

II. LEPANTO (7 OCTOBER 1571)

After capturing Constantinople in 1453 and destroying Byzantium, the Ottoman Turks conquered Egypt and Mesopotamia, advanced into North Africa and the Balkans, and eliminated the old Hungarian kingdom. Two-thirds of the Mediterranean coast passed under their control; their sea power was hardly challenged. In 1570 Emperor Selim II, called "the sot," demanded Cyprus from the Republic of Venice. The latter appealed to a Christendom which was disunited by the Reformation and by rising nationalism which made states mutually distrustful.

The Pope and Philip II of Spain, whose Mediterranean dependencies were threatened, formed a league with Venice to defeat Islam and deprive the Turks of sea communication between the African and Eurasian parts of their empire. Command of the allied fleet passed to Philip's twenty-six-year-old bastard brother, Don Juan of Austria, who was an inspiring leader. His force had over 200 galleys, each mounting five bow guns. A few galleasses, gun ships combining sail and oar in battle, were available. Don Juan carried 30,000 infantry and, among slave and free, about 50,000 oarsmen. While the Turks reposed confidence in the arrow power of their marines, Don Juan had Spanish arquebusiers.

The Turks concentrated their African and Home fleets under Ali Pasha at Lepanto in the Gulf of Corinth. Under orders of the Sultan, Ali pressed to the attack in approximately equal ship strength, but in greatly inferior modern firepower. The fleets each engaged in three divisions and used the familiar ramming, boarding, and fire tactics. Ali rammed Don Juan's flagship, but his boarders were repelled and counterattacked by the arquebusiers. Ali was killed. Christian firepower all along the line provided the margin of victory.

Last of the great galley battles, and the first since Actium, Lepanto heralded the emergence of the Age of Sail and Shot. Turkish losses were heavy in every respect. Yet, although tactically defeated, the Turks retained their holdings because of French intrigue and allied quarrelling. Also, of course, as Potter has written, "while naval victories often make a decision possible, the final decision is usually reached on land." The moral result was more decisive in that Lepanto destroyed the aura of Turkish invincibility and heartened Christendom.

III. THE ARMADA (JULY-AUGUST 1588)

Within seventeen years, a new naval warfare appeared off England. Since naval power primarily supports and protects maritime commerce, its role in a particular conflict varies with the importance of water transportation. It exposes the enemy to attack upon his coasts and, negatively, to the constriction of his own trade. In modern war, the differentiation between land and sea war became distinct, primarily because of the scope of naval operations and the predominance of technology in naval conflict. Given the range of operations, the thinking of professional naval men in general became broader and more flexible than that of their army counterparts.

A. *Age of Discovery*

Improvements in maritime technology growing out of the Renaissance, and the compass—brought to Europe from China—enabled man to embark upon the Age of Discovery. In the fifteenth and sixteenth centuries, the horizons of Europe broadened to embrace the world as we know it, to bring rapid political and commercial expansion, and to provide the fiscal power to finance the emergence of the modern world. Columbus in effect sailed on behalf of the Atlantic nations seeking an alternate oriental trade route to rival that of the Mediterranean community. Vasco da Gama opened such an avenue in 1498 and thereafter the Mediterranean declined as the focal point of Western civilization and became a backwash. Ocean trade powered the rise of the Atlantic nations. In this no country played so great a pioneering role as Portugal, but it was the sailors of Spain who remade the world. Their instrument was the sailing ship which replaced the galley simultaneously as the Gun Age replaced feudal warfare. Thus the Ages of Gunpowder, Sail and Discovery were not only approximately simultaneous in inception, but they interacted with the Reformation to create the modern world.

B. *Anglo-Spanish Rivalry*

Despite the attempt of the Pope to regulate the New World by dividing it between Spain and Portugal in 1493, the northern trading powers quickly entered the lists. The riches of the Aztecs and Incas, and the hope of uncovering similar civilizations, were powerful incentives. Spain, from the standpoint of geography and bullion, was a superstate after she absorbed Portugal in 1580.

In reality, however, she was weakening because of the inflation caused by the New World wealth and her lack of industry which made her a middleman who exchanged gold for Northern European manufactures. The wealth she exported went to maintain the naval power with which the Dutch, English, and French contested her for the trade of her own colonies. Strategically, they sought her bullion at its source by piracy in the New World. Meanwhile Spain's quest for Continental power and her efforts in behalf of Rome to suppress the Protestant Reformation were expensive undertakings on which she squandered her treasure and blood. In 1570 the Pope, despairing of mending the breach with the Church of England, excommunicated Queen Elizabeth and called upon Philip to battle her heresy.

As contending commercial and religious power centers, Spain and England were certain to clash. Inevitably, this reckoning had to take place in a common medium, the sea. England had for centuries used sail rather than oar. Her progress in naval gunnery and technology led to great sailing ships with tremendous firepower. They combined the principal naval virtues: maneuverability, speed, and steadiness as a gun platform. Guns—up to seven and a half inches, hurling a fifty-pound ball to a range of 2,000 yards—were powerful enough to destroy ships.

C. *The Campaign*

Philip planned a large amphibious operation to discipline England, block her support of Dutch rebels against Spain, halt incursions on his own American treasure supply, defend Rome against Protestantism, and acquire predominance in Europe. He intended to enter the English Channel, board, engage hand-to-hand, and capture English vessels that opposed him; seize local naval superiority and cover the crossing to the Thames of his veteran army in the Low Countries. Unfortunately, the Dutch and disease undermined Philip's army and Sir Francis Drake's attack in April 1587 on the Armada assembling at Cadiz delayed operations a year.

In July 1588 the Armada sailed with 124 ships, carrying 1,100 guns and 27,000 men. It was neither well equipped nor provisioned. As at Lepanto, Philip intended to rely on Spanish infantry for a naval victory. England had 136 vessels, mostly armed merchantmen, under Lord Howard of Effingham, with Drake as vice-admiral. These had superior, longer range guns of debatable accuracy, but they enjoyed the advantage of more maneuverability and unequalled seamanship. The English refused to close within range of Spanish guns. Close to their base, they could replenish ammunition while Spanish expenditures were absolute. The English used fireships by night, which so confused the Spanish that they rammed their own craft. Under English attack, ammunition gone, and the army unready to sail, the Spanish started north around Scotland, abandoning the campaign. Storms punished them worse than had the English Navy, bringing ship losses to sixty-three. Not an English vessel was lost.

D. Results

The victory was strategically complete and a tactical landmark. While the Spanish employed line abreast galley tactics, patterned after their success at Lepanto, the English followed the trend of the future by using line ahead for advantage in applying firepower in time and space. The campaign showed the importance of bases relative to command of the sea, and of gunnery as opposed to boarding as a tactic. The gun replaced hand-to-hand fighting in the Age of Sail. The action signaled the shift of the western focus from the Mediterranean to the Atlantic. England went on to capitalize and perfect her naval instrument.

Strategically, the Spanish defeat constituted a decisive victory of Protestantism over Rome. The moral significance was enormous for both contending ideological camps. Philip reportedly commented dryly that he thanked God for making him so powerful that he could create a similar fleet again, but he accepted the Divine verdict. With the Armada vanished his dream of reuniting Christendom and his hope of preventing England from expanding as a naval power. More than any other event, the battle marks the embarkation of England upon the road to great empire and world power. "The defeat of the Armada whispered the imperial secret into England's ear; that in a commercial age the winning of the sea is more profitable than the winning of the land, and though this may not have been clearly understood in 1588, during the following century the whisper grew louder and louder until it became the voice of every Englishman."*

IV. SEVENTEENTH-CENTURY NAVAL TACTICS

The lessons of the Armada were not soon formalized into accepted naval tactics. Groping efforts to do so were typified by the clashes between Holland and England in the mid-seventeenth century. In these, land generals commanded at sea in the old medieval fashion, while the ships themselves were handled by sailing masters. This dichotomy of command obviously created tactical problems which were exceeded only by those of the "general-admiral" in controlling a fleet in action.

Their maneuverability limited by the wind, fleets tended to engage in individual ship-to-ship contests. These commonly took the form of either two parallel lines of contending vessels, or the fleets lost even this limited organization and clashed in a furious melee in which cannon and sword determined the outcome. The Duke of York, later James II, was the first to attempt to break with this lack of an established system by formulating simple fighting instructions. In another century, the whole concept of such regulations fell into abuse and hindered further the evolution of organization and leadership able to deal successfully with technological progress on the sea.

---

* Major General J. F. C. Fuller, *A Military History of the Western World* (New York: Funk & Wagnalls, 1955), II, 38.

CHAPTER VII

War in the Seventeenth Century

IN THE EARLY seventeenth century armies continued to include mercenaries, but formations tended to become smaller and more flexible with a great proportion of firearms. The arquebus definitively replaced the bow and the musket began to replace the arquebus. Cavalry retained importance for reconnaissance and harassment. It received firearms—crude, wheel-lock pistols—because match was difficult for a horseman to handle. By the end of the century balanced standing forces, competitive arms, and balance of power politics were normal.

I. THE THIRTY YEARS WAR

A. *Opening Moves*

Conflict was commonplace, but motivation changed. The Reformation, the religious expression of the ferment surrounding the transition from the medieval to the modern world, touched off an age of ideological war in which quarter was neither asked nor granted. The cold logic of the greatest of the Protestant reformers, John Calvin, was contested by the militant Society of Jesus. Tensions so created led to the battlefield. In 1555, the Peace of Augsburg recognized Lutheranism in the German states where it had already been established. This was only an insecure truce. Germany, the battleground of the Reformation, tensed when in 1609 the Holy Roman Emperor formed the Catholic League to challenge the Protestant Union, brought into existence the previous year by the Calvinists ignored at Augsburg. Bohemia, where the reformed tradition traced from John Hus, became the focal point of the contest when the Emperor attempted to enforce Catholicism in 1618 against the popular will. War was a certainty.

The opposing armies faced each other 8 November 1620 at the Battle of White Mountain. The 12,000 Protestant infantry were formed in eight squares of pikes, supported by musketeers and 10,000 Hungarian cavalry. Although their defensive position between a hill and a swamp was good, the foot broke at the first determined charge of the Spanish pikemen. Within two hours the 28,000-man army of the Catholic League and the Holy Roman Empire had carried the day against the less experienced and poorly disciplined Protestants. Prague, the Bohemian capital, was occupied and the Protestants brutally repressed.

This disaster aroused the interest of the Northern Protestant kingdoms. Only a group of German mercenaries remained in the field against Count Tilly, a native of the Spanish Netherlands who had risen through the ranks to command of the League forces. On behalf of the Protestants, Denmark came forward in 1626 with a somewhat better army. Wallenstein, the greatest of mercenary captains, entered into a contract with the Emperor, whereby he assumed complete responsibility in the field for the Catholic cause. He forced Denmark out of the war and seemed to threaten the Baltic possessions of Sweden. Nevertheless, Tilly once more replaced Wallenstein in command.

B. *Gustavus Adolphus' System*

Sweden's young king had campaigned in support of an aggressive Baltic policy since he was seventeen years old. His empire was held together by naval command of the Baltic but the disciplined, paid army was the primary instrument of power. The bulk of the national income went for this middle-class force, recruited by forced induction of vagabonds plus 10 per cent of all males fifteen to sixty years of age, selected by lot.

Gustavus updated organization, forming six or more 150-man companies into regiments, several of which constituted a combat brigade. A checker-board formation reminiscent of the maniple legion was used with artillery in front and cavalry on the flanks. Gustavus reduced the number of pikemen, and lightened and shortened the weapon. Realizing that the musket was the superior infantry weapon, he lightened it so that the rest was unnecessary, and introduced uniform paper cartridges and the wheel lock. Gustavus had a varied artillery train of lighter guns. Ammunition, prepared in advance and boxed, enabled his guns to fire more rapidly than enemy musketeers.

The greatness of Gustavus lay in the novelty of his ideas and the courage with which he applied them. The King himself often led his men in prayer. He was the first modern general to recognize that mobility is founded upon discipline and discipline upon efficient administration. Therefore, he maintained effective logistics for the care of his men; discipline was strict, but humane, and based upon spirit and dedication rather than flogging. No looting was permitted. Camp-followers were not tolerated. Men wore little armor, relying upon mobility as a solution to firepower. Where possible, the army was sustained by supply levies on occupied territory.

Tactically, Gustavus, the first great field gunner, opened with an artillery barrage which left the field clouded with smoke. Through this cavalry charged at a gallop to drive back the enemy foot. Infantry then advanced to hold the cavalry's gains, and decimated the enemy by volley fire. The cavalry returned to roll up the foe's flanks. Reserves were withheld for use as needed. Cavalry scouts kept the opponent always under surveillance.

These tactical and technological innovations, combined with Gustavus' leadership, were profoundly to influence warfare. Gustavus was notable for his application of the latest technological advances, the precision of his infantry tactics, and his use of artillery. Just as the Spanish *tercio,* the first modern infantry formation to integrate firearms, was a reflection of dying feudal warfare and Swiss mercenaries, so Gustavus' formation—lighter, more flexible, and with greater firepower—was an answer to the seeming invincibility of the Spanish solution. War does not stand still and, as in every age, he who best adjusts military methods to the technological and societal environment of his day looms large in history. Such a man was Gustavus Adolphus.

C. *Breitenfeld (17 September 1631)*

Gustavus' first opponent in Germany was Count Tilly, a product of the Spanish school, who fought with great squares of foot flanked by cavalry. In May 1631 the Catholics stormed and sacked the Protestant stronghold of Magdeburg. This morally strengthened the Protestant cause and Gustavus brought Tilly to battle at Breitenfeld. There Swedish guns outfired the enemy three to one and goaded him into a senseless cavalry charge. Gustavus' Saxon allies fled the field exposing his left. The King wheeled his formations to face the oncoming Tilly and personally led a cavalry charge, capturing Tilly's guns, turning them on him, and carrying the day. Gustavus followed up with a vigorous cavalry pursuit. In the Protestant world, Breitenfeld was a land Armada, and the simple folk took heart at the victory of their new champion.

Gustavus turned southwest and took the supposedly impregnable fortress of Marienburg in which the princes of the Catholic Church had stored their valuables. He assessed a war contribution from the Jesuits and clergy of Mainz. Wisely, the King tolerated no neutral or "uncommitted" states, asserting, "I shall treat neutrality as equal to a declaration of war against me." Wintering in the Protestant Palatinate gave him a secure base and cut Spanish land communication with the Netherlands.

D. *Lützen (16 November 1632)*

The Emperor turned in desperation to Wallenstein, whose terms were absolute control of the army and no imperial orders without his prior consent. In April 1632 he reoccupied Bohemia and raised his army to 60,000. His recruiting method was to offer country lads a choice of coin or a noose. In September he forced Gustavus to lift the siege of Nuremburg by attacking him indirectly, i.e., threatening his supply line. By November, assuming the Swede would go into winter quarters, Wallenstein began casually entrenching himself at Lützen until spring, for he thought the campaigning season was over.

Gustavus seized the strategic initiative and attained complete surprise by marching from Nuremburg to arrive late 15 November with about 18,000 troops. Wallenstein, gout-ridden, wished to avoid battle, but he spent the night feverishly entrenching himself. In the misty morning Gustavus drew up two lines flanked by cavalry; unfortunately, however, while riding in the fog he was killed by an enemy patrol. Instead of destroying his well-trained army, his death filled it with fanatical fury. In the battle, the Swedes carried all before them, scattering Wallenstein's troops by nightfall.

Lützen did not end the war. Gustavus' idea of a great Protestant combination under his leadership died with him. The old Swedish army was squandered in a foolish frontal attack at Nordlingen in 1634. Military bands devastated a Germany so desperate that cannibalism appeared and a third of the population perished for one cause or another. The conflict expanded into a power struggle between France and Austria from which the original religious causes rapidly receded and into which poured the aspirations of contestants soon to include nearly all Europe except England.

E. Rocroi (18 May 1643)

At Rocroi, the long-invincible Spanish tercios went down to defeat before a French professional army employing the Swedish system. The military superiority of Spain passed, again because of failure tactically to progress beyond an initially successful formula. France emerged from Rocroi the principal military power and Spain faded into decline. The inevitable strategic reaction to the unrestrained bloodshed of the long war set in when a new French general, Turenne, finally concluded the Thirty Years War in 1648 by maneuver rather than by pitched battle.

II. THE ENGLISH CIVIL WAR

Scotland and England merged under James I in 1603 and England thereafter had no land frontier. Given her insular position the necessity for standing forces vanished. All fit men remained subject to service, but not outside their counties unless there was an invasion. Consequently, unlike continental monarchs, the King was unable to use force to impose his will upon Parliament or to control the purse. He could summon Parliament to vote revenues whenever he wished, but if he could operate the state on his personal income there was no need for him to call it at all. Such a course required economy and refraining from foreign wars. The earlier Tudor dynasty had managed this feat, in part through supplementing the royal income by raids against Spanish treasure ships.

James I and the later Stuart kings were not so successful and, besides, they possessed an exalted concept of the kingship in conflict with English constitutional development. The result was a friction with Parliament which had religious aspects. When the Church of England was separated from Rome by Henry VIII, the King became its head. Bumbling Charles I permitted attempts to force Church of England practices upon the staunchly Calvinist Scottish Presbyterians. The Scots began preparing for war, and Parliament, rather than vote the King the needed appropriations, intrigued with the rebels. Charles, a weakling, vacillated. Parliament entered the power vacuum and even began to raise its own armed force. The English Civil War rapidly took shape.

A. Forces

The struggle was economically and socially between the dying feudal nobility and the rising urban moneyed commercial classes. The latter controlled the sea and, therefore, customs receipts and the fleet. It could limit the King's importation of foreign arms. Both sides appealed for volunteers and called militia, but they paid irregularly; lack of discipline and desertion were common. Impressment was used and supplies were arbitrarily levied.

Parliament had the trained bands—or militia—of London, which alone in the kingdom were decently drilled. The officers soon urged a permanent force and in December 1644 under Thomas Fairfax and Oliver Cromwell—the latter a squire without military experience—the New Model Army was established. Cromwell realized that leadership was useless without disciplined followers. He selected men of quality dedicated to the Parliamentary cause. Over them he maintained a firm but fair discipline. The force consisted of eleven regiments of cavalry, twelve of foot, and a thousand dragoons—in all, 22,000; the cavalry, under Cromwell's personal command, was the decisive arm. It used pistol and sword, rather than lance. Organized in troops of 100 each, it was employed in the Swedish manner in three lines. The infantry was one-third pike and two-thirds 100-yard range musket. The company was the permanent organization. Several were grouped into regiments as needed. The New Model Army was attired for the first time in the British Red Coat.

B. *Naseby (14 June 1645)*

In the decisive battle of Naseby, Prince Rupert's cavalry drove the enemy left from the field, but could not control the pursuit. When he finally regrouped to return, his horses were blown and he was unable to succor the King's foot which was forthwith defeated by Cromwell's cavalry. The New Model's victory cost Charles both his kingdom and his head.

C. *Results and Legacy*

When Parliament attempted to disband the army without back pay, the soldiers refused to go home, purged the politicians, defeated all opposition, and executed the King. This left England under the unconstitutional control of Cromwell and the 70,000-man standing army which had originally taken up arms to defend the constitution. Although the country was given an aggressive foreign policy, troops were quartered in private homes to prevent revolt; a secret police spied on the nation and even oppressive taxes could not meet the military expenses. The entire nation was divided into eleven districts under Major Generals supported by cavalry and militia. Police, public order, taxation, and enforcement of morality were their duties. Cromwell's was a true standing army, and the English experienced a real taste of military dictatorship which, as a people, they have never forgotten.

After Cromwell's death, General Monk called a new Parliament and the Stuart Dynasty was re-established. The quarrel with the King over the armed forces did not end, and in 1688 James II was deposed. His daughter Mary and her husband, the Dutch William of Orange, implacable enemy of France, came to the throne. William needed troops for his French war and accepted Parliamentary restrictions that (1) a peacetime standing army without Parliament's prior consent was illegal, (2) Protestant citizens had the right to keep firearms, and (3) soldiers would not be permitted in courts or at polling places. Parliament further limited appropriations and the Mutiny Act, upon which the government depended for courts-martial, to a single year.

Cromwell's legacy was remembered by the American founding fathers, is reflected in the Constitution of the United States, and continues to influence civil-military relations in English-speaking countries. Consequently, neither the United States, nor Britain, nor the Commonwealth have ever been adequately prepared for war and suspicion of the professional officer has become an unfortunate part of our heritage. Civilian control, however often inept, has therefore become a fetish.

III. THE WARS OF LOUIS XIV

On the Continent, royal control of the armed forces remained unchallenged. France emerged from Rocroi the strongest military power; Louis XIV pursued an imperial policy aimed at political dominance as well. The process of consolidating royal power, begun as feudalism declined, was pushed to its conclusion with Louis reigning absolutely under the doctrine of the divine right of kings and without regard for the ancient *Parlement* of Paris. His ambition for fame and his desire for greater territory kept France, and much of Europe, at almost continuous, albeit indecisive, war.

But it was a new type of conflict, patterned after the restraint and maneuver of Turenne rather than the brutality of the religious struggles. Armies were composed of long-term professionals, harshly disciplined, paid and maintained by the state and isolated from society. The indirect approach replaced the battle of annihilation as a strategic objective. An age of limited war and armed diplomacy enveloped the Western World.

A. Louvois

For the French Army, War Minister Louvois initiated a program of sweeping reforms. Turenne was an addict of war of the stomach—

of great turning movements to sever enemy supply lines—and Louvois therefore took care for the belly of France. The seventeenth century saw the beginning of the since-unchecked growth of bureaucracy; Louvois blessed the army with professional administrators. He established a quartermaster general's department to supervise the purchase and distribution of supplies. Rigid military administration replaced administrative anarchy. Well-fed and well-equipped forces could be better disciplined. Military roads were improved and at key frontier points magazines were erected for storage of matériel and foodstuffs. This alone was sufficient to alter the character of war by freeing the army from the task of foraging and thereby the population from pillage by rapacious troops. It helped to confine war solely to the sphere of the professionals.

Technological advances were at play. The flintlock mechanism appeared, reducing the chance of musket misfires. The advent of the bayonet rendered the pike obsolete. Consequently, mass formations with pike protecting firearm yielded to linear tactics with musketeers firing in volleys and then fixing bayonets. To be tactically effective, soldiers had to be precisely drilled and trained to act in unison. They had to stand, reload, and fire amidst fallen comrades in the heat of action. Such rigidity could be had only by rigorous, incessant drill. The parade ground therefore acquired a place in military training, which it still retains. Each man marched at an identical pace, weapon held at an identical angle. Each movement of the firing order was simultaneously performed. Uniformity throughout the army was assured by Inspector Generals. War games and maneuvers were held annually. Standardization and centralization for efficiency's sake were preferred to tactical innovation.

Since training such a force to combat readiness took five years, the state's investment in each soldier was high. To derive commensurate benefit, it held him to a long term of service. A valuable man, he was well supplied, employed strategically with care in the field, and given the *esprit de corps* of an honored professional. Fancy uniforms and ribbons distinguished him from civilians. After 1678, France maintained a standing force of over 200,000 of these soldiers.

B. Colbert

The economic support for French military and political policy was directed by another great minister, Colbert. He closed tax leaks and established a fiscal policy which placed France on a sound financial basis. The greatest of mercantilists, Colbert sought to acquire a larger share of the world supply of bullion. This he did by fostering trade, industry, agriculture, communications, colonies, ports, and a powerful fleet. By confining colonial trade to the mother country and seeking a favorable trade balance which would require debtor nations to ship bullion, he aimed at keeping the country economically and financially powerful. All mercantilist policies were designed to increase national wealth relative to other states and to pay standing armies and navies.

The outgrowth of this policy and of political considerations was that the seventeenth century witnessed standing forces, competitive arms, and balance of power politics.

Colbert's program placed a premium upon a merchant fleet and a navy to protect colonial and international commerce. Every French seaman was registered for possible maritime conscription. Naval architects were hired. Within a decade their shipyards produced a force powerful enough to challenge the Dutch and the English. But from a naval point of view, France had two coasts to defend and she divided her defense funds between land and sea. Land war traditionally absorbed her first attention.

In 1685, Louis revoked the Edict of Nantes which had granted toleration to Protestants. The result was the emigration of 200,000 of the country's best craftsmen, businessmen, and industrialists; Colbert's program of internal prosperity failed, and industry and trade began to decline. In time, Louis' constant wars against the coalitions he provoked against himself left his monarchy nearly bankrupt.

C. Turenne

While the wars of Louis XIV are of less military than diplomatic interest, one great general was in the field. Turenne was adept at the skillful maneuver characteristic of war from 1660 to 1763, but so were most generals of the day. Armies were comprised of valuable professionals who could not be squandered in needless attacks, but they also were slow and cumbersome because they fought as single forces rather than in the small combat units of Gustavus. They moved only when provided with six days' supply of bread and operated upon magazines as fixed strong points. Strategically, they were used in limited operations against or for limited objectives.

Turenne, whose generalship improved with age, demonstrated genius in his winter campaign of 1674-1675. Not only did he take the field in winter's snow—unusual due to bad roads—but he cut loose from his magazines and operated with mobility and surprise in Alsace and Lorraine, defeating a force of allied Germans under the Elector of Brandenburg. The example went unemulated by less flexible minds.

D. *Vauban*

Military engineering had steadily progressed since the Italian wars in response to the development of greater offensive fire-power. Military engineers designed works which added to the power of the defensive gun and made less certain the attacker's success. On behalf of the offense, Marshal Vauban, a French engineer, formulated a system for attacking fortified places by constructing three parallel trenches connected by zigzag approaches. As the three parallels closed, artillery was brought up and mines emplaced. Once all preparations were completed, the attacker called for surrender. If refused, he set off his mines and stormed the remaining works. Vauban's siege method was highly successful and was practiced for a century and a half.

As a defensive engineer, the master was equally great, designing fortresses which provided for enfilade fire and infantry counter-attack. These continued to protect France as late as the French Revolution. Vauban also organized the first uniformed, modern engineering corps. The eminence it exercised over siege operations and fortress defense gave it added importance in combination with the basic arms.

E. *Summary*

The strategic reflection of economic, social, and political factors at play and of Vauban's innovations, was slow, methodical warfare focusing upon maneuver and the reduction of strongholds. In these, great stores were stockpiled for armies. In effect, this method of operation was a reversion to feudal warfare in that the defense was ahead of the offense, leading armies to operate upon fixed strong points. Prior to the mass production methods of the industrial revolution, no state could accumulate adequate equipment from current production alone. This fact slowed innovation by delaying the impact of technological advances; stockpiling, however, kept the few armament manufacturers well occupied, and furnished them capital with which to develop other enterprises.

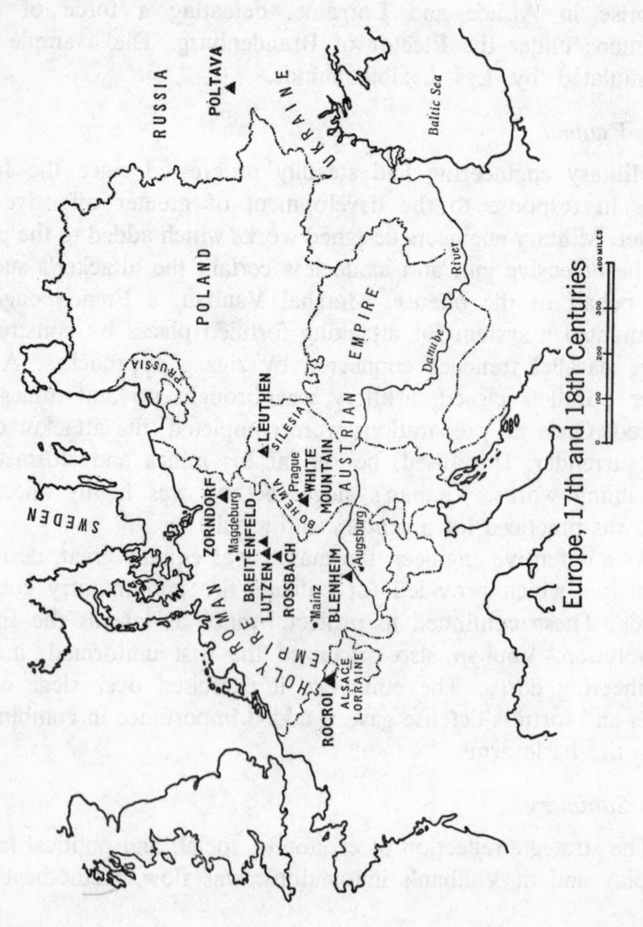

Europe, 17th and 18th Centuries

CHAPTER VIII

Eighteenth-Century Warfare

I. INTRODUCTION

EIGHTEENTH-CENTURY warfare was limited "because of a static military technology and because monarchs could not reorganize their potential military resources without social revolutions which would be more dangerous to themselves than to their enemies."* The absolute monarchs relied upon professional armies as their real power base but employed them for limited political or economic objectives. Logistics also kept war limited. Magazines of food and matériel were positioned at three-day intervals. This practice made armies self-sufficient and obviated foraging, during which soldiers might desert, but it limited the range of operations. Campaigning was restricted to a few months by the availability of green forage for the great hordes of draft animals.

As the economic position of the nobility declined, serving the state for pay grew acceptable. The officer corps was compatible with a gentleman's honor. Therefore, class and military tradition became bound up in the profession. The middle class gradually infiltrated it, however, by purchasing commissions. This was especially true of the engineers and artillerymen, whose technical training was more important than their breeding. Engineering education was originally confined to military purposes.

The standard infantry weapon was the musket, modified with flintlock and the socket bayonet which permitted firing with

* Theodore Ropp, *War in the Modern World* (Durham, N. C.: Duke, 1959), 42.

bayonet fixed. Push of a pike lost importance and there was seldom a bayonet charge. The original ninety-eight steps in the firing order were reduced to less than thirty, but they were still complicated and performed under fire in close order. As improvements increased infantry firepower, cavalry continued its decline. It was most successful in surprise attacks on flank and rear, but was little used for reconnaissance.

Into the linear infantry formations, seeking the effects of later automatic weapons, tacticians crowded as much firepower as possible. Yet, live fire was seldom used in drill and marksmanship was virtually nonexistent. As in the Greek phalanx, physical skill and stamina were paramount. Endless parade drill and dry firing occupied the soldier's time and is an inheritance the modern soldier shares. Not individual initiative, but speed and volume delivery of ¾ inch lead balls, was desired. Since the effective forty-yard range of volley fire could be covered by an enemy bayonet charge in about thirty seconds, fire was delayed for maximum effectiveness until the last possible moment in order to avoid the uncertainty of reloading. With this proximity, the close formation, and the bayonet charge, infantry again groped backward toward the phalanx. Casualties were high; deployment of troops was slow. Battle seldom occurred without mutual consent and was a last resort. Pursuit was rarely effective and sometimes was forbidden for fear of desertion.

Prussia raided and seized men where they were found for lifetime enlistments but, due to desertion, still had a replacement rate of 20% per annum. Every army included persons of other nationalities. In general, however, armies consisted of the nonproductive classes who were not missed, i.e., of the nobility as an officer corps, and the dregs of society as soldiers. Discipline was brutal in order to control the type of irresponsible person who filled the ranks. Tactical formations were designed to use him as an automaton. The public attitude toward him was fear and contempt. The middle class and freeholders under a mercantilist economic philosophy paid the taxes that sustained the military but devoted their attention to production rather than war. They were glad to live isolated from it.

Turenne's system of maneuver and Vauban's fortifications and siegecraft were the highly emulated strategic patterns. Skillful attention to these techniques and to logistics were the keys to success. Armies were almost equal in men and equipment; generalship was the decisive factor. Genius in executing the indirect approach was not uncommon. Three eighteenth-century generals have been ranked among the Great Captains—Marlborough, Eugene, and Frederick the Great.

II. MARLBOROUGH AND EUGENE

A. *War of the Spanish Succession*

When Charles II of Spain died childless (11 November 1700) he left his throne to Louis XIV's grandson, Philip. This threatened the balance of power, which England had been striving to preserve, by at last placing world domination within Louis' grasp. Austria had a rival claimant to the Spanish throne. England was committed to protecting the Dutch against France, and feared loss of her own large clandestine trade with Spanish America. A great alliance was consequently raised against France and Spain. The allies had naval superiority but had suffered a long history of land defeats by the French.

Anticipating the alliance, France reenforced the Spanish garrisons in northern Italy. Austria's brilliant Prince Eugene of Savoy gained the initiative by crossing the Alps over an implausible route in May 1701, deceived the enemy with agile maneuver, and on 1 September at Chiari lured him into a disastrous attack. Displaying innovation, Eugene deployed his men prone behind defenses to decimate the French frontal attack. This campaign brought the German states and Savoy into the war on the allied side and placed France at a moral disadvantage.

John Churchill, Duke of Marlborough, Britain's Captain General and the Deputy Captain General of Holland, was "one of the greatest military geniuses his country has known. He possessed the rare virtue of seeing a war as a whole, and of being able to relate seapower with land power and strategy with politics."*

* Fuller, *op. cit.*, 127-128.

Meticulous in planning and executing his campaigns, he was equally concerned for the provision and welfare of his men. Marlborough was the most successful coordinator of allies prior to General Dwight D. Eisenhower. Unfortunately, his inability to include peace within his expansive view of the full scope of conflict made him a weak grand strategist. Nevertheless, in an age which preferred precise maneuver to aggressive offense, he vigorously sought battle. As such, although he fought but four, he stands as the link between Gustavus and Frederick the Great.

The Duke destroyed French tactical supremacy through his unequalled Dutch infantry and his English cavalry which again used Gustavus' shock tactics. The infantry fixed the foe in position so that he could be broken by the horse which charged in three lines at a brisk trot, sword in hand. While the French relied upon the bayonet, Marlborough preferred disciplined musketry and permitted the other side to fire first. While the enemy reloaded, Marlborough's musketeers acted as their executioners.

B. Blenheim (13 August 1704)

To succeed strategically against France, Marlborough had to prevent England's Dutch and Austrian allies from being overrun. Collaboration with Eugene surmounted the obstacle of France's strong interior position and numerical superiority. The French had decided on a defense against the Low Countries and an offense in south Germany. Austria was in danger of collapse, so Marlborough daringly abandoned his Dutch base 19 May 1704 and marched southward toward the upper Danube with 20,000 men, averaging ten miles daily for six weeks. After such maneuvering, Marlborough and Eugene, who had joined him, achieved tactical surprise by a dawn attack on 60,000 French and Bavarians in a position between the river and hilly terrain. The usual evasive maneuvers were denied. Marlborough fixed the enemy in heavy fighting, concentrated troops to gain local superiority at the decisive point, softened the French with grapeshot, penetrated their line with cavalry late in the afternoon, and pinned part of their force against the Danube. At a total cost of 12,000, the allies inflicted 38,609 casualties on the enemy and captured an immense booty. The tactical decisiveness of the action was rare for the time and reflected Marlborough's skill and great determination, and Eugene's tenacity.

C. *Results*

Louis XIV began to abandon the idea of dominating the world, but Blenheim, greatest continental victory of English arms since Agincourt, did not end the war. In May 1806 Marlborough won again at Ramillies and liberated all of Flanders, and in September Eugene inflicted a defeat so severe on the French besieging Turin that they yielded Italy; it became an Austrian sphere of influence for 150 years. At Oudenarde (10 July 1708), after a forced march, the allies routed the French late in the day, Eugene having the major role. Honorable peace could have been had except for the heavy terms demanded by the allied politicians. Negotiations failed and the war dragged on.

The patriotic spirit of the French and the Spanish rose. At Malplaquet, 11 September 1709, in the eighteenth century's bloodiest and largest battle, Marlborough and Eugene gained a Pyrrhic victory. The only battle which they entered with numerical superiority, it ruined the Dutch army as an effective force and set up a cry in England where Marlborough's political fortunes slipped. The politicians rejected the offensive on Paris by which peace might have been imposed. Consequently, France and Spain gained far better terms in the 1713 Peace of Utrecht. England, however, won Gibraltar and with it naval control of the Mediterranean. She received Nova Scotia, Newfoundland, Hudson's Bay, and trade rights in Spanish America.

III. CHARLES XII IN THE GREAT NORTHERN WAR

By a surprise invasion, Sweden's King Charles XII defeated Denmark in 1700 and secured the western end of Gustavus' old Baltic empire. Surrounded by enemies, he then turned eastward against Russia and Poland, which coveted his control of the eastern Baltic littoral. Although victorious in a sweeping campaign with numerically inferior forces, Charles failed to consolidate politically his military gains before invading Russia in 1708.

Russia's Czar Peter (called "the Great") had been endeavoring to shake his country out of the barbaric stupor in which it had lain since the Mongol era. He twisted Russia's face toward Europe and sought Swedish coastal territory for a defensible port. Peter's army had powerful new artillery. He determined to avoid pitched battle and use space and Russia's winter against Charles, who swung southeast hoping to gain Ukrainian allies. Charles's supply lines were harassed; scorched earth lay before him. Yet he survived the winter and laid siege to the depot town of Poltava in May 1709.

To Poltava's rescue came the Czar with a large force and greater firepower. Charles employed his usually successful tactics of speed and shock but unfortunately, he was wounded and could not personally command. His army was destroyed in the attack on Peter.

Poltava marks the emergence of the sinister, Mongolized Russians as a European military power replacing the attractive Scandinavians in the European power concert. The former "gained a foothold on the counterscarp of eastern Europe."* Peter soon imposed a harsh regime and raised a great army which was "a portent of yet another Asiatic invasion."* The offspring of Peter's marriage of European efficiency to Mongol brutality was the Russian nation.

IV. SAXE

The war of the Austrian Succession, beginning in 1741, was virtually a resumption of the War of the Spanish Succession. France's army was really that of Louis XIV in decay. Her best commander was Maurice of Saxe, bastard son of the late king of Poland, and a professional since he was thirteen. At Fontenoy (11 May 1745) the artillery he had posted in four redoubts in front of his main line poured a deadly fire into the attacking English and Dutch. Their advance was halted with heavy losses on each side. Thereafter Saxe overran the Netherlands. He is most known, however, for his theories on war.

* Fuller, *op. cit.,* 184-185.

Published in 1757, Saxe's *Reveries* contained a better grasp of tactics and leadership than any work since that of Vegetius. He lamented the decline in warfare after Gustavus, which he charged to emulation of forms, forgetting of principles, and raising of troops by fraud or force. He was ahead of his time in desiring breachloading guns and muskets, functional uniforms, company messes, expert riflemen and skirmishers to break up enemy charges, and an end to volley in favor of aimed firing. He suggested a return to pikemen, however, to protect infantry in order to add to musketeers' confidence and get them to take careful aim. He advocated five-year conscription. He stressed redoubts or strong points as preferable to trenches in defensibility. Determined pursuit of a beaten enemy stood high with him. Saxe had a keen appreciation of the morale factor in war, stressing that understanding how to keep morale high was a true trait of the Great Captain. "It is not the big armies that win battles; it is the good ones." Yet, he perhaps moved unsteadily in asserting that "war is a science covered with shadows in whose obscurity one cannot move with an assured step. Routine and prejudice, the natural result of ignorance, are its foundation and support. All sciences have principles and rules; war has none." Reconciled to eighteenth-century warfare, Saxe deprecated acceptance of battle, advancing the possibility that "a general can wage war all his life without being compelled to do so."

V. THE SEVEN YEARS WAR

A. *Introduction*

"The Seven Years War was the climax of the empire building that had begun early in the fifteenth century, when the horizons of Europe were broadened by the Age of Discovery and Exploration. The urge of Atlantic maritime peoples to chart and use the unknown seas was primarily due to jealousy of the monopoly held by the Italian city-states over the Eastern trade that had grown out of the Crusades. Fear of the inexorable encroachment of the Moslem world upon the declining Byzantine Empire was another important factor."* After defeating Spain and eliminating the Dutch as an Atlantic rival, the English resumed in the Seven Years War the contest with France for colonial preeminence based upon sea power. They enjoyed a great advantage in that France was once more dividing her effort between the sea and land war on the Continent. England left the land war to Frederick the Great, her Prussian ally.

B. *Pitt and Colonial War*

American colonies meant different things to the mother lands: to Spain, they were for "God, gold, and glory" and theoretically equal under the crown; to France, they were for missionary work and fur trade mercantilism; to England, they were permanent settlements—safety valves of society—to which English life could be projected. The success of the latter over the French in North America was interrelated with greater prosperity and population (in 1759, 1,300,000 to 82,000). There were American counterparts to European wars because the English and French colonists had economic rivalries and deep Catholic versus Calvinist religious hatreds.

1. FORCES

The English colonists adopted the militia system, which of course traced from the pre-Norman fyrd. Each colony had its own force. Most settlers used weapons in their daily lives but lacked formal training in their use. The gap between officers and men was almost nonexistent and a more individually responsible soldiery than in Europe invited looser formations and greater individual initiative. Only New York had a standing garrison of British regulars and these were of very low quality.

The French had a uniform militia 10,000-20,000 strong—almost the entire able-bodied male population. It was reasonably well trained and generally more effective in the forests than

* Department of English, History, and Government, United States Naval Academy, *Materials in Naval History* (Annapolis: United States Naval Institute, 1952), 1.

were the English. The French in 1753 began constructing along the inland waterways a chain of wooden blockhouses connecting Quebec and New Orleans. In 1754 Colonel George Washington's Virginia militia attempted unsuccessfully to cut this enemy axis of expansion aimed at sealing the English east of the Appalachians. Strategically, however, French North America was weakest in her main river line of communications, the St. Lawrence. Quebec was the jugular vein.

2. BRADDOCK

Tension was high by April 1755 when General Edward Braddock, experienced in contemporary Continental conflict, set out to wrest control of the Ohio Valley from the encroaching French. Irregular woods warfare was completely beyond his ken and in the 9 July Battle of Monongahela his inability to adjust tactically to his enemy led to destruction. An obscure action in a colonial wilderness, it did not mark the end of regulars in America as an effective force. It did signal the approaching demise of parade-ground war, the return of light infantry just as Saxe had predicted and, more important, the advent of the modern age of the citizen soldier. When the British navy retaliated by trying to blockade the St. Lawrence, war resulted.

3. PITT

"I know that I can save this country and that no one else can," said William Pitt when he became Secretary of State for War in 1756. England's fortunes in the Seven Years War were at a low ebb, for she had suffered defeat in the Mediterranean. Pitt gathered all the financial, military and administrative power and waged the first world war. He disengaged England from the land aspect of the struggle, concentrating her efforts. He eliminated inept senior commanders, replacing them with talented young men. He resolved to destroy French power once and for all in Europe, America, and Asia. His intention was to take the strategic offensive where England was strongest—on the sea, and therefore colonially—and to barter sea power for victory over land power at the peace table. Meanwhile, seizure of enemy colonies would provide wealth to sustain the war effort and to subsidize Prussia on the Continent. Further to support Frederick, Pitt conducted amphibious diversions against the coasts of Europe.

4. QUEBEC (13 SEPTEMBER 1759)

Using naval domination of the Atlantic, Pitt broadened war in America into a regular's contest. Light infantry tactics succeeded in 1758 against Fort Duquesne (renamed for Pitt) and up the Champlain and St. Lawrence valleys. The following summer an expedition under Wolfe was sent against Montcalm's French at Quebec.

Montcalm behind his 300 guns, without support from the mother country, employed a defensive strategy. Wolfe unsuccessfully attempted to gain a lodgement on the north bank of the St. Lawrence and then probed the French defenses. On the night of 12 September he crossed the river and ascended a neglected path to the Plains of Abraham. He placed himself between Montcalm—who still was not obliged to fight—and an advancing reinforcement. Wolfe had but a few days' supplies and his communications were by a precipitous trail. He held the irregulars and American troops in scorn and felt certain that the French Canadian militia would desert Montcalm. The latter drew up his forces, throwing away his advantages, and accepted battle, firing first. Worse, he primarily relied upon linear tactics in which his militiamen did not fit well because they dropped to the ground to reload. The British conquered Canada with two musket volleys at 30 yards and a bayonet charge. Both commanders were killed; Quebec surrendered 17 September. Notably, this decisive action was fought primarily by regulars and in the prevailing European manner.

C. *Frederick and Continental War*

Prussia was poor, lightly populated, and strategically weak because she lacked natural frontiers and was surrounded by aggressive nations. She had been fashioned from a group of noncontiguous personal possessions of the exceedingly capable Hohenzollern family. Beginning during the wars of Louis XIV, they founded a frugally efficient domestic bureaucracy and channeled the improved resources of their lands into an army disproportionate to their demographic or economic means. With this force they made themselves felt in Europe and set in motion expansion and consolidation. "It was not Prussia that made the army, but the army that made modern Prussia," wrote Dorn. The king was in person the commander of this expression of the nation.

Frederick II—"the Great"—concentrated in himself the sum of military and political authority. His officers came from the Junkers, the poor but proud and stern rural nobility. Europe's finest and most cohesive military class, they lived a strenuous, dedicated life of loyal service to their reformed church, country, and king. Their professional training was Europe's best. Native soldiers were raised on a territorial basis. Provinces were divided into cantons, each of which raised a regiment.

Since there were never enough Prussians available without disturbing the productive, economic power-generating middle class, the army impressed aliens. The desertion rate was therefore the highest in Europe. Corporal punishment was needed to control the troops. Officers enjoyed life and death powers over men. Training in the prevalent linear tactics was strict in order to obtain the maneuver which Frederick prized. His infantry used an iron ramrod which led to increased firepower.

When Frederick II came to the throne in 1740, his army of 80,000 was Europe's fourth largest after those of France, Russia, and Austria. War of decision seemed futile until—taking advantage of Austria's passing into the hands of a woman, Maria Theresa—Frederick invaded the wealthy province of Silesia. At Mollwitz (10 April 1741) his superior artillery and higher rate of infantry fire proved more than a match for superior Austrian cavalry. In the ensuing War of the Austrian Succession, Frederick made good his Silesian claim, but Austria was left vengeful.

She reversed her traditional alliance with England and Holland against France and turned to France and Russia. Thereupon, the British in January 1756, after colonial war in America was a certainty, allied defensively with Frederick to protect their king's German realm, Hanover. The continental phase of the Seven Years War resulted.

1. ROSSBACH (5 NOVEMBER 1757)

At Lobositz in October 1756 the tenacity of his infantry gave Frederick a victory over the Austrian and Saxon armies. He occupied Dresden, the Saxon capital, looted it, added its resources to his own war chest, and impressed part of the Saxon army. After an indecisive campaign in Bohemia, he found himself threatened on all sides by the enemy allies. After rapid maneuver, he encountered the doubly numerous French and Austrians at Rossbach. Frederick watched their attempt to turn his left and cut his communications develop slowly across muddy ground. Swiftly he redeployed to meet them. The allies mistook his movements for retreat and speeded up. Frederick struck them on the march with 4,000 cavalry supported by artillery and achieved a rout within an hour. Because of the character of his largely impressed army, Frederick could not pursue for fear of desertion. French effectiveness suffered a severe blow; Rossbach confirmed the decline of the once mighty French army. England increased sevenfold her subsidy to Prussia.

2. THE FRENCH ARMY

France's army was still that of Louis XIV in decline. The officer corps, at higher levels, was closely bound up with the court. Intrigue was necessary to maintain and improve military positions, the livelihood of the nobility. Colonels and Generals rarely visited their commands. There was an officer—usually ignorant of tactics and command—for every fifteen men. At times there were more nobles in the army than there were positions because commissions were created for them. They dragged along elaborate baggage trains. Finally, the purchase and sale of commissions and units introduced into the army the class struggle between rising bourgeoisie and old nobility.

3. LEUTHEN (5 DECEMBER 1757)

Frederick still had to contend with the main Austrian army which had overrun Silesia. He marched 170 miles in fifteen days to meet it at Leuthen. The Austrian position was strong but over five miles long. Frederick deceived the enemy with a cavalry feint to the right, and then advanced against the left in an oblique order. The Prussians crushed the Austrian left, turned, and began rolling up the entire long enemy line. Attempts to reform failed and the tightly packed infantry was subjected to severe punishment. As darkness fell, Frederick completed with a cavalry charge his victory over triply numerous forces. By strict adherence to the principles of concentration and economy of force, he gained a great triumph. On this occasion he pursued vigorously. With the Austrians destroyed, Silesia returned to Prussian control. Napoleon viewed Leuthen as "a masterpiece of maneuver and resolution," of itself sufficient to rank Frederick among the Great Captains.

4. ZORNDORF (25 AUGUST 1758)

After a year of inconclusive maneuvering which served to protect Prussia, Frederick met the Russians on the Oder River, as always with numerical inferiority. He maneuvered them into a perimeter defense and won with a frontal attack, albeit with losses so heavy he was unable to prevent Russian withdrawal. Frederick was then beset with added problems. He could not replace the losses of his gravely weakened army. The previously inept enemy commanders were learning from experience. On 14 October at Hochkirchen the Austrians surprised and defeated him by a night march. Then, on 12 August 1759, the Russians avenged Zorndorf by handing Frederick his worst defeat at Kunersdorf where the Prussian threw away 48 per cent of his veterans in a series of poorly coordinated frontal attacks.

Thereafter Frederick employed maneuver defensively, generally from necessity avoiding battle. Prussia was economically incapable of supporting a long war; superior numbers in time began wearing Frederick down. In 1762, with Pitt out of power, England abandoned Frederick to seek a separate peace with France. The allies concerted a plan for combined operations on converging lines. Frederick maneuvered furiously to stave off disaster, but his real salvation was political. The death of the Czarina Elizabeth brought to the Russian throne Peter III, a Prussophile, who threw away victory in a friend's peace with Frederick. France, defeated colonially by Pitt's strategy, could no longer be effective continentally and Austria, virtually deserted, settled with Frederick on the *status quo ante bellum.*

5. ASSESSMENT

Except for Marlborough's, eighteenth-century warfare was generally precise prior to Frederick. Although the Prussian accepted Turenne's views on maneuver against enemy supply lines, he also saw that war of decision required offensive battle. The enemy was his primary objective. His drill and training gave him superior mobility and speed. By seizing and holding the strategic initiative, Frederick employed his army on interior lines against the three largest armies in Europe. Tactically, he perfected the oblique order, advancing one wing while refusing the other, in order to achieve local numerical superiority against an enemy flank. Like Gustavus, he emphasized firepower, both of artillery and musket. Frederick nevertheless adhered to the tactical offense in order to implement a strategic defense. War of annihilation may not have been beyond his thinking, but it was beyond his means.

D. Results of the Seven Years War

In the 1763 Peace of Paris, the war ended with Frederick retaining Silesia. He had been abandoned by England; for this neither he nor Prussia ever forgave her. Austria and Russia lost nothing of importance. England, whose campaigns were the more decisive, acquired France's American possessions east of the Mississippi and in Canada and restricted her in India to a few trading stations. Britain emerged the principal world power. France was finally left—after all her wars—a financial ruin, sapped by deficit financing, her colonies and fleet weakened. She retained, however, key harbors throughout the world and, consequently, the ability to revive. And finally, although England's maritime supremacy was momentarily unchallenged, there was an ill portent for her in that her American colonies, devoid of foreign peril, were left in comfortable security.

VI. THE EVOLUTION OF NAVAL WARFARE

A. Command

Although there was negligible technological advance, the old problem of naval command was near solution by the end of the century. In 1704 the English admiral, Rooke, issued to his captains *Basic Fighting Instructions*. These were unfortunately reprinted as *Permanent,* instead of *Basic,* with the result that on the sea the rule of law, fashion of the Enlightenment, was rigidly applied. Consequently, in 1756 Admiral Byng was court-martialed and shot for breaking the line of ships. There remained one loophole, however, Article 39 which permitted a general chase. This was used most effectively by Hawke in 1759 when he drove a French fleet through Quiberon Bay and up a creek. But such an expedient meant that an admiral relinquished effective control.

The problem remained until Admiral Kempenfelt developed the vocabulary signal book, although it was not perfected until shortly before the 1805 battle of Trafalgar. The book at last conceded admirals the initiative to go beyond mechanical execution of a particular maneuver cited by reference to the *Instructions*. Even the signalling of intentions could not bring victory if captains did not understand their commanders' mind. Nelson solved this problem also by frequent conferences in which he and his subordinates discussed possible combat situations and their tactical solution. This was the "Nelson touch" which made his captains into an effective team.

B. Tactics

During the eighteenth century the British were generally aggressive and took the windward position, while the French defensively preferred the leeward. From there they aimed to cripple their opponent's mobility by bringing down his masts, spars, and sails. For their part, the British attempted to engage at close quarters for the advantage of their rapid firepower—as much as five broadsides in as many minutes from some ships. French vessels were generally faster owing to better design, and to lack of weeds and barnacles from long periods in fresh water. The British periodically suffered from poor matériel, especially weak masts and dry-rotted hulls. Their difficulties were particularly acute during the American Revolution, when French leadership was on the rise.

Ships remained in service in most navies for twenty to sixty years. Thus, for example, the 130-gun *Santissima Trinidad,* the eighteenth century's most powerful ship, was built in the 1760's during Spain's period of naval rebuilding, and she was still flagship at Trafalgar in 1805. Smoothbore guns were little improved, although some were as large as 32 pounders. The one important innovation was the "half-ring" set in the deck which, by allowing a gun to be pivoted, enabled British gunners to traverse their pieces.

Towards the close of the century tactics improved. Admiral Rodney defeated De Grasse in the battle of Saints (1781) in the West Indies by "doubling up," i.e., getting his vessels on both sides of the Frenchman. Admiral Lord Howe on the Glorious First of June 1794 led his fleet downwind to the French and penetrated their formation, thus breaking the line. Although a tactical success, he lost the strategic victory through failure to pursue energetically. Despite poor conditions of service which led to mutinies in the British navy in 1797, it vanquished the Spanish 14 February at Cape St. Vincent when young Captain Nelson broke his line and blocked the enemy while other British vessels came into action. Unlike the hapless Byng, Nelson was rewarded for his initiative. In October, Admiral Duncan signalled a general chase, his only means of bringing a retiring Dutch squadron into action.

Advances of this kind eventually led to Nelson's decisive defeat of Napoleon Bonaparte's combined Franco-Spanish fleet at Trafalgar; in no small measure, however, these developments were the result of Britain's defeat in the war of the American Revolution, which forced her to rethink naval doctrine.

CHAPTER IX

The American Revolution

I. INTRODUCTION

GREAT BRITAIN emerged victorious from the Seven Years War but with her internal debt doubled, with sources of additional revenue dried up at home, and with increased expenses for colonial defense and administration. She was colonially overextended. The watchful French knew she would have to raise money in the American colonies and that this would lead to estrangement. The British, however, had little alternative to obliging the American colonies to help meet these expenses, particularly the cost of their own defense. The means selected included enforcement of mercantilist trade measures for the benefit of the mother country; in 1765 Britain applied the Stamp Act and other new duties. This raised a constitutional issue, since the colonists believed themselves directly under the King and beyond the taxing authority of Parliament. Intellectual and economic opposition in America, coupled with vacillation on the part of the successive ministries of the British oligarchy, provided the tension which spawned the Revolution.

The colonists resented standing armies and European militarism. They did not approve the maintenance of a proposed regular garrison of 10,000 under General Gage. New Yorkers resisted the 1765 Quartering Act which would have billeted the soldiers in inns and empty houses. In March 1770 Boston radicals provoked regulars into firing on civilians. Distrust of standing forces—the legacy of Cromwell—was greatly aggravated.

American nationalism sought to separate pure, undefiled America from corrupt European society. She was the haven of persecuted liberty, where hard work and frugality could be rewarded without artificial limitations of class or status. The Crown held the empire together, but Protestant dissenters, particularly Calvinists, formed an anti-monarchical force.

Colonial discontent coalesced politically in the September 1774 meeting in Philadelphia of the radical-dominated First Continental Congress. Militarily, the colonists began assembling arms and Gage laid preparations for repressive measures.

II. OPENING HOSTILITIES

Gage ordered 1,800 troops to advance from Boston to Concord on 18 April 1775 and seize arms stores of the Massachusetts militia. On the return trip, minutemen (irregular volunteers) inflicted 273 casualties and then laid siege to Boston. Gage carried a frontal uphill bayonet attack 17 June with 2,500 men against 1,600 patriots on Breed's Hill (Bunker Hill) but at the cost of 1,054 casualties. Meanwhile on 10 May, Benedict Arnold and Ethan Allen seized Fort Ticonderoga and lesser posts on Lake Champlain.

From these actions the American politicians derived the erroneous assumption that any citizen could effectively stand against British regulars; a permanent colonial force seemed unnecessary. Furthermore, the Americans quickly assumed the initiative in the war. General Henry Knox hauled the 120 guns from Ticonderoga and emplaced them to threaten Boston. The indecisive General William Howe, remembering the storming of Breed's Hill, thereupon abandoned his stores and evacuated in March 1776 without a fight. In the same month the infant U.S. Navy captured New Providence in the Bahamas and acquired large munitions stores.

III. FORCES

A. American

The Second Continental Congress convened in May and assumed responsibility for raising an army. Averse to standing armies and deluded by early successes, Congress insisted upon civilian control at all times and called peacetime regular forces dangerous to liberty. It authorized the raising of regiments for one year, thus initiating an unfortunate practice of short-term enlistments and reliance on undisciplined militia. George Washington, an untrained militia officer, was appointed Commander in Chief. In July 1775 three divisions under Major Generals Artemas Ward, Charles Lee, and Israel Putnam were organized. Commissions were awarded to anyone who raised a unit. Each state had its own militia which elected its own officers. The colonists had a large manpower pool and a nucleus of trained officers from the Seven Years War. They had some capacity for producing arms—primarily the standard infantry musket—but captured almost all of their guns from the enemy. Cavalry was insignificant and the medical service was atrocious.

Throughout the war, when enlistments were up, the men vanished. On 31 December 1775, Washington was faced with creating a new army, an annual event thereafter. Patriotic reasons alone were not enough to hold men. Therefore, in 1776 Congress authorized bounties, or enlistment bonuses, in an attempt to raise a longer service federal force. Bonuses grew throughout the war as the states and Congress in effect bid against each other. High bounties and low pay stimulated short service. By 6 February 1777, realizing that bounties and voluntary enlistments were a failure, Congress called upon the states to draft men for nine months. Unfortunately, this was used as a means of disposing of bums and criminals. Maryland emptied an insane asylum; Massachusetts inducted British deserters. Virginia by 1779 was offering $750.00, an annual suit of clothing, and 100 acres for duration enlistments. Congress resolved in 1780 to increase the army to 35,211 but left the means to the states. The following year it fixed the regular army at four regiments each of cavalry and artillery, forty-nine of infantry (612 men), and one of engineers. By July 1781, however, the army totaled only 5,835 men. Since all these methods of raising forces proved unreliable, Washington was obliged to adopt a defensive strategy, for he could not be sure of his manpower.

B. British

The British Army was a fairly typical eighteenth-century organization. Commissions and units were bought and sold. Impressment and induction of petty criminals were common practice. A colonel was responsible for maintaining his regiment's strength. He drew funds to pay and sustain it on the basis of the muster. If he was honest, the men were well cared for and fed; if not, they were deprived. The soldiers were overdressed and uncomfortable for parade-ground warfare. Tight shoes pinched their feet, gaiters their legs, and leather collars their necks. The red coat was hot in summer and cold in winter. Surgeons considered a butcher's handsaw their most important tool.

To put down the rebellion, Britain also had German contingents provided mainly by the Duke of Brunswick and the Landgrave of Hesse-Cassel. These British allies received a subsidy for the use of their forces, who were paid and maintained on the same basis as the English troops. Their use added to anti-British sentiment in America.

Finally, a large number of Loyalists fought for their king, since probably one-third of the colonists were apathetic while the remainder were equally divided between patriots and King's men.

IV. NORTHERN CAMPAIGNS

A. Long Island

After Howe withdrew from Boston to Halifax, Washington anticipated New York as his next objective and shifted his own forces. General Howe arrived at Staten Island late in June 1776 with more than 30,000 men supported by a powerful fleet under his brother, Admiral Richard Howe. Washington was obliged by the Congress—which on 4 July declared independence—to attempt to hold the city. He did so by seeking to deny Brooklyn Heights to the enemy. Howe routed Putnam with a skillful envelopment, but the remainder of his campaign was indecisive except for the 15 November storm of Fort Washington where a large booty was taken. Washington employed a Fabian retirement which carried him across the Delaware on 8 December with only 3,000 men remaining. Stragglers from the defeated forces of the captured General Charles Lee brought patriot strength to 6,000. Howe failed to pursue energetically and went into winter quarters. He established an eighty-mile chain of positions from the Delaware to the Hackensack. Howe then returned to his mistress in New York, leaving Colonel Rall, a Hessian parade-ground soldier, in command at Trenton, anchor of the line.

B. *Trenton and Princeton*

On Christmas night Washington recrossed the Delaware, and achieved complete surprise, killing or capturing the 1,000-man garrison. His first victory, Trenton, had a great moral effect in the colonies. It being the end of the year, his men's enlistments were up; only by borrowing money from leading Philadelphians to pay them a fresh bounty was an army kept in the field. General Cornwallis, sent from New York with reinforcements, was outmaneuvered by Washington's night march on Princeton, 2 January 1777, and evacuated western and central New Jersey. The Revolution had been saved and its Commander in Chief had emerged a military strategist capable of executing his plans in the field.

C. *Saratoga (17 October 1777)*

1. STRATEGY

Britain should early have blockaded and constricted the rebellious colonies with a naval strategy while employing the army to occupy the New England hotbed and impose martial law. That this was not done is usually charged to Lord George Germain, Colonial Secretary, who was detested by the army. He determined in 1777, at General Burgoyne's suggestion, to split the colonies along the Hudson-Lake Champlain axis, build a chain of blockhouses supported by water transport, and then clean out New England. The military means was to be convergent operations northward from New York, southward from Montreal, and eastward from Oswego with Albany as the common focus. The strategy was difficult, but not impossible of execution. Unfortunately, Germain failed to issue orders to Howe for the advance from New York and on 18 May 1777 permitted him to ship most of his forces to Philadelphia. Furthermore, since no coordinator was designated, the plan suffered from lack of unity of command. Rugged wilderness terrain made transport and communications difficult. Finally, when Burgoyne, commanding the northern or principal force, arrived at Montreal, he found that the plan had been published in a local newspaper.

2. CAMPAIGN

Burgoyne started south with 8,200 well trained and disciplined British and Brunswicker troops, as well as 500 uncontrollable Indians who provided grist for the atrocity mill. Washington strengthened forces in the upper Hudson Valley. He sent the very able General Benedict Arnold and 500 Virginia riflemen under Colonel Morgan. Arnold repelled the western prong and Clinton, who replaced Howe at New York, did not start north with his 3,000 men until 24 September. Burgoyne arrived near Saratoga and waited in vain for the other forces. His transport and supply situation rapidly deteriorated in the face of an enemy force growing daily with irregulars. He resolved to fight his way out but was repelled by Arnold 19 September 1777 and again on 7 October. Major General Horatio Gates—a retired British major, in over-all command as a result of political intrigue—sat in his tent and failed to support Arnold with reinforcements. Finally outnumbered five to one, Burgoyne surrendered on 17 October. The victory was earned by Arnold's decisive action but the inept Gates claimed the credit.

3. RESULTS

Saratoga was one of the most decisive battles in the history of the world. France had been watching England's colonial troubles with ill-concealed amusement and the victory served notice that the colonists had a chance of success. The moment had arrived for France to avenge herself. Although her finances were creaking, she aided the Americans with money, arms, and, above all, with recognition of the United States of America in February 1778. Spain joined her in war on England in 1779, the Dutch became involved in 1780, and Russia, Sweden, and Denmark formed a League of Armed Neutrality to oppose English practices on the high seas. At home, opinion was divided; a majority probably opposing the war. England found herself alone against the world, with no continental ally to occupy French attention in a land war and with her trade and national income declining. All of these things, the turning point of the war in America's favor, are creditable to the Battle of Saratoga and to its true hero, Benedict Arnold.

D. *Philadelphia (25 September 1777)*

General Howe, meanwhile, had embarked 18,000 men and, after feints along the coast, landed at Elkton at the head of the Chesapeake Bay and advanced overland toward Philadelphia. On 11 September 1777, he enveloped Washington's right at Brandywine Creek, forcing his withdrawal toward the city. After skirmishes the city fell two weeks later. Washington's attempt to regain it by an early morning attack on Howe at Germantown 4 October attained surprise and nothing else. His converging columns fired at each other in the fog and then panicked. Washington withdrew his remnants and went into winter quarters at Valley Forge unmolested by the lethargic Howe.

E. *Valley Forge*

At Valley Forge, Washington received Steuben, a Prussian recruited in Paris by Franklin. As inspector general, Steuben set out to standardize and train the army. He sought to adjust tactics to American advantages—speed and marksmanship. By creating a disciplined establishment, he fashioned an instrument which could stand against British regulars instead of running at their approach. This was a major element in U.S. victory.

F. *Later Operations, 1778-1781*

General Clinton, who replaced Howe as land commander after Saratoga, determined to take the army back to New York and from there to conduct more vigorous operations. Washington paralleled the movement and fought a hard, but indecisive, action at Monmouth, 28 June 1778. He then blocked the land approaches to New York. Thereafter, except for the campaign in the Northwest of George Rogers Clark—culminating in the capture of Vincennes, 25 February 1779—the North remained quiet for the remainder of the war.

V. WAR IN THE SOUTH

A. Georgia and the Carolinas

Unable to split the northern colonies, and sealed in New York, Clinton turned his attention to the South. By December 1778 Georgia was conquered and a year of minor actions followed. In January 1780, Clinton launched a new expedition against South Carolina, capturing Charleston's large garrison by 12 May. Civil conflict then erupted between loyalists and patriots in the Carolinas. The Continental Congress, typically inept in its direction of the war, appointed fifty-two-year-old General Gates to command a new Southern Theatre. On 16 August 1780 he was met at Camden, South Carolina, by Cornwallis who had numerically inferior forces. Gates's militia promptly deserted and he fled with them, abandoning his regulars, and covering 200 miles in four days, a speed which Alexander Hamilton said "did admirable credit to the activity of a man at his time of life."

Congress returned the theatre to Washington, who sent General Nathaniel Greene and Steuben to take command. Greene split his small force in the face of Cornwallis' superior army, but the latter responded in accordance with the reciprocal attraction of forces by doing likewise. On 17 January 1781 at the Battle of Cowpens, the Loyalists under Tarleton were defeated by continental regulars and militia under Morgan. The latter employed extreme tactical ingenuity, utilizing in his own favor the flight of his militiamen who, unable to cross a stream at Morgan's rear, were rallied and brought back to strike Tarleton's flank at the decisive moment. Thereupon, Cornwallis retired northward with Greene constantly maneuvering against him until they fought 15 March 1781 at Guilford Court House, North Carolina. The battle was a tactical defeat but a strategic victory for Greene, because Cornwallis—sustaining heavy losses and finding the country now hostile—elected to withdraw to the coast to make contact with the navy. Greene moved southward and, although tactically defeated in every action, he was strategically successful in liberating all the country except for Savannah and Charleston.

B. *The Virginia Capes (5 September 1781)*

Cornwallis invaded Virginia in April 1781 and maneuvered inconclusively until August, when he moved to Yorktown. Washington, who had been joined by a French expeditionary force of over 4,000 under Count Rochambeau, learned that the French fleet was sailing from Haiti for the Chesapeake. He resolved to screen Clinton at New York and concentrate against Cornwallis. The latter, on a peninsula, was vulnerable if French sea power could be brought to bear. Washington as a grand strategist grasped the relationship of sea and land war, but he had never had a fleet to implement his conceptions. He left New York 17 August with his army in fast march south.

After the Seven Years War, France had begun a naval revival; at the same time, corruption undermined the British navy. Although Washington lacked an effective navy, 800 American privateers contributed to the war effort. John Paul Jones, most famous American commander in the insignificant Continental Navy, on 24 September 1779 defeated the British frigate *Serapis,* although losing his refitted merchantman, the *Bonhomme Richard.* After France entered the war, Washington devoted himself to securing the cooperation of the French fleet for a decisive action.

Admiral De Grasse arrived at the mouth of Chesapeake Bay and on 5 September the British fleet under Admiral Graves hove into view. De Grasse began straggling into a line of battle but, due to confusion over signal flags, the British rear failed to close with the enemy. Consequently, Graves did not cut off the French van. The battle, therefore, was hard fought but inconclusive. The French anchored again inside the mouth of Chesapeake Bay, while the English returned to New York. Graves intended to return with Clinton as reinforcement for Cornwallis. Indecisive tactically, this action was nonetheless—along with Saratoga—a great decisive battle of the Western World.

C. Yorktown (19 October 1781)

After Admiral Graves accepted strategic defeat, Washington embarked his army for the voyage down the bay and by 26 September 1781 had concentrated against the hapless Cornwallis. He had a twofold numerical superiority with an army approximately half American and half French. Gradually the siege of Cornwallis was tightened. The British should have crossed to Gloucester on 11 October, but waited until the sixteenth. A storm scattered their boats. French artillery was the decisive arm in the siege. On the seventeenth, exactly four years after Burgoyne's surrender, Cornwallis asked for terms. He had had but 482 casualties, and surrendered 8,077. With them, in effect, he conceded the First British Empire. The relief expedition from New York arrived by sea a week too late. Although peace negotiations in Europe dragged on for two years, primarily due to the continuing Anglo-French War, American independence had been won.

VI. RESULTS

By wearing the allies down, and gaining the important 12 April 1782 naval Battle of the Saints in the West Indies, Britain was able to emerge from the war with little loss beyond her American colonies. They attained independence in the expanse east of the Mississippi with the exception of Florida, which was returned to Spain. That country also shared the Mississippi border. In losing, Britain strengthened her power base, the navy; in winning, France destroyed her fiscal stamina. Spain, by joining France, contributed indirectly to the loss of her own great American Empire. The United States' example did not go unnoticed in Spanish America. The American Revolution ushered in the age of citizen armies to replace eighteenth-century dynastic armies. Militia, nevertheless, was shown unreliable against regulars. The war reintroduced ideological conflict. Public opinion was subjected to propaganda; psychological warfare was expanded. Effective irregulars and the hostile populace appeared. While men were reluctant to serve in the army, they were quick to defend their own homes against enemy troops. This accounted for the large force which gathered against Burgoyne at Saratoga. Notably, the Continental Army won no open, pitched battles.

The war in America was revolutionary in the sense of tactics. Just as Saxe had foreseen, skirmishers backed up by formed bodies assumed an important role in warfare. The French had already tested such tactics in maneuvers. Rochambeau, a pioneer in this approach, was well prepared when he led French forces to America. The war was a training ground for him, as well as for Lafayette, Berthier, Dumas, and Jourdan—all destined for prominence in the wars of the French Revolution. England reduced her line from three to two ranks. Sir John Moore, later famous as a trainer of light infantry, saw action in America.

The most important lesson of the Revolution, however, was political. The Declaration of Independence, which reflected the ideas of John Locke, was in reality a declaration of war on absolutism throughout the Western World:

> We hold these truths to be self-evident, that all men are created equal, that they are endowed by their Creator with certain inalienable rights, that among these are life, liberty, and the pursuit of happiness. That to secure these rights governments are instituted among men, deriving their just powers from the consent of the governed. That whenever any form of government becomes destructive to these ends, it is the right of the people to alter or abolish it, and to institute new government, laying its foundations on such principles and organizing its powers in such form, as to them shall seem most likely to effect their safety and happiness.

A new political era had been born of Old World sea power and American free men fighting for themselves in the interest of a cause they deemed just.

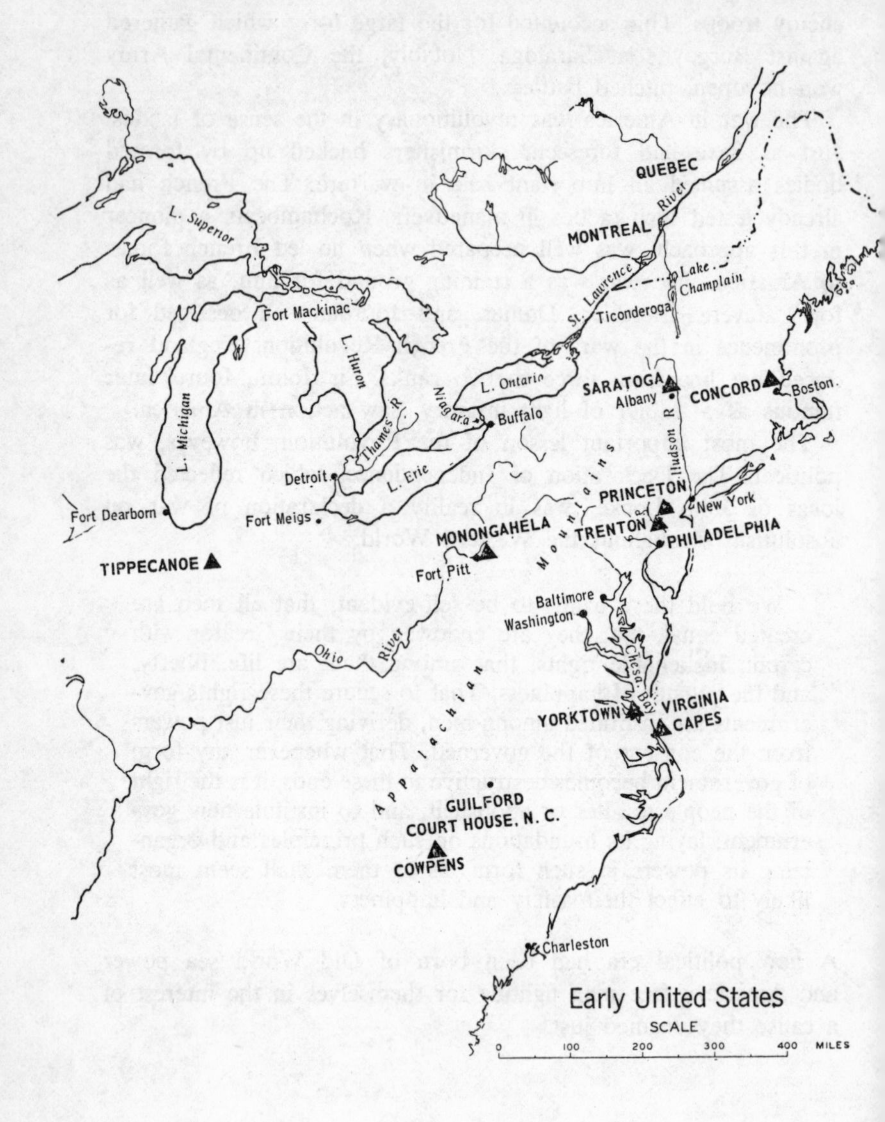

Early United States

CHAPTER X

The War of 1812

I. MILITARY POLICY, 1783-1812

YORKTOWN won American independence, but the war did not end officially until April 1783. In the interim the Continental Congress, a war government, had to maintain a military establishment lest the victory be lost to British troops still on United States soil. It was beset by numerous demands from the Army, mostly concerned with pay and supply. In June, some eighty troops of the Pennsylvania regiments threatened Congress, which moved to Princeton. Peace brought the hasty dissolution of the army. This set an American pattern. In November, Washington resigned and was succeeded by General Henry Knox, who later became the first Secretary of War. Congress in 1784 asked the states to furnish 700 militia for a one-year term to garrison frontier forts. The inadequacy of this expedient brought Congress a year later to resolve 700 three-year regulars for defense of the Northwest.

Meanwhile, Washington's *Sentiments on a Peace Establishment* advocated (1) a small navy and a regular army for garrison and frontier duty, (2) a well organized, uniform militia of all men eighteen to fifty years old, (3) arsenals, (4) military academies, and (5) some type of arms industry. Given his experience with militia, he clearly envisioned a trained, disciplined, organized force. This was compatible with the Founding Fathers' basic military policy of opposition to *large* standing, peacetime forces. The war debt provided fiscal support for this view. Washington estimated 2,631 as an adequate army. Congress took no action on his recommendations.

In 1789 Congress authorized a regiment of infantry, expanded the following year, and a battalion of artillery. Its strength was 1,216. Indian victories motivated authorization in 1792 of the 5,120-man Legion of the United States under General Anthony Wayne. This reborn United States Army won the Battle of Fallen Timbers 20 August 1794 using linear bayonet tactics and an envelopment. Unfortunately, the Legion was dissolved in 1796, after the Indian perils were controlled.

Faced by the depredations of Barbary pirates against United States shipping in the Mediterranean, Congress in 1794 voted a four-ship navy. The force created was employed in an undeclared naval war with Revolutionary France (1798-1800) but privateering remained the chief naval activity. There followed a four-year war (1801-1805) against Tripoli which was partially successful. These struggles should have taught the policy makers that maritime powers must have strong navies. The lesson was unlearned.

The Army experienced a series of vicissitudes under the economy-minded Jefferson administration. Highlights were Lewis and Clark's exploration up the Missouri and across the Rockies to the Pacific, and the opening 4 July 1802 of the United States Military Academy. With 950 men, General William Henry Harrison, Governor of Indiana Territory, repulsed the Shawnees and their allies 7 November 1811 at the Battle of Tippecanoe on the upper Wabash. At the time, the Army had less than 3,000 of an authorized strength of 9,921. Congress did not permit the War Department to coordinate the militia which remained its principal reliance. The armed forces were still deemed a necessary evil in a republican nation.

II. THE WAR

A. Background

British agents were blamed for the Indian troubles in the Northwest. An economic depression in the Mississippi Valley was attributed to British trade restrictions. This, and the desire of some nationalistic frontiersmen for further northward expansion into

Canada at British expense, provoked the War of 1812. Many deemed Canada ripe for the taking. Strategic considerations were unchanged from 1775. The nation was vulnerable to naval war along the Atlantic seaboard and threatened (as it was since colonial days) from the north. In nearly twenty years of fighting against Revolutionary France, Britain had asserted absolute naval dominance of the world. She employed economic warfare against the French-controlled Continent, enforcement of which was felt by some to be damaging to growing U. S. commerce on the high seas. The war in America was for Britain largely a sideshow to her epic struggle against Napoleon. Her small army was tied down in the Peninsular War in Spain.

Against this, the United States had an authorized force of 35,000, actually far below strength. Bounties of $16.00 with a mustering out bonus, after honorable service, of 160 acres and three months' pay were paid to secure five-year regular enlistments. Congress on the eve of hostilities complicated recruiting by providing for 50,000 two-year volunteers and by calling 100,000 six-month state militia. It did not trouble to provide for the equipping of this host, rejected additional naval appropriations and venturesomely pitted puny forces against the mistress of the seas in what of necessity was to be a naval conflict. American victory would have seemed a foolhardy wager.

B. *The Northwest*

The long Canadian frontier was weakly held by about 4,450 British regulars, supported by a similar number of militia and numerous Indians. In war between thinly populated Canada and the expanding United States, the decisive arena was the inland waters and the adjoining land from Quebec to Lake Superior. Command of this line at any point would carry the country upstream. Strategy therefore favored the historic offensive against Quebec or Montreal. Political considerations dictated operations in the American Northwest, however, because if the frontier fortresses fell, the Indians would reconquer the country. Furthermore, it was the frontiersmen, and not the New Englanders who had desired hostilities.

The British under General Isaac Brock seized the outpost of

Fort Mackinac, 17 July 1812. On 15 August, Indians massacred the garrison of Fort Dearborn (Chicago), and on the sixteenth, without a fight, General Hull surrendered Detroit and a garrison of over 1,000 fit for duty to Brock's motley force of some 1,300 regulars, militia, and Indians. These actions eliminated the westernmost thrust of the United States' planned three-pronged offensive and brought thousands of Indians into the war against them. Brock turned his attention to the second thrust along the Niagara. There more than 6,000 Americans assembled. On the night of 12 October about 3,000 regulars and militia crossed the river; with 1,000 men Brock vanquished them. The following January, a fresh defeat was inflicted upon General Winchester in Michigan. Harrison, after beating off attacks on Fort Meigs in July, called for control of Lake Erie as a prelude to successful prosecution of the war.

C. *The Great Lakes Campaigns*

The 18-gun brig *Oneida* supported the army in a raid on Toronto in May 1813. Although on Lake Ontario the war became a stalemate of ship construction, on Lake Erie, Commandant Oliver Hazard Perry built two 20-gun brigs and three schooners destined for important service. Five small British ships held control of the lake until Perry's squadron defeated them decisively 10 September 1813. Although only fifteen ships were involved, the Battle of Lake Erie gave the Americans vital communications lines and destroyed British hopes of constructing an Indian buffer state in the Northwest. After Perry's victory, British forces at Malden withdrew through Detroit, followed by General Harrison. He routed the inferior enemy on 5 October along the Thames River.

D. *Central Operations, 1813-1814*

The conduct of the war had illegally passed to the direction of Secretary of War James Armstrong, an inexperienced civilian who mistakenly fancied himself a better strategist than the generals. Late in October, incompetent General Wilkinson began an ill-prepared advance toward Montreal with 13,000 men. He was repelled by 2,000 British, Canadians, and Indians. By 19 December, the British had resumed control of the Niagara River. The year 1813 saw the United States employ 149,000 troops in all with little success.

Near Buffalo, a bright new commander, Virginia volunteer Winfield Scott, was busy training troops. Again crossing the Niagara at Chippewa Landing 5 July 1814 Scott's brigade advanced steadily under fire, wringing from the enemy the exclamation, "Those are regulars, by God!" After the militia's dismal performance, the appearance in the field of well-disciplined Americans was doubtless amazing to the British. Twenty days later at Lundy's Lane, Scott attacked boldly but was wounded and repelled. He took refuge in Fort Erie, built opposite Buffalo by the United States engineers. As British troops—freed from Europe by the defeat of Bonaparte—began to reinforce Canada, the Americans by year's end returned to Buffalo.

E. Lake Champlain (11 September 1814)

The British, seeking victory for the peace table, concentrated veterans of Wellington's campaigns in Spain for an invasion by the traditional Champlain route. These 16,000 troops were treasonously supplied by New England traders, eager for the dollar. In August 1814 peace talks had begun at Ghent in Flanders. Britain now intended to support her diplomacy with conclusive military action. The success of the invasion depended upon gaining naval command of Lake Champlain.

British shipbuilders, supplied by New Englanders, worked feverishly constructing four vessels on the lake. The opposing navies were approximately equal in tonnage and ordinance. Victory for the American fleet 11 September 1814 had the same effect as the Greek triumph at Salamis—it cost the enemy control of the sea, rendering his land advance untenable. The British abandoned their projected invasion along the route followed by Burgoyne, and the United States was saved.

F. Washington, 1814

To support invasion from Canada, the British launched an amphibious raid against Washington with 4,000 veterans in

August. At Bladensburg, Maryland, on the twenty-fourth, 7,000 United States militia were routed after offering token resistance. The Government abandoned Washington; the Capitol and White House were fired by the enemy, allegedly in retaliation for the destruction of Toronto. The raiders then re-embarked and sailed for Baltimore. After militia had stood firm behind well-constructed field fortifications, Fort McHenry was subjected to a naval bombardment. The British failure occasioned the writing of the immortal "Star Spangled Banner." The fleet sailed for Jamaica and thence to New Orleans.

G. *New Orleans (8 January 1815)*

General Andrew Jackson had been conducting successful campaigns against the British and the Indians in the Gulf Theatre. Anticipating the next enemy move, he marched into New Orleans, 1 December 1814, with 5,000 men and imposed martial law. Britain viewed the city as a pawn for negotiations and a potential check valve on the future heartland of America, the great Mississippi Basin. Jackson understood the capabilities and limitations of his militiamen. Against regulars he employed them behind field fortifications and not in the open. The British veterans, 8,000 in all, attacked frontally, suffering heavy casualties. The celebrated victory did not affect the war; a stalemate peace had been signed 24 December 1814. It did set Jackson on the road to the White House and proved the worth of militia properly employed.

III. RESULTS

For Britain, the War of 1812 was a limited conflict resulting partially from her employment of naval-economic war against Bonaparte. For the United States, it was a means of ending Indian depredations, protecting maritime rights, and possibly acquiring Canada. Naval actions on the high seas were virtually equally divided, with the heavier guns victorious in each case. The decisive actions of the war, all naval, were fought on the interior lakes. The conflict—in which the United States could not even protect their capital—revealed conclusively the bankruptcy of their military policy.

The errors of the Revolution were all repeated: the democratically-conceived militia was the primary reliance; it elected officers; states provided or refused to send their militia; competitive recruiting and bounties made a nightmare of raising forces. Bounties reached $125 and 320 acres by war's end. A regular army of 15,000 well-trained and well-equipped men could have carried Canada early and with it the war. Instead, more than 527,000 served in one fashion or another. With the exception of Scott, Jackson, and possibly Harrison, the general officers were incompetent. The civilian direction by Armstrong was even worse. That of James Monroe, who replaced him after the fall of Washington, was good. Monroe even sought federal conscription, albeit unsuccessfully. Peace brought the usual disbandment and in March 1815, Congress fixed the standing establishment at 10,000.

For the growing United States, an era of general peace was inaugurated which was devoted to internal expansion. In 1818 Jackson, using only regulars, crushed the Seminole Indians and invaded Spanish Florida, from whence they operated. This unauthorized operation stimulated prompt acquisition of the territory by purchase from Spain. A war of consolidation against the Seminoles began in 1835 and lasted seven years. Casualties were about 30 per cent of the regular army. The cost was more than double the combined price of Florida and Louisiana. No solution had yet been found to the problem of a military policy for the republic.

CHAPTER XI

The Liberation of Spanish South America

THE NAPOLEONIC INVASION of the Peninsula disrupted the legal relationship between Spain and her American "kingdoms," which were united only by the person of the monarch. The removal of the lawful sovereign broke this tie; when the *junta central* at Cadiz attempted to assert its authority over the Americas, they refused it recognition. Believing themselves equal to the Spanish, the Americans created their own juntas to hold power in the name of the deposed Ferdinand VII.

I. BOLIVAR

In the principal American cities, however, there were radicals who, under the influence of the *philosophes*—especially Abbe Raynal and Rousseau—and of the American and French Revolutions, longed for full political liberty. Among these men was Simón Bolívar, the Caracas-born scion of a prosperous *criollo* family. On 5 July 1811, Bolívar and other members of the *Sociedad Patriotica* of Caracas succeeded in persuading a congress to declare independence from Spain.

Bolívar was not a professional soldier. He began his career with only political ideas and the force of his will. These he used to subordinate associates, foster national sentiment, and form a military establishment capable of translating ideas into political reality upon the field of battle. In no small measure, Bolívar was in spirit and deed the Venezuelan state. Years of defeat and failure provided a school for his training, but lasting success did not reward his efforts until 1819.

II. SAN MARTIN'S LIBERATION OF CHILE

In contrast to the amateur Bolívar, José de San Martín was a Spanish professional soldier who, after service in Africa and against Napoleon in the Peninsula, arrived in 1812 at Buenos Aires to offer himself to the city of his birth. Following service there and in the north, in 1814 he was appointed governor of the province of Cuyo at the eastern slopes of the Andes and from its capital, Mendoza, he proceeded toward the implementation of his continental plan for securing the independence of Spanish South America.

A. The Continental Plan

The patriots of the United Provinces (Argentina) had attempted unsuccessfully to liberate Upper Perú (Bolivia) by taking the traditional colonial trade route across the mountains toward Lima. San Martín perceived Lima and Buenos Aires as opposing centers, the one steeped in colonial tradition, the other in the vanguard of new thought currents. An expansive military thinker, he conceived a brilliant strategy. His intention was to form a small, well-disciplined regular army at Mendoza, cross the Andes, and establish a friendly government in Chile. Uniting with the Chilean revolutionaries, he proposed to go by sea to Perú and there to eliminate the primary seat of royalist power. His plan thus was a massive, strategic indirect approach.

B. Preparation

At Mendoza, San Martín applied all his organizational genius to the preparation of his forces. A penetrating judge of men, he founded a school to train officers, an intelligence network to pave the way for the invasion of Chile, and wrote regulations to standardize training. He sought to inculcate a strong offensive spirit. San Martín made of Cuyo a small nation in arms whose resources were applied toward the military objective. Daily he saw not only to the well-being of his men, but also to their spiritual needs. Once his political base was secured by the 9 July 1816 declaration of independence and the creation of a viable government, he received his appointment as General in Chief of the Army of the Andes. San Martín had fashioned a splendid professional force.

C. Crossing the Cordillera

In January 1817 he crossed the Andes with 4,000 men against at least 6,000 royalists in Chile. To confuse the enemy, he pushed token forces through four widely separated passes. On the high, arid mountain trails the men suffered intensely from cold, altitude, and lack of water. San Martín's two main columns united in Chile on 8 February following an exploit to rival Hannibal. Of 10,600 food-carrying pack mules and 1,600 horses, only 4,300 of the former and 511 of the latter survived; most of the army, however, remained intact. San Martín's feat was a tribute to his skillful organization and sound logistics and to the application of his powerful will.

D. Chacabuco (12 February 1817)

The enemy, who had long since lost the psychological initiative, was confused by reports of patriots debouching from the Andes on a broad front, but he belatedly attempted to concentrate near Santiago. On 12 February, in the first important victory of criollo regulars, San Martín defeated the Spanish at Chacabuco, a battle marked by maneuver and envelopment. Two days later, he entered Santiago where his Chilean lieutenant, Bernardo O'Higgins, became chief of state as Supreme Director.

E. Maipú (5 April 1818)

After Chacabuco, royalist stragglers regrouped in the south near Concepción where they later were besieged by O'Higgins. With command of the sea, the viceroy of Peru determined to reconquer Chile and on 9 December he sent an expedition which brought royalist strength to 4,612 including 150 artillery and 886 cavalry. The Spanish intention was to beat O'Higgins, transport the bulk of

South American Independence

the army by sea to near Valparaíso and—assuming San Martín would have gone south to join O'Higgins—march on unguarded Santiago. A good plan, it provided for evacuation by sea in case of failure.

San Martín learned early of the enemy's intentions from his clandestine agents in Lima. He reinforced O'Higgins and prepared to halt the Spanish whether from Valparaíso, or below Santiago. O'Higgins, who on 12 February proclaimed Chilean independence, barred the approaches up the central valley from the south. Royalists and patriots maintained cavalry contact.

San Martín planned to lure Osorio, the enemy commander, inland and force a battle where superior patriot cavalry could be exploited, but the initial result was not as he expected. Osorio achieved limited tactical surprise with a night attack 19 March at Cancha Rayada and defeated the patriots, many of whom fled believing that all was lost. San Martín rallied an orderly retreat. He did not lose his spirit and in reality the reversal opened his most successful campaign.

By 31 March, San Martín had 5,000 soldiers. He placed great reliance on his cavalry, scouting south of the Río Maipú, to provide him with prompt intelligence. He resisted the varied counsels of his officers, especially that he endeavor to prevent a river crossing. Osorio, his supply lines now stretched through hostile country, attempted to ford the stream and withdraw to Valparaíso in order to re-establish contact with his fleet. The night of 4-5 April 1818, Osorio was six miles southwest in a left oblique across the patriot front. His artillery commanded the road where it branched to Santiago and Valparaíso. The royalist cavalry was on the left; Osorio's lines lacked both depth and reserves.

San Martín rode out of the city at dawn and, after glancing over Osorio's deployments exclaimed: "Osorio is stupider than I thought! The day is ours!" At 1130 a cannonade opened the battle; at noon San Martín ordered his right forward against the enemy's weaker flank. Osorio had planned an advance at the same moment and heavy fighting resulted. The patriot then committed his reserve to gain a penetration which isolated the Spanish left. By mid-afternoon Osorio's remnant was in poorly directed retreat along the right bank of the river. He had lost approximately 2,000 killed, 3,000 captured and almost all of his matériel.

Maipú was the Saratoga of South America, making good the independence of Chile, securing Argentine liberty, and clearing the way militarily for the final steps in San Martín's continental strategy. A fleet was formed under the brilliant but erratic British Lord Cochrane, who won naval dominance of the eastern Pacific. Political collapse in Argentina and fiscal weakness in Chile imposed painful delays, however, and San Martín could not exploit the momentum of Maipú. Two years passed before the next phase of the Continental Plan was practicable.

III. BOLIVAR'S LIBERATION OF COLOMBIA

A. *Political Ideas*

In May 1816, Bolívar returned to Venezuela from Haiti and formed an alliance with the native cavalry (*llaneros*) of the wild grasslands of the Orinoco Basin, who were led by José Antonio Paéz. With this support and the help of British volunteers, Bolívar consolidated his position in the back country, avoiding direct attacks on Spanish coastal strongholds.

Ever the political figure, Bolívar summoned a congress at Angostura in February 1819 and presented his assessment of the political capabilities of Spanish Americans. With their lack of experience, he said, a federal system would be impossible; they had deliberately been kept in ignorance by Spain and now were exposed to the danger of losing their liberty. Complete freedom, though, would mean Latin American ruin. The people should strive for the practical—a strong government—rather than the ideal. The Congress accepted this advice and established a centralized state with Bolívar as its head.

B. *Boyacá (7 August 1819)*

1. STRATEGY

Meanwhile, Bolívar had grasped the military and political importance of present-day Colombia for its geographic situation, resources, and revolutionary sentiment. Patriots had been active in the country since 1810, but only sporadically successful. Bolívar entrusted to Santandér, his able lieutenant, the task of stimulating revolutionary sentiment in preparation for an invasion. He proposed a plan by which Paéz would operate against the city of Cúcuta to draw and hold the attention of 4,000 royalists in northern Colombia; having accomplished this, Paéz was to return to the Orinoco to protect Bolívar's seat of government from the royalists along the Venezuelan coast. With the beginnings of a concept of the strategic indirect approach, Bolívar set out westward through the flooded upper Orinoco basin.

2. CAMPAIGN

The army crossed river after river and arrived at the foot of the Andes in very poor condition. There Bolívar's 1,850 soldiers were augmented by Santandér with 1,200. Paéz refused to fulfill his part of the plan, claiming that his men would desert rather than cross the Andes. He himself feared the terrain would neutralize the saddleless lancers and deny them the opportunity for the maneuver which made them so effective.

Bolívar selected the more difficult of the available passes, possibly to achieve greater surprise. He marched another hundred miles southward along the foothills to Pore, fording swollen streams and plodding through soggy terrain. Finally, on 23 June 1819, he began the ascent, relying upon his iron will and example to hold his poorly prepared army together.

The heights alarmed the llaneros—just as Paéz had warned—and many deserted. Rain fell night and day, making the steep trail slippery and treacherous. *Soroche,* or mountain sickness, beset the troops. On 27 June, the vanguard under Santandér handily dislodged 300 royalists from an excellently chosen defensive position which could have held up the army indefinitely. After eliminating this Thermopylae, Bolívar once again chose a route considered impassable and turned northwest to enter Colombia by Pisba. The trail passed across the *páramo,* a high cold plateau which brought terrible suffering to the half-nude troops and cost the lives of forty per cent of the men and all of the horses.

When Bolívar on 6 July finally reached the valley of the Sogamosa River, the climate of the 9,000-foot plateau grew more equable and the troops welcomed four days of rest. The royalist's reaction to Bolívar's appearance was to position half of his 3,000 well-disciplined, well-mounted men along the upper river where an eight-hour engagement with Bolívar proved indecisive. The republican forces then outmaneuvered the enemy, bypassed him to the west, and compelled him to retreat. On the twenty-fifth, Bolívar accepted battle in a disadvantageous position after recrossing the upper Sogamosa. By greater energy in holding high ground—and aided by the timely action of his British contingents—he came off the better in another inconclusive contest. He thereupon resorted to his usual recruiting technique to fill the depleted ranks; he issued orders for the impressment of every able-bodied male fifteen to forty years within twenty-four hours under penalty of death.

3. BRITISH VOLUNTEERS

Such methods could scarcely produce the caliber of army which Bolívar indicated in his addresses was needed, nor was it ever as well conditioned as San Martín's force. Except for the British and the llaneros, Bolívar could hardly have hoped to win the war for independence. The British, mostly veterans of the Peninsular campaigns, had been mustered out during a depression. Lacking job opportunity, they chose to sell the trade they knew best: war. Their government responded with the Foreign Enlistment Act, making service for a foreign power, whether recognized or not, illegal. Despite conflicting commercial interests, Spain had been an ally against Napoleon and Britain could not now willingly serve as a recruiting ground for Spain's rebellious colonists. Nevertheless, illegal enlistments for Bolívar continued.

4. BATTLE

After outmaneuvering the royalists once more, this time by night, Bolívar (5 August) captured the 600-man Tunja garrison. Two days later the royalist main body retreated along the shortest route, which bridged the Río Boyacá in a narrow ravine. Bolívar ordered fast march on the main road and overtook the Spanish at 1400 with their vanguard already across the bridge. The remaining forces were strung out for half a mile. While Santandér severed the enemy's head from his body, Bolívar enveloped the latter, capturing the commander and 1,600 men.

5. RESULTS

Immediately he marched on Bogotá, entering the city late 10 August with colors flying. As always, he had sought the political objective (a principal city) rather than the military objective: the enemy's army. This time his choice was the correct one. The population had been uncommitted; Bolívar's dramatic, if inept, crossing of the Andes and victory at Boyacá decided the moral issue. In this campaign he had gained strategic surprise and the initiative, acting in accordance with his view that:

> Every defensive war is ruinous for those who have to maintain it; it weakens without hope of indemnification, while hostilities in enemy country can always be profitable from the good which comes of evil inflicted on the enemy.

Bolívar at once set up a provisional government under Santandér, and well he might, for at Boyacá the independence of Colombia had been assured. He hastened toward the 17 December 1819 creation of Gran Colombia, which included Venezuela and Ecuador. The latter was unliberated and unaware of its new political affiliation.

IV. SAN MARTIN'S PERUVIAN CAMPAIGN

San Martín had prepared 2,347 Argentines and 1,917 Chilenos for operations in Perú against 23,000 royalists. Principal center of wealth and power and key to Spain's position in South America, Perú was unready for independence. Her ruling class preferred the status quo to the uncertainty of political liberty. San Martín therefore proceeded with extreme operative prudence. Landing south of Lima at Pisco (8 September 1820), he promptly freed 600 Negroes and incorporated them into his army.

As a result of the Riego revolt of 1 January 1820, Spain failed to send out forces to support the royalists, and the liberal Spanish constitution of 1812 was proclaimed in America. The new home government ordered conciliatory gestures toward the rebels; consequently, an armistice was established. This was a moral victory for the republicans. Not only did they deal with the Spanish on a footing of equality, but also by so doing they undermined the position of the monarchy which the royalists were defending.

During the short armistice, San Martín prepared for his next move. He launched an expedition into the sierra to isolate Lima by destroying Spanish support in the back country. Sailing north, he entered the Bay of Ancón (30 October), but landed 150 kilometers north of Lima at Huacho on 12 November.

Aware of his great numerical inferiority and the hostile climate of opinion in Lima, San Martín embarked upon indecisive maneuvering accompanied by skillful psychological preparation for the move against the city. Recognizing the futility of a frontal attack upon an unfriendly town, he sought to gain the support of the populace.

By assidously striving for its favor, San Martín won the psychological battle and on 9 July 1821 was invited by convened patriots to enter Lima. Patience and appreciation of political and psychosocial factors enabled him to gain a cheap victory where direct military methods would have invited disaster. On 28 July he proclaimed Peruvian independence. Despite the presence on the continent of strong royalist forces whose final defeat would take three more years, this action, coupled with Bolívar's triumph of June, left the result no longer in doubt.

V. CARABOBO (24 JUNE 1821)

Bolívar had grown restless during a prolonged armistice with the Spanish, and in January 1821 he revealed his anxiety lest San Martín should attain ahead of him the honor of liberating all of South America. Furthermore, Bolívar's army lived at the expense of the land—from contributions and cattle—and was not easily preserved in idleness. Consequently, utilizing incidents as an excuse, Bolívar instructed Santandér to denounce the armistice on 16 April. His plan called for a massive strategic envelopment of General Miguel de la Torre's loyalist forces in coastal Venezuela. This would convert the apparent Spanish advantage of interior lines into a liability. Bolívar envisioned attacks from east and west, with the main blow coming from the south.

On 14 May, Caracas was taken from the east with the royalists shifting to Puerto Cabello. As Bolívar anticipated, La Torre detached forces against this danger, exposing important positions on the road northward to Carabobo. A feint from the west drew off additional enemy strength to protect the vital sea outlet of Puerto Cabello. Bolívar had completely dominated La Torre and compelled the latter to accede to his will. The result was the meeting of La Torre's 5,000 and Bolívar's 6,300 on the plain of Carabobo.

Bolívar, who had created battalions capable of independent operations, formed his army into the classical three "battles" with the van commanded by Paéz. Finding that enemy artillery commanded the valley approach he must use, Bolívar ordered Paéz through an unfrequented path to the west from which he could plunge upon the Spanish right while the main force fixed the enemy. Paéz charged his llaneros directly, only to find himself in a depression 150 feet below the level of the plain. The Spanish poured fire onto the cavalry and only the steadiness of the British Legion's 900 men prevented a rout. Paéz re-entered the plain farther north under cover of trees, struck La Torre's right rear, and destroyed it. Bolívar's main body, arriving by the road, completed the rout.

The road to Caracas was open and 29 June 1821 Bolívar entered the city. The Battle of Carabobo was decisive; the issue had been settled. Bolívar was the undisputed hero and liberator of Colombia and Venezuela and was ready to turn his attention southward toward Ecuador and San Martín in Perú. First, though, he convened a Congress at Cúcuta and obtained a new constitution establishing a united, centralist republic with theoretical states' rights and balance of powers, but in reality with power concentrated in the hands of a single man: the Liberator.

VI. THE AFTERMATH

A. Spanish American Independence Completed

Bolívar's brilliant lieutenant, Antonio José de Sucre, made good Ecuador's independence at Pichincha 24 May 1822. Two months later a brief meeting between Bolívar and San Martín occurred at Guayaquil. Supposedly, Bolívar refused San Martín's offer to serve under him, and promised only a few troops for consolidation operations in Peru. San Martín argued that Perú was wholly unready for republican government and advocated a European prince. This Bolívar vetoed as alien to the spirit of America. Convinced that his presence was an obstacle to the consolidation of independence, San Martín, probably the better man, chose to fade away into European exile. He died at Boulogne 17 August 1850. Not until 1878 were his remains returned to Buenos Aires, where his reputation has justly grown.

Bolívar was now supreme and the able Sucre won the final field action at Ayacucho 9 December 1824, a South American "Battle of Nations" in which Argentines, Bolivians, Chileans, Colombians, Ecuadorians, Peruvians, and Venezuelans fought side by side. Bolívar's political creations fragmented beneath him into the present states of Venezuela, Colombia, Ecuador, Peru, Bolivia and later, Panama. He died at Santa María, Colombia 17 December 1830, a bitterly disillusioned man convinced that "America is ungovernable. Those who have served the revolution have plowed the sea."

B. Evaluation

Bolívar was typically Spanish in his personal life and character, but he possessed shrewd political insight. He attempted to create enduring states, governed under conditions suited to their people. Factionalism mired their strength; regionalism shattered Bolívar's centralized government. Militarily, he operated over the equivalent of New York to San Francisco, a vast distance in 1821 when the trans-Mississippi west was scarcely explored. Primarily, his success was due to his will and to the compelling force of his ideas. Yet he was at best only a gifted amateur whose preparations were hasty and improvised with costly results. As a strategist, after eight years he abandoned strategically frontal assaults on the seats of Spanish power and in his Boyacá and Carabobo campaigns demonstrated real capacity. Of the two liberators, however, Bolívar militarily is the lesser and cannot be ranked among the Great Captains.

San Martín lacked Bolívar's dramatic flair and in political ideas —beyond a sincere dedication to South American independence— was realistic and sober. As a leader he equaled Bolívar in will and dedication, surpassed him in steadfastness, and towered above him as a genius in authentic military matters. He was a superb and careful organizer and planner; an expansive strategic thinker with keen understanding of the influence on military operations of political and psycho-social factors. His conceptions, campaigns, and leadership earned him a role among America's Great Captains.

Together Bolívar and San Martín, and their fellow patriots, altered the political complexion of the Western World by completing one of the three great Revolutions—American, French, and Latin American—which straddle the turn of the eighteenth and nineteenth centuries. By military means they called into existence—along with Brazil's peaceful independence movement—a continent of nations that form a cultural area of vital importance to the free world.

CHAPTER XII

The Napoleonic Wars

I. REVOLUTIONARY WARFARE

WITH THE COMING of the French Revolution and the rise of Napoleon Bonaparte war became a conflict between nations instead of a contention between rulers. War had been for centuries the province of professionals in which civilian populations had little share. When the French Revolution brought popular sovereignty, it validated Rousseau's assumption that the citizen has a responsibility to fight for his nation. The Convention's 23 August 1793 decree of the *levée en masse* implemented this idea, inaugurated the Age of Conscription, and created the nation in arms, or the armed horde. The people, having seized the state, were now summoned to its defense.

Militarily, this event was the most revolutionary in modern history. It led, Fuller has written, "to the greatest political and military transformation the world has yet seen." The era of national, or unlimited, wars had begun, for henceforth the total human and material resources of countries could be mustered and thrown into contention. Although objectives were sometimes limited, conscription changed the character of conflict. Previously, soldiers had been skilled, costly specialists frugally employed. Now, manpower was cheapened and became expendable. Of this fact, more than any other, Napoleonic warfare was born.

Technology also had an important role in the transformation. The Industrial Revolution made possible the outfitting and supply of the mass armies. Interchangeable parts and mass production facilitated the output in quantity of weapons and munitions. Improvements in artillery, already evident in the later years of Frederick, meant greater means of applying firepower in time and space. Standard carriages, interchangeable gun parts, more durable axles, better casting, and the tangent sight gave artillery new power. Better surface transportation and cartography enhanced mobility. It was hardly a coincidence that Napoleon himself first attracted notice as a gunner.

The new armies were massive and necessitated changes in organization and command. They were divided into divisions which could be employed independently or assembled into larger bodies. In Marlborough's day, a five pace interval was maintained between files; there was no close order march, no cadence, and cross country movement was in loose column twenty files wide. Armies had to take the field in battle order, maneuver was cumbersome, and even the aggressive commander was hindered in his efforts to bring on battle. French military thought as early as Folard (1724) contemplated new tactical systems based on closed and realigned columns. By 1754 cadence was introduced, and after the Seven Years War the French adopted innovations in the deployment of the column based upon the methods of the Count of Guibert.

In *Essai Général de Tactique* (1772), Guibert laid down a tactical formula which was adopted in the Ordinance of 1791 and became the basis for four decades of French practice. Guibert adjusted tactics to growing fire power, and devised methods to shift quickly from column to line and back again. His divisions, he believed, could revolutionize warfare by enabling an army commander to divide or reconcentrate units at will. This made possible broad enveloping movements and concentration on the field. Mobility, simplicity, and flexibility Guibert sought. The solution was divisional organization and the revolutionary quick step which gave the French an advantage in being able to maneuver faster than their enemies. Movement in column became the pattern for Revolutionary France.

Armies would no longer form opposite one another before engaging. The less rigidly disciplined, trained and indoctrinated, but high-spirited citizen-soldier was more independent and capable of greater initiative. He had flexibility, often was utilized in a skirmish line, and took greater advantage of terrain. He moved at the one hundred-twenty pace revolutionary quickstep, lived off the land, bivouacked in the open, and fought for a personal cause. Thus the revolutionary armies gained combat superiority over the formalized royal forces of Europe, just as they had in America.

General Bourcet, a distinguished staff officer, advanced methods for employing divisions. He insisted that the commander must always conceal his true intentions for the maximum time. To facilitate this, Bourcet discussed calculated dispersion of the army into several columns, followed by concentration on the decisive point once near the foe. Every plan of campaign should have several "branches," or options to threaten alternate objectives, which would also assist in hiding actual intentions.

Napoleon inherited the military instrument fashioned by the Revolution and he possessed the genius to conceive the strategy and tactics which enabled it to conquer Europe. Bourcet—along with Guibert—provided the ideas upon which Napoleon built to fashion his successful conquest doctrine. Yet, the nation in arms led by him fed on war, thrived on its own ideological inspiration, and had a crucial defect, which ultimately brought Bonaparte's ruin—inability to make a lasting peace. This was the natural result of the revolutionary purpose, which was basically not to acquire territory but to destroy the enemy in order to bring a new order to Europe. The military revolution, therefore, was inseparable from the political.

II. THE RISE OF NAPOLEON BONAPARTE

A. *The Great Captain*

The great Napoleon first gained renown at the age of twenty-four by his command of the artillery in the 1794 siege of Toulon. An obscure professional, he had long been a diligent student of war and military history. While believing that infantry was the primary arm, he recognized that it could not stand before the greater firepower of artillery. On 5 October 1795 he saved the government of the Directory by using his guns against the Paris mob. He accordingly became aware that the revolutionary armed forces could be used as an instrument to control the state itself. The Revolution had in essence established a political anarchy which unleashed the national energies toward foreign war. Thus was created a situation conducive to a strong leader who would provide vigorous direction and employ the coercive mechanism of the revolutionaries.

Napoleon was a man of supreme ambition and ego, driven inexorably toward the fulfillment of his destiny. He was egocentric, tremendously active, and the last great genius who centralized the conduct of war in his own person. "It is the one man who is all," he wrote in his *Maxims*. Consequently, he considered *unity of command* to be the first requisite for successful war. To him this meant the concentration of all available forces in the main theatre under a single commander. But only a Napoleon possessed the capacity, ability, and drive thus to direct the mass armies of Revolutionary France.

Bonaparte had a unique ability to project his own ego to his men, arousing enormous combat spirit by enhancing their vanity. He understood both their virtues and their limitations. He inspired them in the quest for glory and their own destiny. *Personal leadership,* therefore, was fundamental in his method, and responsible for the tremendous loyalty of his soldiers.

Finally, Napoleon's genius was expressed in his *military planning*. Ultimately centralizing in his person both the political and military conduct of war, he meticulously planned both grand and military strategy. Characteristically introspective, he contemplated the probabilities with utmost care before determining his course of action. This necessitated detailed, accurate intelligence in order to establish the enemy's probable intentions and to minimize uncertainty. For this he utilized far-ranging cavalry and espionage.

An analysis of Napoleon's methods by the brilliant General J. F. C. Fuller reveals his emphasis on the offensive, speed (or mobility), strategic surprise, concentration of superior forces at the decisive point, and careful attention to security. Since his armies had been fashioned by the Revolution, and Napoleon's technological support was common to all Europe, his success can rightly be attributed to this, his system of waging war.

B. *The Italian Campaign*

In part because the Directors feared his ambition, in March 1796 Napoleon received the command of the Army of Italy.

Spread along the Genoese Riviera, his troops faced combined Austrian and Piedmontese forces which held the mountain passes into the Po Valley. After rallying his men with prospects of glory and booty, Bonaparte planned to penetrate between his foes and defeat them in detail. Following initial costly repulses, he covered the Austrians and isolated the weaker ally, the Piedmontese, who then abandoned the war. This gave him numerical superiority which he employed to outmaneuver the Austrians, who took refuge in their fortress of Mantua to await reinforcements. Thereupon, by orders of the Directory, Napoleon looted northern Italy; subsequently, he successfully defeated Austrian forces sent to relieve Mantua. After the 14 January 1797 Battle of Rivoli, the besieged fortress capitulated. Napoleon thereupon advanced toward Austria. Militarily weakened by the losses in Italy, Vienna was obliged to sue for peace.

This campaign saw Napoleon victorious because he utilized brilliant maneuver, often by divisions, to defeat Austrian forces successively. But he also won the hearts of his own men and laid the basis for the popular reputation which carried him to the throne.

C. *Egypt*

Faced with a victorious army and the growing political aspirations of its leaders, the Directors agreed to a Napoleonic plan to strike toward India through Egypt. Thus, they hoped, English trade could be damaged. This conception had the virtue of a foreign adventure to absorb the attention of the army, the people, and Bonaparte. Landing at Alexandria on 2 July 1798, Napoleon successfully occupied the ancient country, but inherent French naval weakness foredoomed his campaign. Horatio Nelson vanquished Napoleon's fleet on 1 August at Aboukir Bay. After an indecisive campaign in the Holy Land, Napoleon sailed for home 23 August 1799, leaving most of his army behind. Although adding to Napoleon's renown, the Egyptian campaign brought no benefit to France.

D. *Marengo (14 June 1800)*

While Bonaparte was in Egypt, a Second Coalition was formed

by England, Austria, Turkey, Russia, and Naples to replace the first which had been destroyed by Napoleon's victorious operations of 1797 against Austria. The allies liberated Italy and seemed ready to invade France herself. Faced with a political crisis at home, the Directory was ripe for the coup d'état which Napoleon executed 9 November 1799. He emerged as the first of three consuls whose ten-year rule was approved by plebiscite. The democratic phase of the Revolution had ended.

The First Consul formed a reserve army of 60,000, utilizing the Conscription Act of 1798, which remained the basis of French recruiting until 1870. With his new force, Napoleon debouched through the Alps onto the rear of the Austrians in Italy. The Battle of Marengo at first went against the Consul who was saved from defeat only by the timely arrival of a division which he had earlier detached. Almost too late, Napoleon had learned the value of reserves; his belief in the necessity of keeping open his own lines of communication was confirmed by his close brush with defeat. A few months later an armistice closed the conflict with the Second Coalition.

E. *Defeat at Trafalgar (21 October 1805)*

England—warring on Revolutionary France since 1793—signed the Peace of Amiens in 1802. Napoleon thereupon devoted his attention to consolidating his political power and to effecting significant internal reforms in keeping with his aim of making France prosperous and orderly. Two years later he made himself Emperor of the French—virtually a crowned Jacobin usurper—but distinctly a product of the Revolution. He owed his throne to the will of the people, in part manifest through their military instrument, the popular-based mass army. Bonaparte was fully a man of the Revolution, embodying many of its aspects even while restoring autocracy.

Peace was to be shortlived, however. In May 1803 war resumed with Britain and the Emperor began to concentrate troops for a contemplated invasion of England. Like the Spanish in the days of the Armada, this required that France gain at least temporary naval domination of the strategic Channel. Immediately upon the resumption of war, the superior English fleet blockaded the main French ports. French hope of success died 21 October 1805 when Nelson, using the ultimate development of sailing tactics in a two-column assault, won the decisive naval battle of Trafalgar against the combined French and Spanish fleets. Thus ended the century-long struggle between Britain and France for control of the seas. A side effect was that while Britain's empire received a stimulus, Spain was doomed to lose hers by the destruction of her seapower. For Napoleon, Trafalgar forced a return to the strictly land strategy at which he was adept, but it also meant he would need to find a nonmilitary method to war on England.

F. Ulm and Austerlitz, 1805

Earlier in the year, Britain had formed the Third Coalition with Austria, Russia, and Sweden. Its aim was the destruction of the Napoleonic threat to the established order. Napoleon's Grand Army of 1805 may well have been his best. The officers were experienced, half of the 200,000 men were veterans, and the recruits had been well trained during the years of continental peace.

Calculating that the Austrians would advance into Bavaria, the Emperor before Trafalgar ordered his army eastward in forced marches. Espionage had gained for him detailed knowledge of the enemy intentions. He accordingly screened the Black Forest with cavalry, detached forces to guard against a possible Russian advance east of Munich, and swept around the Austrians to the Danube. The result was the strategic surprise, envelopment, and surrender, without major action, of the advanced Austrian Army on 17 October at Ulm.

Having annihilated the Austrians by surprise and maneuver, Napoleon turned against the Russians. Because of the possibility that Austrian forces in Italy would be recalled against him, the Emperor advanced boldly toward the Russians, then on the River Inn, wishing to fight them as far to the east as possible. A detachment threatened their communications whereupon they retired toward Olmütz. Napoleon elected a defensive deployment east of Brunn with 65,000 men and then ordered isolated detachments toward the 82,000 Russians. He deceived the Czar and the Austrian Emperor with peace overtures. His own position was critical because not only would combined Austro-Russian strength double with new arrivals by mid-December, but also Prussia's entering the war with 180,000 men was a possibility.

Fortunately, a shortage of supplies at Olmütz persuaded Czar Alexander I to attack before Napoleon could complete his own concentrations. The French Emperor had decided to stand near Austerlitz with a deliberately weakened right. The allies directed their main thrust in this sector, with a resultant stretching of the Russian left. Napoleon had built up his own left and at the appropriate moment on 2 December, he penetrated the enemy center, enveloped what the Russians had intended as their own main, or encircling force, and destroyed it. So decisive was the victory that within twenty-four hours Austria asked for peace and the day after Christmas she accepted very hard terms. These included the destruction of the millennial Holy Roman Empire.

Napoleon considered Austerlitz, which fell on the anniversary of his coronation, to be his masterpiece. He gained complete local numerical superiority opposite the decisive point and then, at the culminating instant, he maneuvered to obtain success. Major units were irrevocably committed to a course of action before battle, thus solving the problem of how best to utilize the ponderous mass armies. This signified, however, loss by subordinate commanders of all but local initiative. A seed of Napoleon's ultimate defeat was planted, for independence in his generals was discouraged.

G. *Jena-Auerstadt, 1806*

Belatedly, after efforts to acquire Hanover by dealing with Napoleon, Prussia elected to enter war against the arbiter of Europe. Napoleon had begun remaking the map to establish a league of kingdoms under the aegis of France. Prussia was an obstacle to this continental system. Her large army was still that of Frederick, outdated in command, tactics, and logistics. The Prussians were trained to form up in lines and fire by volley in the eighteenth-century manner. There was no unity of command and the supply trains were long and cumbersome. After chaotic planning in councils of war, the Prussians deployed near the Thuringian Forest to await Napoleon's intentions. He, predictably, moved against their left to sever them from their Russian allies.

At Jena on 14 October 1806, the Emperor achieved a rout, despite his piecemeal frontal attack as his units came forward.

Meanwhile, Napoleon's subordinate, Davout, met the main Prussian army thirteen miles north at Auerstadt. The enemy compromised a nearly two to one advantage by lack of concentration. Davout gained a decisive victory. Immediately, Napoleon began a relentless pursuit which carried all the way to Berlin and utterly destroyed the Prussian and allied Saxon armies.

H. *Eylau and Friedland, 1807*

Still facing the Russians, Napoleon pushed on into East Prussia, but both armies went into winter quarters. He conducted a surprise frontal attack through a snowstorm at Eylau on 8 February, and, although the enemy retreated, his own army was too weakened to follow. Both returned to winter quarters. For the first time, Napoleon had failed in a pitched battle.

In June, after taking serious losses in initial fighting, Napoleon penetrated the main Russian lines near Friedland and drove the enemy from the field with heavy losses. The victory was won purely by offensive power, especially artillery. The Czar was so thoroughly defeated that he not only solicited peace, but also sought an alliance. The Emperor of the French, too, was quite ready for peace.

Czar Alexander I and Napoleon agreed at Tilsit to the partition of Prussia and established their respective zones of hegemony in Europe. Russia consented to join in France's measures against English commerce. Bonaparte stood at the height of his power. With Russia defeated, no continental nation contested him in the field. Only England denied him peace to consolidate his gains.

CHAPTER XIII

The Fall of Napoleon

I. THE CAMPAIGNS OF DEFEAT

HAVING LOST HIS FLEET at Trafalgar, Napoleon had no hope of a direct approach to his implacable enemy, Great Britain. Consequently, he chose an economic instrument, the Continental System announced at Berlin 21 November 1806, with which to seal Europe against English trade. He intended to so reduce her revenues that she would be unable to service the debt incurred during the lengthy conflict. Napoleon hoped that he could destroy Britain's financial capacity for war, drive her toward bankruptcy, and force her to a peace of his own choosing.

A. *The Peninsula*

Portugal, traditionally England's trading partner, was the most serious gap in the French economic cordon. Therefore, on 19 July 1807 Napoleon warned Lisbon to close her ports to English shipping and twelve days later he delivered a similar warning to Denmark. England reacted by sending Nelson to seize the Danish fleet and bombard Copenhagen, an example which kept Portugal in the British camp.

To reach Portugal, Napoleon obliged Spain to permit a French army to cross Spanish territory. Inadvertently he opened an Iberian Pandora's box which, along with his later Russian campaign, paved the way to his fall. This he compounded in March 1808 by overthrowing the Spanish monarchy and seating his brother Joseph on the throne. On 2 May the citizens of Madrid rebelled, thereby igniting a flame which the winds of nationalism swept across the Peninsula. The Emperor assumed that the revolt could easily be crushed, although he safely held only the country which was within range of his men's muskets.

Spanish roads were poor and few, the terrain rugged and mountainous, and agriculture was close to the subsistence level. With a hostile countryside, these factors made it difficult for the French to employ their usual technique of living off the land. The insurgents knew no rules of war, employing practices so savage that the Frenchman who was merely killed was fortunate. This was the original "guerrilla" war of an occupied people against an alien invader.

At Baylen on 19 July a French army surrendered; the invincible army of Napoleon had been beaten! The moral effects for each side were profound; the Spanish never relinquished their advantage. Joseph fled his capital and the Emperor sustained 40,000 casualties that summer. In August the British landed an expeditionary force in Portugal which was in time destined to belittle the conqueror of Europe and, at Waterloo in 1815, to inflict upon him his final defeat. Bonaparte concentrated veteran corps from all over Europe and took personal command. On 2 December he was in front of Madrid and a month later, after covering 214 miles in twelve days despite severe frost, snow, and glare ice, he entered Astorga. He had driven the British before him, but his plan of conquest had been dislocated and the Spanish rebellion had gained time and space to gather strength. Henceforth, the Iberian Peninsula would be a constant affliction for the Emperor who had at last been halted.

Although he returned to Paris, Napoleon left behind a theatre in which the Spanish provisional government had 135,000 under arms and in which French despatches had to be escorted by entire squadrons of cavalry. The new British expeditionary force under Sir Arthur Wellesley aggravated and encouraged the trouble and kept up a constant strain on France.

1. WEAPONS AND TACTICS

The British Army of 1809, like other European forces, used the smoothbore flintlock musket as a standard infantry weapon.

The piece could be fired two or three times per minute by well-trained troops and was accurate to 100 yards. Wellesley's light forces fought in a two-deep "thin red line" in which every man could fire his weapon. The French tactics by this time were built around the columnar attack of a mass of troops twenty-four deep. They relied more upon the psychological impact of seeming invincibility than upon shock. Skirmishers screened the column. When they encountered the British infantry, which usually was deployed along ridges with its flanks protected, the French were subjected to fire on both head and flank. In such encounters the line was never defeated by the column.

B. *Wagram* (*5-6 July 1809*)

Napoleon and France had suffered an enormous loss of prestige in Spain. Consequently, Austria once more entered the field. The French Emperor struck out for the Danube, again separated superior enemy forces by maneuver, and defeated them in detail at Abensberg and Eckmühl in April 1809. Napoleon advanced toward Vienna and attempted to recross the Danube near Essling in the face of the Austrian main body. After attempting to maneuver, Napoleon impatiently fell back on mass and a direct assault, but suffered a repulse which gave further hope to Europe. After making adequate preparations and concentrating vastly superior forces, he faced the enemy again near Wagram in early July. On the first day of battle he delivered an extravagant frontal attack. He repeated the tactic the next day to avert having his left enveloped. By sheer weight, Napoleon managed to stave off defeat before the arrival of crucial Austrian reinforcements. The Austrians withdrew and again made a painful peace, although this was due as much to financial crisis as to the campaign. While to this extent he had succeeded, Napoleon at Essling and Wagram displayed little of the agility associated with his great earlier triumphs; instead, his reliance was on massed artillery and manpower, neither of which was inexhaustible.

C. *Defeat in the Peninsula*

After Austria was again defeated, Napoleon placed over 300,000 men in Spain. Wellesley, now the Viscount Wellington, stood off the French in front of Lisbon and then launched an offensive of his own in early 1811. He had now gained the initiative in the Peninsula. Although vastly outnumbered by the French, he and his Spanish allies kept up a continuing pressure which tied down much of Napoleon's army. During 1812, Wellington waged a successful campaign which forced the enemy to concentrate at the price of relinquishing even more of the country to the Spanish guerrillas. During the following summer he drove the French into the Pyrenees and early in 1814 invaded southern France.

In the Peninsula, Napoleon had met his first serious reverse. The war there became an ulcer which cost him dearly. His failure gave encouragement to all the oppressed peoples of Europe, had tremendous moral significance for his enemies, and denied him important forces in subsequent operations in the main theatre.

D. *The Russian Campaign, 1812*

The alliance of Napoleon and the Czar was short-lived, for Russia soon found it expedient to return to her traditional trade pattern with Britain. Franco-Russian relations deteriorated rapidly after 1810 and in January 1812 the Czar made a secret agreement with London. Napoleon raised an immense army of 680,000 from all of the allied and subject states of Europe, as well as France. The very size of the invading army obliged a direct approach along the line of greatest expectation. On 24 June 1812, he crossed the River Nieman and four days later entered Vilna, where he tarried for two weeks due to logistic problems; at Vitebsk he again delayed a fortnight. Meanwhile, the enemy concentrated at Smolensk by the beginning of August but escaped when the French arrived.

Napoleon now was in a dilemma. He could not go into winter quarters at Smolensk because of his inability to provision the army there and because Sweden (who had entered the lists against him) threatened his rear. Therefore, he had to retreat before winter or continue toward Moscow; he elected the latter bold alternative, hoping that its capture would prove politically decisive and bring peace. After the bloody but indecisive Battle of Borodino (7 September), in which Napoleon again abandoned maneuver in favor of a tremendous artillery barrage and a simple frontal mass attack, he reached the ancient Russian capital a week later. But Alexander I did not yield.

The Emperor faced a guerrilla campaign against his communications, somewhat similar to that in the Peninsula. His system, which depended in essence upon mass and mobility, broke down when the population was actively hostile and the roads notoriously poor. The depth of empty, hostile countryside meant that the French could not live off the land. Furthermore, the Russians had bartered space in compensation for their numerical inferiority. The allied contingents were unwilling warriors who deserted in droves. Due to these problems, with only 108,000 of the men with whom he had started, Napoleon began his retreat on 19 October. Winter actually came late. Snow did not fall until 4 November, but during the withdrawal indiscipline virtually disintegrated the army. On the twenty-eighth and twenty-ninth, the Russians punished Napoleon at the Beresina where command deteriorated and a river crossing became a panic. The Grand Army ceased to exist. The campaign cost Napoleon 500 pieces of artillery and 200,000 muskets; French industry began to fall behind the demands placed upon it for new matériel. As his remnant straggled out of Russia, Napoleon set out posthaste for Paris.

E. *The Leipzig Campaign, 1813*

1. BACKGROUND

The entire character of the Napoleonic wars now changed. Whereas, except in the Peninsula, Napoleon had been opposed by monarchs, now the peoples of Europe rose against France. The armies of the Revolution had carried with them the gospel of popular sovereignty and the rights of man. But they had come not only as liberators but also as enslavers whose purpose eventually became indistinguishable from traditional French imperialism. This the Emperor did not understand.

When in January the Prussian Army of General Yorck von Wartenberg—which had accompanied Napoleon into Russia—defected to the enemy, the signal was given to avenge Jena and Auerstadt. A Prussian *levée en masse* was proclaimed and French methods were adopted for the defeat of France. Serfdom had been abolished and the basis laid for a people's war. Against this threat, Napoleon bent all his energies to the creation of yet another great army. By mid-April he had raised over 225,000 men, but he was short of his favored guns.

Armies had grown in size and theatres had become so extended that Napoleon's command system was no longer feasible. One man could no longer effectively be his own staff. Coupled with this, Napoleon had discouraged the development of his marshals' capacity for independent operations. They were trained to obey. Previously, his campaigns had been offensive, but now he was forced onto the defense and, due to the rise of the downtrodden peoples of Europe, he had to fight in country almost as hostile as the Peninsula and Russia. Finally, Napoleon had grown more dictatorial, more convinced of his own invincibility, and more prone to underestimate an enemy which had finally learned from him. His own methods would now be applied toward his defeat.

2. LÜTZEN, BAUTZEN AND DRESDEN

Napoleon marched eastward toward Leipzig, critically short of the cavalry which had always been his eyes. In the initial action near Lützen (2 May 1813) the allies gained surprise, but were defeated. Although a costly French victory, the battle was indecisive because the Prussians and Russians withdrew in perfect order and were not pursued. They then took up an excellent defensive position east of Bautzen. To forestall any attempt of Austria to take the field, Napoleon proposed an armistice to the Czar. He proceeded with an offensive plan intended to fix the enemy frontally and then envelop him from the north. Due to indecisive execution, the Battle of Bautzen (21 May) was again inconclusive. The allies withdrew skillfully after heavy losses on each side. An armistice was accepted 1 June.

Napoleon lacked cavalry, feared an Austrian declaration of war, and had suffered serious casualties. Nevertheless, the pause in the war, on balance, was detrimental to him. Russia, Prussia, and Britain took advantage of the truce to gain Austrian and Swedish adherence. When Napoleon refused the peace terms which Vienna offered him, war resumed in August. Although the Emperor had built up his strength and enjoyed a central position, the allies planned well. Their intention was to fight forces commanded by Napoleon's marshals and to retreat before Bonaparte himself. This strategy was a successful solution to Napoleon's traditional practice of defeating allies in detail. The marshals sustained successive defeats and the allies gradually closed in on the French ruler.

At Dresden on 27 August, Napoleon himself opened an attack early amid torrents of rain and practically destroyed the allied left. Once again, the Russians and Prussians withdrew and the pursuit was halfhearted. Near Kulm, the retiring enemy crushed a French force and took 13,000 prisoners. On 6 September the allies won another victory which cost France an additional 22,000. This brought the lesser states of Germany into the field against Napoleon. His foes began advancing from several directions on Bonaparte's troops who were concentrating near Leipzig.

3. LEIPZIG (16-19 OCTOBER 1813)

A tremendous cannonade by both sides opened the "Battle of Nations." The allies attacked concentrically in four great columns. The Emperor's attempt to penetrate their southern force failed mainly owing to the intervention of thirteen squadrons of Russian cavalry. Napoleon could have retreated, but he delayed doing so. His enemies received fresh contingents on the seventeenth which brought their strength to 295,000. The following morning they attacked east of Leipzig, but made no effort to envelop the French on the west. Napoleon was pushed back intact and was able to retreat toward the Rhine. He had been decisively beaten and had completely lost the strategic initiative. For the second year, he had lost almost an entire army, as well as huge quantities of arms.

F. The Defense of France, 1814

Napoleon calculated that the allies would not move until spring, but instead they entered France in January 1814. They denied him time to recuperate. Their numerical superiority, considering the contingents of the lesser nations which joined the struggle, rose to about three to one. Napoleon perhaps regretted the huge losses of manpower he had accepted in his later campaigns. He became a dynamo, however, employing his interior lines, mobility, and lack of allied unity, to strike alternate blows and delay the advance of his enemies. As they closed in, the Emperor desperately maneuvered to threaten the rear of the Austrians, raise new forces, and oblige them to withdraw eastward. After much deliberation, the allies in March concentrated their drive on the capital, leaving the remnant of Napoleon's army far to the rear. The last action was fought 30 March when Paris capitulated. Because his marshals refused to follow him any longer, Napoleon abdicated 11 April.

G. *Waterloo (18 June 1815)*

With Napoleon vanquished and the wars unleashed by the French Revolution at an end, the victors restored France to her 1792 boundaries and convened the Congress of Vienna to effect a general European settlement. Napoleon, from his detached position as Emperor of Elba, kept informed of the divisions and deliberations of his enemies and on 26 February escaped to the mainland. By 20 March he was again in Paris. The restored Louis XVIII had fled.

Bonaparte at once began raising another army of about 300,000 for the anti-climax of his career. His enemies intended to crush him by force of numbers, and he to beat them, as he had the Piedmontese and Austrians in 1796, by penetrating between the respective armies and defeating them in turn. Napoleon selected the forces nearest him—Wellington's Anglo-Dutch, and Blücher's Prussians—for his first targets, hoping to destroy them quickly and then turn on the other allies before they could complete their concentrations. He chose Wellington in Belgium for his first main blow; the Prussians for his second.

In Wellington, he met a general who had usually fought with inferior forces—and won. In the Peninsula he had developed linear tactics to a fine science. Deploying with the benefit of natural cover, he welcomed attack and delivered his counterblow once his more effective fire had halted the columns of France. Like that of Napoleon, his was a personal command system, but because his armies were small, for him the method remained effective.

At Ligny (16 June), Napoleon forced the withdrawal of Blücher, gaining initial separation of the allies, but he failed to pursue or to ascertain Blücher's route. Still unscathed, Wellington withdrew from Quatre-Bras, convincing Napoleon that he would retreat toward Brussels. The initial objective of separating the allies had been accomplished due to Bonaparte's skill in choosing the decisive point.

Wellington carefully selected a position along ridges south of Waterloo. The units immediately engaged were approximately equal in strength, although the great French gunner had more artillery. Napoleon attempted to penetrate Wellington's center with a direct attack but it was poorly coordinated. Late 18 June, Blücher—who Napoleon thought was gone—arrived on the French right, bringing the battle to a culmination. The French collapsed. During the night, the fresher Prussians pursued relentlessly. Napoleon Bonaparte, Emperor of the French, had been struck down never again to disturb the peace of Europe.

II. NAPOLEON ASSESSED

The successes of Bonaparte stemmed from a fortunate combination of factors, of which the most important were his own military genius; the ideology of liberty spread by his armies; and the revolutionary spirit unleashed in 1789 which, when enthusiasm faded, left as its legacy the coercive power of the new democratic state.

Napoleon's ultimate failure was due politically to his inability to make lasting peace with England. Economically, the conflict was between protectionism and free trade, contending children of the early Industrial Revolution. Britain therefore raised coalition after coalition to prevent the confederation of Europe under French leadership. Her task was facilitated on the Continent by the repercussions of the French message of nationalism, which finally boomeranged.

Militarily, Napoleon fell because of his overcentralization of command. Although war's expansion necessitated a well-organized General Staff, Napoleon continued to perform all his own intellectual work. He exacted unquestioning obedience from his marshals. His determination not to recognize impossibilities and his unlimited self-confidence had been early assets, but they eventually contributed to his own downfall, as did his own physical deterioration. Burned out at forty-six, some have written that he grew intoxicated with power and success. The vanquished inevitably learned from the victor and by 1813 they employed his own methods against him. During the summer armistice, the allies agreed not to engage the Emperor singly, but to retire until all their forces could be concentrated. Thus he was denied the opportunity to defeat them in detail and his unwieldy command system was made a liability, because his enemies realized that their previous lack of unity had served Napoleon. And finally, cashing the blank checks of conscription against French manpower, he relied more and more upon mass, abandoning the mobility that had brought him triumph. If there is a single lesson to be gained from Bonaparte's failure, it is that a once-successful formula must constantly be re-evaluated within its societal and technological context, lest with time it be converted into a liability.

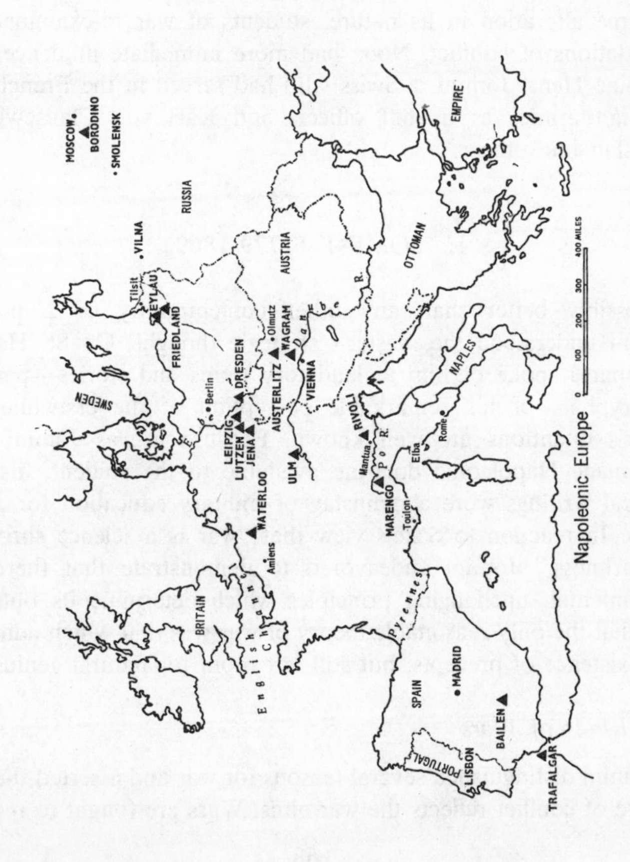

Napoleonic Europe

CHAPTER XIV

Interpreters of Napoleon

BECAUSE THE French Revolution and Napoleon had produced an extreme alteration in its nature, students of war re-examined the foundations of conflict. None had more immediate influence than Antoine Henri Jomini, a Swiss who had served in the French and Russian armies as a staff officer, and Karl von Clausewitz, a Prussian line officer.

I. JOMINI (1779-1869)

Possibly better than any other contemporary of Napoleon, Jomini understood the master's strategic thought. On St. Helena, Bonaparte spoke of him in laudatory terms and stories—perhaps apocryphal—of his remarkable perception of the erstwhile emperor's intentions are well known. Because it was Jomini who first made Napoleonic doctrine available to the student, his theoretical writings were a mainstay of military education for many years. In reaction to Saxe's view that "war is a science shrouded in darkness," Jomini endeavored to demonstrate that there are fundamental, unchanging principles which determine its outcome and that the only reasonable theory of war was that which admitted the existence of precepts, but still left room for natural genius.

A. Kinds of Wars

Jomini distinguished several reasons for war and asserted that the nature of conflict reflects the war aims. Wars are fought to reclaim rights or to defend them; to preserve the balance of power; and for ideological reasons. There are two types of wars of conquest, those which seek to enhance national power and influence through expansion, and those which gratify a simple lust. A senseless invasion, such as that of the Mongols, is a crime against humanity. Trained troops and difficult terrain make invasion extremely difficult, for no army can contend with the resistance of an entire people unless it is strong enough simultaneously to control communications, blanket the countryside, and beat the enemy main force. Jomini, therefore, particularly urged serious study of the Peninsular War.

Preferring "loyal and chivalrous warfare to organized assassination," Jomini hoped that "wars of extermination" might be "banished from the code of nations, and that the defenses of nations by disciplined militia, with the aid of good political alliances" might be adequate to preserve their independence. Apparently an apostle of international organization as the inevitable counter to the intolerable destruction of total war, he was thus far ahead of his time.

Jomini was profoundly apprehensive of total war and yearned for conflict to be circumscribed by international law. He realized that the Napoleonic era had opened the way toward, and that the *levée en masse* provided the means for, wars of annihilation. Considering the impact of the Industrial Revolution, he wrote that "the means of destruction are approaching perfection with frightful rapidity."

B. *Military Policy*

Jomini set forth a number of conditions for ideal military forces, none of which could be neglected without serious consequences. He esteemed the strength of representative governments but cautioned against their peacetime neglect of the armed forces. He specified a number of bases for a sound military policy, including leadership trained for both political and military roles; a high state of readiness of forces and matériel; serious study of military science; an esteemed position for the military profession; peacetime planning; strategic intelligence; fiscal soundness; and operations planning compatible with war aims.

C. Command

The most essential quality of a general is moral and physical courage. His knowledge should be thorough, including grounding in the principles of war. Like Saxe, Jomini stressed natural genius, or born leadership. He warned that "mediocre minds are always jealous and inclined to surround themselves with persons of little ability," for they fear the reputation of being led and fail to realize that the nominal commander receives most of the credit for success, even when he least deserves it. All other things being equal, a good staff officer due to his greater breadth makes a better commander than a line officer. His qualities, however, should be balanced with those of his chief of staff.

D. Strategy

Jomini believed that the art of war, and especially strategy, was the same under Caesar as under Napoleon. The essence of Jomini's advice was energetically to apply mass, at the decisive moment, successively against the enemy's decisive point and his communications, while maintaining one's own security. Furthermore, concentration should be achieved against fractions of the enemy army in order to defeat them in detail. Certainly, Jomini had learned well the basic techniques of Bonaparte.

In general, Jomini favored offensive operations, although—due perhaps to his own observations in the Peninsula—he pointed out that arousing the animosity of the invaded people could be hazardous. For a single operation he deemed the offensive almost invariably advantageous since only thus could force be brought against decisive points. Gaining the strategic initiative should be a primary operational objective.

To explain his ideas on strategy, Jomini divided the theatre into zones, points, lines, and bases of operations. He discussed these in considerable detail and illustrated them with drawings. From this he earned a reputation for advocating a kind of geometric warfare. Yet, in his own statements he emphasized the need for flexibility, made clear that war could not be reduced to geometric figures, and asserted that the genius of Great Captains must be unfettered by such pedantry.

E. The Influence of Jomini

Jomini's writings had tremendous impact on subsequent warfare. Their influence in the establishment of the modern subdivisions of military science was considerable. Much of his terminology is still in common use. He appreciated the changes which had occurred in war as a result of the French Revolution and he dimly foresaw the total war made possible by the Industrial Revolution. This he feared, and wished to restrict conflict to the concern of professionals. He had a strong tendency toward methodical strategy and limited war aims. Unfortunately, he demonstrated negligible understanding of the general relationship of war and society.

II. CLAUSEWITZ (1780-1831)

While Jomini interpreted changes in warfare for professionals, Clausewitz laid the foundation for the modern study of the subject. His major work, *On War,* which was incomplete when he died, was more than an assessment of Napoleon. Originality of thought gave it enormous subsequent influence and enduring value. Clausewitz set out to show the interrelationship of theory and practice, of war and society.

A. What Is War?

Clausewitz described war as an act of violence to compel the enemy to yield to one's will. Force is the means and imposing desires is the end in this process. While the theoretical use of force is without end, in practice limitations are imposed by international law, political considerations, and petty circumstances called "friction." The ruthless employer of force who is willing to accept unlimited bloodshed has an advantage over a foe who places restrictions on the lengths to which he is willing to go. Therefore, to ignore brutality, because of its repugnance, is at best a waste of time and effort.

The primary objective of military action is to disarm the enemy and reduce him to the point where continuing hostilities will appear more detrimental to him than peace. Inevitably this becomes the war aim. Violence tends to escalate to the maximum bounds. Only the extent of means available will limit it; thus, war is abstractly an act of violence to the utmost limits. Clausewitz went on to explain his concept of *absolute* or theoretical war. While this constitutes the ideal, in practice there are distinct military and political restrictions on the application of force. These stem from the fact that war is not an isolated act, nor does it depend on a single decision or blow. Wars accordingly vary widely in the degree of energy they generate and unleash. After the French Revolution had created the nation in arms, the masses acquired an influence on the political leadership which tended to reduce the latter's freedom of action. Napoleon waged something close to absolute war by utilizing unmodified violence, made possible by mass participation, to oblige an enemy to yield completely to his desires. Consequently, Clausewitz felt that theory must place absolute war foremost and take it as a point of departure.

B. *Means and Ends in War*

Disarming a state, or compelling its accession to our will, must always be the war aim. To attain this objective, its armed forces must generally be destroyed, or rendered incapable of continuing the fight. The country must then be conquered and occupied. Finally, the will of the foe should be subdued, his government and allies induced to peace, and his people brought to accept the settlement and its terms.

To destroy the enemy armed forces, Clausewitz believed there was only one means: combat. Therefore, although he admitted that there were other ways to reduce the enemy's will, his thought stressed the great, bloody battle, or decision by arms, toward which all military activity inexorably moved. Since only great, large-scale engagements can produce great results, Clausewitz scornfully wrote "let us not hear of generals who conquer without bloodshed."

C. *Generalship*

If war in its absolute sense is unrestrained violence and the great battle is the best means to the attainment of the war aim, then the role of leadership in ordering forces is of indescribable importance. The talent for war lies in a combination of powers, or tendencies of mind and soul. The more martial a society, the more prevalent will be military genius. Genius requires high qualities of intellect—the vital quality—and physical and moral courage. Daring and boldness often are its manifestations and, the greater the level of courage, the broader the margin that may be conceded to the accidental or unforeseen. Unfortunately, as men rise in rank, boldness becomes less common owing to the pressure of increasingly heavier exterior considerations.

The commander also needs health or stamina and a strong trait of resolution. The latter owes its existence to intellect, but more to strength of mind than to brilliance. Especially, the commander must be tenacious in holding to his convictions and keenly perceptive of the approach of the culminating point of every military action. The type of intellect associated with military genius is searching rather than creative; comprehensive rather than specialized; and cool rather than fiery. The desired combination of characteristics is rare, for out of a thousand truly remarkable men, possibly not one will possess the balance of qualities which will raise him above mediocrity as a general.

He operates under severe limitations, one of which results from military intelligence. Information requires an analytic discrimination in an officer which can be gained by judgment and knowledge. At best, seeing things objectively and correctly is difficult. Most reports, Clausewitz pessimistically thought, were false. Indeed, intelligence separates conception from execution. Therefore, the commander must stand firm against the pressures of the moment, because his first conviction generally will prove valid.

An important Clausewitzian concept is friction, or the trifling circumstances which accumulate to produce obstacles or inertia beyond imagination. Action in war is difficult enough because conflict is in a resistant medium. The general must be mindful of friction, but not overawed by it, for it can only be overcome by his powerful will.

Clausewitz believed that the commander must have clear judgment to resist impressions running counter to his convictions. He distinguished what he deemed vital traits of the great leader, but these can be reduced to a well-balanced temperament proceeding from moral fortitude and intellect. This combination enables the few gifted and qualified great generals to function effectively under enormous responsibility.

D. Strategy

Attack and defense Clausewitz saw as separate forms of unequal force. The defense, rightly understood, is stronger than the offense, both in political and military contention. A sound defense must revolve about the greatest possible preparation of means, an army habituated to war, a general who calmly awaits the foe, and a vigorous people who have no fear of the latter's coming. While he ridiculed the Jominian concept of decisive points, Clausewitz himself was concerned with centers of gravity—which amounts to the same thing in a strategic sense—and he thought that usually they lay in the enemy armed forces. The destruction of these units then is the most valid strategic objective and this end can best be served by a strategic defense.

The entire success of the defensive hinges upon the concept of the culminating point. Strength increases for the attacker due to a number of factors, but simultaneously it is dissipated by others. Ultimately, the attack will reach its culmination, or point of diminishing return. At this moment, the perceptive defending commander will swiftly unleash a vigorous counter offensive. Thereafter, the level of violence will increase rapidly toward the inexorable climax of the great battle. The advantage will have passed from the offense to the defense, and the latter will drive to victory. Thus, Clausewitz really advocated an offensive defense which would derive its superiority from luring the foe to spend himself in offensive operations. The great skill of the successful commander lies in detecting and exploiting the culminating point.

E. War and Politics

Clausewitz is noted for his analysis of the relationship between politics and war. The latter he regarded as always a politically motivated act whose aim is therefore the major consideration in the conduct of war. To be sound, the aim must always be compatible with military reality. The greater the significance of the political motivation, the greater the extent of the resulting violence. War thus tends to be governed by the motives that produce it. From this, it is but a logical step to the famous dictum that "war is a continuation of policy by other means."

Here Clausewitz referred to war as an inseparable part of a societal whole. It reflects national policy and is one of its instrumentalities. For this reason, he cautioned, the military point of view must always be subordinated to the political. Valid theory requires that political conditions determine the war aims before a conflict opens and this within the realm of military possibility.

Clausewitz also penned a pioneer analysis of people's war. A nineteenth-century phenomenon, he understood it as a natural consequence of the vast progression in violence occasioned by the levée en masse. An armed nation, or people, gradually debilitates an invading army. The struggle must ever be conceived as a guerrilla conflict supported by organized forces. Battle should be avoided and reliance placed upon a strategic defense and a limited tactical offense carried out by small units. Rarely should the outcome be left to a single great engagement, because time and space are the people's allies which enable them to defeat the invader through a war of attrition.

F. Clausewitz Assessed

Clausewitz was filled with an inquiring spirit which sought for the absolute or fundamental nature of things. He was a product of contemporary German philosophy and, distinctly, of his time, which marked the transition between disintegrating absolutism and rising nationalism. In reaction to the eighteenth-century scientific approach, he held that since war was undefinable by exact precepts, it was an art and not a science. While he dwelt upon what he called an absolute war, he intended this in a Kantian philosophical sense as a yardstick to measure military actions. Unfortunately, what he intended as abstract theory was grasped uncritically and out of context by practical soldiers who sought actually to wage absolute war. Clausewitz himself admitted and described numerous factors which operate to prevent war from ever reaching perfection, or its absolute form, despite its tendency to escalate to the utmost violence. Consequently, it is grave error to confuse Clausewitzian absolute war with modern total war.

Clausewitz' understanding of Napoleonic war was imperfect and certainly inferior to that of his contemporary, Jomini. But he believed in exhaustive reading of military history and did not confine himself to Napoleon alone. Unique circumstances, he saw, make each campaign different from every other; each age also has its own social, political, and technological characteristics. Therefore, Clausewitz advocated no particular military system and even denied that a universally valid approach existed. He recommended constant study and reflection to enable the leader to produce at any moment and under any circumstances, a sound decision. No fixed rules or principles could provide a shortcut to military success, but he himself set forth several general principles.

A great strength of Clausewitz was that he viewed war as a whole and expressed it as a national affair. He was far ahead of his times and founded the modern basis for the systematic study of war as a field of human knowledge set within its broad societal framework. His view of war as an instrument of policy is his outstanding contribution. Applied to current conditions and problems, this concept means that a peace-time policy can be sound only in so far as it can be supported if necessary by force of arms. Furthermore, a variable balanced military instrument permits a flexible foreign policy able to cope with a variety of situations.

Because Clausewitz' study was incomplete and at times contradictory, one can prove a great many things from it by adopting a "proof text" approach. Misinterpretation or incomplete interpretation led to the term "Clausewitzian," which usually refers to one willing to wage war in its most violent form in pursuit of a political objective. Indeed, this became the one-sided Prussian interpretation which, for a century, stressed Clausewitz' views on offensive violence and overlooked his theory of the superiority of the offensive defense.

CHAPTER XV

The Mexican War

I. TEXAS INDEPENDENCE

MEXICO WAS ONE OF Spain's principal New World power centers until 1821, when the Viceroyalty made good its independence following a series of militarily uninteresting campaigns. Both the new country and the United States were expansionists. Although heir to the Sabine River boundary pacted by Spain with the United States in the 1819 Florida cession, Mexico yearned for additional territories. Wishing to protect her empty frontiers, she sought colonization by industrious Roman Catholic folk; nevertheless she made grants in Texas to Moses Austin of Connecticut. By 1825, when the United States established a legation in Mexico City, relations were tense over damage claims, a projected wagon road from Missouri to Santa Fe, and conflicting boundary ambitions. Each side aspired to more than the Sabine line. The inept diplomats of the early United States further hampered relations.

As Texas grew in population, it desired statehood within the Mexican Republic. Vicissitudes in the national capital—where a successful political formula eluded the politically immature Mexicans—resulted in an unfortunate goading of the Texans. Their 1836 rebellion excited the sympathy of the United States and brought Texas unofficial aid. The issue was decided on the field at San Jacinto 21 April 1836. There, late in the day, General Houston attacked General Santa Anna's army, which was in siesta behind hastily constructed fortifications. Houston achieved surprise and vanquished the government forces. Texas made good her independence, at least to the satisfaction of the United States,

Britain, and France. She maintained it with the aid of an efficient little navy. Mexico refused to accept reality and on 3 November 1843 announced that U.S. annexation of the Mexican national territory of Texas would mean a declaration of war.

Nevertheless, after political maneuvering in Washington, Congress voted annexation 1 March 1845. This was a major victory for expansionists who had a vision of a territorially great nation stretching from coast to coast. Texas and Mexico had contended their border, the former asserting the Río Grande while Mexico City claimed the Nueces. When President Polk chose to press for the former stream, war became certain. In August, Brevet Brigadier General Zachary Taylor was ordered into Texas. His instructions were to protect her and, if necessary, "to drive all Mexican troops beyond the Río Grande." Taylor was later authorized to cross the river and disperse assembling Mexican invasion forces. Clearly contemplated was "a bold and aggressive war." In March 1846 Taylor, disregarding Mexico's warnings, advanced with 2,839 to face her army at Matamoras. Opposite the town he built Fort Brown. A patrol clash on 24 April in the disputed territory north of the Río Grande was regarded as an invasion of the United States and the commencement of hostilities. The Mexican Army began a river crossing in force.

II. FORCES

A. *Mexico*

The Mexican Army in 1845 consisted of conscripted—i.e., impressed—soldiers, mainly of Indian ancestry, who were officered by aristocracy ill-schooled in the art of war. With the exception of the repulse of a Spanish invasion force at Tampico in 1829 and of a French expedition at Vera Cruz nine years later, the army had been an instrument of civil political intrigue. Tactically, in civil strife there was disorganized infantry action usually concluded by a cavalry charge. When properly trained and disciplined, the troops fought courageously and with credit, but generally they were poorly equipped, supplied, and commanded. Controversial Santa Anna was no imbecile in military matters; at times he displayed brilliance, but he was qualitatively erratic. As a whole, in comparison to the contemporary United States Army, the Mexican Army of 1846-1847 was a worthy, if inept, foe.

B. United States

Since the War of 1812, Congress had continued to look with disfavor upon strengthening either the Army or the frontier defenses. Militia retained its historic importance. The War Department had no well-established logistic plans. Faced with a new foreign war, the Army's General in Chief, Winfield Scott, recommended bringing strength to 15,843 through expansion of existing units. Instead, in his 11 May 1846 war message to Congress, Polk proposed volunteers. Congress voted to call 50,000 for one year and, in addition, to double the regular army. Predictably most men preferred a single year with the volunteer units to a five-year regular enlistment. Although this practice re-established competitive recruiting, military policy was improved over that of previous wars. Few militia were used, the percentage of regulars (30) was higher, and the volunteers proved reasonably effective. Of the 104,284 men mustered, however, half saw no action and were a useless expense. In the area of weapons, the United States possessed a new muzzle-loading rifle which fired a long "sugar-loaf" bullet. An improved ramrod with cup-shaped head seated the bullet with ease and precision. The new weapon was accurate at 500 yards.

III. OPERATIONS

A. Early Northern Movements

General Arista, the Mexican commander, occupied a position between Fort Brown and Taylor's supply base, Port Isabel. With about 2,000, Taylor struck the doubly numerous Mexicans at Palo Alto on 8 May 1846. After Arista retired in good order, Taylor the next day attacked at Resaca de la Palma. There all three primary arms proved their mastery over the Mexicans, who fled after their left was enveloped. This established a U.S. moral superiority which conditioned the entire war. Taylor, an indiffer-

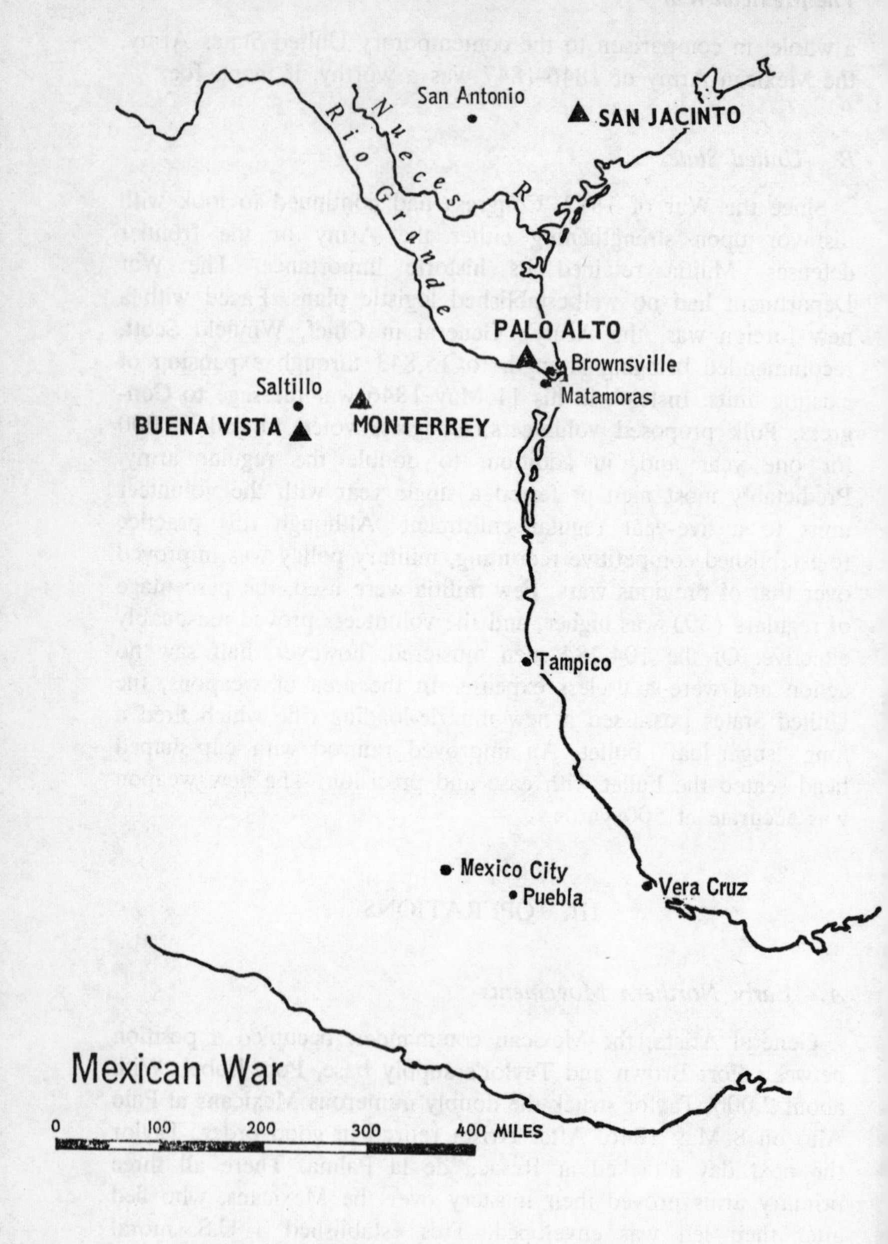
San Antonio
SAN JACINTO
Nueces
R.
Rio Grande
PALO ALTO
Brownsville
Matamoras
Saltillo
BUENA VISTA
MONTERREY
Tampico
Mexico City
Puebla
Vera Cruz
Mexican War
0 100 200 300 400 MILES

ent strategist, but a good tactician and trainer of men, failed, however, to confirm his victory by an energetic pursuit. Nine days later he crossed the Río Grande and waited three months at Matamoras for more wagons. This fortunately provided time which he used to drill his volunteers six hours a day. In August, he invaded Mexico with over 6,000 men. Monterey fell 21 September after three days' fighting, whereupon Taylor conceded an armistice which Washington rejected. Resuming operations, Taylor captured Saltillo on 13 November and moved on Victoria in December.

Meanwhile, Santa Anna—with U.S. assistance—had returned to Mexico from exile on the assumption that he would make a peace favorable to the United States! Instead, he assumed command of an army assembled at San Luis Potosí. Learning that Taylor was being weakened in his effort to provide troops for operations in the South, Santa Anna formulated a Napoleonic conception. He would march north, defeat Taylor near Saltillo, and then, using interior lines, shift rapidly southward to meet the new threat. The government failed to support him with adequate transport or logistics, leading to inordinate losses during the remarkable 200-mile advance through desert country.

B. *Buena Vista (23 February 1847)*

When Taylor learned of Santa Anna's approach, he retired to eight miles south of Saltillo. There he made his stand in rough country straddling the main road. Santa Anna detached a cavalry column to Saltillo, directed a secondary attack along the road, and hurled the bulk of his 14,000-man army against the American left, which disintegrated. Shifting of forces from right to left, and the arrival of reserves under Colonel Jefferson Davis, stabilized the situation. Santa Anna then enveloped Taylor's right. A disaster was averted through the efficient employment of artillery; superior infantry marksmanship was also important. The Mexicans, as night fell, lost heart; neither side was in condition to renew the fighting.

Although the battle was indecisive, Santa Anna elected to withdraw toward San Luis Potosí, leaving the field to Taylor. Personally, the latter had had little to do with the success of his 5,000 men, although he had demonstrated great courage during the fighting. Captain W. S. Bliss, his adjutant, probably had considerable influence on the action. Major operations in the North thus came to a close, for it was strategically a side show, but Taylor rode victory into the White House two years later.

C. *Opening Campaign in the South*

Winfield Scott, General in Chief of the Army, correctly determined that, given the loose political character of Mexico, her capital was her true center of gravity. In a brilliant strategic conception he resolved to strike directly at the national vitals. For economy of forces Taylor was reduced to a secondary role in the North. Familiar with Prescott's recently published *Conquest of Mexico,* Scott chose to emulate the 1519 exploit of Hernán Cortes. In March 1847 the navy put him ashore near Vera Cruz. After taking the city by siege he moved inland. By means of a remote trail he flanked Santa Anna's strong forces—whose fortifications were incomplete—at the narrow mountain pass of Cerro Gordo. The Mexicans were defeated and pursued with little loss to Scott, abandoning considerable matériel. The road to Mexico City was uncovered; by 22 April, Scott debouched onto the high Central Plateau.

A few days later, he sent 4,000 short-term volunteers back to Vera Cruz and with less than 6,000 remaining he abandoned his communications and captured Puebla on 15 May. After resting and receiving reinforcements, he resumed the advance in August with an excellent though small force of about 11,000. It included 300 U.S. Marines. "Scott is lost," observed the aged Duke of Wellington as the American entered the Valley of Anáhuac, "he cannot capture the city and he cannot fall back on his base." Despite political dissension, Santa Anna scraped together yet another army—about 30,000-35,000—albeit an ill-trained one. Consequently, unable to maneuver, he concentrated in the capital and heavily fortified its approaches. Scott therefore abandoned the main road, avoided frontal operations, and advanced indirectly on the city around the lakes to the southeast. This was made possible by the discovery of rough trails passable by wagons.

D. Mexico City Campaign

Working his way through the difficult lava field south of Mexico City, Scott surprised the enemy by a night advance and won a short action at Contreras early 20 August. He pursued, was again victorious late in the day at Churubusco and then demanded the city. Santa Anna asked and obtained an armistice for discussion. Finding this only a cover for desperate Mexican fortifying, Scott terminated the truce 6 September and concentrated within three miles of the capital at Tacubaya. Two days later, acting on erroneous information that cannon were being made in Molino del Rey, a cluster of stone buildings west of the city, Scott ordered a costly attack.

On the twelfth, a heavy bombardment served as a prelude to the main thrust against Mexico City. The 200-foot hill of Chapultepec, site of Mexico's military academy west of the town, received the main assault on the thirteenth. A secondary attack against the city from the south diverted the enemy, who believed it the primary thrust. The Mexicans fought desperately to defend the capital's gates, but Scott carried them by storm. The remnants of Santa Anna's army withdrew. Scott inaugurated an enlightened, well-disciplined military government. The war had effectively ended.

IV. LESSONS AND RESULTS

Although the United States' war with Mexico was small in numbers, it was large in results. By the 1848 Treaty of Guadalupe Hidalgo, Mexico accepted the Río Grande boundary and ceded her northern territory from Texas to the Pacific Ocean for $15,000,000. Most of this area had been occupied by small army expeditions; San Francisco had fallen to the navy. Mexico's loss, nearly 50 per cent of the national territory, was among the greatest suffered by a surviving state in modern times. This result was chargeable to her internal confusion and two-decade failure to find a successful political formula. She could not, therefore, despite invariable two to one numerical superiority, mount militarily strong forces and a united war effort.

An increased regular establishment and the avoidance of large scale use of militia had led the United States to their most successful conflict thus far. Nevertheless, no viable military policy had yet been accepted in Washington. Political disunity hindered the war effort, especially in the legislature. Traditional errors of competitive recruiting and short-term enlistments dogged commanders in the field. The war was a training ground for the junior officers who were to become the generals on each side during the Civil War. Fortunately, the nation was blessed by the generalship of Winfield Scott—one of the United States' Great Captains—whose bold and brilliant strategy avoided a long and possibly disastrous conflict.

CHAPTER XVI

The American Civil War: The Stage and Opening Actions

I. INTRODUCTION

THE WAR BETWEEN THE STATES has probably been the subject of more books than any other war in which the United States participated. Aside from its national interest, it was the first great conflict in which the technological advances of the Industrial Revolution received full play. The struggle was between agrarian society and industrialism. The growing role in modern war of the economic instrument was confirmed in the victory of the North. Jomini's clearsighted recognition that the "means of destruction are approaching perfection with alarming rapidity" was borne out by the impact of new weapons. The struggle was a clear portent of the Age of Total War. Psycho-social factors influenced the outcome of this, the first modern ideological struggle. For both sides the objective was nothing short of total: no compromise was possible.

Progress in missile weapons began revolutionizing the means of applying firepower in time and space. Guns were rifled for greater range and accuracy and strengthened to accommodate more powerful propellants. Bayonets retained little importance as infantry fire increased in range. The increasing use of muzzle-loading rifles accurate to 500 yards served to drive armies into the ground for protection. Spade and axe became important military tools. Mass production of weapons and bullets gave the factory a role. The bullet halted the cavalry charge and led to employment of the arm as mounted, highly mobile infantry.

The railroad revolutionized strategic transport and mobility, especially when operations could be conducted on interior lines. Supply bases could be far to the rear. One facet of Union strength was better organization of the railroads for war. The telegraph reduced communications time and placed a premium upon security and strategic surprise. With swift communications, great movements such as Napoleon's Ulm campaign were rendered almost impossible. Furthermore, the telegraph ushered in the age of the war correspondent, exposing the generals' timeless art to public scrutiny. Publicity threatened vital military security. The telegraph also enlarged the commander's geographic span of control; one man could manage larger, more dispersed forces in the field provided he had effective staff organization.

Armies on each side were based upon the nation in arms. The Confederate States of America had only 5,500,000 Caucasians; yet, by war's end they mobilized over 1,000,000. The North, with more than 20,000,000 people, used 2,375,000 soldiers. In most actions casualties on each side were high. This, and the hasty employment of semi-trained soldiers, led to mass tactics.

II. CONTENDING STRATEGIES

A. The Union

"Democracy at war needs to produce a political leader as head of the state whose grasp of grand strategy enables him to direct war policy."* The constitutional role of the President assured civilian control of military policy, but in the Civil War the distinction between Lincoln's legitimate role and meddling in purely military matters was a narrow and delicate one. Lincoln pursued a long search for a commander whom he could trust and for an effective command system. While militarily unqualified for his task, he learned from experience and was clever in his human relations.

Lincoln's strategic problem was dictated by his war aim—the preservation of the Union. The war must therefore be one of aggressive conquest in order to deny the South its independence. Negotiation was inconceivable because the objective was total.

* Richard A. Preston, Sydney F. Wise, and Herman O. Werner, *Men in Arms* (London: Atlantic Press, 1956), 243.

The Anaconda Plan, presented by venerable General in Chief Winfield Scott, envisioned the seizure of Southern ports—especially those served by railroads—to seal off all commerce. Control would be gained of the Mississippi River and two powerful armies, in East and West, would then be employed to constrict the Confederacy to death. Scott grasped the importance of rivers in the poorly roaded South as alternate transport lines to the vital railroads. Since the "colonial" economy of the agricultural South depended upon Northern and European industrial imports, she was vulnerable to restriction of her trade. Lincoln did not immediately understand the relationship between economic pressure and land attack; therefore, he did not appreciate Scott's conception although he blunderingly carried it to implementation piecemeal over the years.

Lincoln initially went part way, proclaiming on 18 April 1861 a naval blockade of the South. The fallacy of this blockade was that—unlike Scott's proposal—it left the ports themselves open. Although these were gradually captured, some were free until 1865. This made possible large-scale blockade-running and seriously limited the effectiveness of the entire policy. Furthermore, since the Navy was unable to implement the proclamation, it was a paper blockade without status under international law.

Lincoln at times was a strategic visionary who understood what should be done, but he did not know how to do it. A series of second-rate commanders complicated his problem. The best example is his early appreciation of the vital importance of Chattanooga and his subsequent diversion to the indecisive Eastern Theatre.

B. The Confederacy

Jefferson Davis, a West Point graduate and former regular officer, had distinguished himself in the Mexican War. He was Secretary of War in the Pierce administration and served in the House of Representatives. Such a background appeared to qualify President Davis ideally to lead his country in its war for independence. Unfortunately, he held an exaggerated opinion of his military qualities, literally exercised his constitutional position as Commander in Chief, and was a poor judge of men. He was "autocratic, and forever standing on the pedestal of his own conceit, a man of little humor, who could dictate, but who could not argue or listen, and who could not tolerate either assistance or opposition."*

Southern strategy was simpler than Northern. The South's aim was Independence and, therefore, her strategy should have been defensive. She enjoyed the Clausewitzian advantage of its being easier to defend than to acquire. Further, she could successfully operate on interior lines with numerically inferior forces. From the standpoint of grand strategy, her survival as a nation depended upon the same factors that controlled the Revolution of 1776; a war of attrition to tire the enemy, and foreign recognition and aid to consummate independence. To gain this end, Davis relied upon a mistaken belief that demand for cotton would oblige Britain and France to come to his rescue; in England, 20 per cent of adult males lived by the textile industry. Instead, other sources of cotton were found and Confederate diplomacy met defeat.

Davis failed to recognize that the political and strategic boundaries of the Confederacy did not coincide. The former ran along the Potomac, Ohio, and Missouri rivers and included Kentucky and Missouri, while the latter were the Potomac, Appalachian Mountains to Chattanooga, and thence along the Tennessee to Shiloh, overland to Fulton, and finally to Little Rock. The strategic decisive point was Chattanooga because it was geographically the gateway to the heart of the South and it was also the outer rail center. Railroads were admirably situated for defensive strategic mobility on interior lines northeast to Washington and west to the Mississippi at Memphis. Atlanta, as the hub of the interior coastal rail network, was the inner center of gravity. For these reasons, the militarily decisive theatre lay in the West. The East, favored by many historians, was the political theatre with the two capitals in contention. Capture of Washington would conceivably have brought European recognition and led to Confederate victory.

III. FORCES

A. *The North*

Lincoln, upon taking office 4 March 1861, faced the same confused military affairs as his predecessors, but his need was urgent.

---

* Major General J. F. C. Fuller, *Decisive Battles of the U.S.A.* (New York: Thomas Yoseloff, 1942), 181.

How mobilization should be conducted was an unresolved question. States' rights over militia remained a liability. Initially, he resorted to the Militia Act of 1795 to call part of the 3,000,000 enrolled men to the defense of Washington. Scott advised that 300,000 ably generaled troops would be needed for two or three years. On 15 April, however, Lincoln summoned 75,000 ninety-day men; this drove four more states to secession. On 3 May, Lincoln called for 42,034 three-year volunteers and an increase in the regular establishment to about 26,000. Although the men were forthcoming, the War Department lacked plans and logistics for their support. Congress, reconvening 4 July, repeated historic errors and authorized 500,000 for six months to three years service. State governors handled commissions, except for general officers.

During 1862, recruiting was entirely in Federal control, but on 3 April 1863 it was returned to state governors. News of heavy casualty figures dampened early enthusiasm for military service. State drafting for the militia was hardly effective. Competitive bounties and $300-hired substitutes added to the confusion. By 1863 a national conscription was begun for three years or the duration. In New York City citizens rebelled and rioted against their military obligations. Finally, colored troops were employed to the number of 123,156.

At the start of the war, the 16,357-man Regular Army was dispersed in garrison duty. Of the 1,098 officers, 313 resigned to take service in the South. General Twiggs took a sixth of the army with him when he turned the Department of Texas over to the Confederacy. Aside from the augmentation of 1861, the regular establishment was not expanded. Junior regular officers saw themselves advanced slowly and serving under civilian political appointees, often of negligible quality.

B. The South

The South began the war without a regular army, but with a nucleus of excellent former regular officers who were advanced and employed on merit rather than seniority. In effect, while the North kept the old army, the South obtained its brains. Davis himself, with his experience as Secretary of War, supervised the raising of forces. He appointed all general officers. The Confederacy

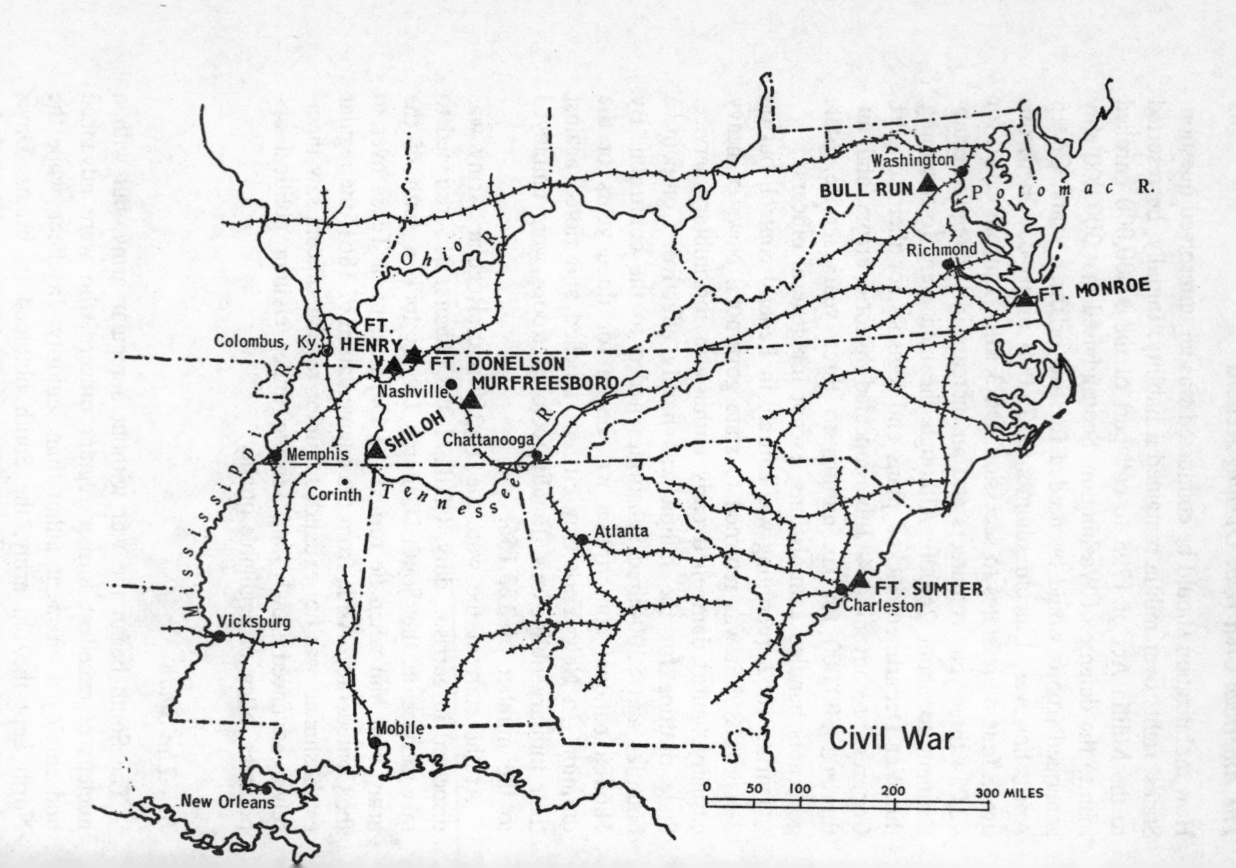

Washington
BULL RUN
Potomac R.
Richmond
FT. MONROE
Ohio R.
FT.
HENRY
Colombus, Ky.
FT. DONELSON
Nashville
MURFREESBORO
SHILOH
Chattanooga
Memphis
Corinth
Tennessee R.
Mississippi R.
Atlanta
FT. SUMTER
Charleston
Vicksburg
Mobile
New Orleans
Civil War
0
50
100
200
300 MILES

obtained the three professionals initially best qualified for high field command: Lee and the two Johnstons. Voluntary enlistment was first employed; by 16 April 1862 calls had been issued for 65,000. Resort was taken to conscription, but as at first, the states were relied upon for troops.

Confederate soldiers were self-reliant and unsurpassed as skirmishers, but they were ill-suited to disciplined regular methods. Their commanders wisely adjusted tactics to the character of their men, who were adept at field fortification. Though less "military" than the U.S. Army, the Confederate Army was more flexible and creative. Northern techniques were conventional and bound to the textbook, Halleck's translation of Jomini being the standard. Both sides employed costly frontal attacks against tactically decisive points. Failure stemmed from the power of the bullet hurled from behind field fortifications. The Confederacy managed to arm its soldiers by seizing 100,000 stands of rifles in arsenals, by domestic manufacture (although industry was far weaker than the enemy's), by capture, and through the blockade from Europe. In general, however, they were poorly supplied and equipped.

IV. FIRST BULL RUN (21 JULY 1861)

Regardless of the ideological issue of slavery, or the economic struggle of the factory against the farm, the war opened over the issue of the right of seceding states to acquire federal property in their territory. On 14 April, Fort Sumter in Charleston Harbor surrendered to the Confederates. Six days later Robert E. Lee resigned from the U.S. Army and was entrusted with the defense of Virginia. He sent General Joseph E. Johnston and 11,000 to Harper's Ferry and 22,000 under General P. G. T. Beauregard to Manassas Junction. On 10 June, Colonel John B. Magruder defeated Union forces near Fort Monroe, Virginia, and left them isolated; 12 July the western counties of Virginia were kept in the Union by a Confederate defeat at the hands of Major General George B. McClellan.

By virtue of his professional education in France, Major Irwin McDowell was advanced to Brigadier and given 35,000 hastily raised troops at Washington. In the entire country, the only officer who had ever commanded over 5,000 was Scott and he was too aged and infirm to take the field. He preferred to wait until the army was fully trained before launching offensive operations, but public and political opinion overruled professional counsel and McDowell's plan for an advance "On to Richmond" was adopted. The army required two and one-half days to march twenty miles to Centreville against Beauregard. Johnston left a cavalry screen under James E. B. Stuart to contain 18,000 Federals below Harper's Ferry. He then entrained to join Beauregard (18 July) in the first important instance of the use of the railroad for strategic mobility.

While McDowell frittered away his opportunity, Beauregard by 21 July received 12,000 reinforcements and contemplated taking the offensive. McDowell planned to hold enemy forces with a feint and a secondary attack down the Warrenton Turnpike and across the Stone Bridge. His main blow was intended as a sweeping envelopment to the northwest. Instead, the feint was ineffectual and the action degenerated into fierce fighting on Henry House Hill, where the brigade commanded by Jackson stood "like a stone wall," gaining him a nickname. About 1600 hours General Kirby Smith's brigade, last of Johnston's rail-transported units to arrive, was decisively committed against the Union right. McDowell's withdrawal turned to a rout as his troops fled toward the defenses of Washington. The Confederates, with Commander-in-Chief Davis personally present, failed to consummate their victory with a vigorous pursuit although the war's decision lay within reach. Instead, Davis gained an elevated idea of the prowess of his soldiers, whereas the outcome was owed to generalship.

On the following day, McClellan was called to Washington and given command of all troops in the area. These he promptly set about training into the Army of the Potomac. Lincoln was so terrified by Bull Run that thereafter the protection of Washington acquired exaggerated importance. In November, Scott retired and McClellan—the new General in Chief—began meticulous preparations for offensive operations. He was a man of great organizational skill who readily won the enthusiastic support of his men, but he was unproven in the field.

V. FORTS HENRY AND DONELSON (6-16 FEBRUARY 1862)

On 5 September, Brigadier General Ulysses S. Grant, who had returned to active services with Illinois volunteers, seized Paducah, Kentucky. Grant, an 1843 West Pointer and Mexican War veteran, had been forced out of the Army in 1854 for drunkenness. In the West there was no unity of command; Missouri and Ohio were separate departments under Generals Henry W. Halleck and Don C. Buell. The Confederacy, however, had placed all forces from Arkansas to Cumberland Gap under the very capable General Albert Sidney Johnston. Strategically, Johnston held a thin, overextended cordon defense across Kentucky, which enjoyed the single advantage of lateral rail communications. In the sparsely roaded West, however, rivers formed natural avenues of approach. The Confederacy lacked the industrial capacity to construct an effective river squadron; therefore, forts were erected to guard the streams. Near St. Louis, the Union formed a powerful squadron, the Western Flotilla. Grant fully appreciated that naval power had to be combined with land forces to capture the enemy's river forts, cut his rail lines, and destroy his outer defenses in the northwest. On 1 February 1862, Halleck authorized Grant to implement his strategy for an advance upstream against Fort Henry on the Tennessee River.

Fort Henry had been hastily built on low ground on the Tennessee's east bank. It could offer but weak resistance to the Union gunboats and capitulated 6 February. Most of the garrison withdrew overland twelve miles to Fort Donelson on the Cumberland. Grant landed his army and advanced unopposed. The gunboats took command of the river as far as Alabama, cutting the Memphis and Ohio Railroad. Donelson was high above the river and strongly garrisoned; its guns held off the flotilla, but Grant's army approached overland. Johnston divided his forces, reinforced Donelson with 12,000 men under former Secretary of War John B. Floyd, and withdrew his right from Bowling Green, Kentucky, to Nashville. By 14 February, Grant had surrounded Fort Donelson's land approaches.

Floyd resorted to a council of war with Generals Gideon Pillow and Simon Bolívar Buckner, his subordinates, and decided to abandon the fort he had just entered. The morning of the fifteenth a breakout was accomplished and the Confederates were in position to roll up the enemy flank and gain a victory. Instead, Grant re-formed his right; Pillow lost his nerve, throwing away success by ordering a return to the trenches. That night another council resolved to surrender, but Floyd and Pillow themselves escaped up-river with about 1,200. The great cavalry leader Nathan Bedford Forrest departed overland with 1,500. On 16 February, Grant demanded, and received, "unconditional surrender" from Buckner. This gave the Union flotilla control of the Cumberland and the vital rail bridges. Furthermore, Confederate command of the Mississippi at Columbus, Kentucky, was strategically turned. On 24 February, Buell entered Nashville, Johnston withdrawing to Murfreesboro. The outer Confederate cordon defense line had been shattered and the North had a new hero, U. S. Grant.

VI. SHILOH (6 APRIL 1862)

Immediately, Beauregard came west with a plan for concentrating at the important rail hub of Corinth, Mississippi, to take the offensive. There, 40,000 were quickly assembled by bringing Generals Leonidas Polk by rail from Columbus, Johnston from Murfreesboro, and Braxton Bragg from Mobile. Grant's forces moved up the Tennessee to Pittsburg Landing. On 11 March, unity of command was finally achieved under Halleck, who ordered Buell from Nashville. General John Pope's 25,000 men in Missouri were contained by small Confederate forces on Island No. 10 in the Mississippi. By 5 April, Grant had six divisions of 33,000 in a poorly guarded, unfortified camp against the river. Unaware that the enemy was only two miles distant in the dense timber, he felt no apprehension.

Johnston's intentions were to envelop the Union left, denying waterborne reinforcement. His attack developed in columns as the troops debouched in line from the woods along two available roads about 0600, 6 April. The assault became confused as units intermingled; all available men were quickly committed as they arrived. No reserves were withheld. By noon, the Confederates were advancing all along the front but against an orderly, fighting retrograde Union movement. By mid-afternoon, Grant's left finally yielded, but there were no Southern reinforcements available to exploit the success. Johnston himself was killed and command passed to Beauregard. Grant concentrated artillery and stabilized his lines. As a stormy, rainy night set in, both sides bivouacked in position. Beauregard felt he had won, but Grant realized that the victory would go to whoever first attacked in the morning.

That night, Buell's newly arrived forces began pouring across the Tennessee River. These 25,000 fresh troops overwhelmed the enemy on the seventh and in the afternoon Beauregard ordered his gallant men to retreat. Although he had gained tactical surprise and had fought a hard, indecisive action, the Confederate was strategically beaten. His attack had been poorly executed and overextended. Not only did he withdraw from the field, but he had failed to halt the enemy invasion. His return to Corinth was covered by the brilliant Forrest; Halleck, assuming personal command, required three weeks to pursue thirty-one miles.

VII. NEW ORLEANS (18-24 APRIL 1862)

New Orleans was the Confederacy's largest and wealthiest city, the natural trade center of the entire mid-continent. The Union navy, however, ended the city's hopes of dominating her trade area. The approaches to the port were defended by powerful Fort Jackson and a boom of cypress trunks and chains. There was a small river gunboat squadron. The garrison, however, had been reduced for operations in Tennessee. Two weeks after Shiloh, Admiral David G. Farragut bombarded the forts with mortar ships, penetrated the boom, ran the forts on 24 April, and defeated the defending flotilla. On 1 May, General Benjamin F. Butler occupied the burned-out city. This was a severe blow to Confederate hopes for French recognition, since Napoleon III desired a strong South capable of furthering his own Caribbean policy.

VIII. CONCLUSION

While the first year of the war in the East was marked only by the unexploited Confederate victory at Bull Run, in the strategically decisive West, the tide ran strongly against the South. Grant's campaign destroyed the outer defense line and opened the river approaches toward Chattanooga, Confederate center of gravity. The lethargic Halleck failed to exploit his gains and finally disbanded his army after Shiloh, sending Buell back to Nashville, Grant to Memphis—which was captured after a gunboat victory 6 June—and leaving General William S. Rosecrans with 23,000 facing the enemy. Beauregard skillfully withdrew to Tupelo, Mississippi. Confederate communications with the trans-Mississippi West were reduced to a single vulnerable avenue through Vicksburg.

Columbus, Ky.
Mississippi R.
Nashville
MURFREESBORO
CHATTANOOGA
LOOKOUT MT.
MISSIONARY RIDGE
CHICKAMAUGA
Corinth
ATLANTA
VICKSBURG
Jackson
WESTERN THEATRE
0 50 100 200 Miles

CHAPTER XVII

The American Civil War: The Culminating Point

I. THE PENINSULA CAMPAIGN, FIRST PHASE

A. Strategy

McCLELLAN devoted the winter of 1861-1862 to training and organizing his army and to the recruiting, supply, and movement of troops in all Departments. His dual role both as General in Chief and commander of a single field army added to his problems. He did nothing positive, however, about Johnston's army, only thirty miles from Washington at Centreville. McClellan relied for information—since the army had no intelligence service—upon the Pinkerton Detective Agency; it invariably exaggerated Confederate strength. Consequently, he formulated an indirect approach to Richmond by way of the Chesapeake Bay and the lower Rappahannock.

Lincoln favored a strategically frontal overland advance, lest Washington be exposed. McClellan correctly perceived that the city's defenses were adequate and that Johnston would be obliged to follow him southward. By the time the President approved the plan in March 1862, Johnston—whose espionage system was excellent—withdrew to Culpepper. Faulty security thus forced McClellan to modify his conception in favor of a landing at Fort Monroe and an advance on Richmond from the southeast. Lincoln consented, relieved him as General in Chief so that McClellan's full attention might be devoted to the field, and personally assumed the supreme command. This Lincoln exercised through Secretary of War Edwin M. Stanton, with considerable interference by certain Senators. From the military viewpoint, unity of command was destroyed because the President lacked ability to coordinate his numerous independent commands.

B. Hampton Roads (9 March 1862)

In April 1861 the United States Navy scuttled the 50-gun frigate *Merrimac* and fired the Norfolk Navy Yard. Gallant Virginia militia rushed in, quelled the flames, and saved the largest store of modern ordnance in the hemisphere. These guns were then emplaced for defense of coastal and interior waterways. The execution of McClellan's strategy on the Peninsula required absolute naval control of the adjacent waters. The Confederacy raised the *Merrimac* and wisely converted her to an ironclad. Only one Southern rolling mill was able to turn out plate; railroad rails were the metal source. Union agents reported progress to Washington, thus hastening Northern countermeasures. Recommissioned the CSS *Virginia,* the ship mounted three 9-inch, two 6-inch, and two 7-inch guns. A heavy iron ram protruded from her bow. She was easily capable of vanquishing any wooden Union vessel.

Washington's answer to the *Virginia* was the USS *Monitor,* built in the fall of 1861. An ingenious craft, she featured over forty innovations in ship construction. She was low and flat with a nine-foot turret twenty feet in diameter, and carried two 11-inch guns. On 8 March 1862 the sluggish Confederate ship emerged from Norfolk and sank two enemy frigates. Apparently, the blockade could be demolished and McClellan's attack on Richmond neutralized. Even as the battle ended, however, the *Monitor* was approaching after a trying voyage from New York. At 0630 the next day, the *Virginia* steamed forth to complete the destruction of the enemy squadron. A two-hour gunnery duel at under 40 yards failed to damage seriously either ironclad. This achieved a stalemate; the *Virginia* returned to port; the *Monitor* did not again accept battle. A new era of naval warfare had, nevertheless, been born.

C. Yorktown and Williamsburg

With the Confederate naval threat obviated, McClellan landed 121,500 at Fort Monroe by 5 April 1862 and encountered defenses from Yorktown across the Peninsula. He learned that Lincoln, who feared for Washington because of Jackson's presence in the Shenandoah Valley, had cancelled sailing orders for McDowell's last corps. With a garrison of 40,000 already in Washington, Lincoln's action was needless. General Johnston was massing all possible strength against the Army of the Potomac. McClellan settled in front of the enemy line for a month, although it was manned by only 15,000, and prepared for a water-borne envelopment. Johnston, however, withdrew toward Richmond under cover of General James Longstreet's rear guard action at Williamsburg. Heavy rain and muddy roads hampered both sides. Johnston's action negated a Union landing near the head of the York River at West Point. McClellan's pursuit was slow but on 25 May he concentrated above the Chickahominy, only five miles from Richmond. Meanwhile, under pressure, Norfolk was evacuated on the tenth and the *Virginia* destroyed by the Confederates, thus opening the James River.

II. THE VALLEY CAMPAIGN

Johnston informed Davis that there was no hope of defeating McClellan in a war based upon artillery and engineering. The South must open offensive operations. McDowell's corps, which had advanced to the Rappahannock, posed a deadly threat if it should advance south and join McClellan. McClellan, who had a two-to-one numerical superiority, overestimated Johnston's strength at 200,000. Lee, who had become military adviser to Davis, reinforced Jackson in the Valley, setting in motion a brilliant diversionary operation.

During the winter, Jackson had contained a corps under General Nathaniel P. Banks at the mouth of the Shenandoah Valley. The Valley offered the South a natural avenue of approach to the North above Washington and to the Baltimore and Ohio Railroad; as such, it gravely concerned Lincoln. Offensively it was of no importance to the Union since the southern exit of the Valley threatened nothing of significance. In March, Banks advanced south through Winchester and on the twenty-third Jackson suffered a defeat at Kernstown. Nevertheless, Lincoln was so alarmed that, for the first time, he ordered McDowell not to join McClellan. Avoiding battle, Jackson retired to Swift Run Gap. At this point he received the order to divert McDowell, who was again moving toward Richmond.

General John C. Frémont, on the western slopes with 18,000, threatened Jackson's left. The latter entrained ostensibly for Richmond, but instead moved west and defeated Frémont at McDowell, Virginia. He then moved down the Valley, shifted through the Massanutten passes, expelled the enemy from Front Royal on 23 May, inflicted a second defeat on the retiring Banks by enveloping his right at Winchester, and drove him across the Potomac. Secretary of War Stanton again ordered McDowell to detach 20,000 against Jackson who thereupon faced 50,000 converging troops. Moving rapidly, Jackson escaped a trap. He then successively defeated Frémont, who had returned down the Valley, and McDowell's advance division. McDowell's orders to Richmond were cancelled for the third time. With 16,000, Jackson had contained 70,000 Union troops. Properly employed in conjunction with McClellan's offensive on the Peninsula, these troops could easily have ended the war.

III. THE PENINSULA CAMPAIGN, FINAL ACTIONS

A. *Fair Oaks (31 May 1862)*

McClellan had pushed his III and IV Corps across the Chickahominy, expecting McDowell's arrival to complete his dispositions. When Johnston learned of the latter's diversion to the Valley he attacked 31 May, although he had only 63,000. The execution of his well-planned operation was piecemeal and Johnston himself was wounded. McClellan failed to counterattack. On the following day Lee took personal command in the field, reorganized his force as the Army of Northern Virginia, and began entrenching and constructing field fortifications to protect the capital.

B. *The Seven Days' Battles (25 June–1 July 1862)*

McClellan gradually moved his 105,000 troops across the stream, but then spent his time emplacing siege guns. He displayed his usual reluctance to seize the initiative. Lee was eager to do just that and 12-15 June he sent Stuart's 1,200 cavalry to reconnoiter behind the enemy to the north. This so alarmed McClellan that he began preparations to shift his base to the James River. Lee, whose weaker forces could not endure a battle of attrition, chose to attack the enemy right. He ordered Jackson to join him by rail from the Valley. Once he arrived, Jackson was to turn Union communications and force retreat. Enemy agents discovered these intentions. Lee, by stripping his own right, acquired local numerical superiority against McClellan's right, for he correctly assessed the latter's weak generalship. The excellent plan failed 26 June at Mechanicsville because of Jackson's unexplained indecisiveness, and because of the ill-conceived frontal attack of General Daniel H. Hill. McClellan, overestimating Lee's strength by 100,000, resolved to retire to the James River.

The next day, frontal assaults and Jackson's lack of initiative again cost victory at Gaines' Mill, but the enemy line had been broken and retirement commenced. Savage fighting ensued in semi-jungle White Oaks Swamp as Lee struggled to halt the retreat or to convert it into a rout. On 30 June at Frayser's Farm and again at Malvern Hill the next day, the Union fought successful rear guards and the Confederacy lost opportunities. Coordination was poor, Union artillery was deadly, reconnaissance and maps were deficient, and genuine results were negligible. The battles cost the South 20,000 whom she could less readily replace than could the North her 16,000 casualties. Through aggressive action Lee had saved Richmond and gained strategic victory with inferior forces. Tactical success was denied him primarily because of Jackson's failures. McClellan's Army of the Potomac remained on the James at Harrison's Landing until August, when it was evacuated to the Washington area.

IV. SECOND BULL RUN (29-30 AUGUST 1862)

During the Seven Days' Battles, Lincoln placed Banks, Frémont, McDowell and the Washington garrison under the command of General John Pope, who had fought well in the West. On 11 July, the President summoned Halleck to Washington to be General in

Chief; this really signified the failure of Lincoln's personal attempt to direct the war. Pope aspired to seize the important rail center of Gordonsville, but the swifter Lee already had Jackson at the town with 12,000 veterans. Halleck decided—over McClellan's objections—to evacuate the Army of the Potomac to Aquia Creek to combine with Pope's Army of Virginia. When Lee learned of this, he immediately decided to move north with 55,000, get between Pope and Washington, and defeat him before McClellan's arrival. This he attempted unsuccessfully 18 August, Pope escaping up the Orange and Alexandria Railroad. The armies faced each other across the Rappahannock 24 August.

Lee knew that with McClellan's troops already disembarking at Alexandria and Aquia Creek, speed was necessary before 130,000 concentrated against him. Lee perilously split his army to send Jackson northwest and then east to Mannassas Junction. There he blocked Pope's line of communications from Washington. Pope sought to annihilate Jackson, who took up a defensive position behind an unfinished railway embankment west of the Stone Bridge. For a time Pope lost his enemy because of faulty cavalry reconnaissance. Fearing Pope would retire toward Washington, Jackson deliberately revealed his position late 28 August.

Pope had issued orders for a concentric attack but he overlooked Longstreet's presence at Thoroughfare Gap only ten miles from Jackson. Pope's piecemeal attack was frontal and Jackson held. General Fitz-John Porter's corps—after fighting well on the Peninsula—had already joined Pope and discovered the approaching Longstreet. Pope refused to accept this information and ordered Porter to attack Jackson's right. Pope's overly optimistic order for "pursuit" of Jackson intensified the results of his original error. Consequently, Longstreet's artillery enfiladed the Union attack 30 August. He pressed an infantry attack in conjunction with Jackson, placing Pope in a nutcracker. Lacking forces to complete the encirclement, Lee could not prevent the vanquished from retiring across Bull Run by night. He did, however, send Jackson to threaten once more the Union rear. Tired and hungry, Jackson's army was incapable of victory in the 1 September Battle of Chantilly. Pope nevertheless retired within the defenses of Washington, a beaten man. On the fifth, he was relieved. His army was merged into McClellan's.

Lee's daring and his retention of the initiative had virtually cleared Virginia of enemy troops in less than three months. He had reversed the June situation; it was now the Confederate States Army which lay outside Washington, not the United States Army outside Richmond. But its inadequate logistics and numerical inferiority made a siege impossible. Even to remain in the field Lee had to find supply country. Strategically, he needed to retain the advantage of the initiative. Therefore, on 3 September, he informed Davis that the moment seemed propitious to invade Maryland, enemy territory but with a large proportion of friendly people. Unfortunately, the Army of Northern Virginia was unequipped for such an operation. Lee also considered it timely to attempt negotiation with Washington on the basis of Confederate independence. Certainly, at this moment Lee underestimated his enemy both militarily and politically.

V. ANTIETAM (17 SEPTEMBER 1862)

Lee's first invasion of the North was aimed at (1) luring Maryland to secede, (2) strategically supporting Bragg's invasion of Kentucky by cutting the Baltimore and Ohio Railroad, Union supply route to Ohio, (3) capitalizing upon Union war-weariness, (4) indirectly threatening Washington, and (5) gaining European recognition. By 7 September, Lee had crossed the Potomac, concentrated at Frederick, Maryland, and screened his actions with Stuart's cavalry. He then unwisely scattered his army, sending Jackson to capture Harper's Ferry and Longstreet to Hagerstown.

McClellan moved slowly northwest from Washington. On 13 September good fortune fell his way in the form of a copy of Lee's Special Order 191 detailing Confederate plans. Immediately Lee learned of this and shifted forces in an unsuccessful attempt to block the mountain gaps. Next, he elected to reconcentrate his divided army at Sharpsburg and accept battle. This decision was unnecessary. It disregarded the defensive essence of wise Confederate strategy. The South could ill afford the resulting losses. McClellan delivered his attack successively from right to left; General Ambrose E. Burnside squandered soldiers in a frontal attack across a bridge over an easily fordable stream. Union

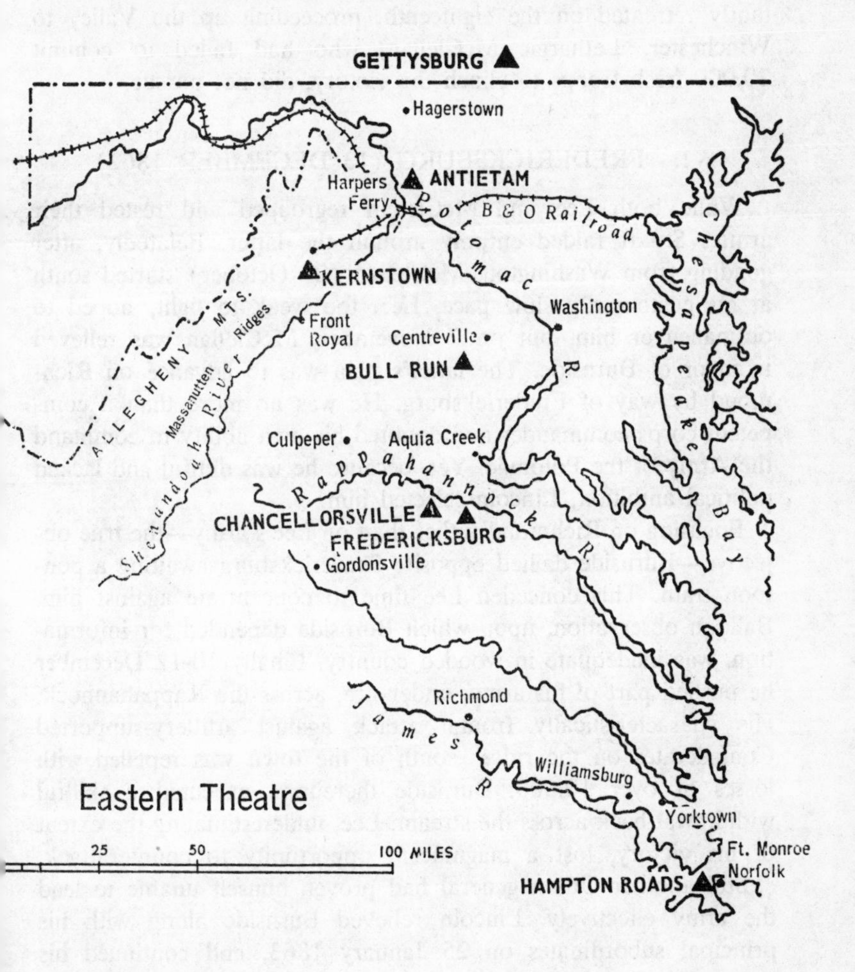
GETTYSBURG
Hagerstown
Harpers Ferry
ANTIETAM
B & O Railroad
Potomac
KERNSTOWN
ALLEGHENY MTS.
Massanutten
Shenandoah River
Ridges
Front Royal
Washington
Centreville
BULL RUN
Chesapeake Bay
Culpeper
Aquia Creek
Rappahannock R.
CHANCELLORSVILLE
FREDERICKSBURG
Gordonsville
Richmond
James R.
Williamsburg
Yorktown
Ft. Monroe
Norfolk
HAMPTON ROADS
Eastern Theatre
25
50
100 MILES

artillery—superior as always—inflicted a slaughter. Lee reluctantly retreated on the eighteenth, proceeding up the Valley to Winchester. Lethargic McClellan, who had failed to commit 20,000 fresh troops to clinch the victory, did not pursue.

VI. FREDERICKSBURG (13 DECEMBER 1862)

While both Lee and McClellan regrouped and rested their armies Stuart raided entirely around the latter. Belatedly, after goading from Washington, McClellan (26 October) started south at his customarily slow pace. Lee, too weak to fight, hoped to outmaneuver him, but on 7 November, McClellan was relieved in favor of Burnside. The latter's plan was to advance on Richmond by way of Fredericksburg. He was no more than a competent corps commander and doubted his own ability to command the Army of the Potomac. Yet, because he was dutiful and lacked political ambition, Lincoln selected him.

Focusing on Richmond rather than on Lee's army—the true objective—Burnside dallied opposite Fredericksburg awaiting a pontoon train. This conceded Lee time to concentrate against him. Balloon observation, upon which Burnside depended for information, was inadequate in wooded country. Finally 10-12 December he pushed part of his army, under fire, across the Rappahannock. His characteristically frontal attack against artillery-supported Confederates on the ridges south of the town was repelled with losses of over 10,000. Burnside thereupon executed a skillful withdrawal back across the stream. Lee, underestimating the extent of his victory, lost a magnificent opportunity to counterattack.

Still another Union general had proven himself unable to lead the army effectively. Lincoln relieved Burnside along with his principal subordinates on 25 January 1863, and continued his search for a competent general by entrusting the army to General Joseph Hooker.

VII. MURFREESBORO (31 DECEMBER 1862–3 JANUARY 1863)

After the Confederate evacuation of Corinth, Halleck had sent Buell to Nashville. Raids against his railroad communications by

Forrest and General John H. Morgan alone prevented Buell from advancing on Chattanooga. Bragg shifted most of his troops from Tupelo, Mississippi, to Chattanooga by rail through Mobile and prepared to force Buell north by an indirect approach, i.e., invasion of Kentucky. In support, General Kirby Smith advanced from Knoxville to Lexington in August 1862. Bragg marched north from Chattanooga to Munfordsville. Buell withdrew through Bowling Green after finding Bragg astride the Louisville and Nashville Railroad. Buell regained the initiative, however, in an attack at Perryville, whereupon Bragg retired unmolested through Cumberland Gap. His attempt at recovering Kentucky had failed for lack of local support. His strength had been inadequate for the sounder task of strategically enveloping the entire Union west by invading Ohio.

Buell was replaced 30 October by Rosecrans, who concentrated at Nashville against Bragg at Murfreesboro. Rosecrans' reputation stemmed from his victory at Corinth 4 October over General Earl Van Dorn. He was under heavy political pressure to attack, but first he carefully reorganized. His march was harassed by enemy cavalry. Bragg lay in a defensive position astride Stone's River. On 31 December each general attempted to envelop the other's right. Bragg, who struck first, threw a crescent around Rosecrans, but piecemeal use of reserves late in the day probably cost him a victory. Rosecrans doggedly refused to accept defeat, held the field, and crossed the river on New Year's Day with part of his force to dislocate Bragg's offensive. After Rosecrans received a large supply train 3 January, Bragg skillfully withdrew, conceding the strategic victory after fighting a tactical draw.

VIII. CHANCELLORSVILLE (1-6 MAY 1863)

When Hooker took over the Army of the Potomac its morale was very low. The new commander displayed unexpected organizational skill, improved conditions of the troops, established an intelligence service, and tightened discipline. Hooker was a man of many faults, not the least of which was a low standard of personal morality, but he was a brave, aggressive combat leader. He brought all his cavalry together into a corps for greater effectiveness, but he decentralized his artillery. "May God have mercy on General Lee," he boasted, "for I will have none." By the end of April 1863 he had the best army the continent had ever seen—122,000 infantry, 12,000 cavalry, and 400 guns. Hooker knew that Lee had only half his own strength, but the Confederates had fortified the Rappahannock line inland from Port Royal. He therefore planned a turning movement far upstream to descend upon Lee's left and cover the river crossing of his own main body. This operation was executed 29 April.

With three corps on Lee's rear at Chancellorsville, a crossroad in the wilderness, Hooker ordered a fatal pause, dug in, and waited for reinforcement. Lee decided to hold 40,000 Federals under General John Sedgwick at Fredericksburg and concentrate 43,000 against Hooker's main force of 73,000. His intention was to fix Hooker with only 17,000 while using his remaining troops under Jackson to envelop the enemy. Stuart brought reports that the Union right was exposed and vulnerable. When Jackson began his move at 0600, 2 May, Hooker convinced himself that the enemy was retreating. Twelve hours later, although Hooker had been fully warned, without his taking action, Jackson attacked down the enemy's trench line and routed him. Seeking a route in the dark to prevent Hooker's escape, Jackson was shot by his own men. Hooker attempted a feeble night counterattack, but made no further effort to regain the initiative. Lee's army was split; Sedgwick successfully broke through at Fredericksburg and was coming down on his rear. Lee correctly perceived Hooker's inactivity, left Stuart—who had assumed command of II Corps upon Jackson's death—to face him, and swiftly reconcentrated against Sedgwick. Late 4 May he drove the latter back across the river. All the while, Hooker did nothing. Lee then planned on all-out offensive against him for the sixth, but the Army of the Potomac withdrew during the night.

IX. GETTYSBURG (1-3 JULY 1863)

After Chancellorsville, the armies returned to their former positions. Lee, whose forces were at a peak of morale, reorganized into three corps with integral artillery and an oversize cavalry division under Stuart. The general Confederate situation was deteriorating. European recognition had not come; the anti-war, Copperhead movement in the Midwest was failing; domestic finance was collapsing; in the West, Grant was besieging Vicksburg and Banks was at Port Hudson, Louisiana; the blockade was beginning to hurt seriously. Lincoln's Emancipation Proclamation had shattered all hope of compromise.

In this situation, Longstreet came forward with a brilliant strategic conception. He proposed to hold the inactive Hooker with two corps while he himself and all other available troops in the East moved by rail to Chattanooga. There he would concentrate with Bragg and Johnston—who was at Jackson, Mississippi—and launch a grand operation against Rosecrans. This, he believed, would constitute an indirect approach to Grant, bring him away from Vicksburg, paralyze the North, and threaten invasion in force of Kentucky and Ohio. This was a masterful plan utilizing railroads for strategic mobility on interior lines. It was perfectly in keeping with a sound strategy for the South, as discussed earlier. Lee, however, was at heart Virginia's general, unconcerned with grand strategy and Davis feared for his capital.

Lee instead returned to the erroneous strategy of directly invading the North. Considering his own usually atrocious logistics and the high morale of his army, Pennsylvania as a source of supply was an attractive goal. He felt the war could not be won defensively and that Hooker would be obliged to follow him north. He hoped then to inflict a decisive, war-winning defeat. Hooker correctly deduced these intentions and wished to counter with an advance on Richmond, but Lincoln vetoed this in favor of the enemy army as an objective. Hooker thereupon began paralleling Lee's movement. By 28 June, Lee was in the vicinity of Chambersburg, Pennsylvania, with his advance forces outside Harrisburg. Pennsylvania was in a panic; Washington was gravely alarmed, especially because Stuart raided as far as Rockville, Maryland. That night Lee, who had lost the enemy army, learned that it was near Fredericksburg under General George G. Meade. Hooker, who had been handling the army adeptly, had that morning resigned because of Washington's meddling with his troop dispositions.

Meade determined to lure Lee to battle south of the Susquehanna. His instructions from Halleck were to maneuver and fight to protect Baltimore and the Capital. Lee began a concentration near Cashtown, but with Stuart gone he had inadequate reconnaissance. A Confederate brigade seeking a reported supply of shoes blundered into enemy cavalry at the road center of Gettysburg. On 1 July successive elements of each army entered the fray, which grew in intensity. Lee was drawn by his subordinates into a battle not of his own choosing. Late in the day, General Richard S. Ewell, acting under discretionary orders, lost an opportunity to seize the commanding Cemetery Hill. Lee planned an attack for the next morning, but it did not develop until afternoon. Longstreet favored luring the enemy to attack, but Lee, as always, stood for the offensive. In part, this reflected his logistic inability to remain long at Gettysburg. The former's assault was late, and failed to carry Little Round Top. Ewell's blow from the north also failed.

Meade's commanders voted in a council of war the night of 2 July to stay and fight. Their position covered the ridges, but was virtually enveloped on the north and open on the south. Meade's superior logistics were an important factor; he obtained almost unlimited supply from Baltimore. Lee's supply was weak, but he had 15,000 fresh troops under General Pickett. He massed 159 guns and elected another frontal attack in preference to Longstreet's recommended move against the open enemy left. At 0100, 3 July 1863, the artillery opened and expended almost all of the ammunition; presumably, the enemy guns had been silenced. In a mile-wide line down Seminary Ridge and across the intervening half-mile valley Pickett's brave soldiers charged into Union artillery, which at once broke its silence to decimate the Confederate ranks. Lee assumed the full blame and prepared for Meade's counterattack which never came.

Each side had lost over 20,000. Lee held his position through the cloudbursts on the fourth while his wounded were evacuated. Then he withdrew, his generalship at a nadir. The campaign was based upon two misconceptions—the invincibility of Confederate infantry and the willingness of Washington to make a compromise peace. Lee erred grievously in employing his cavalry improperly when his need for its reconnaissance was greatest. He had been careless, lacked vigor in his orders, and had resorted to a foredoomed frontal assault without diversionary actions. He underestimated his enemy and overesteemed his subordinates. Only his brilliant retreat with an enormous wagon train of spoils was worthy. Meade's lethargic pursuit enabled Lee once more to cross the Potomac during the night of the thirteenth. With him went the hope of winning the war, for English recognition—which almost certainly would have followed victory at Gettysburg—was now forever lost.

X. VICKSBURG (4 JULY 1863)

While Lee was retreating on 4 July 1863, a greater disaster befell the Confederacy in the West. Following the October 1862 victory at Corinth, Grant pressed Halleck for permission to "get on with the war." When this was obtained, he attempted an overland advance from Memphis to Vicksburg, the key link between the eastern Confederate states and the trans-Mississippi West. Grant ordered Sherman downstream by boat to complement his own land march; 26 December 1862 the latter general began disembarking above Vicksburg. Grant, subjected to successful raids on his rail line by Forrest and Van Dorn, abandoned his own advance; Lincoln set in motion a new two-pronged operation by ordering forces upstream from New Orleans. General John C. Pemberton, CSA, repelled Sherman and the move from the south under Banks was blocked by Confederate defenses at Port Hudson. Grant took personal command at Vicksburg on 29 January 1863.

He could not effectively move until rains and floods subsided in the spring. Therefore, to busy the enemy, the politicians, and his men, he engaged in various experiments. The well-fortified city lay atop bluffs which made it most easily assailable over dry ground stretching eastward. Efforts at landing and attacking from the north had failed. Grant consequently resolved to get past Vicksburg, cross the river downstream, and approach indirectly—from the East. The operation was covered by Colonel Benjamin H. Grierson's raid through Mississippi; on 30 April, Grant crossed the river. Learning that Banks was unready to cooperate, Grant daringly chose to sever his communications completely and to plunge inland. Aware that Johnston was assembling forces at Jackson, he adopted a Napoleonic strategy of getting between enemy forces to defeat them in detail. The Union general applied his powerful will to achieve rapid execution of the difficult operation. This deceived Pemberton, who thought Grant had communications vulnerable to his own attack. By 14 May, Sherman had expelled Johnston from Jackson, Mississippi, and Pemberton's own advance from Vicksburg had been blocked. Although still able to fight, the latter retired into his original defenses. Grant's assault 19 May failed and the city fell under siege.

Within Vicksburg were about 37,000 troops, but Grant gradually received reinforcements until over 70,000 faced the hapless Pemberton. Johnston had ordered him to withdraw before the opportunity was lost, but Donelson was repeated when a council of war resolved that this would be impossible. Johnston then attempted to mount a relief force, but the garrison was starved out and surrendered 4 July 1863. Johnston withdrew eastward with Sherman in pursuit. To complete the campaign, Port Hudson surrendered 9 July.

The culminating point of the war had been reached. First, the South had been split along the Mississippi which was now controlled by the Union Navy. This denied her access to vital western meat and grain. Furthermore, it ended her importation through Matamoros of European arms which had been acquired in exchange for Texas cotton. Second, with the arrival of Rosecrans at Chattanooga, the strategic center of gravity of the Confederacy was at last exposed. Third, hope of foreign recognition—upon which Southern policy hinged—was hopelessly lost. Finally, the North had at last produced a general capable of winning the war by defeating the enemy.

CHAPTER XVIII

The American Civil War: Defeat of the South

I. CHICKAMAUGA (19-20 SEPTEMBER 1863) AND THE BATTLES AROUND CHATTANOOGA (24-25 NOVEMBER 1863)

AFTER WITHDRAWING SOUTHWARD from Murfreesboro early in January 1863, Bragg took up a strong position screened by cavalry. Outnumbered, and with Vicksburg having priority on troops, he had to remain on the defensive in order to cover vital Chattanooga. Rosecrans was under continuing pressure from Washington to advance, but he had lost his taste for action. Finally (26 June), he moved rapidly, outmaneuvered Bragg at Manchester, Tennessee, and pressed him so hard that he could not stabilize the situation and was driven into Chattanooga on fateful 4 July 1863. Bragg established light cavalry detachments along the Tennessee River for about seventy miles in each direction and strengthened the city's defenses. Rosecrans procrastinated until 16 August before again moving toward the river; he began crossing south of the city four days later. This he covered by deceiving Bragg with a demonstration in front of Chattanooga. Rugged terrain, however, lay between Rosecrans and the Western and Atlantic Railroad, Bragg's supply line.

As reinforcements Bragg received a division from Johnston, and Longstreet's corps belatedly moved by rail from Virginia. He withdrew to Lafayette, Georgia, and concentrated for battle. Rosecrans blundered forward, his forces widely spread, inviting defeat in detail but Bragg, although aggressive, lost his opportunity. He attacked on 19 September piecemeal, although with approximate numerical equality, in an attempt to envelop the Union left. Instead he crushed it, but the right under General George H. Thomas held firm until ordered back. Bragg had early committed his reserves and, despite forceful remonstrances from Forrest, failed to pursue and consummate his victory.

Rosecrans withdrew into Chattanooga, surrendering the initiative. Bragg foolishly contented himself with investing the southern approaches to the city and with cavalry raids against Union communications. The North sent Hooker and two corps from the Army of the Potomac by rail as reinforcements and Lincoln placed Grant in over-all command in the West. Thomas replaced Rosecrans, who had personally collapsed from his defeat. Hooker opened a rail supply route into the city below Lookout Mountain. By November, Grant was ready to take the offensive. On the twenty-fourth, Hooker took Confederate positions on Lookout Mountain and the following day Thomas stormed Missionary Ridge. Grant had planned a double envelopment, but Sherman's force was checked on the left. Bragg's men fled unpursued to near Dalton, Georgia. The gateway to Atlanta was opened, the Appalachian line was turned, and the South's strategic center of gravity was lost.

II. THE WILDERNESS-COLD HARBOR CAMPAIGN

A. *Actions of Late 1863*

By the end of July 1863, the Army of Northern Virginia once more faced the Army of the Potomac across the Rappahannock. Each rested and reorganized. Confederate morale was low, but the leaders felt that retention of the initiative was imperative. Accordingly, Longstreet was finally detached to reinforce Bragg at Chattanooga, leaving Lee with only 47,000. Meade planned an envelopment, but the necessity after Chickamauga of detaching two corps to the west turned the tables. Lee attempted a turning movement (9 October) and began following Meade northward, but the latter gave him no opportunity to attack. The armies therefore returned southward and on 7 November Meade pushed across the Rappahannock. An attempted blow at Lee failed; the armies went into winter quarters along the Rapidan.

B. Command Changes

Lincoln called Grant to Washington and made him General in Chief on 9 March 1864, reducing Halleck to the new post of Chief of Staff. As such, the commander was at last relieved of administration connected with the war effort. Grant established his headquarters with Meade's army, leaving to the latter tactical direction of the war in Virginia. At last the North had fashioned a capable command system. Grant's intention was to defeat the armies of Lee and Johnston. Excepting Sherman's march to the sea, forces rather than geography finally became the objective.

C. The Wilderness (4-7 May 1864)

Late 3 May the Army of the Potomac began crossing the Rapidan to turn Lee's right. Each side displayed indecision worsened by poor cavalry employment. In the densely undergrown

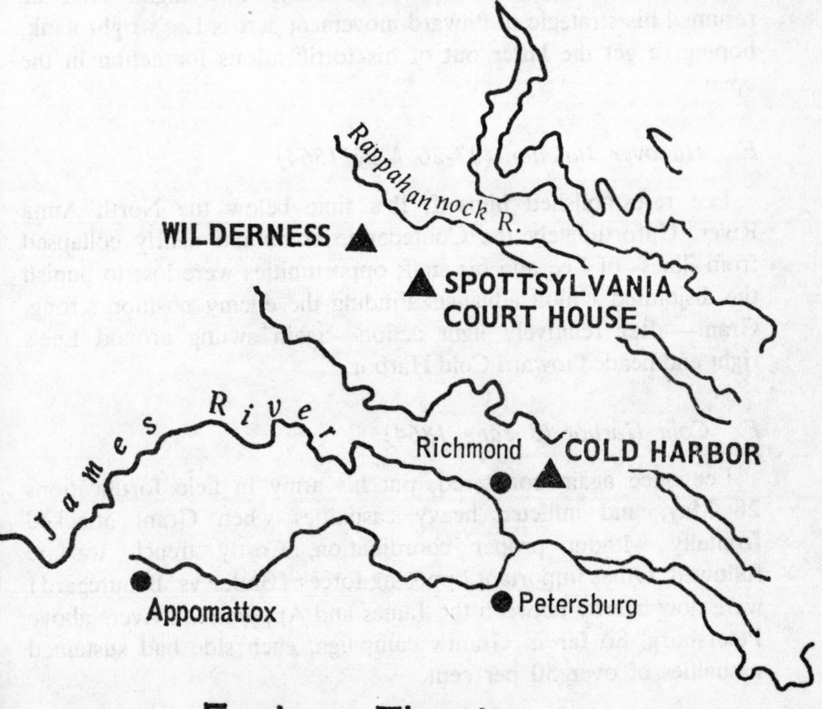

Eastern Theatre

wilderness, an indecisive battle gropingly developed without adequate control. Casualties mounted on each side. Previously, Union armies under similar circumstances had withdrawn, but Grant instead resumed his southeastward advance.

D. Spottsylvania Court House (9-19 May 1864)

Lee moved to block his tormentor near Spottsylvania. From there General Philip H. Sheridan's cavalry raided clear to Richmond and killed Stuart, but achieved little else. Lee entrenched, emplaced artillery, and established strong field fortifications. On the tenth, Grant launched a costly frontal attack and two days later took a salient in Lee's line. The Union Army attempted to shift tactically against the enemy right, but bad weather slowed the operation and saved Lee from a serious surprise. He completed a counter move. Failure, meanwhile, of diversionary Northern operations in the Valley and the Peninsula freed reinforcements for Lee. Grant's fresh attacks floundered 18 May. Two nights later he resumed his strategic southward movement across Lee's right flank, hoping to get the latter out of his fortifications for action in the open.

E. Hanover Junction (23-26 May 1864)

Lee re-established himself, this time below the North Anna River. Unfortunately the Confederate command nearly collapsed from illness of Lee and his staff; opportunities were lost to punish the disjointed Union advance. Finding the enemy position strong, Grant—after relatively light action—again swung around Lee's right and headed toward Cold Harbor.

F. Cold Harbor (3 June 1864)

Lee once again countered, put his army in field fortifications 28 May, and inflicted heavy casualties when Grant attacked frontally without proper coordination. Costly trench warfare followed. Other important opposing forces (Butler vs. Beauregard) were now nearby between the James and Appomattox rivers above Petersburg. So far in Grant's campaign, each side had sustained casualties of over 50 per cent.

G. *Crossing the James*

Recognizing the importance of the rail center of Petersburg to the defense of Richmond, Grant decided to cross the James River, take Petersburg, swing north, and sever the Danville Railroad into Richmond from the west. This strategy would have left the Confederate capital virtually surrounded along with—hopefully—the bulk of the enemy army.

The night of 12 June 1864, Grant withdrew and began crossing the James on a great pontoon bridge. Lee again shifted southward, whereupon a long Richmond-Petersburg front took shape. Union attacks (16-18 June) floundered against the Petersburg defenses. An attempt to penetrate the Confederate line by mining failed on 30 July with the loss of 4,400 men. Static trench warfare characterized the Petersburg front. With heavy losses, Grant was virtually where McClellan had been in 1862. He had failed to win the war prior to the November election.

III. THE ATLANTA CAMPAIGN

When Grant was called to Washington, his Military Division of the Mississippi was given to Sherman. It consisted of the Army of the Cumberland under Thomas, that of the Ohio under General John M. Schofield, and the Army of the Tennessee commanded by General James B. McPherson. Grant intended to fix Lee in Virginia while Sherman defeated the South from the rear. Bragg was replaced by Johnston and, despite his sorry performance, went to Richmond as military adviser to the President. Grant instructed Sherman to vanquish Johnston, get into the interior, and inflict all possible damage upon Confederate war resources. Sherman gradually became obsessed with the latter part of his mission, interpreting it very broadly indeed.

On 7 May 1864 he began driving Johnston slowly before him. The Confederate waged a model Fabian action, fighting over successive fortified positions. At Kenesaw Mountain (27 June), he was obliged to withdraw after Sherman, who at first attacked frontally, resorted to his more typical, skillful turning movement. Although Johnston was fighting perhaps his most brilliant battles,

Davis was displeased and (17 July) turned the army over to rash General John B. Hood. Three days later Hood struck at Peachtree Creek in an oblique order, but fell back on Atlanta where on the twenty-second he again attacked with great cost. Once more (28 July) he hurled six assault waves at Sherman without success. Sherman correctly assessed Atlanta's defenses and employed an indirect approach, cutting the city off from the Macon Railroad on 31 August. Hood consequently evacuated the city; Sherman moved (2 September) into the interior rail center of the South. He had fulfilled part of his mission by penetrating into the vitals of the Confederacy, but he had failed to destroy the enemy army. Sherman now grew lethargic, permitting his men to lie about in idleness, while he imposed a harsh occupation policy. But his victory strengthened Lincoln in the presidential elections, possibly enabling him to defeat McClellan and the peace-seeking Democrats.

IV. FRANKLIN AND NASHVILLE (30 NOVEMBER AND 15-16 DECEMBER 1864)

President Davis visited Hood (27 September) and agreed that the general should approach the enemy indirectly by striking at Chattanooga. Thus Sherman could be obliged by the reciprocal attraction of forces to evacuate Georgia and to follow Hood. The latter hoped eventually to lure him to battle on terms favorable to the South. Supplies for the Confederate Army would be obtained from Alabama along the Blue Mountain and Selma Railroad. On the twenty-ninth, responding to Forrest's cavalry raids in Tennessee, Sherman sent Thomas back to Nashville to prepare defenses. On the same day, Hood set his army in motion. Sherman followed with 55,000. By agile movement the Confederate evaded his pursuer.

Hood turned west to Gadsden, Alabama, having decided that the morale of his men would not permit a battle. At this point, he decided to destroy Thomas, invade Kentucky and recruit as he went. If Sherman followed, Hood would fight in Kentucky; if he did not, then Hood would turn east through Cumberland Gap to join Lee against Grant at Petersburg. Sherman reinforced

Thomas, but on 2 November he received Grant's approval for his long-desired march to Savannah. By the tenth Sherman was marching back toward Atlanta and two days later started for the sea after firing the city. To this extent, Hood had already failed.

After tarrying for supplies near Florence, Hood started northward on the nineteenth. An engagement occurred near Spring Hill (29 November) in which Hood's subordinates deprived him of the chance to destroy outnumbered General Schofield, who was retiring from Chattanooga. The next day at Franklin, Schofield fought again. Although Forrest urged an envelopment, Hood foolishly employed a frontal assault at the cost of 6,252, which he could ill afford. That night Schofield withdrew, Hood losing a chance to punish him on the march. Knowing that morale was poor, Hood feared his army would disintegrate if he now retreated. Because Thomas had a decided superiority, Hood hoped to take up a strong defensive position. Unwisely, he detached Forrest's cavalry against Union communications. On 15 December, Thomas feinted at the right and then shoved back the Confederate left. Hood retired by night and entrenched, his men getting very little sleep or rest. Late the next afternoon, his left was virtually enveloped. This time, the exhausted, once proud army of the Confederate States of America broke and ran. Hood collected the remnants and retreated in deteriorating weather. Forrest rejoined him in time to cover the withdrawal toward Tupelo, Mississippi, where Hood's army ceased to be an effective combat force.

V. GENERAL EARLY IN THE VALLEY

Lee ordered General Jubal E. Early (12 June 1864) to drive ravishing Union forces from the Shenandoah Valley and relieve pressure on Richmond by the old method of threatening Washington. This Early partially accomplished by passing up the Valley and crossing the Potomac 5 July. On the twelfth he was at the outskirts of Washington but decided he was too weak to attack. He then returned to clear the Valley again and to raid as far as Chambersburg. Grant ordered Sheridan (7 August)—with a new Army of the Shenandoah—to track Early down and devastate the Valley so that not even a crow could find sustenance there.

Meade supported the operation by blows against Lee south of Petersburg. This had the effect of stretching the Confederate lines slowly southwestward, forcing Lee with his limited manpower into a cordon defense. Troops were of necessity recalled from Early, who consequently met with defeat despite the agility and daring of his operations.

VI. PETERSBURG TO APPOMATTOX

The winter was hard for the poorly provisioned, exhausted Army of Northern Virginia. On 15 January 1865 the fall of Fort Fisher in the mouth of Wilmington harbor to an amphibious landing closed the last channel to external assistance. Excellent rail communications, natural defenses, and proximity to Bermuda for blockade runners gave Wilmington importance second only to New Orleans among Confederate ports. The defenders fought fiercely, but were overrun. The South at last was enveloped strategically. Grant, with his inexhaustible reserves of men and matériel could now grind Lee into submission.

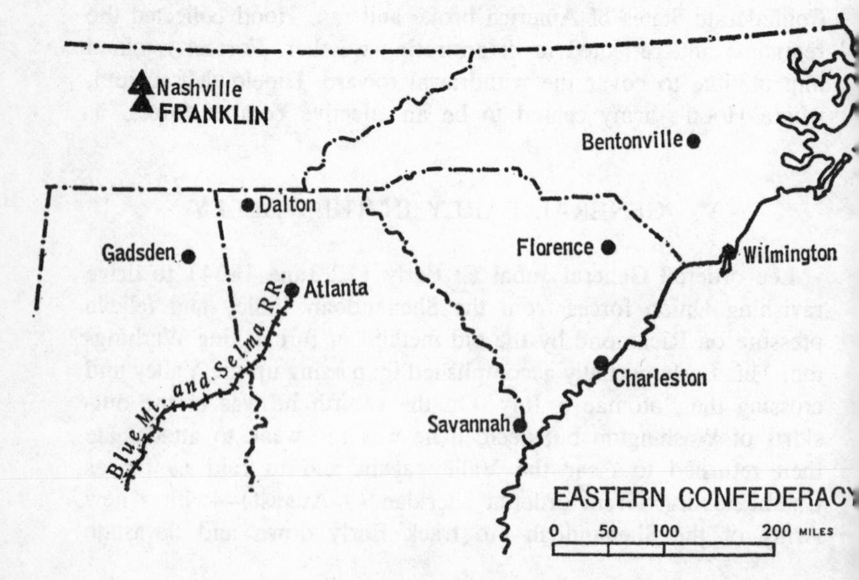

A hopeless Confederate plan called for Lee to defeat Grant, leave small forces to cover Richmond, join Johnston to defeat Sherman, and then to bring the entire Confederate States Army back against Grant. Lee's attack jumped off 25 March, but failed with heavy casualties. Sherman rejoined Meade, giving Grant better than two-to-one numerical superiority.

Grant opened a fresh attack on the twenty-ninth against the enemy right. Dismounted cavalry held off a desperate Confederate counterattack, struck again the next day, virtually wiped out Lee's flank, and closed the South Side Railroad. Realizing the hopelessness of the situation, his supply nearly halted, and his men beginning to melt away, Lee ordered withdrawal 3 April 1865. Grant directed a circling pursuit with cavalry to cut off the retreating shadow of the once mighty enemy. When his own cavalry failed to break the Union forces on 9 April, Lee had no alternative to surrender at Appomattox, Virginia.

VII. THE NAVAL-MARITIME WAR

Although the Confederacy had negligible sea power, it inflicted considerable damage upon Union forces. Apart from the development of ironclads, rams, and mines (torpedos), the Southerners grew expert at *guerre de course*. From Confederate and British ports a number of steamers preyed upon Northern commerce. The most famous of these raiders were *Florida, Shenandoah,* and *Alabama;* for the depredations of the last named, Britain eventually compensated the United States with $15,000,000. The raiders demonstrated the vulnerability of commerce to modern warships, a lesson which both the Russians and the French later took to heart.

The Union Navy had insufficient ships to maintain an effective blockade of the entire Confederate coast. Therefore it concentrated on the passages through the outer banks where major Southern shipping moved seaward, and on a campaign against the port cities themselves. Consequently, by the close of 1862 only three principal ports remained open—Wilmington, North Carolina; Charleston, South Carolina and Mobile. Farragut, after opening the Mississippi, forced his way past the forts guarding Mobile on

5 August 1864 and occupied the bay. This neutralized the harbor, but the city did not capitulate until 12 April 1865. On the Cape Fear River, Wilmington was protected by Fort Fisher which held out until 15 January 1865. The Union attempted to assault Charleston amphibiously in April 1863, settled into a long and desultory siege, and was not successful until Sherman opened the back door on 18 February 1865.

VIII. THE MARCH TO THE SEA

Sherman, meanwhile, left Atlanta in November 1864 with 62,000 men on a virtually unopposed march of devastation to Savannah. He had completely abandoned his communications and lightened his army. Fuller has compared the advance to abuses by Tilly and Wallenstein during the Thirty Years War—an exaggeration—because destruction was the policy; on 21 December "Savannah fell to Sherman's pillaging horde, now followed by thousands of plundering Negroes." Yet, the campaign was morally and economically decisive against the enemy rear. The foodstuffs of Georgia no longer flowed to the army and the state was demoralized. The road to peace was opened by destroying the will of the enemy people.

Later, Sherman started north to join Grant in a final great concentration to complete the destruction of Confederate dreams of independence. Johnston, restored to command, attempted to stop him 16 March at Averysboro, North Carolina, but Sherman's march was inexorable, in part because his objective was never apparent. Johnston failed again three days later at Bentonville; on 15 April he surrendered near Durham. But for minor actions in the west and on the sea, the War of Southern Independence had come to an end. That night, Lincoln was assassinated in Washington.

IX. GRANT AND LEE

Robert E. Lee won battles, but he fashioned no strategy which could win a war; Grant did both. Lee's vision was limited by order and desire to Virginia; Grant's encompassed the entire country. Lee attempted to command Napoleonically; Grant efficiently employed a modern staff system. Grant accurately judged his opponents; Lee understood only some of them. Yet, Lee served a losing cause, fought at times brilliantly with few resources beyond human courage, and did so with a dedication and heroism which will never lose their appeal. He resembled Washington and as such he was a man of the eighteenth century, fighting for an agrarian society against the modern Northern generals of industrialism, who were in method precursors of the twentieth century. Grant had unlimited resources of every kind—human, material, economic, and political, which he directed vigorously against a clear objective: destruction of the South's armies. He was successful because he understood the new warfare.

The American Civil War was new in many ways which have already been summarized. Dominated by the rifle bullet and the trench, it was a clear prognostication of the character of World War I, but this was largely unappreciated by the next generation of soldiers of America and Europe.

CHAPTER XIX

Small Wars and Growing Tensions

I. INTRODUCTION

DESPITE the prognostications of Clausewitz, the century following the final defeat of Bonaparte was remarkably free of generalized armed strife. This was partially a reaction, politically manifest by the Concert of Europe, to the Napoleonic Wars. It also reflected the anti-military spirit of liberalism, as well as the attention of some of the powers to internal development in the age of industrialization and of others to the preservation of the social order. The British Navy—superior to all others combined until the 1880's—imposed a kind of global *pax britannica.* Although tensions existed, especially in connection with the unification of Italy and Germany, the powers basically were satisfied to maintain the status quo. Hope was widespread that the impact of war upon society could be limited.

II. DEVELOPMENTS IN MEANS

The nineteenth century witnessed tremendous improvements in firepower. The Industrial Revolution enabled man to progress rapidly in perfecting means of destruction. Breech-loading, rifling, smokeless powder, brass cartridges, and automatic firing revolutionized weaponry. The Minié ball, or expanding bullet, eliminated the smooth bore by making rifling easier. In 1841 appeared the Prussian Dreyse needle gun, the first practical European bolt-action, breech-loading rifle, and it was followed by the improved French *chassepot* which doubled effective range. By 1884 smokeless powder facilitated concealing the firer and left the field smoke-free. Artillery was improved by rifling, breech-loading, advanced ballistics, and better recoil mechanisms. Repeating rifles were used in the Civil War and the Gatling gun—the first true machine gun—also saw action; the *mitrailleuse* failed to live up to expectations in 1870 because it was used as artillery; the more effective Maxim was produced by 1885.

The railroad, steamship and later, the motor vehicle, revolutionized transportation and, coupled with greater productive capacity, radically altered strategy and logistics. Means of violence could be applied over greater space in less time than ever before. More resources could be brought to bear in support of larger armies. The beginnings of the population explosion occasioned by medical science furnished vast available supplies of manpower. To control these increasingly complex forces, the staff system perfected by Prussia gained rapid acceptance after 1871. The wars of the late nineteenth century provided the field test of new weapons and methods. Fruits of science, they were mass-produced by the factory which gave industry a vital role in modern war.

These factors of means brought forward a new type of general—one who emerged from the poorly tracked Mississippi Valley. General U. S. Grant may have understood little else, but he knew how to apply with brutal thoroughness the resources of the modern state toward the attainment of a politico-military objective.

III. EUROPEAN ARMED FORCES

Following the Napoleonic Wars, European armies generally settled into lethargy. Austria neglected staff work and technological advances. Russia did likewise, because Nicholas I was not interested in reforms although he supported a huge military establishment. France reinstated conscription but only to fill the ranks of an army made up primarily of long-term professionals. Britain, which grew from nineteen million to twenty-eight million people in the quarter century after Waterloo, was concerned with her industry and trade. Her army, still viewed by Parliament as a necessary evil, resisted change and innovation. Among all the powers, service fell heaviest upon the rural classes at the very time when they were losing their economic and social dominance. With the exception of Prussia, which will be considered separately, and possibly of England, no country encouraged the study of military theory, but where it existed, Jomini was the standard fare.

IV. THE CRIMEAN WAR, 1854-1855

Fundamentally, this struggle stemmed from Russian ambition against the Ottoman Empire and British and French desires to protect their Near Eastern interests. As Clausewitz had predicted, popular opinion limited the action of the political leadership and demanded extreme solutions. Following an indecisive campaign in what was to become Rumania (April-July 1854), the Allies determined to seize the Russian naval base of Sebastopol in the Crimea. For this adventure they lacked maps, intelligence, adequate staff work, or even a reasoned appreciation of the situation. The entire British command and logistic systems were deficient. After an amphibious landing north of the city on 14 September, the Allies gradually advanced against preliminary resistance. The defenders blocked the harbor with sunken ships and constructed strong fortifications. Before the latter lay entrenched riflemen. Yet, while the French and British utilized muzzle-loading rifles, most of the Russians still had muskets. The defense proved highly effective; a tremendous naval and siege gun barrage failed to damage the fortifications seriously.

As the Allies settled for an investment, sickness and disease swept their camps. Thousands died of illness, but the advent of the telegraph and war correspondents brought war for the first time close to the home front. One result was greater concern for suffering soldiers, which led to better field medicine and Florence Nightingale's nursing system. By the time Sebastopol was carried by storm (8 September 1855), casualties had risen very high indeed.

The conflict preserved the Turk, but it struck a blow against the Concert of Europe and evoked a major reaction in Britain and France to the cost of warfare. The Geneva Convention of

1864 was a humanitarian outgrowth of the Crimea, as was the International Red Cross. The Convention sought to limit the violence of war by international agreement.

V. THE ITALIAN WAR, 1859

Due to the requirements of an ambitious foreign policy, Napoleon III led France into brief hostilities on behalf of the Piedmontese program for Italian unification. Piedmont had participated in the Crimean War to curry the Emperor's favor. In the first war in which both sides carried rifles, the French and Piedmontese defeated the Austrians at Magenta (4 June) and in the accidental Battle of Solferino twenty days later. Due to greater firepower, losses were high on both sides; the French medical service broke down and the Emperor was so appalled by the bloodshed that he entered into an armistice. The French erroneously attributed their success to the bayonet, whereas in reality their rifled guns—with double the range of the enemy's—were primarily responsible. The Austrians withdrew to a strong defensive position in Venetia and Napoleon III compromised the Allied war aims. Nevertheless, the fighting paved the way for the unification of Italy and her emergence as the sixth major European power.

VI. THE WAR OF THE TRIPLE ALLIANCE, 1864-1870

Although obscured from Europe in the interior of South America, the epic struggle of Paraguay against Brazil, Argentina, and Uruguay was not devoid of tactical lessons. Provoked by Brazilian threats to the Río de la Plata balance of power, the war at first revolved about Allied efforts to pass Humaitá, a powerful riverside fortification on the Río Paraguay. There, in positions built by British engineers, the Paraguayans employed artillery and well-acclimated troops to hold off superior enemy land and naval forces. The growing strength of the defense was confirmed. When finally the Paraguayan armed forces were ground down in a war of attrition, a people's war broke out which necessitated virtual destruction of the nation. Clausewitz appeared confirmed as violence approached its utmost bounds.

VII. THE RUSSO-TURKISH WAR, 1877-1878

Greatly enhanced firepower had already invigorated the tactical defense and served to drive men into the ground to escape the bullet. Against field fortifications, the Napoleonic mass frontal attack failed. While this had been demonstrated in both North and South America, Europeans did not comprehend the trend, for it was unclear at the time. At Plevna in 1877, outnumbered Turks—firing U.S.-made rifles from improvised positions—thrice stood off Russian attacks. While a few began to appreciate reality, nineteenth-century European soldiers were conservative in political beliefs, social outlook, training, experience, and tactical approach. They resisted adjusting tactics to keep abreast of technology.

VIII. COLONIAL CONFLICT, AND THE BOER WAR, 1899-1902

The final wave of European expansion was due to economic, strategic, and religious causes. In the ensuing small colonial struggles such objectives as the enemy's army or his capital were of limited value. Regulars found it difficult to bring mobile guerrilla fighters to battle. War took on a brutality perhaps beyond Clausewitz' expectations when, for example, the Ethiopians castrated their Italian prisoners after Adowa (1 March 1896). Economic warfare against the natives' source of livelihood gained importance. Although acquisition of the rifle gave him new strength, razing his home and property could still destroy his will.

In the hearty, Dutch-descended Boers of South Africa, the British faced an unusual colonial foe. Primarily mounted riflemen, the Boers with their Mausers were superb shots. They were highly mobile, albeit poorly disciplined. In the early campaigns of 1899-1900, they enjoyed a numerical advantage, but a concerted British offensive under Lord Roberts in the southern winter of 1900 ended organized resistance by August.

The Boers then launched a people's war against British lines of communications and small units. They were finally crushed by Kitchener, who compartmentalized the country with barbed wire and blockhouses, placed Boer civilians in concentration camps, and then used superior mobile forces (250,000 to 45,000) to clean out each enclosure.

Like the Crimean War, the conflict had important repercussions in British military policy. After experiences in Russia, a series of army reforms had been introduced which included the 1871 end to the sale and purchase of officers' commissions. After the struggle against the Boers, the Esher Committee examined the conduct of the war and made recommendations which culminated in the Committee of Imperial Defense; the establishment of the Imperial General Staff; and the Haldane Reforms which included a territorial army in place of the militia which was traceable to the fyrd.

By the time the last Boer capitulated, a new age of irregular operations had been ushered in to parallel the nascent totality of conventional conflict. The world was at the threshold of what Ropp has called "the Age of Violence."

EUROPEAN WARS, 19TH CENTURY

CHAPTER XX

The Wars of German Unification

I. INTRODUCTION

THE NAPOLEONIC DESTRUCTION of the Holy Roman Empire created in central Europe a power void which the German Confederation did not adequately fill. The two German Great Powers, Prussia and Austria, were rivals for leadership in the restoration of German unity. The latter Empire, a polyglot state containing important non-German nationalities, was ill equipped for the task. Equally so were the well-meaning, but impotent liberals who endeavored to achieve unification by constitutional means. The solution of the problem lay in the military instrument of Prussia, in the "blood and iron" panacea advanced by Prussian Minister-President Otto von Bismarck.

II. THE PRUSSIAN GENERAL STAFF

When William I became King in 1861, he set about reorganizing his army for its political task. Plans for updating it in line with modern technology required military reforms. He wished to make Prussia into a nation in arms by pouring money into large-scale training of conscripts. Military thought in Prussia had been largely cast in the Clausewitzian mold; its dissemination was by way of the small but professionally adept General Staff.

Created in 1812, the Prussian General Staff had largely been shaped by Gneisenau, its second chief, who encouraged flexibility of thought; established continuing peacetime planning, study, and doctrine-shaping; developed the system of general directives, which left subordinates considerable freedom of action; and influenced thinking toward the great enveloping battle of annihilation. In 1857, widely read, well-rounded Helmuth von Moltke was named Chief of the General Staff. Moltke gradually achieved the transformation of the body into an agency furnishing cohesion through jurisdiction over all matters of command and secured recognition of its chief as the highest military adviser to the monarch.

III. THE IMPACT OF THE RAILROAD

The railroad changed the nature of war by revolutionizing mobility. It speeded mobilization and reduced concentration time, thus allowing urban reservists to take part in opening actions. Rapid employment of vastly greater forces necessitated more efficient transportation planning down to the precise capacity of forward rail sidings and exact timetables. The French failure to understand this would contribute to their collapse in 1870, although German planning was hardly perfect. Rail resupply permitted troops to be committed with light equipment. Wounded could be evacuated swiftly to home hospitals, thus increasing civilian awareness of war. The railroad became in another sense a conveyor belt between the new mass production factories and the front lines, just when breech-loading, longer range guns and rifles in the hands of plentiful conscripts demanded a mammoth, efficient supply service controlling everything from raw materials to factories. Von Moltke pioneered sound military strategy based upon these developments.

IV. MOLTKE'S WARS

A. The Danish War, 1864

Denmark's incorporation of the ancient Germanic duchy of Schleswig, which had been ruled autonomously by her king, aroused opinion throughout Germany. Bismarck secured Austrian agreement for joint military action, but he was looking beyond toward the unification of Germany under Prussian hegemony. Despite heroic Danish resistance, the outcome of the war was never in doubt. The General Staff had negligible influence on operations until Moltke was appointed Chief of Staff of the Field Army. Bismarck parlayed the disposition of Schleswig and neighboring Holstein into a war to expel Austria from Germany.

B. The Austro-Prussian, or Seven Weeks' War, 1866

1. PLANS

Moltke, who as Chief of the General Staff had won the right to issue orders on his own authority, planned to concentrate four armies against Bohemia to forestall an Austrian advance through Saxony. Long concerned with Prussia's lack of natural defenses, he had quickly grasped the strategic possibilities of the railroad. He believed that rapid troop movement by rail made possible conquering space with time in order to improve the Prussian strategic position. Her rail net admirably suited this purpose; five lines were available for the war on Austria, while the enemy depended upon a single railroad. Moltke's dispositions covered 260 miles, for he planned to operate on exterior lines and concentrate on the field.

The Austrians mobilized first and assembled in Moravia with the vaunted advantage of an interior position, intending to await attack. They had superior cavalry and artillery, but were inadequately trained. To prevent a possible invasion of Silesia, one Prussian army was shifted from the main plan, albeit against the wishes of Moltke. When his forces entered Austria's ally, Saxony, the Saxon Army also withdrew into Moravia.

2. SADOWA (3 JULY 1866)

Utilizing railroads, Moltke concentrated near Sadowa. The enemy, still armed with muzzle-loaders, held a compact position in front of the fortress of Königgratz. Although Moltke envisioned a massive double envelopment, his army commanders advanced shoulder to shoulder in what amounted to a frontal attack. Yet, he was fully confident in his plan and refused all requests for its modification during the battle. The action went strongly in favor of the Prussians, whose breech-loading rifles enabled them to fire prone. Morally, the Austrians had lost before the fighting began because their commander had succumbed to defeatism. Only the brilliance of their cavalry averted a rout. There was no pursuit because Prussian objectives were limited.

3. RESULTS

The war was decided by a single battle, although Prussia's Italian allies had been beaten both in Venetia and in the naval battle of Lissa. The peace nevertheless gave them Venetia. Prussia emerged the leader of a new North German Confederation. Austria's lesser German allies were brought under the denomination of Berlin and she herself was eliminated from Germany. Prussian superiority in leadership, organization, weaponry, training, and railroads had actually resolved the issue prior to Sadowa. Moltke's belief was confirmed that the breechloader made the defensive the stronger form of war and that henceforth little could be expected from frontal attacks; turning flanks would be preferable.

C. *The Franco-Prussian War, 1870-1871*

Because France was determined to prevent disruption of the balance of power through the appearance of a strong, unified Germany, still another struggle faced the politico-military duo of Bismarck and Moltke. A common war of all the German states against their traditional enemy offered an opportunity to consummate unification. When Moltke assured him that the military was capable of defeating Napoleon III's Empire, Bismarck's diplomacy brought the French to declare war 19 July 1870.

1. FORCES AND PLANS

The French had returned to the professional principle in raising their armed forces. As in the eighteenth century, their peacetime organization was regimental with great units formed only for war. Training was inferior and the staff system was quite inefficient. Although his initial plan was defensive, Napoleon—under the pressure of popular demands—decided to invade south

Germany. For success this project required a rapidity which French logistics, plans, organization, and railroads could not provide.

Moltke's General Staff plans were predicated upon French inertia and the usual Prussian speed. His basic intention was to launch an offensive as soon as possible. Mobilization time had been reduced to eighteen days. Moltke believed that the initial concentration was the most important portion of a campaign. Operations themselves could be planned only one engagement at a time because each battle created the conditions for the next. Therefore, his 1870 battle plan was flexible. Moltke's command system relied upon the general directive, which established a task but left the details of its accomplishment to the initiative of subordinates. This required daring, calculation, perception—high intellectual qualities—in Moltke's generals.

2. THE FRONTIER BATTLES AND METZ

The French decided upon a reconnaissance in force by three corps near Saarbrücken (2 August). Moltke's Third Army pursued the enemy across the frontier, inflicting two separate defeats during 6 August despite the superior fire of the French chassepot rifle; this weapon inflicted heavier casualties than Napoleon's men suffered. A major factor in these German victories was superior massed artillery. The French lost the initiative to the allied German states and their two armies—under Marshals MacMahon and Bazaine—withdrew northwestward amidst various combats.

The Prussians swept around Metz from the south and on 18 August, west of the fortress near Gravelotte, the contending armies clashed in the unique position of facing their respective bases. This amounted to disaster for the loser since his line of retreat was already closed. French fire halted the Germans and even brought them to panic in some sectors. They managed, however, toward nightfall to turn the enemy right, whereupon Bazaine ordered retreat into Metz. Exhaustion prevented immediate pursuit. Further, the Germans considered the fortress unassailable. A general more daring and resolute might have saved his army, but once besieged Bazaine's force was effectively out of the war. The surrender of his 173,000 French troops occurred 27 October.

3. SEDAN (1 SEPTEMBER 1870)

Moltke lost little time after Gravelotte. He ordered an army toward Paris while another moved toward MacMahon (who was marching to rescue Bazaine), cut him off from the capital, and caused him to concentrate around the small fortress of Sedan near the Belgian border. The position was so unfavorable that Moltke could not believe the French would remain there. The Germans closed in, crushed them, and secured the capitulation of both the army and Napoleon III himself. The second French Empire fell in one of the great disasters of military history, its army destroyed as a fighting force.

4. PEOPLE'S WAR

Prussia and her lesser German allies had won the war in six weeks—a tribute to combat capacity and to the skill of the General Staff. French field forces were eliminated, but popular will was not subdued. Leon Gambetta, the Interior Minister, organized a new resistance. Only part of the country's resources had been mobilized and the capital was well fortified. Paris was invested 19 September, but it fought on. Moltke felt that the popular struggle gave war a hate-inspired character that amounted to a return to barbarism. In January 1871 a methodical bombardment tore the city, bringing it to its knees.

Meanwhile, 80,000 remaining French forces in the southwest entered Switzerland and were interned. France was left prostrate.

5. RESULTS

The Prussian Army gained global renown and the General Staff became a model for emulation. Germany, whose unification as an empire under the King of Prussia was the major result of the war, replaced France as the foremost military power. Her triumph was a victory for the nation in arms, which she had reinstituted, over the professional army, to which France had reverted. Leadership in military science passed from France to Germany. So did the rich, industrial frontier provinces of Alsace and Lorraine. Yet, the war aims had been limited and, once attained, a moderate peace ensued. France, however, was left embittered and vindictive.

V. THE DEVELOPMENT OF GERMAN MILITARY THOUGHT

Moltke had taken astonishing risks against France, but he had succeeded because of the brilliance of his subordinates and the incompetence of the French High Command. He was not satisfied with the peace, believing that France should be completely crushed. Nevertheless, he recognized civilian supremacy and the subordination of the military to the political. Moltke was a good student of Clausewitz and accepted war as a political instrument, but he believed that political considerations should prevail before hostilities to determine war aims, after a war to negotiate peace, and not at all during a war itself. In wartime, strategy should be independent of politics.

A. The Influence of Moltke

Moltke's views came to be accepted by generations of German military men. He fashioned a distinguished group of General Staff officers—dedicated, highly responsible, holding to a common body of doctrine, and exercising decisive influence in the army. Unfortunately, though they were militarily outstanding, they tended to isolate themselves from society. Moltke himself was in that respect the last true Clausewitzian—well-read, balanced, and educated. While he had established the area of competence of the General Staff and gave it a pattern of thought, he did not succeed in preventing it from becoming in many respects inflexible.

Moltke grew certain that another great war was inevitable and he foresaw that it would be a long one. By 1879 he thought that any war, even for the victor, was a misfortune. He planned for future hostilities against a Franco-Russian alliance which would force Germany to fight on two fronts from a central position. He envisioned an offensive first against France but, after she had fortified her frontier in the 1880's, he changed in 1887 to a defense in the West and an offense in the East.

B. Schlieffen

Count Alfred von Schlieffen, Chief of the General Staff (1891-1906), brought to the position a singleness of purpose which made him insensitive to human relations. He was a narrow professional who prided himself on being "unpolitical" and who served his Emperor blindly and uncritically. Obsessed with the problem of two-front war, he became convinced that the only way for a weaker army to win was by a large-scale enveloping attack to bring on a great battle of annihilation. Only thus, he believed, could swift, decisive results be obtained. Schlieffen did not believe nations could fiscally support wars of attrition, owing to the enormous cost of huge modern forces. Swift decision was the key to his strategy; otherwise, he rightly feared for the social order.

Schlieffen returned to a rapid offensive in the West as the best means to prevent a protracted war. The Russians had improved themselves with fortifications and railroads, which made them less attractive for the initial blow than they had seemed to Moltke. On the other hand, France's concentrated strength invited a strategy of annihilation. Therefore, Schlieffen gradually evolved a plan by 1905 which, utilizing Germany's central position, aimed at concentrating maximum strength against one enemy. Holding the other with few troops was made feasible by defensive firepower and the probable slowness of Russian mobilization. To turn the French fortifications running from Switzerland to Belgium, Schlieffen planned to violate the latter, sweep through the Seine Basin with his right, and pin the entire French Army against his left along the frontier. The ratio of strength between right and left he placed at 7:1. Whereas Moltke used strategy as a guide and allowed subordinates initiative, Schlieffen turned to a rigid master plan, but his major error was that he failed to realize—despite his study of history—that the great Cannae-like battle of annihilation had rarely been politically decisive.

VI. FRENCH MILITARY THOUGHT

The defeat at the hands of the Germans pointed up for France the need for military reforms starting at the top. A common view was that the war had been lost because of the inability of the High Command to exploit enemy mistakes. The study of theory was limited, mainly to Jomini, until the 1880's.

A. DuPicq

Posthumously there appeared a small book, *Etudes sur le combat,* authored by Colonel Ardant DuPicq, an obscure professional killed during the frontier battles. In reaction to industrialization and modern firepower, DuPicq asserted that man remains the decisive instrument in battle. He examined what makes men fight and produced a respectable treatise on combat psychology. Unfortunately, he decided that the moral element in war is superior to the physical, that is, that mind can overcome matter. Victory or defeat therefore results entirely from a state of mind, not from material strength. It is the valor of the individual fighting man that wins battles.

B. Foch

These ideas were built upon by Lieutenant Colonel (later, General) Ferdinand Foch in a series of lectures delivered at the new *Ecole de guerre*. Foch borrowed his conception of the importance of battle from Clausewitz, who had previously been little known in France. He asserted, however, that the offensive alone can gain results in war, because the attacker enjoys moral superiority. War is the domain of moral force; consequently, his famous dictum (really lifted from Joseph de Maistre) held that "a battle won is a battle in which one refuses to acknowledge defeat." Defeat, to Foch, was a mental condition induced by the pressure of moral and material elements simultaneously employed. Mass times velocity was the primary route to success. The best strategy for undermining enemy will, Foch asserted, is the battle of maneuver which gains surprise and thereby destroys morale. Foch also distinguished the parallel battle, or general engagement, but he considered it an inferior type.

C. The Planners

Foch misunderstood the effect of automatic weapons and even argued that increases in firepower favored the offense. Coupling this with the notion of moral force, or DuPicq's "spiritualization of war," led Foch's disciples in the French General Staff to conclude that French infantry was irresistible in the attack. The planners built a strategic conception atop this shaky foundation. They believed that, following a heavy artillery barrage, infantry should be advanced to within 400 yards of the enemy, whereupon it would attack with fixed bayonet. Bayonet and will would be decisive, because the courage of French soldiers made them unbeatable in a charge. This was the "mystique" of the offense at all costs. To win a war against Germany, therefore, French Plan XVII envisioned concentrating 800,000 men in five armies along the frontier for an all-out, uncontainable offensive. It assumed that Germany could not mobilize and commit reserve corps in the initial actions and that she would, consequently, be too weak simultaneously to fight in Lorraine and Belgium. This was an error, but the greatest French fallacy was deeming mind superior to bullet.

VII. BLOCH

Ivan S. Bloch, an amateur civilian societal military thinker, perceived with far greater clarity the portension of the new means and methods of war. Unlike Clausewitz, Bloch understood the role of economics in the spectrum of conflict and unlike the French theorists, he had a healthy respect for bullet power. Interrelating modern communications, the growing role of industry, and the tremendous progression in firepower, Bloch foresaw wars of horrible slaughter. Because generalship lagged behind social developments, directing war by old methods would fail to attain decision in the great battle. Thereupon, the issue would pass to the economic sphere. The destruction of resources would disrupt the social order. War, Bloch concluded at the turn of the century, was henceforth possible only at the price of national suicide. Peaceful means of settling international disputes were imperative.

CHAPTER XXI

The Coming of Twentieth-Century Seapower

I. INTRODUCTION

ON THE SEA, as well as on land, tremendous technological changes occurred during the nineteenth century. Steampower, applied through the screw propeller, drastically changed naval strategy. Wind lost its control of sea war, reducing the element of chance. Iron ships permitted greater size, cellular construction, longer range, and more stable gun platforms. The Crimean War proved the operational superiority of such ships. A race developed between naval gunnery and armor, with first one and then the other dominant. The torpedo was a partial tactical answer to better ships and the submarine, as an offensive-defensive weapon, added a new dimension to maritime conflict by the end of the century.

The effectiveness of the Paixhan shell gun was demonstrated by the Russians against a Turkish squadron at Sinope in 1854. The French in 1859 produced the first ironclad, *LaGloire,* and the British followed with HMS *Warrior*. The U.S. Navy under Admiral David Porter reverted after the War Between the States to full-rigged sailing ships. Yet, not only did the clashes between ironclads in that war herald a new era, but at the battle of Lissa in 1866 the Austrians set a precedent by ramming and sinking the American-built Italian flagship. Thereafter, most warships were fitted with ram bows which, though rarely used in battle, provided buoyancy needed forward in the new slim, heavy, metal hulls.

In general, throughout the nineteenth century most navies

devoted their time to showing flag and force against recalcitrant native princes. Generations of officers attained flag rank without ever having seen action against an enemy fleet. Ossified in their ways and incapable of tackling new inventions, they generally left the products of modern technology to very junior officers. Certain new navies such as the Japanese, and the German under Tirpitz, as well as eventually the Royal Navy under Sir John Fisher and the U.S. Navy under Sims, took some heed of these developments.

II. WAR OF THE PACIFIC, 1879-1883

Modern naval forces received an important test in the struggle of Chile against Peru and Bolivia. Basically, war stemmed from boundary contention affecting ownership of nitrate wealth in the bleak Atacama Desert. The Peruvian navy included two English-built ironclad frigates and two U.S.-made monitors. Chile had two vessels which were superior both in armor and firepower. Her seamen also were better. In the first action, they took one of the Peruvian frigates, but the other subsequently raided their coast until 8 October 1879. Then, in the first major high seas action between modern ships, Chilean firepower crippled the vessel and she was captured. This gave Chile a naval advantage which ultimately enabled her to impose a peace that deprived Bolivia of her seacoast and Chile's two enemies of their nitrates. These minerals invigorated her economy for several decades. The naval war aggravated the armor-firepower race and stimulated the United States in its transition to iron ships.

III. MAHAN

In the mid-1880's battleship construction almost halted world-wide on the assumption that the power of such vessels was neutralized by torpedo boats and cruisers. A great nation, however, needed a powerful fleet to protect her trade and colonies and she needed colonies as coaling stations for the navy. The new surface ships had greater speed, but coaling limited their range. This placed emphasis upon the base and stimulated colonial expansion. Of all the naval powers, Britain was vastly the strongest because her bases straddled all the major sea lanes except the Dardanelles.

Alfred Thayer Mahan, the only first-rate military thinker the United States produced, was concerned with the supreme importance of seapower in the development of nations to such greatness. Especially interested in cause and effect relationships in war, he decided that historically control of the sea was a vital, although unrecognized, strategic factor. It stemmed from a number of elements which determined whether people seriously took to the sea. These included a country's geographical position, terrain, territorial extent, population, national character, and political institutions. A small maritime country with rugged coasts, a growing energetic population, a perceptive and ambitious government, and a position on important waterways was best equipped to become a naval power. Mahan stressed the interrelationships of internal development and production with peaceful shipping and colonies. He emphasized strategically located naval bases on the world's major waterways in order to control the medium (sea).

Mahan clearly demonstrated the role of seapower relative to national policy and power. Influenced by Jomini, he advocated a central position, the concentration of force against the enemy's fleet (his decisive point) and offensive operations. Mahan's theory of seapower gave imperialism a final impetus, as nations sought overseas possessions to enhance power and it accelerated large-scale naval construction.

United States naval thought before Mahan had hardly progressed beyond coastal defense and commerce raiding. By 1890, building of a capital ship fleet had begun. Mahan stressed the importance of the Caribbean. He saw the isthmian canal as the decisive point for U. S. seapower and he pointed out the necessity of dominating its approaches. Cuba, he wrote in 1897, is the key to the Caribbean and therefore on that island is found the paramount single strategic position, Guantanamo Bay. Although at home these ideas had impact upon only a small group of alert, able men, Mahan was lionized in England and Germany.

IV. THE RUSSO-JAPANESE WAR, 1904-1905

In the latter nineteenth century, insular Japan relinquished her traditional isolation and embarked upon a stunning modernization and industrialization which included a national standing army and naval purchases. To gain strategic security relative to China and Russia, she undertook an imperialist program to gain domination of adjacent waters and to project her power to the mainland. In 1894 she attacked China on the sea and in Korea and Manchuria. The fruits of the Sino-Japanese War were Formosa, the Pescadores, and Port Arthur. The first two cleared the southern approaches to Japan; Port Arthur dominated the western approach. The acquisition of Port Arthur brought on direct rivalry with Russia who, by diplomatic pressure, secured the return of the port to China and then took it herself in 1897. Thereupon, Japan began preparing for another war.

A. Port Arthur and Mukden

After Russia refused her demands, Japan initiated hostilities in February 1904 both on land and sea, despite numerical inferiority. She received a logistic assist from a gap in Russia's Trans-Siberian Railroad at Lake Baikal. Bottling up the enemy fleet in Port Arthur, the Japanese invaded Manchuria to isolate the naval base. The Russian ships finally emerged 10 August, but were driven back into port by superior gunnery. The Japanese then accepted enormous casualties and gradually overran the Port Arthur trenches and redoubts.

The Japanese soldier was well disciplined, dutiful, and morally superior to the reluctant Russian troops, who stressed the bayonet. The Japanese also were up to date in their German-style staff system and their regulations which were modeled after those of Western Europe. They employed machine guns, modern artillery, the field telephone, and even observation balloons. Yet, when they attempted to bring on a great conclusive battle in February 1905, the struggle settled into a trench war of attrition near Mukden. More than 300,000 were employed on each side, but earthworks

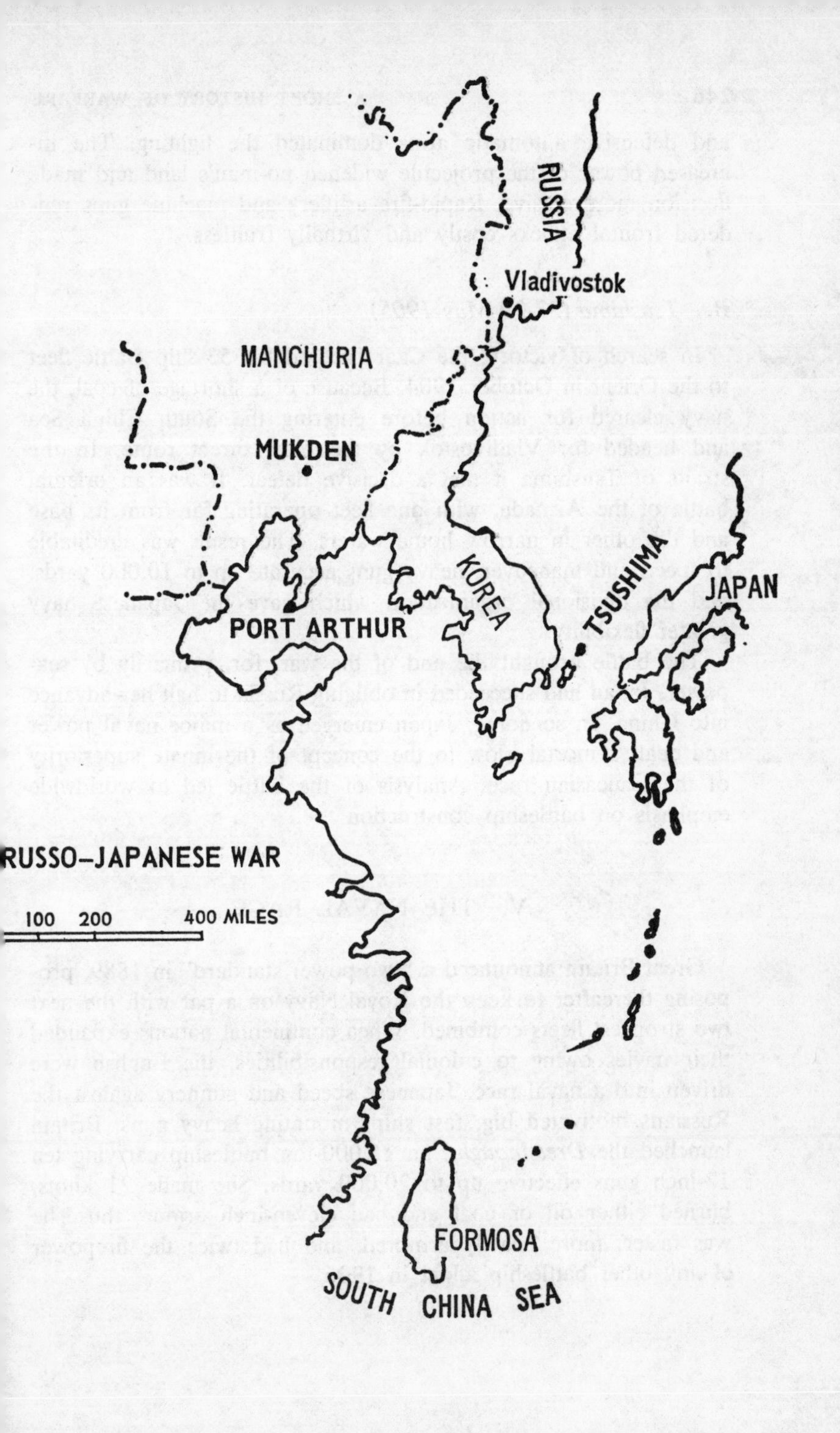
RUSSIA
Vladivostok
MANCHURIA
MUKDEN
KOREA
TSUSHIMA
JAPAN
PORT ARTHUR
RUSSO–JAPANESE WAR
100 200 400 MILES
FORMOSA
SOUTH CHINA SEA

and defensive automatic arms dominated the fighting. The increased power of the projectile widened no-man's land and made decision more elusive. Rapid-fire artillery and machine guns rendered frontal attacks costly and virtually fruitless.

B. *Tsushima (27-29 May 1905)*

In search of victory, the Czar ordered his 53-ship Baltic fleet to the Orient in October 1904. Because of a shortage of coal, the navy cleared for action before entering the South China Sea and headed for Vladivostok by the most direct route. In the straits of Tsushima it met a decisive defeat. It was an oriental battle of the Armada, with one fleet operating far from its base and the other in narrow home waters. The result was creditable to speed and maneuver, heavy guns accurate up to 10,000 yards, and the divisional organization which gave the Japanese navy greater flexibility.

The battle brought the end of the war, for, primarily by seapower, Japan had succeeded in obliging Russia to halt her advance into China. In so doing, Japan emerged as a major naval power and dealt a mortal blow to the concept of the innate superiority of the Caucasian race. Analysis of the battle led to worldwide emphasis on battleship construction.

V. THE NAVAL RACE

Great Britain announced a "two power standard" in 1889, proposing thereafter to keep the Royal Navy on a par with the next two strongest fleets combined. When continental nations expanded their navies owing to colonial responsibilities, the English were driven into a naval race. Japanese speed and gunnery against the Russians motivated big, fast ships mounting heavy guns. Britain launched the *Dreadnought,* an 18,000-ton battleship carrying ten 12-inch guns effective up to 20,000 yards. She made 21 knots, burned either oil or coal and had eleven-inch armor; thus she was faster, more heavily armored, and had twice the firepower of any other battleship afloat in 1906.

Germany responded by laying several comparable vessels and other powers hastily followed suit. "A big battleship navy had become a visible evidence of national virility," Ropp suggests. Under the influence of Admiral Tirpitz, Germany endeavored rapidly to construct the world's second best navy. She needed such a force in the event of war with France and in the Baltic against Russia. Her program also was based upon the "risk theory" relative to Britain, that is, that destroying the German fleet should be made too costly to be a rational undertaking for Britain in the event of war. Unfortunately, the naval race and British popular fears of the German Navy did much to strain relations and bring on World War I.

VI. THE ITALO-TURKISH AND BALKAN WARS, 1911-1913

With a view to the division of Africa among the powers, and her own strategic needs, Italy on 29 September 1911 declared war on Turkey in order to seize the latter's North African provinces. Although they performed poorly on land, the Italians employed superior seapower to isolate the defenders strategically and to occupy the Dodecanese Islands.

Meanwhile, after Tsushima, Russia returned to adventures shelved since Plevna and encouraged the nationalism of the Balkan peoples. Bulgaria proclaimed independence from the Ottoman Empire in 1908, whereupon Austria, not to lose out, annexed Bosnia and Herzegovina. The Balkans then formed a league against both Austria and Turkey and went to war with the latter 18 October 1912, only five days after Constantinople had accepted its losses to Rome. Serb and Greek offensives—enjoying numerical superiority—attained success, but the Bulgarians were contained and received an unsatisfactory share of the territorial spoils. They consequently provoked a new conflict in which Serbia, Greece, Rumania, and Turkey defeated them badly.

From these minor wars—the one decided by naval power and the other by massed infantry—the Bulgarians emerged bitter and eager to disrupt the new status quo; the Serbs looked to Moscow for protection; while the Ottoman Empire lost its Mediterranean and African dependencies and retained only a small corner of Europe. Realizing that changes were imperative in their military establishment, the Turks engaged the services of the German General Liman von Sanders. All of these developments would soon affect World War I.

CHAPTER XXII

The Spanish-American War

I. INTRODUCTION

FOLLOWING THE DEFEAT of the Confederate States of America, the restored United States gradually reduced their army to 25,000 officers and men. This force was scattered among more than 200 small garrisons in forty-two states and territories. Congressional economy initially imperiled effectiveness against frontier Indians and led to a high desertion rate.

The years between 1865 and the Spanish-American War were formative for the American military profession. Without foreign threats the public was apathetic, a paucity of contracting denied the army economic influence and large bodies of opinion were hostile to the military establishment. Frontier posts were geographically isolated, just as the officer corps was socially and intellectually isolated. Aloofness from politics was encouraged for fear that political meddling would destroy the services. Professional journals, advanced military educational institutions, and gradual reforms in the personnel system shaped the profession. The standards of dedication, regard for civil authority, abstinence from politics, and professional development which have long been exemplary in the U.S. armed forces evolved during the thirty years of official neglect following 1865.

II. THE INDIAN WARS

Postwar westward expansion was met by the most determined Indian opposition yet encountered. The nomadic plains Indians, moving with the buffalo herds, ranked among the best light cavalry in military history. The army was charged with maintaining order and supporting the policy of confining the natives to reservations, but its numerical weakness prevented concentration against scattered bands totaling possibly 300,000 braves.

Reduction of the Indians was accomplished by several means. Economic warfare, focused upon destruction of the buffalo, destroyed the livelihood of the Indians. Breaking their tribal organization and confining them to reservations undermined their will. Force of arms, however, was a frequent necessity; the ten regular cavalry regiments bore the brunt of the fighting. Some nineteen separate conflicts were waged. In time, the railroad facilitated speedy shift and concentration of forces and spelled doom for the wild savage.

The most significant Indian fighter was General George Crook, who pacified Arizona in 1874 and then was ordered against the northern tribes led by Crazy Horse and Sitting Bull. Crook traveled light and fast to achieve mobility comparable with that of the enemy in what has become the best known campaign of the Indian Wars. On 25 June 1876 in the Battle of the Little Big Horn, Custer's Seventh Cavalry was vanquished by probably the largest force of Indians ever assembled. The Army's Commanding General, Sheridan, stripped the western garrisons to place about 2,000 men each under Generals Crook and Alfred Terry. In a winter campaign the Indians were beaten into submission. Renewed Apache rebellion persisted, however, until the capture of the vicious Geronimo in 1886. Although another Sioux uprising required military action four years later, the Census Bureau reported that the frontier had ceased to exist.

III. THE WAR WITH SPAIN, 1898

A. *Introduction*

With the frontier gone and in possession of an industrial base which already had made them a major power, the United States were ready to turn to new fields. The colonial idea with its social, economic, political, and religious aspects was enhanced by the strategic concepts of A. T. Mahan. These tenets—abetted by a sensationalistic press—stimulated a vigorous foreign policy which led to the acquisition of an American empire. The peaceful annexation of Hawaii secured the Pacific approaches to the United States, but domination of the Caribbean required the complete expulsion of Spain from the New World.

Cuba had remained faithful to the mother country during the Spanish-American Wars of Independence but a serious ten-year insurrection commenced in 1868. Renewed rebellion in 1895 became a subject of major concern because of the long-time political and economic interest of the United States in Cuba. When the battleship *Maine* blew up in Havana harbor, war sentiment swept the nation.

B. *Forces*

The United States was, as usual, unprepared for war. The army had only 28,000 regular troops and the War Department lacked plans for mobilization, adequate intelligence, or even proper stores. Congressional neglect had fostered maladministration and inefficiency. After the war was declared in April, calls were issued for more than 200,000 volunteers. Plans finally crystallized in an expedition to Cuba, which was assembled at Tampa, Florida.

Spanish--American War

The navy, which had been favored with a building program, was completely superior to the enemy and this partially offset army unpreparedness.

C. *The Cuban Campaign*

Spain ordered to Cuba a squadron of four armored cruisers towing three torpedo boats. News of their sailing under Admiral Pascual Cervera, who lacked enthusiasm for the enterprise, panicked the eastern seaboard. The Navy was obliged to commit unnecessary ships to coastal defense. Cervera, unable to obtain adequate coal in the West Indies, put into Santiago where he was blockaded; a better choice would have been Cienfuegos where he would have been connected by rail with Havana and able to acquire coal. On the other hand, the presence of Cervera's virtually impotent squadron contained most of the superior United States Navy and dictated the strategic conduct of the war in the main theatre.

The Navy, unable to reach Cervera, seized Guantanamo Bay from Spain as a forward base and called for land forces to take Santiago. Thus, the stage was strategically set for a situation similar to that of Port Arthur. The V Corps (Major General William R. Shafter, 16,888 men) was hastily embarked at Tampa and arrived off Cuba 20 June. Santiago, although defended by about 36,000 soldiers, was relatively isolated from the rest of the island. The American approach to Santiago was marked by the 1 July storming of San Juan and Kettle Hills. Two days later, Cervera under orders made a suicidal attempt to escape and lost all his ships. The 14 July surrender of Santiago concluded the campaign.

During late July and August, General Nelson A. Miles occupied Puerto Rico, almost without casualties, thus bringing the war in the Caribbean to a conclusion.

D. *The Philippine Campaign*

When war began, Commodore George Dewey's Asiatic Squadron was in Hong Kong and there received orders initiated by Under Secretary of the Navy Theodore Roosevelt to attack the Spanish squadron at Manila. On the night of 30 April he entered Manila Bay and destroyed the enemy ships. Except for insurgent natives under Emilio Aguinaldo, Dewey lacked land forces until the arrival of the VII Corps (General Wesley Merritt). After a token attack to save Spanish honor, Manila capitulated 14 August 1898.

E. Results

Politically, the Spanish-American War brought the United States the responsibilities of an imperial power. Acquiring Guam, Puerto Rico, and the Philippines and a protectorate over Cuba, not only implemented Mahan's ambition for the Caribbean to become a U. S. lake, but also projected United States power across the Pacific to the fringe of Asia. Thus, the victorious nation emerged as an intercontinental world power, while hapless Spain sank into oblivion. Militarily, these developments were primarily attributable to modern naval power operating to blockade and to command the sea.

IV. THE PHILIPPINE INSURRECTION, 1899-1902

Dewey had brought Filipino leader Aguinaldo from the mainland to Luzon and had tacitly encouraged him, at least in the formation of a native army. By August 1898, Aguinaldo controlled Luzon and had laid siege to Manila. With U. S. policy unclear, he acted boldly and proclaimed independence. To reach the Spanish, American troops had to pass through Filipino lines. Although this was accomplished by negotiation, Aguinaldo's soldiers were prohibited from entering Manila. Relations deteriorated, no power recognized the Filipino government, and when it became apparent that the islands simply had acquired a new owner, hostilities erupted 4 February 1899.

By May, defeat forced the native Congress to contemplate peace; Aguinaldo's army, however, continued organized resistance until it was crushed in November. The insurgents then opened a people's war lasting two and one-half years. Local populations protested friendship for the Americans by day, but turned guerrilla by night. Although the U. S. Army fought each day from the villages it controlled, it was subjected to almost constant attack at home from anti-imperialists who thus stimulated the naive faith of the native leaders in eventual Filipino success.

To pacify the Philippines, the United States employed more than 100,000 men and spent close to a billion dollars. This included several years of operations against the Moros in the Sulu Archipelago. The Army was ill equipped for counterinsurgency operations, but the fighting bore some tactical resemblance, in the mobility of light forces tracking enemy irregulars, to the Indian campaigns. More important, it blooded the United States armed forces in colonial warfare and demonstrated the requirements of imperialism. Henceforth, duty in the far-flung posts of the empire was a part of every professional officer's career.

V. THE ROOT REFORMS

The Spanish-American War and the Philippine Insurrection drew attention to deficiencies in the military establishment. The War Department had been unprepared for foreign war although, of course, the pauperish budget it had long received was partly to blame. On the other hand, the command relationship between the Secretary and the Commanding General was confused. The chiefs of the army Bureaus, who had virtually life tenure, built up their political ties and presided over frequently ineffective agencies.

Elihu Root, a lawyer selected to head the War Department because of its new military government functions, saw the only solution as a general staff system such as most nations had already adopted. The General Staff Act of 1903 established a command line from the President through the Secretary to a Chief of Staff who replaced the former Commanding General. Chosen by the President from the entire general officer list for a four-year tour, the latter became the true link between the army and civilian authority. Through the control which he obtained over the Bureaus, he was able to direct a more effective administration aimed at better preparation for the exigencies of modern war.

CHAPTER XXIII

The First World War: The Failure to Achieve a Quick Decision in 1914

I. INTRODUCTION

THE RUSSO-JAPANESE WAR ten years earlier had provided a forewarning of the impact of developments in firepower, but European military leaders failed to heed its significance. Politicians, also unappreciative of the effect of the new technology on war, were as convinced as their military advisers in 1914 that the coming conflict would be short and decisive. As a result the conduct of war suffered. It was to be a matter of years, rather than of weeks, before the makers of grand and military strategy realized that this was a total war which required the planned coordination and exploitation of each nation's entire resources. The allocation of manpower to munitions factories became equally as important as conscription into the big batallions, for of necessity industry which furnished the means took its place alongside armed forces in determining military decisions.

II. THE COMING OF THE WAR

A. Origins

Postwar pacifists blamed World War I on the armaments race, but this explanation was far too simple. Contributory causes were the belief in racial superiority shared by both the Germans

Scapa Flow
NORWAY
SWEDEN
St. Petersburg
NORTH SEA
IRELAND
GREAT BRITAIN
Jutland
BALTIC SEA
London
HOLLAND
Berlin
BELGIUM
GERMANY
RUSSIA
Paris
FRANCE
SWITZER LAND
Vienna
AUSTRIA HUNGARY
ITALY
RUMANIA
SPAIN
ADRIATIC SEA
SERBIA
BULGARIA
BLACK SEA
Rome
ALBANIA
GALLIPOLI
TURKEY
MEDITERRANEAN SEA
GREECE
0
400 MILES
Suez

EUROPE, 1914

and the British; French desire for revenge after the humiliation of 1870, and for the return of Alsace-Lorraine; and Anglo-German colonial and commercial rivalries. There were also jingoism, national pride, stupidity, and personality factors, as well as a feeling that war was inevitable. Empires were tottering on their foundations and their prestige was at stake. In opposition to the Germanic peoples the Russians had long backed a Pan-Slav movement, using it also as a means of dismantling the Ottoman Empire. Russia had lost face in 1908 when Austria annexed Bosnia and Herzegovina. The Russians could not back down again. The Austrians were determined to humble Serbia whose virulent Slavic nationalism appealed to minorities within the Empire and threatened the regime. The Germans had been vanquished by the British and the French in the Agadir diplomatic crisis of 1911. The two alliance systems—the Anglo-French-Russian Triple Entente and the Austro-German-Italian Triple Alliance—tended to solidify, albeit with the exception of Italy.

The actual spark which ignited this tinder was the assassination of the Austrian Archduke at Sarajevo in recently-acquired Bosnia. He was killed by a member of a secret Serbian nationalist society. The pistol shots of 28 June 1914 set in motion both diplomatic and military machinery.

B. *Diplomacy and Mobilization*

Austria, having obtained a free hand—the "blank check"—from Germany without consultation, sent a 48-hour ultimatum to Serbia on 23 July and despite a conciliatory reply, Vienna decided on war and began to mobilize. Although Europe still hoped to localize the struggle, Russia too prepared to fight; and Serbia actually did so.

It was now clear that a major war was coming as Russia could not afford to back down and Germany was hampered by the "blank check" she had given Austria. The German Emperor appealed to the Czar, who ordered mobilization confined to the Austrian frontier, but the Russian General Staff lacked plans for such limited action and on the thirtieth proceeded with full mobilization. The British Foreign Secretary believed that he could not act without the support of Parliament, although staff talks dating from 1906 had committed the British Army to aid France. On 31 July Germany sent an ultimatum to France and Russia. Assured of French support, Russia remained firm because of her Balkan commitments. German war plans provided for beating France before Russia could concentrate and commit her strength, a force which Germany overestimated because she considered only manpower and not total resources.

On 1 August, therefore, the German Empire declared war on Russia, seized Luxemburg, and invaded Belgium on the fourth as the Schlieffen Plan was applied. The violation of an 1839 treaty guaranteeing Belgian neutrality and her military agreements with France brought Britain into the war.

C. *The Forces Available*

When mobilization was completed some 335 infantry divisions faced each other, the largest number (114) belonging to the Russians. In addition, there were some 50 cavalry divisions and administrative and training forces totalling 6,500,000 men. Another half million were in the belligerent navies. The armies varied in discipline, equipment and leadership. The Russian was the poorest, the German the steadiest, the French most imbued by the spirit of the attack (*"L'offensive a outrance"*) of Colonel de Grandmaison, and the British the outstanding example of the élite professional army. The Germans initially had the best matériel, except for France's 75-mm artillery. Although soon surpassed in hand and rifle grenades, they tended to retain their advantage in respect to numbers of machine-guns per battalion. The Russians were almost weaponless. No nation had the munitions and supplies with which to wage a long war. All were dependent upon railways, which favored the defensive, and upon horses or mules to take supplies from the railheads to the battle lines. The infantry still moved on foot and once detrained its speed was no better than that of the Napoleonic armies.

Neither on sea nor land was leadership brilliant. The outstanding men either did not command in the major theaters, or tried to handle inferior forces. Conrad von Hötzendorf of Austria is reckoned by Cyril Falls to be the best strategist of the opening days; Serbia's Marshal Putnik the most imaginative; Joffre, the

French commander, better than the nervous namesake nephew of the great von Moltke; Russian's Grand Duke Nicholas, an enigma (since the Russian Revolution has prevented studies of his actions); and Britain's Sir John French, merely competent.* Other scholars are less kind.

The morale of the troops in general was very high. The Serbians had emerged victorious from two Balkan wars. The Germans and the French both had complete confidence in their military systems. Their forces, even considering large reservist groups, were well trained. The British Expeditionary Force sent to France was a professional group with Boer War experience. As in Manchuria the Russians were merely obedient. The Austrian army was debilitated by fourteen different nationalities, their various rivalries, and their lack of common interest in the conflict.

D. *Strategy*

Both grand and military strategies were deplorably simple. They aimed either at the restoration of the smaller injured parties or at the settlement of international tensions by the complete defeat of a major opponent. Much of the lack of planning was due to military optimism, engendered by more than a generation without a war between major powers in Europe. Also responsible was the naïvete of the statesmen of the day, none of whom had Bismarck's iron vision of the need for limited objectives. For the first two years, the war was largely left to the soldiers, whose only objective was victory without regard for political considerations, because these they did not understand.

III. THE OPENING CAMPAIGN IN THE EAST

A. *The Serbian Front*

The Austrian conception of the war envisioned a punitive operation against Serbia. The plan of campaign made no allowance for a Russian attack on Galicia. Therefore, when the Russians moved faster than expected, the Austrians had to divert most of an army

---

* Cyril Falls, *The First World War* (London: Longmans, 1960), 17-19.

from the Serbian front. The Serbs in turn had to cover the Bulgarian frontier, thereby weakening their force although the Bulgars did not enter the war against them until 11 October 1915. After the Serbs repulsed a major Austrian attack on 12 August 1914, a series of indecisive battles followed until by 15 December the invaders were pushed back across the Danube, with losses of 227,000 men versus the Serb's total of 170,000 casualties.

B. *The Russian Front*

On the Galician front the Russians mobilized four armies stretched over the 175 miles from Lublin southeastward to the Dniester. Facing them were three and one-half Austrian armies under Conrad von Holtzendorf. Neither had a clear idea of the other's location. Owing to the unorthodox Russian use of cavalry to fill gaps in the line rather than for reconnaissance, Austrian cavalry was often stopped first by Russian infantry fire rather than by Cossack patrols.

On 23 August the opposing armies blundered into each other at the northern end of the line. Three days later as the encounter was ending, the next armies down the line engaged and once again the Russians failed. They were saved when the third Austrian army became cautious since its flank was not yet protected by the forces dispatched from the Serbian front. Conrad realized on the twenty-eighth that his right was in trouble, and ordered a strategic withdrawal, but the panic of certain units in front of Lemberg spoiled his plan. The Grand Duke Nicholas, who had now taken command in the field, then attempted an envelopment with his superior armies. Because his staff made the fatal mistake of sending the orders uncoded the Austrians were enabled to retire intact to a line 140 miles west of Lemberg, where at last Conrad could be reinforced by the Germans, who by 3 October were freed of the menace to East Prussia.

C. *The East Prussian Front*

Here in exactly the place where no one expected a quick victory, the Germans obtained it. To help the French, the Russians moved before they were fully mobilized. In the north an army under Rennenkampf advanced with but scanty support from a southern force commanded by Samsonov. The Masurian Lakes separated the two forces. On 17 August Rennenkampf crossed slowly into East Prussia, hindered by lack of transport. On the twentieth Samsonov began an advance around the southern end of the lakes. Moltke removed the timid German commander, Prittwitz, and sent Colonel Ludendorff, fresh from a victory at Liege, to East Prussia as Chief of Staff to 67-year-old Paul von Hindenburg, who was brought from retirement.

By the time they arrived, Lieutenant Colonel Max Hoffmann of the staff in East Prussia had already made the arrangements for victory. He ordered troops by foot and by rail from in front of the tedious Rennenkampf to deal a sharp blow at the less cautious Samsonov then advancing on Tannenberg. A touch-and-go battle then ensued in which the Germans managed a double envelopment by shifting four corps west-about by rail to reinforce the one at Tannenberg (22-23 August). The issue remained in doubt until, on the twenty-seventh, two more corps which had marched south from in front of the Russian First Army appeared in the flank and rear of the Second Army. The battle ended three days later with 90,000 Russians taken prisoner; dejected Samsonov committed suicide. Reinforced by two corps nervously transferred by Moltke from the Western Front—using the strategic mobility afforded by the superior German rail network—the Germans proceeded to repeat their victory on 15 September when they drove the Russians back of the Masurian Lakes and captured another 30,000 prisoners. East Prussia was freed. What had been planned as a holding operation thus ended in an impressive victory.

IV. THE WAR IN THE WEST

A. The Schlieffen Plan in Motion

When Moltke the Younger succeeded Schlieffen, he altered the plan so as to avoid the invasion of Holland in order to leave that country as a neutral port. Otherwise, basically, the idea employed in 1914 was that envisaged in 1894—a sweep through Belgium to avoid the defended Franco-German frontier. Everybody knew it and the French were on their seventeenth counter-plan when the war came. The one change Moltke had made was to reinforce the German left (southern) wing. As far as the Germans were concerned, much depended upon the French reaction, intelligent generalship, and railway timetables.

To oppose the 1,500,000-man German army, the French had 800,000 and expected a British Expeditionary Force of 150,000. Since victory in the offensive normally depends upon a 3:1 superiority, the French offensive Plan XVII, modified by Joffre under the influence of Foch, was defective from the start.

1. BELGIUM

Attacking 4-6 August, the Germans pushed two armies through Belgium, bypassing the supposedly impregnable fortress at Liege. Ludendorff, utilizing the superior firepower of howitzers and mortars, required only 11 days to reduce Liege, though planning had not envisioned that much delay. The Belgians were forced to fall back under the guns first of Brussels and then of Antwerp, where they were joined by British marines. On 20 August, General von Kluck took Brussels. On the German left, the French tried to skirt Metz and deliver with five armies a vital blow at the shoulder of the German attack. Joffre hoped that a drive between Mezieres and Belfort, begun on the fourteenth, would allow a breakthrough on either side of Metz, but the French armies were repulsed in the wooded Ardennes valleys and forced to retreat since their artillery was inferior to the German guns.

On 17 August, the last of the Liege forts succumbed to heavy artillery fire and the German rear was cleared. Two days later their great envelopment resumed its advance. By 1 September, von Kluck's First Army had advanced 180 miles on foot.

2. ALLIED ACTIONS

Meanwhile, the shoulder and the extended upper arm of the German sweep were attacked by the French. The cavalry assigned to this task was inadequate. The French blundered into superior forces and were repulsed. The Germans, however, were also cautious and failed to exploit French imbalance. Yet, the German right wing was well beyond the French and the enveloping movement was proceeding effectively.

Meanwhile the B.E.F. under Sir John French began debarking at Le Havre on the seventh. Fear of invasion had kept back two of his divisions and limited him to only 90,000 men. Nevertheless this was a Boer War-hardened outfit and they harassed the spear-point of the German advance at Mons on 23 August with their rapid Lee-Enfield rifle-fire. A British strategic withdrawal became a retreat, however, when the French on their right pulled back. This continued until Joffre directed a counter-attack on 5 September, and Kitchener, the British War Minister, ordered Sir John French to stay in the line.

Although Joffre was puzzled and unsure about what was occurring, he was inadvertently assisted in effect by Moltke. As already mentioned, the German commander ordered two corps to East Prussia, thus weakening his enveloping force under von Kluck at the critical time when all possible strength was needed. Furthermore, the logistic system proved deficient due to the demands which it imposed upon the inadequate Belgian railroads. Joffre struck the Second German Army on the twenty-ninth, halting it for two vital days. He also created a new army near Paris, while at Verdun the French held firm and at Nancy a German attack was beaten off. The latter offensive was ill-advised for it failed to conform to the plan of sucking the French right forward into Bavaria so it could be destroyed.

Then von Kluck also decided further to vary the Schlieffen Plan and, instead of passing west of Paris, to swing east of the capital in pursuit of the French. This played into Joffre's hands, situated as his new Sixth Army was outside the German right. Kluck's change of direction was spotted from the air on 3 September and Gallieni, the commander of Paris, at once asked if he should prepare an attack. On the fourth, the German passage of the Marne was reported and Gallieni set his forces in motion. Joffre delayed the counter offensive until the sixth. The battle of the Marne, which lasted five days and was fought on a hundred mile front, had begun.

3. THE MARNE (6-11 SEPTEMBER 1914)

The B.E.F. advanced cautiously through heavily wooded country into a gap which had opened when the First (Kluck) and

Second (Bülow) German armies, obeying Moltke, turned southwest. Alarmed by the resulting situation, Moltke sent Hentsch, a general staff officer, to visit the various German armies. He had authority to order a general retirement and upon reaching Kluck's area agreed, on 9 September, to plans the latter had already made for such a move.

The Germans now retired skillfully upon the rivers Aisne and Vesle. So far in a war of mass maneuver neither side had lost more than time or ground; the fighting forces remained intact. But the higher German leadership was dejected because the Schlieffen Plan had failed. Despite the victory at Tannenberg, the general prospect was for what Prussia had always feared—a two-front war.

On the night of 12 September, sufficient troops arrived for the Germans to form a new Seventh Army to plug the hole between von Kluck and Bülow. Two days later the Emperor replaced Moltke with Eric von Falkenhayn, the Prussian Minister of War.

B. *The Coming of Position Warfare*

1. THE RACE TO THE SEA

The Allies launched a series of hasty, ineffective offensives—the Aisne (15-18 September), Picardy (22-26 September) and Artois (27 September-10 October). Von Falkenhayn, however, initiated a flanking movement toward the north. Each successive effort was met by Allied counter moves. To protect the open flanks, after each engagement the troops began to dig in. Gradually a primitive line of trenches spread northwards in what is commonly called "the Race to the Sea." The B.E.F. sped north to protect its communications through the vital Channel ports. It arrived on a new front near Ypres in mid-October, just in time to bolster the remnants of the Anglo-Belgian force with which King Albert had held Antwerp until 10 October.

2. FLANDERS

Both sides now sensed that their last chance for a breakthrough before winter was at hand and a series of bloody struggles was fought in the soggy Flanders soil in front of Ypres and along the Yser. They began with a gigantic German cavalry advance, which was broken up by B.E.F. infantry, whose standard short rifle outranged the German cavalry carbines. In the new fighting, gains and losses were measured in yards. One engagement merged into another. The Germans broke the exhausted Belgians and crossed the river Yser, but on 29 October the Belgians opened the sluices and sea water flooded the low-lying lands. On the thirtieth the Germans attacked on a 20-mile front in a big question-mark about Ypres, with little result beyond the destruction of their young reserve battalions. French attacks near Arras proved equally fruitless. By the time the autumn fighting ended, the elite professional British Army had been ruined, but the opposing lines were, if anything, more rigid than before.

The war of maneuver had come to a permanent end. In the East, Hindenberg's offensive had collapsed and he had been reinforced with Austrian troops after the battles of Lodz and Lowicz. The Russians, despite a defeat near Cracow, rolled forward to the crest of the Carpathians. There they halted for the winter.

C. *Reasons for the Stalemate*

None of the commanders was accustomed to handling such large forces in the field. None of them had thought seriously about a long war, for all expected a rapid decision. The new firepower of machine guns and artillery came to dominate the field of battle, just as they had done in Manchuria. The defense was strengthened till it was about three times as strong—with the same number of men—as the offense. No thought had been given to the problems this posed and opponents were generally evenly matched numerically.

As no one had planned for a long war, no country had the munition stockpiles nor the prepared industrial machinery to supply the great armies which were conscripted in an effort to counter bullet power with manpower. The superiority of the defense owed as much to the mass-production of barbed-wire as to that of guns and supplies.

Strangely, the only top commander who was removed at once

was Moltke, who might have won in the West if communications and reconnaissance had been better, and von Kluck more skillful. Under Moltke's direction the Germans had conquered the area from which France drew 40 per cent of her coal and 90 per cent of her iron ore, matter of tremendous significance in the industrial war of attrition which faced Europe as winter's arrival imposed a lull in the fighting.

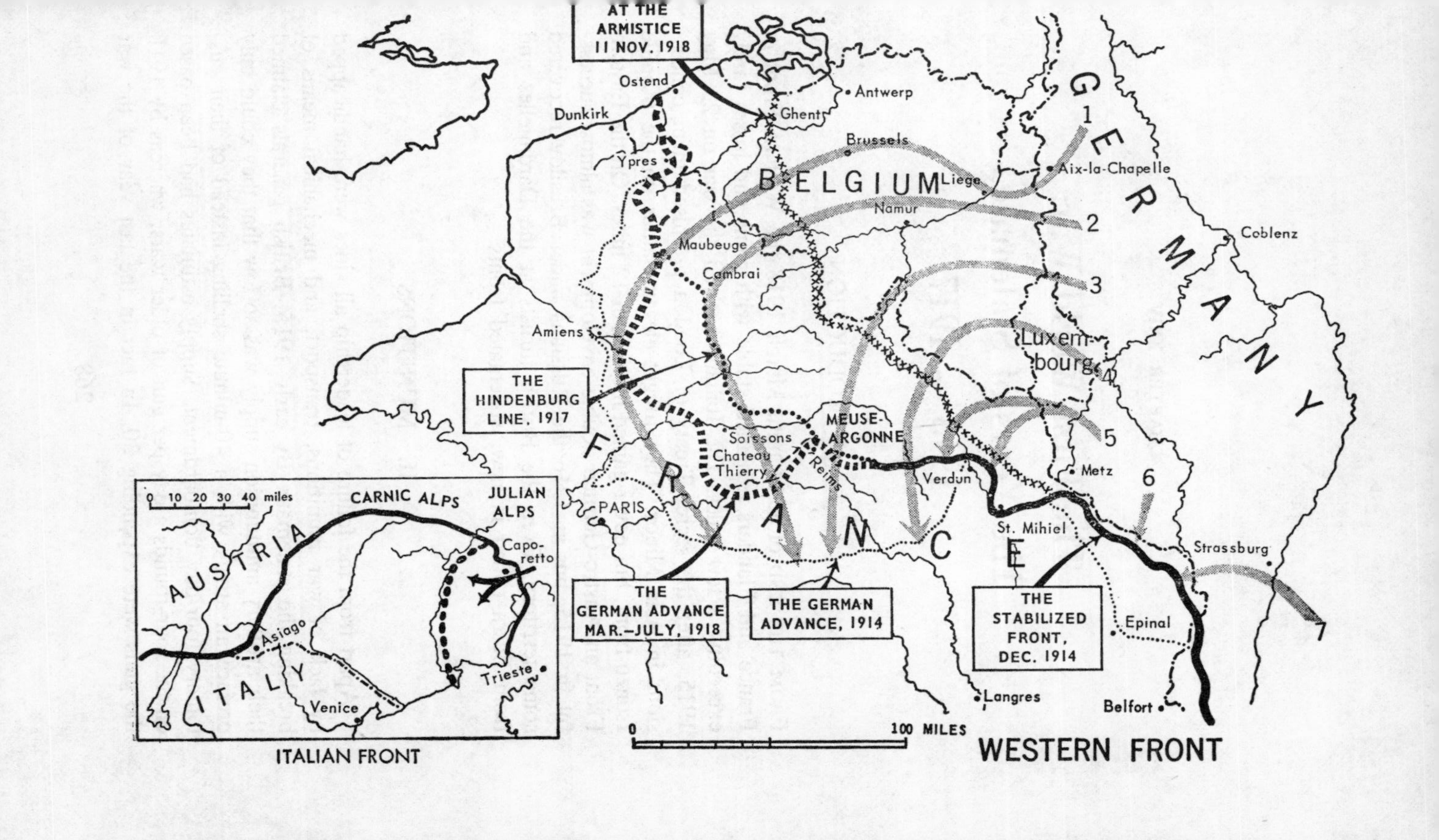
AT THE ARMISTICE 11 NOV. 1918
Ostend
Dunkirk
Ghent
Antwerp
Brussels
Ypres
BELGIUM
Liege
Aix-la-Chapelle
Namur
Maubeuge
Cambrai
GERMANY
Coblenz
1
2
3
4
5
6
7
Luxembourg
Amiens
THE HINDENBURG LINE, 1917
MEUSE-ARGONNE
Soissons
Chateau Thierry
Reims
Verdun
Metz
St. Mihiel
Strassburg
FRANCE
PARIS
THE GERMAN ADVANCE MAR.-JULY, 1918
THE GERMAN ADVANCE, 1914
THE STABILIZED FRONT, DEC. 1914
Epinal
Langres
Belfort
0
100 MILES
WESTERN FRONT
0 10 20 30 40 miles
CARNIC ALPS
JULIAN ALPS
Caporetto
AUSTRIA
Asiago
ITALY
Trieste
Venice
ITALIAN FRONT

CHAPTER XXIV

The First World War: The Years of Stalemate, 1915 — 1917

I. INTRODUCTION

FROM THE END of 1914 until March 1918 the Western Front in France and Flanders remained stable with gains and losses rarely exceeding a few miles. The Italians entered the war on 23 May 1915, after the secret Treaty of London promised them concessions in Asia Minor. They fought eleven battles on the 60-mile Isonzo front, but never gained more than 12 miles. On the Eastern Front an Austro-German double envelopment was almost successful in 1915, but in 1916 the Russians under Brusilov recovered some territory. Even the British thrusts at the Dardanelles and from Basra ended in new, stalemated fronts.

II. MUNITIONS

Apart from the failure of leadership all sides were handicapped by lack of war munitions, transport, and mechanical means of breaking the stalemate. By early 1915, British generals claimed their artillery ammunition supply was so low that they could only preface an attack with a 40-minute shelling instead of their customary four-day bombardment. Supply estimates had been based on the four-rounds a day per gun of older wars, whereas by 1918 the guns were expending 30. In fact in the last year of the war the Anglo-French forces consumed 12,710,000 rounds a month, a feat made possible in part by an 18,000 per cent increase in the production of 75mm shells over the standard peacetime American allotment of 125 per gun a year. For the Allies, by having Americans manufacture the finished article, 18/19ths of the shipping space of raw materials was saved. Mass-produced barbed-wire and machine guns were formidable obstacles not only to the offensive, but to supply as well. The war required a 4,700 per cent increase in the manufacture of machine-gun ammunition. The generals assumed that the answer to these mass-produced defenses was their obliteration by a great barrage of shells such as the 19-day, 321 train-loads (a year's production of 55,000 workers), with which the British deluged the battlefield before Passschendaele in 1917. Yet even then every square mile gained cost them some 9,000 casualties. Moreover, the great barrages generally made the ground impassable for infantry or cavalry and thus strengthened the defense, which itself was turning to reinforced concrete pillboxes. The Russians were hard hit by lack of arms; the success of German offensives in the East in 1915 was largely due to lack of Russian firepower coupled with inadequate railways to move troops and supplies. The Dardanelles offensive was designed to knock Turkey out of the war and to open a supply route to Russia to make her more effective. The situation was less acute in France and Germany; nevertheless, enormous efforts had to be made on the civilian front to organize logistical systems, curtail civilian production and assign manpower. In Germany, this quickly led to a further extension of the State-planned economy. The shell shortage in England transformed the Liberal Government into a coalition in which David Lloyd George became Minister of Munitions in charge of military procurement. The Allies began to buy arms in the United States, from whom the Germans also made some small purchases.

Because on the whole the fronts depended on railways, keeping the trains running became a major operation. Light railways were also established and considerable industry and manpower had to be devoted to operating these forward from the standard-gauge railheads. The organization and operation of shipping and ports also became a primary consideration. When U-boats grew increasingly effective during the period of unrestricted submarine warfare in 1917, convoys were at last organized, at considerable cost to the smooth flow of supplies, until the new system was functioning regularly.

Aircraft manufacture was virtually a new industry which made many demands especially in terms of skilled workmanship and high-class materials, and thus competed with the needs of the Army. Naval procurement added to the strain on the economy; during October 1914-May 1915 more than 1,000 new British vessels from super battlecruisers to patrol boats were ordered, not to mention non-rigid airships, airplanes, and all the other paraphernalia of war.

World War I is also important as the first major conflict in which scientists played an important role. So many of them were employed that their identities were submerged into that of teams delegated to develop specific weapons or counter devices. Except for one or two special cases, such as the 1917 convoy issue, they were not called upon to do operational research or development work. Nevertheless, they did produce the hydrophone and the depth charge, more accurate streamlined shells, geophones to detect underground mining operations and by triangulation to locate enemy guns, field telephones and the like, all of which made mass destruction more complete. The Germans were the first to turn to the pure scientists in an effort to break the stalemate. This led to chlorine gas and gasmasks, and to new methods of obtaining nitric acid for explosives. The Allies followed suit to obtain gas, smoke, incendiaries and flamethrowers, and their researchers went on to industrial, sanitary, aeronautical, as well as statistical, planning and other fields.

III. THE CONTEMPORARY MENTAL OUTLOOK

In 1912 many people had argued naively that war was impossible because it would be far too horrible. The actual development of the war exceeded all conceptions. Men spent days and weeks in cold and mud, but their morale did not immediately break. Losses in air and land attacks were appalling; yet both sides fought on. The belief prevailed on most sides that the participants were engaged in a righteous war with God on their side. More than this, the Higher Commands were imbued with the idea—stemming in part from military necessity and in part from social Darwinism —that the other side was composed of inferior people who would crack first. This led to the great battles of attrition, such as Verdun in 1916. The generals usually failed to realize that the attackers suffered more than the defenders. An additional factor was probably that the mass of conscripted soldiers on both sides were still relatively stolid, uneducated members of the lower classes. In 1915, again in 1916 and still again in 1917 the generals assured the political leaders that they would end the war by a great offensive to achieve a penetration of the enemy lines. It was not until mid-1917 that the Allied politicians began to doubt the fulfillment of these forecasts and to plan in earnest for a war which might last till 1920.

IV. MINOR THEATRES

A. Middle Eastern Operations

On 2 August 1914 the Turks made a secret treaty to enter the war on the side of the Central Powers, but delayed when German defeat appeared likely. The army had been reorganized by the German General Liman von Sanders after the disastrous Balkan Wars, but fighting efficiency and equipment varied with the distance of the units from Constantinople. The Turks, however, began the war with Russia on 28 October by naval bombardment of Odessa. The Turkish War Minister, Enver Pasha, then concocted a plan to invade Georgia in southern Russia. This Caucasian campaign cost the Turks 77,000 of the 95,000 engaged, largely because of winter weather.

Since the southern edge of Turkey was in Arabia close to the Suez Canal, the British stationed a force there which included the Anzac (Australian and New Zealand Army Corps) Division. Its position remained static until Sir Archibald Murray's offensive in support of a rebellion in Arabia by the nationalistic desert sheik, Hussein, began on 15 November 1916. The real advance began after Sir Edmund Allenby was appointed to command on 28 June 1917.

In the meantime, to protect the Anglo-Iranian Oil Company's fields—in which the Royal Navy had an investment—and to encourage the sheiks to rally to the British flag—an Indian army expeditionary force was landed on 6 November at the head of the Persian Gulf. It advanced from the main base at Basra and beat off a Turkish counter-attack (11-13 April 1915) with twin columns reaching up the Tigris and Euphrates rivers. The campaign changed from an offensive-defensive into an attack upon Bagdad, which proved fatal as neither men nor equipment were adequate. The result was the encirclement and surrender of Townshend at Kut (3 December 1915-29 April 1916). A Russian offensive through western Persia made contact with the relief force, but failed to extricate Townshend. Turkish counter-attacks drove the Russians back, and also out of Armenia.

"The lifeline of the British Empire" was also endangered by Turkish attacks on the Suez Canal (3-4 February 1915, 23 April, and 19 July-4 August 1916). In the Fall of 1916, Sir Stanley Maude assumed command in Mesopotamia and on 13 December began a new advance on Kut, took it (9 January-24 February 1917), and captured Bagdad (11 March). Despite the failure of the renewed Russian campaign in western Persia, the British continued to advance and by the end of 1917 held Ramadi and Tikrit.

B. *The Dardanelles* (*Gallipoli*)

The successful escape to Constantinople of the German warships *Goeben* and *Breslau* on 11 August 1914 brought the Turks closer to war. The British hoped to keep them neutral and the Straits open for war matériel and commerce with Russia. With deadlock on the Western Front and Turkey on the side of the Central Powers, Churchill, Lloyd George, and later Kitchener, urged a blow to knock out Turkey and reopen the road to Odessa, so that Russian manpower could be supplied with arms and used effectively against Germany. The "Easterners" wanted to return to the traditional British policy of using seapower against the perimeter of Europe, while their French Continental ally held the Western Front. Although some French generals were sympathetic, Sir John French and Joffre were hostile.

The Easterners suggested several plans of action: cutting the railway near Alexandretta, operations from Salonika and an attack on Constantinople from a landing in the Dardanelles. But these schemes were shelved until the Russians, in January 1915, asked for a diversion to relieve Turkish pressure on the Caucasus. The plan was further delayed by Russian suspicions of the Greeks, whose army had been included in the operational conception.

Surprise had already been compromised by the Royal Navy's bombardment of the Dardanelles forts in November 1914 and February 1915. On 18 March, Admiral de Roebeck attempted to force a passage of the Straits, after marines had spiked Turkish guns, but he retired prematurely when a number of ships struck mines. The Turks under von Sanders now garrisoned the area with 100,000 well-dug-in men. On 25 April, 75,000 troops under General Sir Ian Hamilton landed at the tip of the Gallipoli Peninsula. The whole operation was badly handled from beginning to end. Leadership was lacking; equipment had been misloaded; the troops landed in the wrong place and prepared defenses on

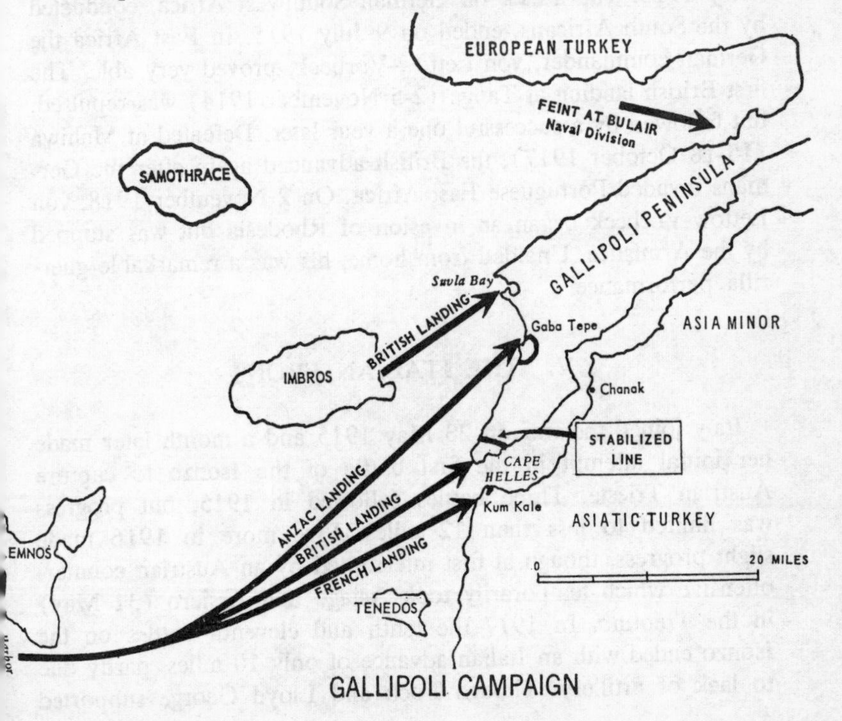

GALLIPOLI CAMPAIGN

the beach instead of rapidly occupying the high ground. Consequently, the Allied forces were soon confined to their beachheads and position war similar to the Western Front set in. On 6 August an additional landing at Suvla Bay, seeking to turn the Turkish lines, repeated all the former mistakes besides being timid in execution. Hamilton was recalled. On 19-20 December 1915 and 8-9 January 1916 the Allies evacuated with a skill that was the only success of the operation, which cost 252,000 casualties out of 480,000 Allied men involved.

Gallipoli was a campaign of destiny. If it had succeeded, the Russian Revolution might not have taken place.

C. *Colonial Operations*

Most of the German colonies overseas were swiftly overrun by superior Allied forces capitalizing on command of the seas. Some, such as the actions in the Cameroons, dragged on until 19 February 1916. The attack on German Southwest Africa, conducted by the South Africans, ended on 9 July 1915. In East Africa the German commander, von Lettow-Vorbeck, proved very able. The first British landing at Tanga (2-5 November 1914) was repulsed, but followed by a successful one a year later. Defeated at Mahiwa (15-18 October 1917), the British advanced again after the Germans invaded Portuguese East Africa. On 2 November 1918, von Lettow-Vorbeck began an invasion of Rhodesia but was stopped by the Armistice. Unaided from home, his was a remarkable guerrilla performance.

V. THE ITALIAN FRONT

Italy joined the war on 23 May 1915 and a month later made her initial attempt in the first battle of the Isonzo to capture Austrian Trieste. Three battles followed in 1915, but progress was limited to less than 12 miles. Five more in 1916 made slight progress, though at first interrupted by an Austrian counter-offensive which temporarily took Asiago and Arsiero (31 May) in the Trentino. In 1917 the tenth and eleventh battles on the Isonzo ended with an Italian advance of only 10 miles, partly due to lack of artillery. Though Foch and Lloyd George supported

Italy's pleas for reinforcements to drive weary Austria out of the war, the Western Front's priority was higher.

Ludendorff meanwhile had beaten Serbia and Rumania (a late entrant in the war) and decided to reduce Italy. Six German divisions sparked a breakthrough at Caporetto on 24 October 1917. The Italians, their spirit undermined by frustration, broke at once. French and British units were brought in (3-4 November) to avoid a rout and, as the Austro-German forces outran their supplies, the front was once more stabilized on 26 December on the Piave. The Italians lost 300,000 prisoners and an untold number of deserters. Both the commanding general and the cabinet changed during the course of the battle.

VI. THE EASTERN FRONT, 1915-1917

The year 1915 started with some inconclusive February fighting on the northern part of the front. In March the Russians endeavored unsuccessfully to break through the Carpathian passes into Hungary. The Tenth German Army bolstered the Austrians on the Galician front and acted as part of the southern force of an enveloping movement. On 2 May they began a great drive and made a real breakthrough at the Battle of Gorlice-Tarnow. A Russian rout ensued. The front restabilized after a 300-mile advance overextended the supply lines. Other reasons for stopping the advance were the tenuous position on the Italian front, the French attacks in the West, and Gallipoli, though the latter had failed by the end of the summer. The Turks, however, could not be aided until the Serbians were thrown off the railway to Constantinople. The Russians lost over 300,000 prisoners and 3,000 guns. On 5 September the Czar assumed personal command in the field thus relieving the more effective Archduke.

In 1916 the Russians planned a great offensive for June at the earliest, but French appeals for relief of the pressure against Verdun persuaded them to attack on 19 March in the battle of Lake Naroch, which ended inconclusively on 30 April. Then the Italians called for help when the Austrians attacked Trentino. The Czar again ordered Brusilov to start an offensive promptly, assuring him of the co-operation of the armies to his north who

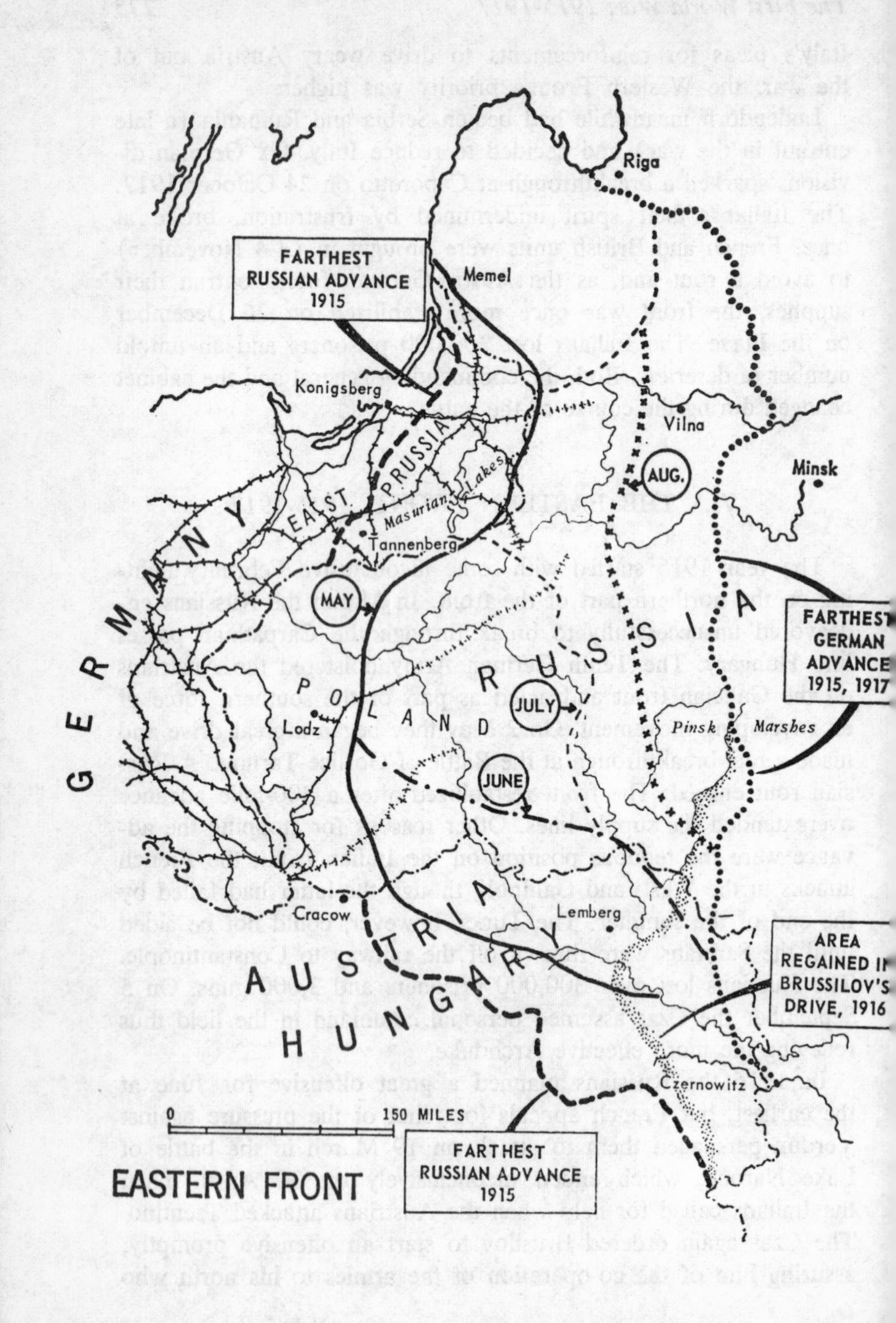

FARTHEST RUSSIAN ADVANCE 1915
Riga
Memel
Konigsberg
EAST PRUSSIA
Masurian Lakes
Tannenberg
Vilna
Minsk
AUG.
GERMANY
MAY
POLAND
RUSSIA
JULY
JUNE
Lodz
Pinsk Marshes
FARTHEST GERMAN ADVANCE 1915, 1917
Cracow
Lemberg
AUSTRIA
HUNGARY
AREA REGAINED I
BRUSSILOV'S DRIVE, 1916
Czernowitz
0
150 MILES
FARTHEST RUSSIAN ADVANCE 1915
EASTERN FRONT

were to undertake the main offensive, but also warning that he would not receive reinforcements. Intended to complement Joffre's 15 June attack on the Somme, Brusilov's offensive opened prematurely on the fourth. Advancing on a 300-mile front, he drove the Austrians before him for a maximum penetration of nearly 100 miles. Although he failed to take the important railway junction at Kovel, he confirmed the decline of Austrian spirit by taking 500,000 prisoners. The drive was halted in September for several reasons: the arrival of 15 German divisions from the Western Front, inertia in sustaining the advance, declining morale, total losses of a million men, and the complete failure of the northern armies to play their part. Some Russian generals even refused to order an attack against the Germans, for whom they had gained a fearsome respect.

After negotiating through the summer, Rumania declared war on 27 August 1916. She had by then missed the chance to aid the Brusilov offensive and was roughly handled by German and Bulgarian forces, which quickly overran the country after an abortive Rumanian attack on Hungarian Transylvania. The Rumanians retired to Jassy leaving the Central Powers in possession of valuable oil and wheat fields.

The March 1917 Revolution in Russia, a product of war weariness and defeat, empowered the middle classes who were determined to win the war efficiently. Brusilov began a new offensive on 1 July and thrust into eastern Galicia, but was turned back by the Austro-Germans 18-28 July. The latter launched an offensive in the North, took Riga (3 September), and pushed up the Latvian coast. The Kerensky government failed. On 7 November the Bolshevik coup d'etat broke the weary Russian back by destroying discipline in the army and navy. On the twenty-eighth Lenin offered the Central Powers an armistice, on the grounds that then the capitalists could destroy each other in the West. Fighting on the Eastern Front stopped 15 December 1917.

VII. THE WESTERN FRONT

On neither side had the leadership yet awakened to the fact that entirely new tactics would be necessary to break the deadlock. Commanders in both armies still talked of a breakthrough winning the war. A series of massive offensives led to virtually no change in the fighting line, while the adoption of war of attrition merely expended vast quantities of men, ammunition, matériel and other national resources. Few generals seem to have understood that they were engaged in siege warfare, for by 1916 the depth of the line was four to five miles. A penetration was almost impossible. Even when a hole was temporarily opened, it could not be exploited before reinforcements re-established the front.

A. 1915

A series of battles were started by the Germans at La Bassée Canal (8 January-5 February 1915), followed almost at once by a French offensive in Champagne and a British attack at Neuve Chapelle. The French then struck the St. Mihiel salient without success. The Allies planned a great offensive in the Second Battle of Ypres (22 April-25 May), but this was frustrated by a premature German chlorine gas attack. Although the results exceeded expectations, the Germans were unready to exploit the Allied collapse. As a result the British were prevented from co-ordinate operations with the French second Artois push (9 May-18 June), which bought a three-mile gain for 400,000 men.

After a quiet summer, the Allies conducted a second ineffectual battle of Champagne (22 September-6 November). Joffre had failed and Sir Douglas Haig replaced Sir John French as British commander (9 December 1915).

B. 1916

1. VERDUN

Haig wanted to secure the Channel ports by rolling up the German right wing along the coast, but was persuaded by Joffre to co-operate on the Somme instead. However, plans were disrupted by a German attack on Verdun whose forts had been denuded of guns, but which was a key salient of the French line and the symbol of French resistance. Falkenhayn, having failed in offensive operations, planned to wage an offensive defense in a key sector and lure the French to bleed themselves white through attrition. The Germans massed 1,400 guns on an eight-mile front and drove forward starting on 21 February 1916. Henri Pétain was brought in as the French commander and succeeded in stemming the attack by running divisions quickly through the Verdun meat grinder, some 65 passing through his command which averaged 24 divisions in the line at one time. The French lost 315,000 men to the Germans' 281,000; morale declined seriously and the French army became mutinous.

2. THE SOMME

Falkenhayn was compelled to let the fighting die down to meet another futile British offensive which opened 1 July on the Somme. Verdun had reduced the French contribution to the Somme offensive from 40 divisions to 16 and the front from 25 miles to 10. The heavily-laden infantry, though enjoying a superiority of six-to-one, simply could not keep to schedule and lost 60,000 men in one day. The barrage did not destroy the deep dugouts of the Germans; their machine-gunners appeared at once and decimated the advance. Though Haig as usual thought of a breakthrough, the field commander from the first envisaged the battle as one of attrition. On 15 September the British used tanks for the first time. Only 49 were available and of these only 18 reached the front line, but the Tank Corps learned much from the experience under fire. Rain and mud ended the Somme (18 November), a minor French counterattack at Verdun recovered two forts and raised morale, and the armies settled into the earth for a third winter.

3. COMMAND SHIFTS

At the end of 1916 there was a general change of commanders at home and abroad. Lloyd George replaced Asquith in England (4-7 December); the Viviani cabinet in France resigned (29 October) and was replaced by one headed by Briand, who on 12 December followed Lloyd George's example in creating a five-man inner War Cabinet; there was a change of government in Italy (11 June); the Austrian prime minister was assassinated (21 October) and the Emperor Francis Joseph died (21 November). In the field Haig had replaced French (9 December 1915); Nivelle succeeded Joffre (12 December 1916); the Hindenburg clique forced the demotion of Falkenhayn from Chief of Staff to commander in Rumania and his replacement by Hindenburg, with Ludendorff as actual second-in-command (29 August 1916).

C. *1917*

1. THE NIVELLE OFFENSIVE

At the beginning of 1917 the Germans partially withdrew to the more easily defensible Hindenburg Line. The French cabinet then tried to persuade Nivelle to give up an offensive he was preparing, but it capitulated to public opinion when he threatened to resign. The massive offensive (16-20 April) on the Aisne and in Champagne was a dismal failure, for security had been ignored, forewarning the Germans. Fighting did not die down till five days after Nivelle had been dismissed (16 May). Sixteen corps of the French army mutinied, refusing to attack again. Pétain was called to save the critical situation. At home 23 civilian pacifists were executed to stiffen the nation.

2. PASSCHENDAELE

The rest of the year was devoted to the hopeless third British offensive of Ypres, which followed a successful attack on Messines Ridge. Sometimes known as Passchendaele, the great drive ground out a five-mile gain between 31 July and 18 November at the cost of 83,000 British, 39,000 French and 130,000 German casualties per mile. The only bright spot was the successful surprise tank attack over hard ground at Cambrai (20 November), where 380 machines were used. The long-sought penetration could have been achieved if the infantry had not been exhausted in keeping up with the tanks, which had plunged through the third line of defenses. A German counter-attack recovered most of the gain (30 November). The lesson, which the prophetic General J. F. C. Fuller later preached, was that infantry, ammunition and supplies had to be carried in tracked vehicles over the shell-torn battlefield if a breakthrough was ever to be exploited.

D. Summary

The end of 1917 saw both sides a year nearer exhaustion than in 1916, with still greater losses including now virtually all of the old professional lower ranks of 1914 and with nothing to show for it but increased war production at home. The situation on the Western Front seemed hopelessly stagnant, though the future depended largely on whether the Germans could defeat the Allies before the Americans could arrive in the trenches to compensate for Allied casualties.

CHAPTER XXV

The First World War: At Sea, in the Air

I. INTRODUCTION

When war was declared in August 1914, the Germans had a number of potential raiders scattered about the high seas. Others slipped to sea over the next few months. The main naval theater was the North Sea where the British Grand Fleet—backed by a highly skilled Naval Intelligence section in London—stood ready to meet any challenge of the German High Seas Fleet. Both sides began to use air services and for most of the war, naval airmen were perhaps more original and better equipped than their land-based brethren.

At sea fleets were measured in terms of battleships. The British had 24 modern vessels, the Germans 17, the French 6, and the Italians 3. All sides had neglected small craft except as part of the armada surrounding the capital ships; yet it took 78 British ships to catch and destroy a single raider such as the German light cruiser *Emden*.

II. THE NAVAL WAR

A. Early Actions

When on 23 August 1914 Japan declared war on Germany, the latter had eight cruisers overseas. Admiral von Spee at once headed into the Pacific. Along the South American west coast off Chile's Easter Island von Spee was joined by *Dresden* from the West

Indies and *Leipzig* from California. Against von Spee from Cape Horn came Admiral Craddock, who failed to concentrate his three older cruisers and an aged battleship. On 1 November off Coronel, Chile, von Spee's superior tactics and gunnery sank two of his ships. The British at once formed another force under Admiral Sturdee which included two new battlecruisers. Off the Falkland Islands, Sturdee sank four of Spee's five ships (8 December 1914). *Dresden* escaped, but was cornered at Juan Fernández Island and scuttled (14 March 1915). Meanwhile after bombarding Madras *Emden* was caught at the Cocos Islands and destroyed. *Konigsberg* also pursued a destructive raiding career until cornered in the Rufigi River, Tanganyika, where monitors and aircraft wrecked her in July 1915. The Japanese cleaned out the remaining Germans in the Far East and the Pacific. Though briefly disruptive, the German raiders could not hope to emulate the Confederate *Alabama* owing to the advantage wireless gave the pursuers.

The submarine proved the most deadly commerce raider after February 1915 until the sinking of the British liner *Lusitania* (7 May) with the loss of many American lives caused President Wilson to protest. The Germans ignored him until after *Arabic* was sunk (19 August), whereupon their ambassador convinced them that unrestricted submarine warfare would lead to war with the United States. Assurances were consequently given by the German Imperial Government (1 September) and no more incidents occurred for the rest of the year.

B. *Home Waters*

In the opening days of the war both sides feared an invasion, especially the Germans, whose Kiel Canal had only just been opened to dreadnoughts. Therefore, the High Seas Fleet clung to its bases and did not molest the B.E.F. crossing over to France. To provoke the former to action, the British under Beatty staged a raid on the Heligoland Bight, lured the Germans and sank four of their ships whereupon they countered with mine-laying and U-boats. Although the British had pioneered the use of submarines, their surface-ship commanders had but a hazy idea of their destructive potential. On 22 September the submarine *U-9* sank *Aboukir, Hogue* and *Cressy*. After an attempted submarine raid on Scapa Flow, the half-finished base in the Orkneys, the Grand Fleet was withdrawn to the west coast of Scotland. This left the High Seas Fleet free to raid the east coast of England in late 1914. At the same time the British broke the German naval wireless code.

Except for the slow tightening of the Anglo-French blockade and contraband rules, which now regulated the flow of goods to neutrals who were believed to be sending them on to the Central Powers, 1915 was a dull year at sea. The German counter-action —the unrestricted U-boat campaign—was withdrawn under diplomatic pressure. In February 1916, the Germans warned the United States that armed merchantmen would henceforth be treated as cruisers and a new sink-at-sight campaign was begun on 1 March. The sinking of *Sussex* on 24 March, however, caused another near-rupture with the United States. Woodrow Wilson got his way when the campaign was called off on 10 May.

C. *Jutland (30 May-1 June 1916)*

1. THE SITUATION

At the beginning of 1916, the Royal Navy had not fought a major engagement at sea since Trafalgar in 1805. Admiral Sir John Jellicoe, commander of the Grand Fleet, well aware of the nature of new weapons, but without experience in how to handle them, believed that any enemy attempt to turn away in action would be designed to draw him over a minefield or into a submarine trap. He was determined never to meet the Germans without superior force and never to risk that advantage.

After von Falkenhayn's appraisal of the grand strategic situation, which regarded the West as the primary enemy and hinted that the Navy was not doing its part in breaking the British blockade, the Kaiser sanctioned more offensive operations. Admiral von Scheer, placed in command of the High Seas Fleet, at once conceived a plan to entice part of the Grand Fleet into just the trap Jellicoe feared. Von Scheer's hope was to reduce the enemy to parity which might give him control of the North Sea in a fleet engagement. Jellicoe's objective was to use the ambush technique to bring on, as soon as possible, a decisive engagement and thus free British sea power.

2. THE BATTLE

Scheer started his campaign with a bombardment of Lowestoft on 16 April, hoping that public opinion would force Jellicoe to divide his force. He next planned to hit Sunderland and sent out U-boats as part of the trap, but he could not sail until early on 31 May. Already the Grand Fleet had been warned by Naval Intelligence and had sortied. In the afternoon Beatty's scouts spotted Vice-Admiral Franz Hipper's battlecruisers of the van. Accord-

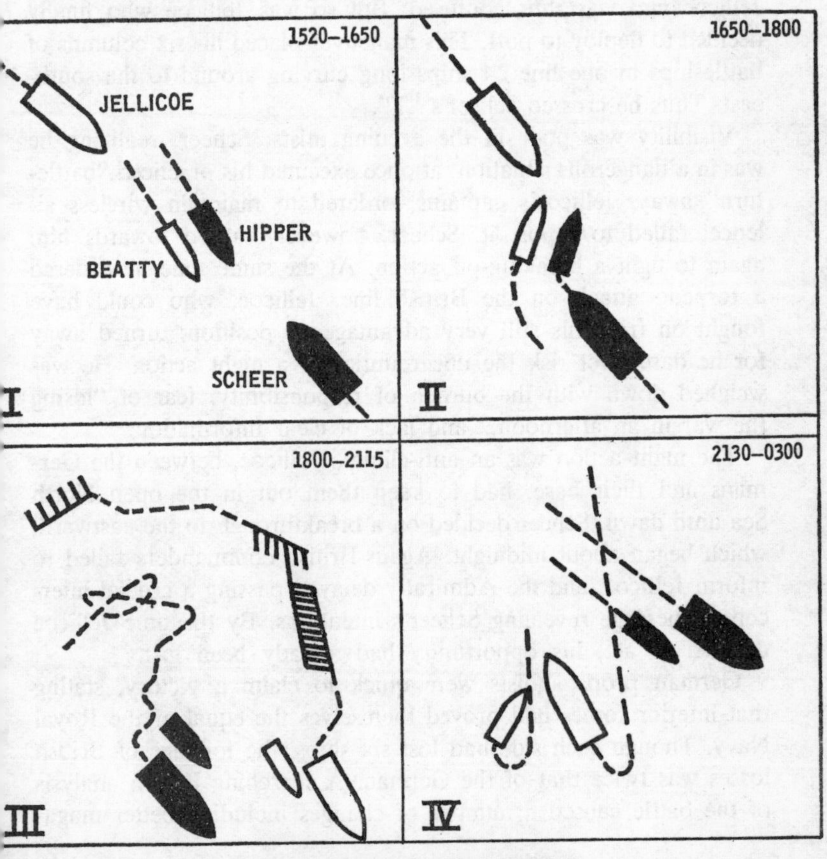

BATTLE OF JUTLAND

ing to plan, Hipper turned tail and lured Beatty south into the maw of the High Seas Fleet. In this running battle German optical range-finding, better shells, and tactical discipline compensated for Beatty's advantage in numbers; moreover Beatty failed to make use of the superior range of 15-inch guns in his four new battleships. He lost battlecruisers *Indefagitable* and *Queen Mary*.

Just when the odds against Hipper became dangerous, the High Seas Fleet came up. Caught unawares, Beatty turned north, doubly reversing the tables. Having been trapped himself, he was now leading von Scheer into a similar surprise. Jellicoe, however, was 53 miles northeast with Rear-Admiral L. H. A. Hood to his east. On sighting the Grand Fleet, Scheer mistook Hood for Jellicoe and was thus confused. But so was Jellicoe who finally decided to deploy to port. This maneuver placed his six columns of battleships in one line 24 ships long curving around to the southeast. Thus he crossed Scheer's "T".

Visibility was poor in the evening mists. Scheer, realizing he was in a dangerous situation, at once executed his practiced "battle-turn" away. Jellicoe's captains, ordered to maintain wireless silence, failed to report it. Scheer, however, turned towards him again to fight a breaking-off action. At the same time he ordered a torpedo attack on the British line. Jellicoe, who could have fought on from his still very advantageous position, turned away for he dared not risk the uncertainties of a night action. He was weighed down with the burden of responsibility, fear of "losing the war in an afternoon," and lack of clear information.

The night action was an anti-climax. Jellicoe, between the Germans and their base, had to keep them out in the open North Sea until dawn. Scheer decided on a breakthrough to the eastward, which began about midnight. Again British commanders failed to inform Jellicoe, and the Admiralty delayed passing a crucial intercepted message revealing Scheer's intentions. By the time Jellicoe decided to act, his opportunity had already been lost.

German propagandists were quick to claim a victory, stating that inferior forces had proved themselves the equal of the Royal Navy. Though each side had lost six ships, the tonnage of British losses was twice that of the German. A searching British analysis of the battle caused a number of changes including better magazines and handling procedures aboard ship, complete redesign of armor-piercing shells (not available to the fleet till 1918), eventual removal of Jellicoe to the Admiralty and elevation of Beatty to command the Grand Fleet.

Notwithstanding all this, the British could with justice claim a strategic victory. The High Seas Fleet thereafter remained at its bases, except for some raids on the English coast (19 August, 26-27 October 1916) and one abortive sortie late in the war. Nuisance raids were carried out again in 1917 and early 1918, but only two attacks on Scandinavian convoys (17 October and 12 December 1917) had serious repercussions, forcing Beatty to provide battleship escorts. During the remainder of the war the Grand Fleet, reinforced by six American battleships, carried out sweeps of the North Sea with increasing air cover, but with little success.

D. The Indirect Approach; U-boats versus Convoys

Increased submarine warfare in the latter part of 1916—begun at the insistence of a German Army increasingly pessimistic about winning the land war—proved effective in getting at British strength. When the Lloyd George government came to power at the end of 1916, Jellicoe was brought to the Admiralty to deal with a rapidly deteriorating situation. Despite significant reorganization of the Admiralty, he pressed for intensified hunting operations, although studies showed loss rates on cross-Channel coal convoys and on the Scandinavian run reduced from 25 per cent to almost nothing by the adoption of convoy. The High Command failed to recognize that the submerged submarine lacked both vision and speed and that merchantmen could be taught to sail in groups. Furthermore ports could be organized to receive them and economy be achieved in the use of escort vessels. The change was brought about through the intervention of U.S. Admiral William S. Sims and through Lloyd George's own use of Admiralty statistics. On 30 April 1917 the Admiralty agreed to try an experimental ocean convoy, although it regarded this as a purely defensive measure. Naval officers had yet to learn that the best offensive might be a good defensive organization—in which the principle of concentration of forces was observed.

On 4 May 1917 the first American destroyers began operating from the eastern Atlantic base of Queenstown, Ireland. Thereafter the loss of merchant shipping, which had reached 875,000 gross registered tons, declined from a high of 10.6 merchant-ship sinkings per U-boat in April to .2 in December. In July and August regular ocean convoys were instituted and in November these were extended to the Mediterranean. Losses there also fell sharply. But even though the British admiral provided adequate, including Japanese, escorts, U-boats still got under the nets stretched across the Straits of Otranto because the Italians failed to patrol them.

The U-boats then moved to the Channel and the Irish Sea where they still successfully employed guns and torpedoes against ships sailing independently. They inflicted losses twelve times as high as those of convoys (May 1917-November 1918). All this damage was inflicted in 1917 and 1918 by fewer than 50 submarines, as mounting repairs and falling production reduced the number of boats at sea.

The large British and American shipbuilding programs accelerated so rapidly that by the beginning of 1918 launchings exceeded sinkings and consequently the Germans had to start a new building program. Ironically it was just hitting its stride of 30 new boats a month when the war ended.

In addition to convoys, the Allies instituted intensive, coordinated air operations in which—after mid-1918—some 300 airplanes and airships took part daily. Though aircraft carried no lethal weapons, they exercised a deterrent effect upon submarines. Towards the end of 1917, a successful mine barrage was laid across the Straits of Dover and a field 230 by 15 to 25 miles and at depths down to 240 feet was sown from Scotland to Norway. Less than a quarter of the estimated number of mines for the North Sea Barrage were needed owing to the American development of the antenna mine. While more than 70,000 mines were laid, the field was too large to be patrolled—the secret of success of the Dover effort—and probably only one U-boat was lost in it. Possibly even more successful were British hunter submarines, which accounted for 19 enemy boats destroyed and had a greater effect upon morale. Another attempt to deal with the U-boat menace was the Zeebrugge raid led by Admiral Keyes (22-23 April 1918).

E. The End of the Naval War

The High Seas Fleet lay at its anchorages during most of 1918. Its best crews had gone to submarines and morale was low. Communist-inspired mutinies erupted just as the Allies broke through in the West and began to mop up the U-boat and destroyer bases. After the Armistice, the Fleet sailed for England and surrendered (21 November 1918). Moved to the Grand Fleet's old base at Scapa Flow, the High Seas Fleet scuttled itself on secret orders (21 June 1919). The submarines and some of the surface ships were distributed to the various Allies as war booty.

The Germans never won a decisive victory at sea, but their combination of the fleet-in-being, which hypnotized the British, and of the indirect approach through a submarine campaign against the sinews of British power along the sea lanes, very nearly proved successful. On both sides, the offensive gripped the admirals as firmly as it did the generals and it took younger, less inhibited men to apply new avenues, such as statistics, to show that a combination of methods and newer weapons could break the stalemate at sea. The war ended before the offensive-defensive pendulum swung back to the U-boat.

III. THE WAR IN THE AIR

A. The Origins of Air Forces

Although before the war France led in developing airpower, Germany and Britain employed it most effectively during the conflict. Both sides also used airships and captive balloons.

About 1910 the United States and the nations of Europe began seriously to consider the possibilities of military aviation. The French created an air battalion as did the Germans, who added anti-aircraft groups. Most armies had at least some airplanes in 1914. On the outbreak of war France, the leading air power, had 27 squadrons with 220 pilots. In the U.S., aeronautics was assigned to the Signal Corps, and relatively little was done until 1917, when an overly ambitious plan for mass-production of pilots and machines produced some flyers and almost no aircraft.

B. *Early Use of Airpower*

At first military airplanes were used only for reconnaissance. Since this was usually followed by artillery bombardments the infantry called for air cover as a protection not against bombs but against artillery spotting and later photo-intelligence. The first aerial combat took place on 5 October 1914, but by mid-July 1915 only eight enemy aircraft had been shot down by French pilots, all but one with carbines! The struggle for air superiority had begun; however, the French officially had created fighter units (*La chasse*) on 1 March. Others did likewise and a rapid turn over in aircraft designs ensued. The British put 40 different types into service during the war, the French 50, the Germans and the Italians 30 each, and the Americans 9 European models. For the greatest possible speed, climb, and maneuverability, single-seat fighters were introduced, but they did not become efficient until the Dutch Fokker was produced in April 1915. A successful synchronization mechanism enabled machine-guns to be fired through propeller arcs and the whole plane to be aimed as a weapon. The next step was the development of mass or formation tactics in early 1916.

The bulk of operations were dangerous from the moment of take-off. The flimsy, unreliable machines were devoted to reconnaissance, artillery spotting, and interdiction. In theaters other than France or Italy, the presence of even a few aircraft on one side—as at the Dardanelles—produced moral results far beyond their actual effectiveness. On the Western Front several squadrons were necessary to make an impression.

C. *Quest for Air Superiority*

The struggle for mastery in the air over the front began in October 1915. General Hugh Trenchard, who had succeeded to the command of the Royal Flying Corps in the field, was of the same offensive mind as Haig, whom he served as air adviser. The result was the British fought a long and bloody aerial war in which pilots sometimes went into action with only 18 hours total flying time. This indecisive operation produced rivalry at home between the RFC and the Royal Naval Air Service for aircraft and engines, and led to stockpiling, questions in Parliament, and the formation of the Royal Air Force. The French under Commandant Rose also developed a fighting force, but used it less continuously and more effectively to gain local domination.

Meanwhile air supremacy came into the Allied camp following the introduction of new aircraft developed from drawingboard to operational status in a matter of ten months. It stayed there from July through September 1916, when the Germans received their own new machines and perfected formation tactics. In 1917 the British and French once again re-equipped and regained the upper hand. By 1918 their tactical superiority was marked and aircraft were frequently used for strafing. At the same time a force of British bombers independent of the commanders in the field was established to undertake the bombing of munitions centers in Germany. Unfortunately, for political reasons, it was given to Trenchard, who used it largely in aid of Haig's offensives.

By war's end, the Royal Air Force which, under the Air Ministry (created 1 January 1918) included both the RFC and the RNAS (as of 1 April 1918), was the largest air force in the world. It comprised 300,000 officers and men and 30,000 aircraft, which it consumed at the rate of 66 per cent per month. The power of air forces on the Western Front increased greatly during 1917 and in 1918 it was possible for the American commander, Billy Mitchell, to place 1500 aircraft in operation over the Chateau Thierry battlefield, thus gaining tactical air superiority to the great benefit of the infantry. By the Armistice, Allied air forces had command of the air and Germany's *Amerika* aircraft building program had been bankrupted, despite failure of U.S. air matériel to appear in quantity. During the war the French produced 51,000 aircraft and 92,000 engines; the Germans 48,000 aircraft and 41,000 engines. The French aircraft industry alone absorbed 186,000 persons, 65 per cent of them women.

D. *Airships*

Both the British and the Germans experimented with airships. After a number of disasters, Count von Zeppelin in 1912 produced successful naval airships; the "Zeppelin" was developed not only for naval reconnaissance, but also for strategic bombing.* Raids on England began 19 January 1915, and nineteen followed during the year, producing negligible physical damage, but considerable impact upon the British government. Much effort was put into anti-Zeppelin measures, which also became entwined with anti-invasion defenses. The great raid of 2 September 1916, in which 14 airships were concentrated against London, was not followed by further success because the British by then had sirens, guns, searchlights and fighters which could intercept the Zeppelins. This caused the Germans to build "height-climbers" with an operational ceiling of 24,000 feet, but they also caused little damage.

E. *Strategic Air War*

1. BRITAIN

Before the end of the Zeppelin attacks, German airplanes began to bomb England (28 November 1916). A series of raids followed, the most important being the two daylight strikes of 13 June and 7 July 1917. These upset the War Cabinet and brought on the Smuts Report from which the Royal Air Force was born. Again, however, the damage was negligible, and the defense slowly mastered daylight and then night attacks. On the whole, the results were political, psychological, and doctrinal, the last primarily after the war.

British naval airmen also developed strategic bombing starting with raids against the Zeppelin bases (Dusseldorf on 22 September 1914, Cologne on 8 October, and Friedrichshafen on 21 November) and continuing with attacks from fields in northern France against U-boat docks and enemy cities. They pioneered night bombing and developed long-range Handley Page bombers. British analysis of the psychological impact of these operations, especially of the work of Sir Hugh Trenchard's "reprisal" Independent Air Force of 1918, was to have profound significance for the development of post-war bombing doctrine.

---

* The difference between *strategical* and *tactical* in the British Army was that anything involving the area to the rear of the enemy's tactical dispositions was strategic and came under Army headquarters. Later it came to mean something different; a source of much confusion.

At sea the development of air co-operation was frustrated at first by exaggerated claims of the airmen and the consequent disenchantment and disillusionment of the admirals. It was not until after the submarine menace developed in 1915 that the Royal Naval Air Service (founded in 1912) began to come into its own. Soon it had a regular system of coastal airship and airplane patrols and, as equipment improved, moved further afield. In 1917 its large flying-boats—based upon the designs of the American, Glenn Curtiss—hunted Zeppelins and submarines in the Heligoland Bight and compelled the Germans to take defensive action.

2. THE CONTINENT

The Germans were slow to develop strategic bombing by other than Zeppelins until late 1916. Then Gothas—large, long range bombers—came into favor and were dispatched against London and Paris. The results were physically insignificant, but on both sides air raids against civilians caused enough popular outcry to create Home Defense forces which absorbed manpower badly needed elsewhere. The French began some raiding beyond the front lines as early as 1914, but their fear of retaliation prevented development of a large force. The Italians kept up a desultory offensive across the Adriatic on Austrian U-boat bases at Pola and Cattaro and on 9 August 1918 they even bombed Vienna.

The Russians developed large, long-range, multi-engine aircraft, but employed them only in sporadic raids due to lack of suitable targets, production difficulties and the coming of the Revolution just as bombers matured. The Russians and Germans had naval and military air forces. The German was employed in protecting naval operations in the Heligoland Bight and the Baltic against both surface and air forces. This was largely unheroic, routine work with a good chance of a wet death. The Russians, including Alexandre P. de Seversky—later a vigorous American prophet of air power—operated in the Baltic, a theater the German Navy dominated.

The French air arm was not divided into land and sea wings as was the British; the bulk of it was in reconnaissance rather than fighter squadrons. During the war, however, the naval side of the French Air Force grew from the 14 seaplanes of August 1914 to 1264 manned by over 11,000 men in 1918.

IV. AIR THEORY

The war naturally made airmen consider their role in modern warfare and thus generated air doctrine. Though Trenchard's unrelenting offensive was very similar to that of Haig, others had a wider vision. Sir Frederick Sykes, commander of the RAF in 1918, built on the work of the engineer F. W. Lanchester and predicted annihilating air blows. Mitchell, learning from Trenchard, the French, and perhaps from Douhet, was more astute and immediately practical. He conceived the use of aircraft to leap over the stagnant front lines and thus with firepower and manpower to disrupt the enemy's rear. In general his ideas were tactical, while wanting an independent air force. In Italy, Guilio Douhet developed his own ideas of devastating, decisive air blows as another means of countering the futility of ineffective frontal infantry attacks against entrenched machine guns. His work had little circulation until the late thirties when it was applied in the Spanish Civil War; about that time he began to receive undeserved fame as the founder of air power theory. The airmen had had enough combat experience upon which to build their doctrine for war's new third dimension.

Air actions in World War I were much overrated and their impact primarily psychological, though in peripheral theaters their direct military effect was considerable. The chief importance of the aerial fighting in the West was its political, psychological, and doctrinal influence on the post-war development of air forces and the older arms.

CHAPTER XXVI

The First World War: The Road to Victory

I. AMERICA ENTERS THE WAR

A. Introduction

WHEN THE WAR broke out in 1914, the American people were divided in their loyalties. Many recent immigrants and important older Middle Western groups had come from the Central Powers, and the Irish minority was of course anti-British. Both belligerent alliances conducted heavy propaganda campaigns. Wilson proclaimed neutrality, protested against the German war zone about the British Isles (15 February 1915), warned Berlin after the sinking of the *Lusitania* (7 May), and forced the Kaiser to restrict submarine warfare after the *Sussex* incident (24 March 1916). Meanwhile the Allies were purchasing large stocks of war matériel in the United States on a cash-and-carry basis.

B. Early Preparations

By 1916 Americans—made tense by German efforts in Mexico and sabotage and propaganda in the United States—were ready to accept a program of national defense. Secretary Daniels muzzled the Navy, but a campaign for armament was run semi-officially and gained momentum under the leadership of General Leonard Wood, Secretary of War Garrison, and Theodore Roosevelt. The road to preparedness was by no means easy. While the admirals had plans for an expanded Navy, the generals had difficulty thinking in mass terms where the Army was concerned. Both Daniels and Garrison urged their staffs to widen their vision. The result was the defense program of December 1915, which aimed only at stopping a German invasion of America and in which the National Guard was written off. The latter at once forced revisions. The War Department began to think instead of an army of intervention in Europe. In June 1916 Congress passed the National Defense Act which authorized a 175,000-man regular army, a new, federally-controlled National Guard of 475,000, a Reserve, and a Volunteer Army. Simultaneously the Navy was given authorization for a "navy second to none" (29 August 1916). Both build-ups were planned to take ten years. At the same time the Merchant Marine Act strengthened logistical support. Meanwhile, Pancho Villa's raid from revolution-torn Mexico had caused the mobilization of the Army—an invaluable pre-war test—in which the new federal National Guard was included (18 June 1916) as military action in Mexico loomed. The United States found itself with a mass Continental-style army, supported after April 1917 by conscription of men and industry.

Upon his re-election, Wilson sought to bring about settlement of the war. Germany, however, renewed unrestricted submarine warfare (31 January 1917) in a calculated gamble for victory; the Zimmerman note which had been intercepted by British Naval Intelligence had been made public; and the Anglophiles had their way when Congress declared war on Germany, 6 April. The United States, however, never formally became one of the Allies.

C. *American Preparations, 1917-1918*

The major American contribution to the Allies had been munitions. Vast shipbuilding, gun-making, and aircraft production programs were accelerated. Time was at a premium if the Germans—aided by the weakening of Russia as the result of the Revolution—were not to win by starving the British and toppling the French. Selective Service passed, destroyers were sent overseas as escorts, an American Expeditionary Force (the AEF) was trained, railroads were operated by the Government, and farmers were urged to produce more food. Unfortunately, neither the War nor Navy Departments were prepared for intervention and plans had to be hastily made. Since the General Staff had never been asked to draw up plans, it had not taken the initiative in doing so. Now this was largely handled by General John J. Pershing at his headquarters in France, much to the annoyance of the Chief of Staff in Washington, Peyton C. March. Pershing complained so effectively about the failure of the bureau chiefs when supplies failed to arrive, that in mid-1918 the supply service was placed directly under the General Staff. Meanwhile Pershing refused to allow American units to be used piecemeal to strengthen the Allied line. Backed by President Wilson, he held out instead for a million-man American Army, ready for action by 1 June 1918. Though opposed by the Allies who held back shipping, he achieved his end. As the military situation deteriorated, they realized that only with large-scale U.S. participation could they gain the offensive superiority necessary to impose their will on Germany.

II. THE END OF THE WAR, 1918

A. Background

The year 1918 opened gloomily for the Allies, but encouragingly for the Germans. Wilson imitated Lloyd George with his peace aims known as the 14 points. This was intended to counter the German success in reducing Russia to a non-belligerent. The Russian state disintegrated upon the independence of the Ukraine and peace was signed at Brest-Litovsk in March. The Germans, who had achieved their full war aims in the East, had now either to make peace or proceed to total victory. They decided on the latter. The blockade was strangling the Central Powers and the Allies were constantly being strengthened by matériel from America, though not yet by men. But, as Fuller points out, the Germans made one fatal mistake when they concentrated in the West their 70 divisions—freed from the Russian front: instead of attacking the war-weary French, they struck at the stubborn British. Their failure to break the British line cost them the war.

B. *The German Offensives*

Haig was planning a new attack, but the Germans beat him and launched theirs on 21 March. Through the fog and gas shells the infantry advanced in the new combat-team formations developed by the German Osker von Hutier and battle-tested at Riga and Caporetto. Armed with automatic weapons, light artillery, and using the tactical surprise of a short bombardment, these forces sustained the momentum of the forward penetration by leap-frogging and by-passing strongpoints and leaving them to wither on the vine. (Hutier tactics, coupled to tactical air, mechanized, and motorized forces as theorized by Fuller, Liddell Hart, and Guderian, later became the basis of the World War II *blitzkrieg.*) A dangerous salient was pushed forward through the weakly-held southern flank of the British front and there was a chance that the Germans would succeed in rolling the British back into the Channel. They advanced some 40 miles before their logistical support broke down and ground became impassable to their reserve divisions.

The first German thrust led the Allies to take the long-resisted but logical step of supplementing the newly-formed (27 November 1917) Supreme War Council in Paris with a Generalissimo, who would control all available reserves. Foch was first appointed to coordinate operations on the Western Front (26 March). After the second German offensive at Lys (9-29 April) began, he was named Commander-in-Chief (14 April).

Like the attack towards Amiens, that on the Lys resulted only in another salient. The Germans then turned on the French and advanced once more to the Marne in the Third Battle of the Aisne (27 May-6 June). Here Ludendorff was foiled by the first use of the newly-arrived American troops. Once again Ludendorff achieved a 40-mile advance which so surprised him that he gave up his idea of defeating the British in Flanders and prepared to turn all his forces against the French. By this strategy, he expected to distract the British reserves which, he hoped, would be moved to protect Paris.

The Battle of the Matz (Noyon-Montidier) (9-14 June) was hastily prepared and there was no tactical surprise as in the previous three drives; the French containing tactics succeeded and the Germans gained little ground. The first significant American contribution came in the defensive battle at Chateau-Thierry on 4 June. The fifth and last German attack opened on 15 July and attempted to penetrate around both sides of Rheims. The battle-weary German troops now facing much reinvigorated Allied forces made no progress and, after three days, Foch ordered the decisive counter-stroke.

C. The Allied March to Victory in the West

Foch's attack threw Ludendorff off balance and drove him back to the line Rheims-Soissons. He was unable to penetrate the new French system of strongpoints in depth, reinforced by artillery. Ludendorff could not make up for the million casualties he had suffered, but the Allies could replace theirs from a fresh manpower pool: the new American divisions. These large units of 28,000 men each were the equivalent to a French corps. This manpower reserve was the deciding factor in the war.

Foch had retained careful control of the newly-created central Allied reserve and from 18 July-6 August he launched it in the Aisne-Marne offensive by which the German salient between Soissons and Rheims was eliminated to improve communications laterally along the front. The line restabilized along the Vesle and the Allies gained moral ascendancy.

On 8 August, Haig opened the Battle of Amiens with 450 tanks. (General Fuller claims it led not only to the collapse of the German armies, but also to a revolution in warfare.) The Germans surrendered in large numbers and the front moved back to the Hindenburg Line (3 September) from whence it had started in March. The American First Army then proved in the reduction of the Saint Mihiel salient that it could be effectively used in the field under its own commanders, as Pershing had always insisted.

Foch thereupon determined to initiate a major offensive which would seize the two main railway centers, Mauberge and Sedan, through which the Germans would have to withdraw on their way back to Germany. If these centers were taken, retreat might become a rout. With this objective in view, he opened the Meuse-

Argonne attack (26 September-11 November). The American First and Second Armies slogged forward and cut the Metz-Mezieres railway, while in the North the British plodded east to Lille and Cambrai. But both ends of the line advanced slower than anticipated.

In the meantime, internal collapse of the Central Powers was steadily weakening the position of Germany. Ludendorff called for an Armistice on 27 September and the Government proposed the formation of a democratic ministry to throw the blame for defeat onto the political Left. Negotiations for peace were opened with President Wilson. Ludendorff's resignation was accepted on 27 October, after he had decided to fight on. During October the British had advanced along the coast to Bruges and the Americans to the east reached Sedan on 10 November. The Kaiser, advised of his army's possible disloyalty, fled to Holland (10 November).

The Armistice was signed in Foch's railway car early on 11 November. The agreement forestalled any ideas the enemy commanders might have had of renewing the struggles after a truce which amounted to surrender. The Germans had to evacuate all territories west of the Rhine as well as Rumania, Austria-Hungary, Turkey, and Russia, to surrender 5,000 each of trucks and locomotives, 15,000 freight cars, 160 U-boats and the High Seas Fleet. The Allied occupation of Germany began on 1 December.

The war was over, but fighting did not stop until 1922.

D. The Other Theatres

1. ITALY

On the Italian front Diaz opened a new offensive across the Piave in June 1918, but was driven back with the loss of 100,000 men. Morale in the Italian Army slid again. On 24 October, Diaz tried another offensive at Vittorio Veneto. With the disintegration of the Austro-Hungarian Empire already in progress, victory was at last assured. The Italians entered Trieste (3 November) and Fiume (the 5th).

2. THE EAST

On 3 March 1918 the Bolsheviks signed the Treaty of Brest-Litovsk abandoning Poland, Lithuania, the Ukraine, the Baltic provinces, Finland, and Transcaucasia. The Germans and Austrians at once sent troops to clear Bolsheviks out of the great Ukrainian granary and took Sevastopol (1 May). Six days later civil war in Finland was ended by German troops. Rumania was driven out of the war in a brief campaign at the end of 1917 and signed the Peace of Bucharest (7 May 1918).

Bulgaria, on the other hand, was defeated by the reorganized Allied armies under Franchet d'Esperey, which pushed north from Salonika on a broad front from Albania to the river Struma. The Bulgarians had sent out peace feelers in June, but the final impetus came from the Serbian success in the battles of Monastir-Doiran (15-24 September 1918). Once the Bulgarians had signed the truce at Salonika, the Allies crossed the Danube (10 November) and moved into Thrace with the object of opening the Straits. They liberated Rumania on 8 November and the Rumanians re-entered the war. In the meantime the Italians advanced up the Adriatic coast, reaching Antivari on 4 November, while the Serbians had taken Belgrade, their own capital, three days earlier.

3. THE MIDDLE EAST

In the latter half of 1917 General Sir Edmund Allenby took over the British command north of the Suez Canal. He advanced in October and in the Third Battle of Gaza succeeded in breaking the Turkish line, a feat Murray had been unable to accomplish by frontal assault in the First and Second battles (March-April 1917). On 8 December, Allenby entered Jerusalem. Further action was delayed by the needs of the Western Front after the German break-through in March 1918, but on 18 September 1918 Allenby attacked at Megiddo with fresh reinforcements. The battle was a masterpiece. Whereas at Third Gaza he had feinted to the left and had then rolled back the Turkish right, at Megiddo he did the opposite. After effective deceptive measures and with complete air superiority, he drove along the coast using armored cars and cavalry to strike through the vital passes and cut the Turkish railway lines. Air power helped make the defeat a rout. By the end of October, Allenby, aided by T. E. Lawrence's Arab irregulars, had rolled 300 miles up the coast to Aleppo. The Turks agreed to the Mudros

Armistice on 30 October. On 12 November the Allied fleet sailed up the Dardanelles and occupied Constantinople, the capital of the Ottoman Empire.

III. THE PEACE

A. Versailles

The Allies officially began the settlement of the war on 18 January 1919. The Germans were excluded until the draft treaty was ready (7 May). The French insisted as a matter of national security on the cession of the left (West) bank of the Rhine. The British, Americans, and Italians refused, but agreed to French control of the Saar coal basin. France accepted an Anglo-American treaty providing for assistance in case of German attack, but this never became effective as it was not ratified by the United States. France, however, felt insecure until the Locarno Treaty of 1926.

The Germans signed the Treaty of Versailles on 28 June after seriously considering the resumption of hostilities. Their army was limited to 100,000 men with no large guns, tanks or aircraft, with the period of service to be twelve years for men and twenty-five for officers, in order to prevent the Germans using their post-Tilsit technique of passing a continuous stream of men through the Army to create a formidable reserve. The Great General Staff was forbidden. The Navy was limited to six cruisers, a few old battleships and a corresponding number of other ships; submarines were forbidden and Heligoland was to be defortified. The Allies were to occupy the Rhineland for 15 years and a zone 30 miles wide on the right (east) bank of the Rhine was to be demilitarized. In addition to other economic penalties Germany was to bear the cost of the armies of occupation. These conditions made virtually inevitable a revival of German nationalism and the ultimate restoration to power of the military.

B. Other Treaties

The loose ends of the war were tied up by a series of pacts, generally limiting the armed forces of the defeated. The Austrians agreed to the Treaty of St. Germain (10 September 1919); the

Bulgarians signed at Neuilly (27 November). Meanwhile the settlement with newly-independent Hungary was delayed because of invasions by her greedy neighbors, who were finally persuaded to withdraw in December 1919. Hungary, now one-fourth its former area and with barely 30 per cent of its old population, accepted peace at the Trianon (4 June 1920).

C. *Turkey*

The Turkish settlement was complicated by the fall of the Czarist regime in Russia and by the disavowal of interest by the Bolsheviks who published the secret treaties, by the rise of Kemal Ataturk's effective nationalist movement and by the disinterest of the United States in the Straits and in Armenian questions. The Italians attempted to carve out their area in Anatolia (29 April 1919). On 15 May 1919 the Greeks with Allied support landed at Smyrna and pushed inland. The Allies occupied Constantinople (16 March 1920). The Sultan signed the Treaty of Sèvres (20 August 1920) demilitarizing the Straits and renouncing all claims to non-ethnic Turkish territory, but the nationalists refused to accept it. Mustapha Kemal persuaded the Italians to withdraw and made a separate peace with Soviet Russia. The Greeks began an offensive (23 March 1921) but failed to reach Ankara due to stubborn Turkish defense at Sakkaria (24 August-16 September). The Allies then attempted to extricate themselves by arranging a settlement between Greece and Turkey. The Turks counter-attacked (18 August 1922) and drove the Greeks into the sea at Smyrna (9-11 September). Britain landed a small force at Chanak, but was forced to negotiate the Mudania Convention and evacuate. The Straits were finally neutralized under international control and the Turks accepted the Treaty of Lausanne (24 July 1923).

IV. THE RUSSIAN CIVIL WAR AND ALLIED INTERVENTION

A. *Intervention in Europe*

Even while the Peace Conference was in progress at Paris, some twenty-two minor wars continued. The British had landed at

Murmansk (23 June 1918) as a counter to what the Allies regarded as the German-Red Russian movement. In August, Archangel was taken with French aid and a puppet White Russian government supported, but this project was later abandoned (12 October 1919). In the Baltic the Allies made various attempts to sort out the local, Russian, and German forces and to counter Bolshevik use of the Russian fleet. The Allies also patrolled the Black Sea and gave support to the White Russian armies.

B. *The Russian Civil War, 1918-1920*

During the great civil war the volunteer Bolshevik Red Army was gradually forged under Trotsky into a regular, conscripted, disciplined fighting force. With the physical advantage of interior lines and the moral of fighting to defend the homeland, the Red Army gradually destroyed its divided opponents, White Russian and Allied. The Ukraine was taken by the Reds (April 1919), was recaptured by the Whites under Denikin in August, but was lost again to the Reds in December, only to be invaded by the Poles in May 1920. The Poles were driven out at the end of the year.

In the meantime, the Whites under Yudenich had advanced on Petrograd in October 1919 but were beaten off. The capital was moved inland to Moscow, a safer and more central location. In the Caucasus, rich in oil, the Whites under Wrangel and Denikin repulsed a Red attempt to recover the territory after the Germans and Austrians withdrew (January 1919). Denikin then swept rapidly north in an offensive and retired equally swiftly (April 1919). He then struck at Odessa (18 August) and took Kiev (2 September), but was forced back by December. When the Bolsheviks took his last base, Denikin turned over his command to Wrangel (27 March 1920), who was forced into the Crimea from whence he was evacuated to Constantinople in November.

C. *Japanese Intervention*

The campaign based upon Vladivostok started with Japanese occupation (30 December 1917-25 October 1922) and with Soviet battles against departing Czech legions eastbound around the world to the Western Front (June 1918). The Czechs advanced westward to Ekaterinburg (26 July) and joined up with Admiral Kolchak leading the White Russians from Omsk. His success was limited and the Bolsheviks were by early 1919 in control of all eastern Russia except the area about Vladivostok in which American troops remained until the spring of 1920 and the Japanese until October 1922.

D. The Russo-Polish War

Hardly was the civil war over when the Poles attacked (25 April 1920) and overran the Ukraine. But their victory was short-lived and the Russians drove to the gates of Warsaw by 14 August. With the help of the French General Weygand, the Poles forced the Russians out of Central Europe for the next two decades—a result confirmed by the Treaty of Riga (18 March 1921). All these wars, Allied blockade, and internal troubles led to a collapse of the Russian economy in 1921.

V. CONCLUSIONS

World War I marked a turning point in Western history. Neither side had thought out the implications of a long war with the result that all were unprepared to handle a stalemate, not to mention the traumatic effects produced in European societies. The clash of industrial societies in which mass-production flooded the battlefield with matériel quickly demonstrated that the leadership of the day, trained in the nineteenth century, was inadequate. With few exceptions, it was unable to cope with mass armies supplied with machine-guns and artillery with unlimited ammunition. The war at sea and that in the air showed the same results.

On the one hand there was trench-warfare which made the defense in depth snug behind sandbags and barbed-wire, and machine guns secure against the standard frontal assault. On the other hand, at sea the refusal to adopt a defensive organization for merchant shipping as opposed to one for the Grand Fleet, nearly cost Britain the war. Gradually the reaction to the slaughter on land and sea resulted in new techniques—on land the Hutier tactics of the Germans, the tank of the British, the deception of Allenby; at sea the German U-boats and the British convoys. In the air individual combats gave way to formation tactics and bombing raids extended from purely tactical close support to strategic and grand strategic operations against enemy political and economic capitals. The war ended before any great changes had taken place in tactics. The year 1919 with its proposed armored and airborne campaigns would have been much more interesting militarily than the four previous years.

CHAPTER XXVII

The Interwar Years

I. INTRODUCTION

PEACE BROUGHT A large reduction in the armed forces of all the belligerents. Demobilization of men and materials—except in France—was generally aimed at returning to either 1914 standards or to 1919 treaty limitations. For the major powers an unaccustomed lack of enemies made long-range military planning difficult, especially in England where the Services were told in August 1919 that there would be no major war for ten years and in America where isolationism flourished. Despite inflation and the high costs of new equipment—or perhaps partially because of these things—budgets were returned to prewar levels and remained inadequate until after Hitler assumed power. In order to secure minimal essential funds, the military had to engage in politics; the depth of this involvement depending on the national character.

The period 1918-1939 witnessed a number of minor conflicts and peace-keeping actions which, after the Japanese invasion of Manchuria in 1931, grew larger and led directly to World War II. When the Geneva Disarmament Conference (1932-1934) collapsed, most nations began to rearm. The revival of the armed forces coincided with technological changes which produced internal difficulties. The 'thirties also saw important changes in the higher commands in Britain and the United States and bloody purges in those of Germany and Russia.

A. Land Forces

The interwar armies adjusted to peace according to their luck in the Great War. Those who had done badly made some reforms to avoid the earlier mistakes. The Germans and the Russians, therefore, mechanized. The victors, on the other hand, either sought safety in Maginot Lines (originally designed as offensive shields) or closed their eyes to reality and returned to pre-1914 colonial-type forces. Until the beginning of World War II, the cavalry fought a rear guard action against mechanization within each army. In terms of matériel, the vanquished bettered the victors in inventing and perfecting new automatic firearms for the infantry and in improving artillery, tanks, anti-aircraft guns and tactical aircraft. Tremendous Allied military inventories perhaps served to discourage technological advances.

B. *Sea Forces*

After the war the principal navies were the American, British, Japanese, French, and Italian. The attitude which each adopted towards new weapons was conditioned by its traditional position and potential enemies. The United States developed the carrier, as did Japan and Britain, but French and Italian naval power was conditioned by rivalry in the Mediterranean. The smaller navies viewed the submarine as the best defense against a superior opponent, whereas the British, who well knew what it could do to their lifelines, wanted it banned. The future roles of the battleship, aircraft, and submarine were also obscured by future technological uncertainties. Many of these confusions were reflected in the various naval conferences seeking to establish parities: Washington (1921-1922), Geneva (1927), and London (1930 and 1935). The battleship-building moratorium inaugurated at Washington in 1922 ended in 1936 and the powers at once began to build capital ships. In the meantime, the Germans concentrating upon getting the most out of their treaty-limitation ships, developed the pocket-battleship.

C. *Air Forces*

In the interwar years, as air forces sought to achieve an independent role, airmen demonstrated the potential military value of their machines in spectacular ways, such as long-distance hops, endurance flights, and ever rising speed records. Technological developments were slow until the early 'thirties, but in the last few years before World War II they accelerated rapidly. Yet the concept of deterrence, or the preservation of peace by the threat of a powerful counter-strike, did not begin to be practical until after 1935.

D. *Theorists*

Interestingly, it was in victorious Britain, where the revulsion was strongest against the apparently incompetent way in which the war on the western Front had been fought that a major fountainhead of theory appeared. Though Admiral Sir Herbert Richmond, Major-General J. F. C. Fuller and Captain B. H. Liddell Hart had little influence in their own country, they were widely read abroad. Only within the Royal Air Force were the military intellectuals a power. Elsewhere, apart from the Italian Guilio Douhet, General Billy Mitchell in the United States propagandized airpower and fought the Navy; Colonel Charles de Gaulle supported armored forces in France; and the Germans tried out their ideas in Russia and Spain.

II. NATIONAL ARMED FORCES

A. *The United States*

The government had sought ways to expand the armed forces rapidly so that mobilization could take place before America entered World War I. This led in 1916 to the Naval and National Defense Acts. The wartime emergency legislation moved rapidly ahead from the modest beginnings. In 1919, with Wilson's eyes on the League of Nations, a formula for a peacetime establishment once again had to be found.

1. LAND

The army recognized the value of the machine-gun, but did not fully appreciate the truck, tank, or airplane. Basically the new National Defense Act of 1920 reverted to the mobilization plans of 1917. It envisioned an infantry army, but failed to provide a selective service system by which the necessary manpower could be raised. Instead, the Army became a 288,000-man cadre of regulars augmentable in wartime by federalizing a large National Guard and calling up an Organized Reserve. College ROTC's continued to prepare officers. Even these provisions of 1920 were emasculated by isolationism which ultimately cut the Regular Army to 119,000, hardly more than a token force.

2. SEA

Characteristically, the Navy in 1919 myopically revived the 1916 program to continue as though the war had not eliminated most potential enemies and technologically rendered obsolete many of the ships under construction. The Harding administration revived the 1916 Act's disarmament clause and called the Washington Naval Conference. By a combination of ratios and political treaties, the need for a two-ocean navy was obviated, a vast global scrapping program undertaken, and the U.S. Navy whittled down to a new peacetime size. Deprived of battleships—made suspect by Mitchell's experimental bombing of the *Ostfriesland* in 1921—the Navy concentrated under Rear-Admiral William A. Moffett on carriers and airships and formulated the doctrines which would lead its carrier task forces to victory in the Pacific in World War II. It also developed long-range submarines, and after 1935 returned to battleship building in search of a more balanced, modern fleet.

Amphibious warfare, in the meantime, was being developed by the U.S. Marine Corps which in 1933 established the Fleet Marine Force at Quantico, Virginia, and began to study the lessons of Gallipoli. Refueling at sea from oilers gave the Navy greater supporting mobility.

3. AIR

After World War I the Army's Air Service—though long controlled by earth-bound generals—was ably championed by its wartime hero, General William Mitchell. He was, however, ahead of his times both politically and technically. He furthered the aims of the airmen, but so antagonized both the Navy and his own high command by going directly to the people and Congress with a propaganda campaign that he was court-martialed and left the service in 1925. Whether an independent air force could either save the country from invasion or win a war by itself was at the time technologically beyond proof. Committee after committee investigated the airmen's claims until the Dwight Morrow Board's recommendations led to the 1926 Act creating the Army Air Corps. For the rest of the interwar years the Air Corps, and after 1935 the GHQAF (a tactical unit of the Army) dedicated themselves to developing the doctrine of strategic bombardment and a vehicle capable of carrying it out. The prototype B-17 of 1935 at last afforded the air theorists an instrument to prove their assertions.

B. *Britain*

The immediate British reaction to peacetime was to reduce the two older Services to 1914 budgetary levels and to attempt to abolish the independent air force. Although neither the Army nor the Navy had a clearly defined role, the R.A.F. was saved by propaganda and events.

1. LAND

The British Army, tied as always to the army in India and the needs of the Northwest Frontier, fought mechanization. Despite the presence of Fuller and Liddell Hart and the publication in 1929 of a field manual, the growth of armored forces was extremely slow. The result was that although British tanks were technically superior to German in 1940, the bulk of them were still tactically and doctrinally bound to the entrenched infantry, whereas the Germans worked with motorized forces.

2. SEA

The Royal Navy was slowly reduced by economy-minded politicians and disarmament treaties. The number of cruisers dropped from "an absolute minimum" of 70 to 44. Little effort was devoted to submarines, aircraft carriers, or, most important of all, to anti-submarine warfare. Only in 1938 was work at last begun in earnest on the equipment needed to protect the island's vital maritime commercial lifelines. The blame fell largely upon the dominating influence of reactionary gunnery officers. They disregarded the new dimensions in naval warfare, created by aircraft and submarines—ironically weapons which the Navy itself had pioneered—and reposed confidence in the methods of Tsushima Straits, already made suspect by Jutland.

3. AIR

The Royal Air Force demonstrated that by using air control techniques it could police primitive tribal areas far more cheaply than could the army, and that home defense could be handled effectively by neither of the older Services. Trenchard, Chief of the Air Staff, decreed that the best defense was a good offense and brought the counter-strike deterrent force into theoretical being, although it always lacked equipment. The air force remained until 1936 a mixture of bomber-deterrent and frontier police force; then it was reorganized to deal with a probable European war. Its inability potentially to deter Germany was only discovered at the time of Munich (September 1938). Fortunately by then an emphasis on home defense had already taken place; the stress on fighters rather than bombers just saving Britain in 1940.

C. *France*

Fear of a revived Germany dominated Paris after her allies failed to approve the Anglo-American Guarantee Treaty of 1919, which would have secured France against Germany. Therefore, all through the 'twenties she maintained the most powerful army and air force in Europe and, with her Little Entente allies (Poland, Czechoslovakia, and Yugoslavia), attempted to form a *Cordon Sanitaire* around Germany. The danger of moral collapse, an ever present legacy of 1917, and belief in superiority of the defense led at the end of the 'twenties to construction of the Maginot Line, a supposedly impregnable and more comfortable way to fight another 1916-style trench war. Increasingly, the army became involved in politics on the Right, with disastrous results as the people pacifistically moved to the Left. The air force also suffered, especially because Leftists, in power in 1936, nationalized the aircraft factories. By 1939 the industry was impotent. Despite efforts of a small band (whose spokesman was Charles de Gaulle) which called for a strong, mechanized, professional army (*L'armée de métier*), the military forces were in a deplorable state by 1940.

The Navy, meanwhile, favored the submarine and focused planning largely upon the Italian fleet. Only late in the interwar years did it begin to consider aircraft-carriers and to revive battleships.

D. *Italy*

The advent of Mussolini's Fascist government in 1922 revived the waning prestige of the armed forces which had declined in World War I. The Army was modernized and lightly mechanized with its role largely defined as colonial operations and defense of the Alpine passes. The Navy also was updated and re-equipped with some extremely fast vessels. Experiments were conducted with motor-torpedo boats and underwater warfare. The Air Force achieved full independence; the writings of Douhet became its official doctrine. Long distance flights were a specialty. Italian forces were exercised in the Ethiopian campaign of 1935-1936 and again as "volunteers" alongside the Germans supporting Franco in Spain from 1936 to 1939. But as World War II began, the Italian armed services were in decline, because they had neither the modern matériel, the economic basis, nor the morale for the war they were to fight.

E. *Japan*

The interwar years saw a continual struggle within Japan between the "positive policy" of General Giichi Tanaka and the civilians seeking to widen democratic participation in government. Tanaka retired in 1929, but his policies continued in the invasion of Manchuria which was designed by the Army as a means of seizing power at home. The active participation of the military in politics as autonomous cabinet members added another dimension to Army and Navy rivalry.

1. LAND

The Army, still dominated by the feudal *samurai* tradition, continued to develop along German lines. It had seen little action in World War I. In the interwar years it concentrated on mechanization as much as upon mobility and operations in jungles and other awkward territory. From 1931 it fought in China, where it grew into a tough, efficient force. During the 'thirties the army air force made rapid progress and developed some very efficient aircraft, but as these were rarely faced by a first-class opponent, technical developments were neglected. The best aircraft were swift, maneuverable firing platforms, but they lacked armor and were cheaply constructed.

2. SEA AND AIR

The Navy was not neglected and under early British instruction made great strides in carrier operations, so that Japan entered World War II with the best shipboard aircraft of the day. Moreover, by 1941 her cruisers and destroyers were excellent and her torpedoes were highly potent weapons.

The Japanese created no strategic bomber force, largely because they did not realize the need for it. Their growing suspicions of the United States; Anglo-American reluctance—due partly to practical limitations on naval operations—to act over Manchuria; and United States softness over the sinking of the gunboat *Panay* (12 December 1937), all encouraged plans for a Greater East Asia Co-Prosperity Sphere—an expansion plan implemented with military backing.

F. Russia

Badly demoralized by the 1917 failure of Czarist leadership, Russian forces, eager to re-establish themselves, proved their new mettle in the Polish wars. The Soviets, as with totalitarian movements elsewhere, made mechanization the symbol of the Revolution. With German help, British thought, and American ingenuity, the Russian Army was rebuilt by World War II into a mobile force equipped with infantry-carrying tanks built to operate over the soft, flat Russian countryside. Cossack cavalry, however, continued to play its part up to 1945.

The 1920 Polish War, though it made the Red Army a national one, also showed that it could not rely upon "liberated" peoples for its supplies. A supply corps had, therefore, to be established. Marshal Tukhachevsky was compelled constantly to employ various units to suppress mutinies and rebellions; a hasty demobilization to rid the Army of trouble-makers only transferred the problem to civil authorities. By 1925, however, discharges had been harmonized with conscription.

At the same time Trotsky worked out a compromise between the desires of the ex-Czarist officers and of the Communist Party. Both a military and a political general staff were created which hampered the Army at all levels until 1944. The Army was also hindered by the supicion with which the Party viewed its older officers; after Stalin disposed of Trotsky, a series of purges were made possible by the increasing numbers of party-oriented officers turned out by Bolshevik Marshal Frunze's military educational system.

The new Red Army consisted of 41 divisions for frontier duties, with a 46-division territorial militia. Frunze, who succeeded Trotsky, encouraged mechanization, standardized formations, conscription, and tightened discipline. Upon Frunze's death, Stalin appointed Marshal Voroshilov Commissar for the Red Army and Navy, a post he held until 1940. Since he had the advantage of no retarding, inherited traditions, Voroshilov was able to make the Army in some respects more modern than most in the West.

In the meantime the air force was reborn. Some 300 Fokkers were purchased in 1922 and agreements made for training by imported Germans. By 1925, both the military and industrial base for a large modern air force had been created. Into this air transport was integrated. In 1926 under Tukhachevsky, then Chief of Staff, the Germans were invited to help mechanize the ground forces. Their advice was also sought to rehabilitate the Navy, which had been left to itself after the 1917 and 1921 mutinies.

By 1928 all components of the Red military were ready for expansion and mechanization. Stalin was prepared and, in part, he industrialized for this purpose. But no strategic air force was created and although the Navy was modernized in cruisers and submarines, it never achieved the status or power of the Army.

Increasingly after Hitler came to power emphasis was placed upon keeping the Germans out of the Ukrainian breadbasket and the Third Five-Year Plan was devoted to bringing the armed forces logistically up to strength. Hitler struck before this work was complete.

G. Germany

1. LAND

The most significant interwar military developments probably took place in Germany. Deprived of power by treaty, irritated by defeat, but saved by the myth that the surrender signed by civilian politicians had been "a stab in the back," the German General Staff worked behind the scenes to repair the damage. The Army proceeded to experiment and to remold its doctrine. German officers were sent to Russia to run training schools and to test new doctrines. At home the 100,000-man regular establishment became a cadre of officers ready to expand rapidly when the word was given. Under von Seeckt in the 'twenties and von Blomberg in the 'thirties, the works of Liddell Hart and Fuller were translated and then elaborated by the Germans themselves. When Hitler came to power, the Army enjoyed additional support, managed to avert the danger of a rival Nazi political army of Brownshirts (1934) and at once began to expand. Though the re-occupation of the demilitarized Rhineland in 1936 was still a horse-drawn affair, by 1938 mechanization had proceeded apace and panzer divisions (armored forces) and equipment were being tested in the Spanish Civil War. The General Staff openly resumed its pre-Versailles power.

2. SEA AND AIR

Under Grand Admiral Raeder experts were sent abroad to develop new U-boats in Spain, Holland, and Finland. At home the Navy sought, not very successfully, to recoup its prestige after the 1918 mutinies. It also engaged in developing warships, such as the 10,000-ton pocket battleships which made maximum use of the treaty limitations on size. After Hitler took power, the keels were laid for the very powerful battleships *Bismarck* and *Tirpitz* and for an aircraft-carrier. The Germans intended that these ships should act first as raiders and later as a challenge to the Royal Navy.

The Luftwaffe under Goering mushroomed in 1935 out of a

cadre of air transport staff, gliding clubs, and a carefully prepared aircraft industry. When its first Chief of Staff, Wever, was killed in 1936, however, it lost its lone exponent of strategic bombing. Thus the Germans developed only a tactical air force mainly suited to close ground support in the lightning threats and strokes with which Hitler intended to have his way with Europe. No attention was paid to home defense, or to the needs of a long war.

H. Summary

Each of the major nations treated its armed forces in the interwar years as its diplomatic position and national characteristics dictated. In one way or another the disarmament movement acted as a brake until its collapse at Geneva in 1934. Thereafter there was an almost universal shift to rearmament especially in the air.

III. THE THEORISTS

Despite the general pacifism of the day, military writers flourished in the interwar years. Prominent were the British writers Sir Herbert Richmond, J. F. C. Fuller, and B. H. Liddell Hart.

A. The Surface Forces Pundits

Richmond called for a return to Britain's traditional use of sea power as an adjunct to a Continental campaign in which her troops would not normally participate. With this idea Liddell Hart and Fuller agreed. Richmond called for limitations on the size of warships and rebelled against compromising British maritime needs by agreement to limitations on the number of cruisers. Overly concerned with commerce raiders, he badly underrated both submarines and aircraft. His most famous work, *Statesmen and Sea Power,* was not published until 1946 when he was 75.

J. F. C. Fuller, responsible for tank-planning on the Western Front, dwelt constantly on two themes—the importance of weapons and the value of good generalship. He was convinced that since

1864-65, the rifle and machine-gun bullet had revolutionized battle-field tactics and that machine-power had to replace muscle-power, whether of man or horse. Thus he was the blunt spokesman of the armored forces.

In the trenches of 1916, Liddell Hart came to the conclusion that new tactics were imperative. He worked out the combat team, moved from there to the idea of armored infantry (1919), and later became closely allied to the Fuller school. But his view was more that of Jomini than of Clausewitz and his concern was to save lives by winning battles without fighting them, as demonstrated in *Strategy* (1929) in which he advanced the concept of the indirect approach. In the 'thirties Liddell Hart, concerned with Britain's seeming defenselessness, advocated dynamic defense of the main base so that England would have a fortress within which to mobilize for a later offensive. He was highly influential (1937-39) in British governmental circles. Writing in a similar vein was the German von Leeb whose *Defense* (1938) dealt with the perennial problem of a two-front war and which once again revived concepts which the nineteenth-century interpreters of Clausewitz had neglected or suppressed.

B. *The Air Power Authors*

The most outspoken theorists were those dealing with air power. Exaggerated credit has generally been given to the Italian Douhet. Mitchell was aware of his work, but many of Mitchell's ideas came from French and English sources. The Royal Air Force developed on its own the doctrine of the counter-strike deterrent in World War I. What all airmen had in common was their belief that the frontier was obsolete as a line of demarcation between the services and that the logical extension of the Clausewitzian doctrine of striking at the enemy's will to war was to attack his political center of gravity, his capital city and force the civilian leadership—through public clamor—to capitulate. They theorized upon scanty evidence, frequently ignored the long history of war, and possessed considerable naïvete as to the actual power of their weapons. The classic exposition of their case, Alexandre de Seversky's *Victory Through Air Power* was not, however, published until 1942.

IV. PEACETIME WARS

The interwar years saw a number of minor conflicts. The most significant either strategically or tactically were the Japanese invasion of China, the Chaco War, the Ethiopian War, and the Spanish Civil War.

A. *Colonial Campaigns*

World War I had scarcely ended before the British were involved in the Third Afghan War (10 May-8 August 1919), in Iraq and Aden, and in attempting to suppress the Irish Rebellion (26 November 1919-6 December 1921). In Morocco, the Spanish tried to pacify the Riff tribesmen, but met with disaster at Anual (21 July 1921) when Abdel Krim killed 12,000 out of a force of 20,000. The Riff War rambled along through political squabbles, with French assistance (26 July 1925 onwards), to its conclusion in July 1927.

B. *The Chaco War and Zarumilla Campaign*

Deep in the South American hinterland, Bolivia and Paraguay battled over disputed territory from 1932 to 1935 in the Western Hemisphere's greatest struggle since the American Civil War. The lessons of World War I—particularly the superiority of defensive firepower and the necessity of trucks for mobility—were re-emphasized in the Chaco. The return of genuine maneuver to warfare marked Paraguay's brilliant General Estigarribia as a precursor of the World War II tank generals. Only the Germans recognized that his sweeping double envelopments demonstrated a solution to the vaunted superiority of the defensive; lack of airpower, whose use he probably understood, denied Estigarribia total victory. Six years later, in a miniature *blitzkrieg* of probable Italian doctrinal inspiration, Perú's airpower smashed Ecuador in the hemisphere's last war, but Perú's victory in the 1941 Zarumilla campaign was tarnished by her ground forces' crude use of mass against a few tattered Ecuadorian battalions.

C. The Japanese Invasion of China

Chinese obstructionism in the usurped Japanese province of Manchuria led the latter to seize Mukden (18 September 1931) and to occupy three eastern provinces. The Chinese were hindered from taking effective action by floods and Communist dissidents. Continued boycott of their goods resulted in the seizure of the port of Shanghai by 70,000 Japanese (28 January-4 March 1932). Jehol was occupied in early 1933, but further attempts at conquest without military occupation were resisted. Chiang Kai-shek made temporary peace with the Communists and presented an ostensibly united front to the enemy.

Japan started an undeclared war (7 July 1937). Inferior in equipment, the Chinese could only slow the campaign in North China and lost Peking and Nanking (29 July and 13 December 1937). In August, a Japanese naval force landed at Shanghai, but was soon in difficulties with a large hostile army; reinforcements arrived, however, and the city fell 8 November. The enemy at once moved up the Yangtze, shocked world public opinion by bombing Chinese cities, and effected a blockade of the whole South China coast. The Chinese obtained aircraft from Russia, but in 1938 the Japanese continued their advance in the north to the Yellow River. Nevertheless, their power was generally limited to the railways and large cities, since Chinese Communist guerrillas controlled the northern hinterland. In mid-year the Japanese reached Anking (12 June) and took advantage of the Munich crisis in Europe to seize Canton (21 October). Shortly thereafter, they occupied Hankow and thus isolated the Chinese from Western seaborne supplies. The struggle then dragged on into World War II, with the Japanese becoming more brash after each success, especially after the fall of France in 1940 allowed them to take over Indo-China.

D. The Abyssinian War

The Italian invasion of Ethiopia (Abyssinia) followed a border incident at Ualual (5 December 1934) and feverish diplomatic negotiations. On 3 October 1935 Italian forces invaded but made slow progress. The League of Nations applied empty economic sanctions, for it had no real force. In November, Marshal Badoglio assumed command, reorganized, advanced into the mountains, and finally took the capital of Addis Ababa on 5 May 1935, when resistance ceased. Italy's defeat at Adowa (1896) was avenged. The campaign was notable for the use of air power, gas, and tanks against a primitively armed people. During the conflict Britain and Italy came near to war, but the Royal Navy was restrained both by timidity in London and by lack of air and anti-aircraft weapons.

E. The Spanish Civil War

The internal political conflict between Right and Left in Spain—similar to that in some other countries in the interwar years—came to a head on 18 July 1936 when the Army in Morocco, led by General Francisco Franco, revolted. Assisted by German air transport, they rapidly seized the Iberian garrison towns, including Cadiz, Seville, and Burgos. The government managed to prevent a coup d'état by holding Madrid, the capital, and Barcelona against the insurgents. Franco with almost full army and partial air force support soon received substantial German and Italian "volunteers" and matériels. Russia aided the Government (Republicans or Loyalists). After successes both in the Tagus Valley, where Toledo fell (28 September) and in the north at Irun (4 September), the insurgents attacked Madrid, but failed to take it despite a "fifth column" inside the city.

The German "volunteers," having discovered in the airplane a mobile artillery—such as Hindenburg lacked to enable his infiltration tactics to break through the Allied defense in depth of 1918—proceeded to develop their ideas of blitzkrieg. The Loyalists countered by turning Spanish villages, with their stone construction, into fortresses which gradually halted an offensive. The war also showed that strategic bombing was less effective than proponents of the deterrent counterstrike theory claimed; Russian and German tactical air doctrine was decisively influenced by experience in Spain.

The insurgents captured Malaga (8 February 1937), but were then forced by the stalemate around Madrid to concentrate on Bilbao, which fell on 18 June 1938. Meanwhile, the Western

Powers had instituted non-intervention patrols and an embargo on arms, which hindered the Loyalists more than their opponents, since the Germans and Italians only paid lip-service to it. Attacks by Italian "pirate submarines" caused the British to take action.

A war of attrition then set in. From 16-18 March 1938 Barcelona was bombed 17 times and casualties rose to 3,300. But these raids ordered by Mussolini backfired; Franco objected, the world was horrified, and the inhabitants responded defiantly. The war in Spain showed that bombing neither cracked civilian morale nor produced the expected casualties. The Loyalists undertook a counter-offensive to stop the insurgent conquest of the north (5 December 1937-15 February 1938), but it failed for lack of equipment. Franco then drove from Teruel to the sea and all summer fought the bitter battle on the Ebro, after which Mussolini withdrew his much-battered Italian divisions. Early in 1939 Franco's forces took Barcelona and all of Catalonia. The war ended with the surrender—after internal dissensions—of Madrid on 28 March 1939. Casualties amounted to 700,000 killed in battle, 30,000 executed, and 15,000 dead from air raids. This left Spain so exhausted that she remained neutral throughout World War II, despite her adherence to the Anti-Comintern Pact (7 April 1939). Hitler, although tempted, failed to use her to seize Gibraltar and end British access to the Mediterranean in 1940.

F. *Conclusion*

The interwar years were characterized by normal military peace-time problems: economy, cutbacks, stagnation, exhaustion and complacency among the victorious democratic powers, while the defeated, authoritarian states solved the psychological and economic aspects of unemployment by expanding and modernizing the armed forces as a symbol of progressive industrialization. World War II put these developments to the test and added the trial of logistical stamina.

CHAPTER XXVIII

The Second World War: The Opening Phase, 1939-1941

I. INTRODUCTION

WORLD WAR II began with the Treaty of Versailles of 1919. Hitler came to power in 1933 determined to right wrongs and to expand. By the use of psychological warfare, "quislings," demonstrations, intimidation, and surprises he opted the grand strategic initiative and kept his opponents off balance as he pursued the expansion of German territory just as he had predicted in his *Mein Kampf* (1925). His prewar maneuvers destroyed France's European hegemony; yet he hoped not to antagonize England. His ultimate goal was control of the Continent by the Third Reich, for which he needed Russian oil and wheat fields. From the military point of view he succeeded with the expansion of the armed forces in 1935, the re-occupation of the Rhineland bridgehead in 1936, the *anschluss* (union) with Austria in March 1938, and the indirect approach through Munich to the dismemberment of Czechoslovakia in September 1938 and March 1939; the elimination of Poland was the next step in his plan.

The western Allies had no real plan beyond the status quo. Britain, France and Italy, the natural allies against a revived German state, had allowed themselves to be spilt so that Italy joined Hitler to form the Rome-Berlin Axis (27 October 1936). French internal troubles in the later 'thirties—aggravated by the Left—combined with a British "business as usual" attitude to delay practical military discussions until the eve of Munich, September 1938. Whereas Hitler had an economic objective and a valid conception of how to obtain it, France and Britain based their approach on mere hatred of the Nazi system. They hoped to destroy it without angering the German people. Moreover, where the Germans were mentally and physically prepared for modern war, neither the British nor the French armed forces or people were ready for it. The correct French counter to the German strategy of annihilation would have been one of attrition based on land and air power, complemented by British strategic reliance upon air and sea power. Instead, the Allies accepted war prepared to resume the conflict on the Western Front where they had stopped in 1918, with the exception that the British would undertake strategic bombing.

In March 1939, Hitler absorbed the remainder of Czechoslovakia in violation of the Munich agreement. Too late, the Allies determined that Germany must be stopped and chose to grant a guarantee of Polish integrity, which could not be honored. Hitler countered with the opportunistic Russo-German Pact in August, which assured him peace in the East and indeed Soviet cooperation for the annihilation of Poland. Much to Hitler's surprise, when he attacked Poland on 1 September 1939, Britain and France declared war.

II. THE POLISH CAMPAIGN

The 1939 Polish armed forces were still organized on a 1919 basis, reliving the Battle of Warsaw. Moreover, Poland's industrial vitals were all close to the 850-mile Polish-German frontier. Because of this the Poles felt obliged to establish a cordon defense with all the faults such a decision entailed. They were unprepared for the lightning war, or blitzkrieg, unleashed by the Germans on 1 September. Dawn bombings disrupted headquarters, destroyed aircraft on the ground, and left the Poles demobilized and demoralized. The Germans, furthermore, could easily reach their own East Prussian frontier because their naval forces controlled the Baltic. Thus they were able to employ a massive double-envelopment. Two northern armies under Bock drove the Poles into the Vistula bend and cut them off, while to the South three armies under von Rundstedt first isolated the Polish Silesian forces and then swept north to meet Bock in driving the remaining Polish forces to the east of Warsaw, which was besieged and capitulated

(27 September). But already by the seventeenth, when Russia moved in to secure the eastern half of Poland, major Polish resistance was at an end. Politically the war ended on 6 October.

The German success was achieved by speed, especially of motorized and armored forces, by using the air force in a tactical role to paralyze the Poles so that strategic bombing would have been meaningless, and by the use of sympathizers already behind the Polish lines. The Germans had clearly demonstrated that the offensive was once again feasible, especially if there was a balanced combination of motorized infantry, armor, and air under a single commander.

III. THE SITZKRIEG

The blitzkrieg in Poland was not counterbalanced by even significant action elsewhere on the part of Poland's guarantors. The French deployed defensively in the Maginot Line and watched the opposing German Siegfried Line. The British Expeditionary Force dug in along the Belgian frontier. The R.A.F. took up leaflet dropping since it lacked the capacity to undertake offensive bombing. There was also political reason for restricting operations —notably fear of retaliation, despite the fact that the war had not opened with German air blows on London and Paris. Daylight raids were abandoned when German fighters proved more than a match for British bombers in tight formations. The French Air Force was held primarily to defensive actions. At sea, a small force of U-boats immediately began to make themselves felt with the sinking of both the *Athenia* on the day war was declared (3 September) and the battleship *Royal Oak* at Scapa Flow (14 October). The Germans also laid magnetic mines about British ports. The British rounded up raiders, including the pocket battleship *Graf Spee* at Montevideo (13 December 1939) in the Battle of the River Plate.

IV. THE RUSSO-FINNISH WAR

In the meantime, the Russians, long irked by Finland's independence, sought by military action to provoke a Communist take-over in that country. The Russian plan was to use some 100 divisions in imitation of German tactics in Poland. But Field Marshal Mannerheim's three Finnish divisions made maximum use of forests, hills, lakes, and snow to bring to a standstill the Russian offensive, which opened on 30 November 1939. The Russians reorganized and finally employed a mass air, infantry, and artillery attack (2-15 February 1940) to grind the Finns into submission by 13 March. Though a minor conflict, the war pointed up the usefulness of highly mobile semi-guerrilla forces, the danger of not taking an opponent seriously, and the need to adjust tactics and weapons to the ground over which they would be used. It led Hitler to under-estimate the ability of the Red Army, but it also afforded the Russians a practical test which was invaluable in altering their doctrine and organization before Hitler struck. The failure of Russian strategic air power to break civilian morale discredited bombing and, along with experience in border clashes with Japan, brought tactical air advocates into complete control of the Red air arm.

V. GERMAN SUCCESS IN THE WEST

A. *Norway and Denmark*

Britain having rejected his peace proposals in the Fall of 1939, Hitler determined to crush her. To attain this grand strategic objective of defeating the traditional anti-totalitarian power, Hitler had to be able to destroy British maritime power and at the same time make France into a subservient state. Thus, his military objective in the West was the coastline of Europe and in three months he gained control of it from the North Cape to the Spanish border. While the plan was offensively aimed at British war-making potential, it defensively assured Germany of vital ore supplies from Norway, ball-bearings from Sweden, and coal from France.

The attack on Norway was a masterpiece of unorthodox warfare. It was planned before the British and French announced the mining of Norwegian territorial waters to halt the flow of iron ore from Narvik (8 April 1940). German soldiers were sent in merchant ships to key Norwegian ports, fifth columnists were organized ashore, and on the critical morning of 9 April through air attacks and airborne landings the enemy seized all the Norwegian airfields and other vital points. Aided by the geographic fragmentation of Norway, the Germans seized Oslo and other strategic points the first day, thus forestalling British counteraction. Denmark also fell that day to forces which simply walked up to the palace gates in Copenhagen and took power.

The swiftness of the entire operation caught the Allies mentally and physically unprepared. Some minelaying was carried out in the Skagerrak between Norway and Denmark, but this had little effect as the Germans utilized air resupply. Not until the fifteenth did a British force arrive at Narvik, followed in the next two days by more meaningful landings at Namsos and Aandalsnes. These were planned as diversions for a direct attack on Trondheim, but this was abandoned owing to the danger the fleet faced in operating without suitable air cover since neither proper carrier forces nor airfields ashore were available. The result of this abortive relief operation was an evacuation on 2-3 May which cost equipment and ships, but few lives. The Norwegians capitulated officially on 9 June. The main result of the campaign was to enhance Hitler's prestige with neutrals and oust the unfortunate Neville Chamberlain, who was succeeded as Prime Minister by Winston Churchill. But it also neutralized the North Sea and demonstrated again the mobility of tactical air power, the strength of coordinated joint operations, and the value of surprise and the principle of security, especially when founded upon sound planning and preparation.

B. *Holland and Belgium*

The main German move against France was preceded by the strategic annihilation of Holland, Belgium, and Luxembourg. While the Germans practiced for the offensive, the Allies considered various static defense plans, but were hampered in making a move by the positive neutrality of the Dutch and the Belgians. Eventually the Allies decided to advance their left to the river Dyle, pivoting on Sedan. The hinge was held by the weakest group in the French Army. (The Maginot Line had not been continued to the sea because the French had lacked the manpower simultaneously to garrison it and to maintain a field army.) Against this strictly

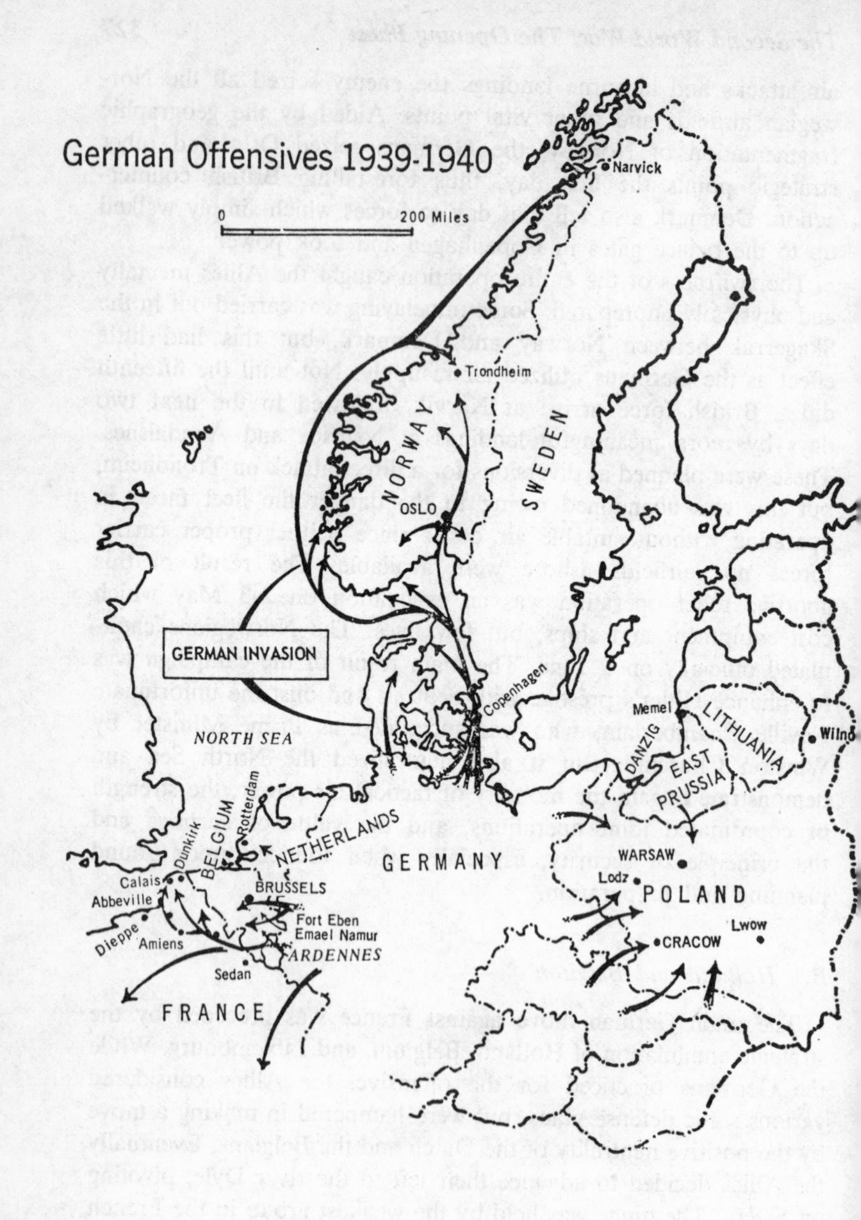
German Offensives 1939-1940
0
200 Miles
Narvick
Trondheim
NORWAY
SWEDEN
OSLO
GERMAN INVASION
Copenhagen
NORTH SEA
Memel
LITHUANIA
Wilno
DANZIG
EAST PRUSSIA
Rotterdam
Dunkirk
BELGIUM
NETHERLANDS
GERMANY
WARSAW
Lodz
POLAND
Calais
Abbeville
Dieppe
Amiens
BRUSSELS
Fort Eben
Emael Namur
ARDENNES
Sedan
CRACOW
Lwow
FRANCE

defensive Allied deployment, the Germans planned an armored penetration through what the French regarded as the impregnable massif of the Ardennes. If successful, this drive was to be followed by two curling armor-headed prongs aimed at thrusting the left of the Allied line back to the sea and rolling the right down the rear of the Maginot Line. The Germans had the advantage of numbers, equipment, and co-ordination, though certain Allied matériel was excellent, if incorrectly employed. By astutely employing their successful formula of mutually supporting armor, motorized, tactical air, and psychological warfare, the Germans achieved tactical surprise and exploited the resulting confusion and congestion. Streams of demoralized refugees soon hindered Allied movement.

On 10 May the Germans delivered air and airborne attacks on Dutch airfields and bridges. Paratroops seized Belgian bridges, railways were bombed, and glider troops took the key fortress of Eben-Emael. Next day the Albert Canal was crossed and the Belgians withdrew to join the Anglo-French forces advancing to their aid. Armored columns rapidly plowed on through the Dutch defenses and isolated The Hague. On the fourteenth, the Germans demanded surrender of the Netherlands and bombed Rotterdam. Dutch resistance ceased. French morale was badly affected by these developments.

C. *France*

For Anglo-French forces, 10 May opened with heavy German air raids on headquarters, supply dumps, and airfields. The First Army group of forty divisions manning the lines from Sedan to the sea was ordered to pivot to meet the German thrusts, thus evacuating fairly well prepared positions in favor of temporary field fortifications. This pleased the enemy. The question was whether Sedan, the fixed point of the maneuver, would hold. Unfortunately, the French Second Army was composed of second-rate troops considered adequate for a quiet sector.

1. THE OFFENSIVE

Against the line from Namur to Sedan, the German Commander, von Rundstedt, hurled the main panzer attack force.

French reinforcements, requested on the tenth, were not due to reach the defenders for a week or ten days. On the twelfth, von Kleist attacked positions on the Meuse and forced a bridgehead, whereupon the Germans streamed into France preceded by a shield of Stukas dive-bombing tactical objectives to confound the Allies. The Allied command was confused, for this was not orthodox 1918-style war! By the nineteenth the Germans were in Amiens, took Abbeville next day and on the twenty-third reached the English Channel. The northern or left wing of the Allied Army was now besieged. The Northeast bastion—held by the Belgian Army—capitulated (28 May) after the British commander, Lord Gort, had already been ordered to withdraw to the coast.

2. DUNKIRK

At last within fighter range of England, the remnants of the B.E.F. were evacuated from Dunkirk (26 May-3 June) together with some of the French rear-guard. That this was possible was due first to a German decision to conserve the armor, which gave Gort from 23 to 27 May to strengthen the beachhead defense of dikes and canals against which tanks could not be used, and second to the Luftwaffe's bombing of Ostend rather than Dunkirk and Calais. In addition Goering got Hitler to entrust the Luftwaffe with completing the annihilation of the B.E.F.

3. THE FALL OF FRANCE

Two days after Dunkirk, the Germans attacked Weygand, who had replaced Gamelin as the French Supreme Commander and drove his army back past Paris (evacuated on 11 June). This brought a change of government as the old man on horseback—the "hero of Verdun"—Marshal Pétain came to power. Immediately he called for an armistice, which was signed on 25 June. Thus fell France. But not before Italy had entered the war on the tenth with an attack across the Maritime Alps to regain the territory Cavour had ceded to Napoleon III eighty years before.

In many respects the campaign in France was fought exactly as Fuller and Liddell Hart had advocated years before. Fast armored and motorized forces with suitable heavy weapons, using aircraft as artillery when they outran their surface support forces, employed with surprise, concentration, maneuver, superb training, command and logistics, smashed through a weakly-held position defense line in "impossible" country and then moved so rapidly as to create confusion in the defenders' rear. It repeated the Polish campaign on a much larger scale. With nine months' warning, there was much less excuse for its having succeeded once more except that like the Poles, the French had the misfortune of having their vital industrial area close to the menaced frontier. Even so, their defense was tactically unsound. The Allies had no really mobile armored divisions, though the equipment was available with which the invasion could have been countered. Doctrine, training and, in the French case, morale were left over from 1918.

VI. THE BATTLE OF BRITAIN

For the Germans the strategy of annihilation had succeeded against France. The problem now was to bring it to bear upon England. The naval bases for a submarine blockade had been obtained, but blockade was a slow and uncertain method. Hitler was, therefore, anxious to force Britain out of the war. The only method was invasion. Here, however, the Germans faced considerable difficulty as they had not planned for a seaborne operation, had none of the necessary amphibious equipment or doctrine, and had yet to win from the Royal Navy and the R.A.F. the local sea and air superiority to cover a mass Channel crossing.

"Operation Sea-Lion," as the German plan was christened, was dependent, therefore, upon Goering's making good his boast to win a war of attrition against the R.A.F. In this he was severely handicapped by the lack of a heavy bomber, by the limited range of his fighters, and by the British system of fighter direction based on radar and radio area coverage, which enabled ground controllers to vector superior formations of defending fighters against his attacking squadrons. Thus Lord Dowding was able to win each phase of the Battle of Britain.

In the first phase (10 July-7 August) the Germans detailed parts of two air fleets to clear the Channel by attacks on convoys. These were partly effective for British radar could not pick up low-flying formations early enough to allow fighters to be scrambled to intercept before convoys were attacked. Moreover the British also suffered losses: their faulty peacetime fighter tactics were just being remedied as the lessons of air fighting over Dunkirk were evaluated. The second phase (8-23 August) consisted of two weeks' attrition starting with an intensification of bombing, but was primarily aimed at achieving German air superiority. Dowding defeated this move by refusing to commit all his forces and by withdrawing his fighters to bases beyond the Luftwaffe's range. The third phase (24 August-6 September) saw the intensification of attacks on R.A.F. airfields and control mechanisms with scattered raids at night continuing to cover almost the entire United Kingdom. The fourth phase (7-30 September) resulted in a change of tactics stemming from raids on Berlin in retaliation for an accidental one on London (25 August). Hitler and Goering, therefore, decided on the Warsaw and Rotterdam morale-breaking approach and were backed by Luftwaffe field commanders who believed that R.A.F. Fighter Command was almost finished. Massive attacks against London, Kesselring believed, would draw in all the British reserves so they could be finished off and the invasion take place. Goering took personal operational command and massed formations intact now crossed the coast against the capital.

The critical turning point was reached on 15 September when the R.A.F. claimed 185 (actually 60) enemy aircraft shot down. Two days later the already delayed invasion was indefinitely postponed. By the time the fifth and final phase opened (1-31 October) the Germans had already lost 1,653 aircraft. Goering now changed to high-altitude fighter-bomber raids which were more difficult for radar, the Observer Corps, and controllers to match. Moreover, the R.A.F. had sadly neglected night tactics in peacetime and was poorly prepared to meet nocturnal raids. By November the battle was over.

The Luftwaffe could surmount neither Fighter Command nor the weather. Although a tactical force, it showed it had neither the equipment nor the tactical knowledge to fight a strategic air offensive. It never gained the necessary air superiority to enable the invasion to take place. Ultimately, incorrect air doctrine in this campaign cost Germany the war in the West. Even before the battle was over, Hitler had issued orders to abandon an attack on Britain and to prepare instead for the invasion of Russia. In this he made the fatal error of leaving an enemy in his rear. Britain's vital area was not only its own industrial Midlands, but also the American arsenals across the Atlantic.

VII. THE MIDDLE EAST, 1940-1941

A. *Introduction*

With Britain isolated, the center of attention properly should have shifted to the Middle East. The demands of grand strategy—in repetition of Napoleon in 1798—called for the elimination of Egypt as the means of shattering British sea power and of seriously weakening the Empire. Moreover, the time was ripe. As later events showed, a single German panzer division under Rommel sent to aid the Italians in the summer of 1940 could have scored a decisive success which would have given Hitler control over both the Middle East and the Turkish gateway to the Russian oil fields. But Hitler left the task to Mussolini, who failed.

The British under Field Marshal Wavell, however, were deprived of the fruits of victory by misguided directions from London, which involved them once again in a disastrous Continental strategy. London resolved to give assistance to Greece, a calamitous repetition of the 1915-1918 Salonika campaign. This politically-inspired action expended piece-meal the vital tank and aircraft strength with which the Italians might have been driven out of North Africa before Rommel arrived, thus ultimately making the invasion of Sicily instead of North Africa the first Anglo-American counter-stroke in 1942.

B. *The Early Offensives in Libya*

When Italy attacked on 10 June 1940, Wavell had in the Middle East some 81,000 ill-equipped troops with which to face 215,000 Italians in Libya and another 200,000 in East Africa. Moreover, until June he was prevented from taking adequate defensive steps. His supply route through the Mediterranean was precarious, although the Italians failed to storm Malta, and his line through the Red Sea was menaced from Eritrea. Italian strategy should have been to strike at Cairo from west and southeast, thus splitting the British command in two.

Instead, Wavell, long noted for his unorthodox peacetime maneuvers, gained the initiative and struck at the enemy in the first of seven Libyan campaigns. Employing the 1918 Allenby tactics of deception he vastly exaggerated his force in Italian eyes. The first Libyan campaign consisted of raids which harassed and captured outposts. The Italian Graziani, a most cautious man, at the same time invaded Egypt in September and erected a chain of seven forts, none of which were mutually supporting. On 28 October, Wavell decided on the second Libyan campaign, but had to postpone its start when Mussolini that same day declared war on Greece. Wavell, therefore, was ordered to occupy Crete.

Meanwhile, reconnaissance established that there was a gap between the Italian posts. After building advanced supply dumps, the British boldly drove through the gap against numerically superior forces and on 9 December began taking the Italian forts from the rear. General Sir Richard O'Connor, commander of the British Western Desert Force, had remarkable successes, and what had been planned as a reconnaissance in force turned into a campaign. The battles of Sidi Barrani (9-11 December), Bardia (9 January 1941) and Tobruk (22nd) were carried by assault.

The demoralized Italians retreated along the coastal road where they were harried by low-flying aircraft and naval bombardments, and Wavell decided to try yet another gamble against them. He sent his remaining armor directly across the desert at the base of the Cyrenaican bulge to cut the coastal road south of Benghazi. The Italians ran into the British advance outpost at Beda Fomm and by 7 February 1941, when the situation had stabilized, they had lost 130,000 at a cost to Wavell of 2,000 casualties. O'Connor was now overextended, Wavell had been ordered by London to send three divisions to Greece and his strength was inadequate to continue the pursuit to Tripoli. The Italians accordingly retained their base for future operations.

C. *The East African Campaigns*

While the Libyan campaign was under way, Wavell ordered forces from the Sudan and Kenya to clean up Italian East Africa.

Because the Italians evacuated Kassala, the advance began ahead of schedule on 19 January. Averaging 35 miles a day, the attackers entered Addis Ababa on 4 April and forced the surrender of the Duke of Aosta at Amba Alagi on the eighteenth. This dual campaign eliminated another 200,000 Italians, secured the Egyptian rear, and cleared the Red Sea supply route. Success was due in part to the Abyssinian guerrillas and to the almost complete lack of interference by the Italian Air Force.

VIII. THE BALKAN CAMPAIGN

A. *Yugoslavia and Greece*

On 22 October 1940 Hitler peacefully occupied Rumania by agreement with her de facto ruler, Marshal Antonescu. Mussolini declared war on Greece on 28 October as an extension of his Albanian adventure, begun on 7 April 1939. He did not give Hitler prior notice of his intention, intending in this way to confirm Italian independence of action. Thus, when Bulgaria joined the Axis on 1 March 1941, Yugoslavia was virtually surrounded. After she rejected the Axis, the Germans altered their timetable for attacking Russia, turned south on 6 April 1941, and in eleven days compelled the bulk of the Yugoslav forces to surrender.

Meanwhile at the end of February the Greeks, with British, and later Yugoslav support, decided on a linear defense position—the Metaxas Line—along the eastern Rhodope Mountains. This once again played into German hands. Against it Field Marshal List used geography and his panzers. A four-pronged thrust began 6 April and entered Salonika two days later. The British then withdrew to Thermopylae, exposing the main Greek Army retreating into the Epirus, where it surrendered on the twenty-first; thereupon the British decided to evacuate. Further orderly withdrawal was disrupted by a German paratroop seizure of the only bridge over the Corinth Canal, an operation quickly supported by a motorized column. From 26-28 April the British managed to evacuate about two-thirds of their force, but were forced to abandon all of their equipment, largely due to lack of armor and air power with which to hold a defensive perimeter. The Greek campaign to bail out the Italians delayed the German attack on Russia by five weeks and may well have cost Hitler victory there.

B. *North Africa*

Meanwhile, on 24 March 1941, Rommel, who had reinforced the Italians with panzer divisions, struck in the third Libyan campaign, swiftly overrunning Neame. The advanced British petrol dump at Msus was prematurely destroyed by its guards. The 2nd Armored Division was captured and, no more tanks being available, Wavell decided on a full-scale withdrawal, leaving a garrisoned Tobruk as a thorn in the enemy's side. Rommel invested the port on 11 April and coasted to Sollum, where he halted when his supply lines reached their immediate limit.

C. *Crete*

British Commonwealth forces had been on Crete six months before the assault came, but little had been done to repel an invasion by sea or air until the retreat from Greece; nor had fighter aircraft been available owing to the Greek and Libyan commitments, the few sent being withdrawn on 19 May. The next day the Germans delivered an airborne assault on the airfields, reinforced by air on the next two days. Despite lack of air cover, the British Navy prevented two attempts to reinforce the attackers by sea, but this defensive work was costly (three cruisers and five destroyers sunk then and during the evacuation). On the twenty-seventh, with 20,000 Germans facing some 27,000 British, evacuation was again decided upon and carried out on the nights of 28 May-1 June.

For the Germans this was almost a Pyrrhic victory, so costly that thereafter they abandoned airborne operations. The British, however, finally became convinced of their utility, and along with the Americans, proceeded to put a great deal of effort into them. As a tactical operation Crete was overrated. Its success lay in the ill-equipped and demoralized state of the defenders, and their lack of aircraft, adequate logistics, or understanding of defense. In general, airborne assaults have only been successful when immediately given support on the surface.

IX. CONCLUSION

By June 1941, when Hitler prepared to invade Russia, the first phase of the war in Europe had come to an end. The strategy of annihilation had seemed to be successful everywhere from Norway and France to Greece and Libya, with one notable and ultimately fatal exception. The Germans had not won the Battle of Britain. Moreover, Rommel had been sent to Africa too late to change the course of the war by seizing the Cairo-Suez area, the vital center of the British Empire.

CHAPTER XXIX

The Higher Direction: The North African and Italian Campaigns, 1942-1945

I. GRAND STRATEGIC PLANNING FOR GLOBAL WAR

MORE THAN ANY other war in history, World War II was directed by the democratic Allies with unique cooperation. Churchill's knowledge of Marlborough's difficulties in the War of Spanish Succession and his own experience with Allied problems in World War I coupled with Roosevelt's interest in command decisions enabled them to create a Combined Chiefs of Staff organization located in Washington which coordinated world-wide strategy and effectively balanced it against available resources. In this task it was buttressed by other boards which tackled special aspects of production and logistics. To ensure harmony and to keep strategy ahead of developments as well as to maintain personal touch a series of eleven high-level conferences were held during the war similar to those held by Castlereagh in the latter years of the Napoleonic struggle. These, which had been preceded by staff talks in early 1941 and by the Atlantic Charter Meeting in August were:

1. Washington (December 1941) at which it was firmly agreed to defeat Germany first, to hold Japan, and to maintain essential lines of communications.

2. London (April 1942) where it was decided to keep Russia in the war by a major operation in Western Europe in 1943, the abortive "Roundup" proposal, to be preceded if necessary by a

diversionary attack on France, "Sledgehammer," and to limit the Pacific forces to those required to hold the Allied position there.

3. Washington (June 1942) and London (July) during which "Sledgehammer" was abandoned and "Roundup" postponed in favor of an attack on North Africa ("Torch").

4. Casablanca (January 1943)—after the patent success of "Torch"—where the leaders decided that the Battle of the Atlantic was to be intensified and Russia receive more aid, that Sicily would be taken by "Husky" in July 1943 and the preparation for "Roundup" accelerated. Most important of all was the directive to develop the strategic bombing attack on Germany assigning priorities to German submarine construction, aircraft manufacturing, transportation, oil refineries, and other war industries in that order.

5. Washington (May 1943) where agreement was reached to take all possible measures to win in the Atlantic, to further the air attack on the German economy so as to undermine morale at home by 1 April 1944, to concentrate 29 divisions in Britain in order to secure an initial lodgement on the Continent in May 1944, to knock Italy out of the war, and to destroy the Ploesti oil plants; in the Far East to increase the airborne supplies to China to 10,000 tons a month and to mount an offensive to open the Burma Road; and in the Pacific to eject the Japanese from their outposts in the Aleutians, Marshalls, Carolines, Solomons, Bismarcks, and New Guinea.

6. Quebec (August 1943) resulted in directions to invade Italy in September ("Avalanche"), force her surrender, and use this base as a springboard for a co-ordinated attack on southern ("Anvil"), while "Overlord" (ex-"Roundup") hit northern, France; in the Pacific to seize the Gilberts and Marshalls on the road to Truk, neutralize Rabaul while advancing in New Guinea, create the Southeast Asian Command with the intention of recapturing upper Burma in February 1944, and open the road to China.

7. Cairo and Teheran (November 1943) saw the first meetings with Chiang Kai-shek and Stalin, respectively. "Anvil" and "Overlord" were given top priority with an advance in Italy to Pisa; in the Pacific the Southwestern forces were to reach the Philippines in October 1944, while a drive from the Central Pacific took the Marshalls in January and the Marianas in October. The Burmese

campaign was delayed, but B-29 bases were to be established in China by May 1944.

8. Quebec (September 1944) approved invading Germany and making studies for the redeployment of the forces used in Europe to the Pacific, establishing bases in the Marianas, opening a sea route to China, and recapturing the whole of Burma.

9. Malta (February 1945) provided Combined Chiefs' approval for Eisenhower's plans to defeat Germany.

10. Yalta (February 1945) reconfirmed approval of Eisenhower's plans, including reinforcements from the Italian theater, gave the Russians a completely free hand in eastern Europe, and called for the capture of Iwo Jima and Okinawa in the Pacific.

11. Potsdam (Berlin, July 1945) at which the new western team of Attlee of Britain and Truman of the United States agreed to increased British participation in the earliest possible defeat of Japan and invited Russian co-operation through an attack in Manchuria, and decided to drop the atomic bomb.

The first effects of these conferences appeared in the North African campaigns in which the general Allied objective was to clear the Germans from the South shore, so that the Mediterranean could be opened and an assault launched against "the soft underbelly of the Axis," especially against the weaker Axis partner, Italy. By a series of moves Italy was forced out of the war—within a year from the opening of the Allied offensive,—but the Allies failed to fill the void by not taking Rome, the Germans moved in, and the campaign dragged on another eighteen unprofitable months.

II. THE NORTH AFRICAN AND ITALIAN CAMPAIGNS

A. Introduction

The strategic initiative in June 1941 remained in German hands. Hitler's objective should have been to annihilate Britain before turning against Russia. Worse, he misjudged the importance of the Middle East and elected to attack Stalin without even first securing North Africa. There, in a contest of communications and generalship, the initiative was won by the Allies in the summer of 1942 with twin campaigns which led to the expulsion of the Axis from Tunisia early in 1943.

Their next objective was to drive Italy out of the war. Among the decisions which prevented this from being done efficiently were Roosevelt's suggestion at Casablanca in January 1943 to demand unconditional surrender and the determination to carry out a strategic air offensive against Germany, which divided the Allied air effort. The demands of the Pacific war, despite the Washington agreement of late 1941 to defeat Germany first, caused a steady drain of matériel, especially landing craft and aircraft carriers. Consequently, full advantage could not be taken of a maritime strategy in the Mediterranean. Moreover, once the political objective had been achieved, the Italian campaign degenerated strategically into a holding operation absorbing troops who might have been better employed elsewhere since they could not be quickly landed in the industrially vital Po Valley.

B. *The Later Libyan Campaigns*

In the summer of 1941 Field Marshal Auchinleck and Air Marshal Tedder replaced Wavell and Longmore. For them—as for Rommel—the problem was reorganizing and re-outfitting before the enemy could attack. The British profited from the aggressive defense of Tobruk and from the harassment of the Axis supply line across the Mediterranean, accomplished from Malta. The Germans responded by despatching 25 U-boats to the Mediterranean where—with Italian help—they reduced British sea power to a handful of cruisers and destroyers by the end of 1941.

At the end of August, Auchinleck created the Eighth Army to face the Afrika Corps (15th and 21st Panzers and 90th Light Division) supported by some Italian divisions. Rommel enjoyed superiority in aircraft and in tank and anti-tank guns. Both sides contemplated attack, but the British struck first on 18 November 1941. After indecisive fighting Rommel ended the fourth Libyan campaign by withdrawing westwards to regroup and resupply. Owing to the excellence of the German tank recovery system (not imitated by the British until October 1942), his losses were not fatal.

Rommel's matériel situation improved rapidly once his supply lines were shortened and on 21 January 1942, he opened the fifth campaign with a lightning blitzkrieg which carried him back

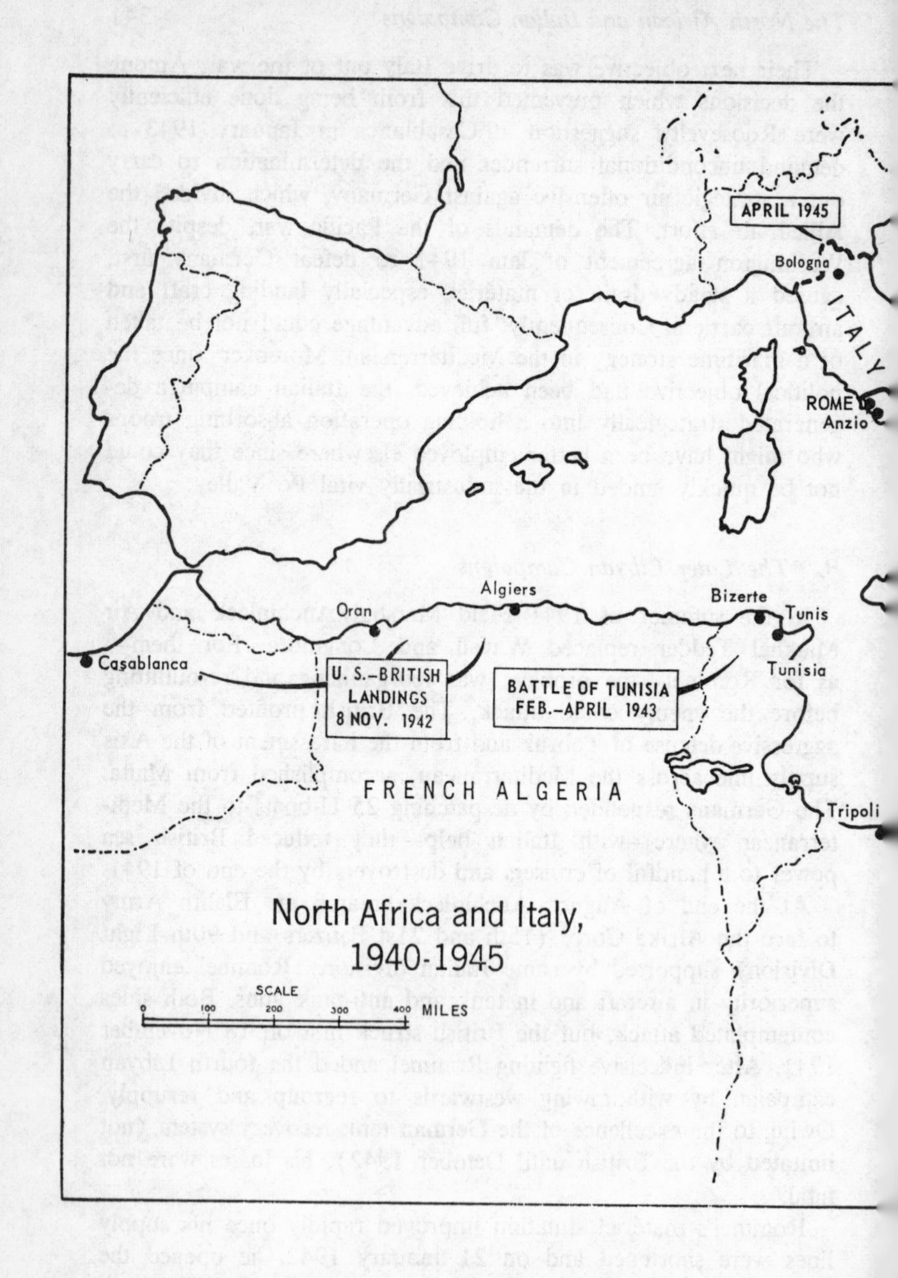
APRIL 1945
Bologna
ITALY
ROME
Anzio
Algiers
Oran
Bizerte
Tunis
Casablanca
U. S.-BRITISH LANDINGS 8 NOV. 1942
BATTLE OF TUNISIA FEB.-APRIL 1943
Tunisia
FRENCH ALGERIA
Tripoli
North Africa and Italy, 1940-1945
SCALE
0 100 200 300 400 MILES

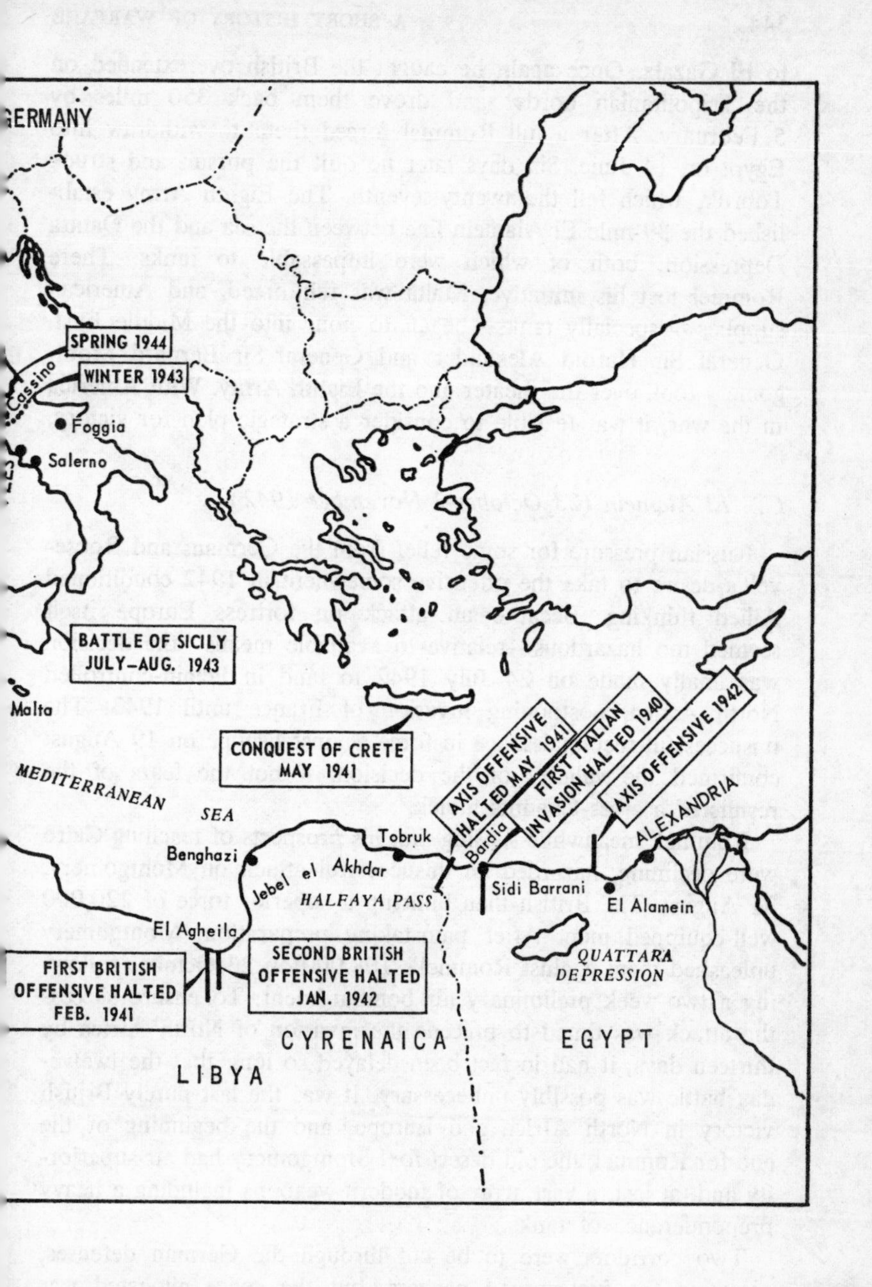
GERMANY
SPRING 1944
WINTER 1943
Cassino
Foggia
Salerno
BATTLE OF SICILY
JULY–AUG. 1943
Malta
CONQUEST OF CRETE
MAY 1941
MEDITERRANEAN
SEA
AXIS OFFENSIVE
HALTED MAY 1941
FIRST ITALIAN
INVASION HALTED 1940
AXIS OFFENSIVE 1942
ALEXANDRIA
Bardia
Tobruk
Benghazi
Jebel el Akhdar
HALFAYA PASS
Sidi Barrani
El Alamein
El Agheila
QUATTARA
DEPRESSION
FIRST BRITISH
OFFENSIVE HALTED
FEB. 1941
SECOND BRITISH
OFFENSIVE HALTED
JAN. 1942
CYRENAICA
EGYPT
LIBYA

to El Gazala. Once again he caught the British overextended on the Tripolitanian border and drove them back 350 miles by 5 February. After a lull Rommel forced them to withdraw into Egypt on 14 June. Six days later he quit the pursuit and struck Tobruk, which fell the twenty-seventh. The Eighth Army established the 39-mile El Alamein line between the sea and the Qatara Depression, both of which were impassable to tanks. There Rommel lost his initiative; Malta was reinforced, and American supplies—especially tanks—began to pour into the Middle East. General Sir Harold Alexander and General Sir Bernard Montgomery took over the theater and the Eighth Army. With America in the war, it was feasible to consider a strategic plan for victory.

C. *El Alamein* (*23 October-2 November 1942*)

Russian pressure for some relief from the Germans and Roosevelt's desire to take the offensive somewhere in 1942 conditioned Allied thinking. Because an attack on fortress Europe itself seemed too hazardous—relative to available means—the decision was finally made on 24 July 1942 to land in Pétain-controlled North Africa, postponing invasion of France until 1943. The unsuccessful reconnaissance in force against Dieppe on 19 August confirmed the validity of the decision, if not the fears of the results of a cross-Channel attack.

Rommel, meanwhile sensing that his prospects of reaching Cairo were declining, hazarded an unsuccessful attack on Montgomery, 31 August. The British then built up a superior force of 220,000 well-equipped men. After painstaking preparation, Montgomery unleashed them against Rommel's 108,000 on 23 October following a two-week preliminary air bombardment. To ensure success the attack was timed to precede the invasion of North Africa by thirteen days; it had in fact been delayed so long that the twelve-day battle was possibly unnecessary. It was the last purely British victory in North Africa and Europe, and the beginning of the end for Rommel, the old desert fox. Montgomery had air superiority and, at last, a vast array of modern weapons including a heavy preponderance of tanks.

Two corridors were to be cut through the German defenses, engulfing the fuel-starved panzers, but the space allocated was inadequate and the thrusts failed. Neither infantry nor armor—still under separate command—could break through. By 25 October the battle was in doubt. Not till 1 November did the offensive begin to move and then on a new plan. On the second the last great tank battle of the desert war was fought and then Rommel retreated—a withdrawal made mandatory by the Allied landings in Algeria. Violent German and Italian counterattacks had failed, but Montgomery's orthodox, even 1915-style generalship allowed Rommel to depart at his own pace. This has been blamed on the refusal of the R.A.F. to become a tactical part of the army. Though for the first time it had adequate transports to do this, it lacked the tactical doctrine. After a 1,200-mile chase the British finally came up with Rommel in position outside the Mareth Line, west of Tripoli at the base of the Tunisian bulge, on 13 February 1943.

D. TORCH—the Invasion of North Africa

The American Chiefs of Staff decided early in 1942 that an invasion of Europe should be made to secure a beachhead, but Churchill convinced Roosevelt that the only place suitable was in North Africa where three major ports outside of Luftwaffe range could be seized. Roosevelt so ordered on 25 July 1942. Resources at this time still were limited. The Western Naval Task Force carried 35,000 troops directly from the United States to Casablanca. The Central Task Force with 39,000 sailed from Britain to Oran, and the Eastern Task Force also started from Britain and attacked Algiers. Assuming the French would be more likely to welcome an American-led force Lieutenant General Dwight D. Eisenhower was selected as the Allied Commander-in-Chief with Air Chief Marshal Sir Arthur Tedder as his Deputy, while overall naval command went to Admiral Sir Andrew Brown Cunningham.

Much depended on French reaction—which, it was hoped, would be sympathetic—and upon the weather; D-Day of 8 November was the last date before heavy Atlantic surf could be expected. The assault was spearheaded by airborne forces staged directly from Britain to the Oran airfields. Hitler lacked the troops to counter the Allied move by occupying Franco's neutral Spain, or by attacking Gibraltar. The Allies therefore landed virtually unopposed at Casablanca, Oran, and Algiers on 8 November 1942. Admiral Darlan, the Vichy French deputy leader, unexpectedly ordered an end to the fighting, 11 November. This, though hoped for, caught the Allies by surprise. The Germans promptly occupied Vichy France, whereupon the remainder of the French fleet at Toulon scuttled itself (27 November); the other vessels had been immobilized either by the British bombardment of Oran (3 July 1940), by the attack on Dakar, or by the United States in the West Indies. German troops were rapidly flown into Tunisia. Eisenhower accordingly ordered an advance, even though transports had not yet put his vehicles ashore.

E. Tunisia

Between 15 and 18 November, American forward units made contact with the enemy on the line Medjez el Bab—Gafsa. Bad weather and the swift German build-up forced a stalemate until February. When the rainy season ended and the Eighth Army passed under Eisenhower's control, assaults were undertaken on the two Axis armies in Tunisia. As usual, Rommel opted the initiative and thrust his armor through the American defenders at Kasserine Pass, but was repulsed by reinforcements and Montgomery's threat to his rear (14-26 February 1943). The German turned unsuccessfully against the Eighth Army (6 March) and the British countered by enveloping the right of the Mareth Line (20-27 March), this time with heavy close tactical air support. Rommel himself then returned to Germany.

A general offensive by both the Eighth Army from the South and the U. S. First Army in the North applied numerically superior forces, but achieved limited success. Alexander, the overall field commander, then decided on an assault using secondary pressure along the whole front and an armored thrust straight from Medjez el Bab to Tunis. The British opened a hole on a 3,000-yard front 6 May and early the next morning their tanks were in Tunis. The demoralized Axis forces fled towards Cap Bon, a natural fortress, but Alexander ordered an aggressive pursuit. By the twelfth resistance had ceased, more than 250,000 men had surrendered and Africa for the first time in three years was cleared of enemy soldiers.

The Allied African success was a victory for the mobility and initiative which sea and air power provides, but it also bore the ominous marks of a return to the battles of mass and matériel of World War I. A new group of commanders took strategic command of combined operations. Their air supremacy greatly facilitated the offensive, but teamwork and concentration were the keys to success.

F. The Sicilian Invasion

After debating a number of courses of action at the Casablanca Conference (January 1943), including invasions of southern France, Greece, and Italy, the Allies determined to attack Italy —weakest of the Axis partners—and demand its unconditional surrender. In addition to clearing the Allied supply line to the Far East through the Mediterranean, they hoped thus to draw off German troops from Russia, encourage the Turks to enter the war, and obtain airfields near Foggia for a strategic bomber offensive against Germany. The demands of air cover, owing to the lack of a long-range fighter, actually prevented the bypassing of Sicily.

The initial airborne assault on 10 July 1943 was badly prepared and did not go according to plan, but the seaborne forces— the American Seventh Army (General George Patton) and the British Eighth Army (Montgomery)—landed against slight opposition. Many Italian coastal defenders deserted their posts and the Germans were diverted by feints against Sardinia and Greece. From Licata and Gela, Patton quickly swung northwest to Palermo (22 July) with one corps while the other pushed due north and reached Messina (16 August). In the meantime Montgomery rolled north from his beaches below Syracuse, but bogged down at Catania. The Germans had time to withdraw both their men and heavy equipment across the Straits of Messina.

G. The Invasions of Italy

To retain the initiative, the Allies crossed to the Italian mainland 3 September and began a mopping up advance with a diversionary landing at Taranto (9 September). Meanwhile, on 25 July, Mussolini resigned and unconditional surrender was discussed with his successor, Marshal Badoglio. Terms were finally settled on 2 September and the Italian fleet sailed to Malta (8 September). The Germans reinforced Field Marshal Kesselring with 13 additional divisions. Possibly, since the Italian center of gravity lay in the Po Valley, an amphibious landing should have been delivered there, which would have strategically enveloped all the German forces in Italy. The Allies unfortunately had neither the aircraft carriers or the long range fighters to provide fighter cover, nor the landing craft necessary for such an operation.

1. THE WINTER CAMPAIGN

Given these circumstances, the main invasion of Italy took place in the Gulf of Salerno on 9 September. The Fifth Army (General Mark Clark) landed and fought a critical battle largely aided by tactical air power until the heavy armor began to arrive. On the sixteenth contact was achieved with the Eighth Army. The advance then rolled northward. The Foggia airfields were taken and Naples, needed as a supply port, fell on 1 October. The Germans meanwhile evacuated Sardinia (20 September) and Corsica (4 October). Kesselring fell back first to the Volturno, then to the Sangro, and finally stood on the Garigliano River (Gustav Line). Eisenhower, Tedder, Bradley, and Montgomery had decided on landings at Anzio to envelop Kesselring's natural castle strategically but in December they were recalled to Britain to take over the D-Day operational planning. Sir Henry Wilson took Eisenhower's place, Leese was given the Eighth Army and Ira Eaker assumed command of the Allied Air Forces.

A secondary frontal attack was attempted against the Garigliano Line on 18 January 1944, which fixed Kesselring's attention. Four days later, the Anglo-American VI Corps landed at Anzio, achieving complete surprise, but insufficient means cost it the initiative and it was soon pinned down, rather like the British at Gallipoli (1915). The Germans sealed the beachhead and sustained their Gustav Line. There followed a dismal series of battles amid snow and mud against the town and monastery of Cassino (29 January-23 March). Intense air and artillery bombardment only made the roads impassable for tanks—reminiscent of World War I —and the infantry made no progress. The tactical air force was finally shifted to an interdiction campaign which constricted German supply and limited most movements to night time.

2. THE ROME CAMPAIGN

On 11 May the Rome campaign opened with a main attack on the Garigliano Line, avoiding Cassino. Kesselring decided to withdraw when his line was penetrated on the right. On 4 June the political objective of Rome was attained. Two days later the Allies landed in Normandy. Kesselring now retired north to the Gothic Line, yet another strong natural position with its flanks on the sea, which guarded the vital Po Valley. Alexander's forces were reduced by ten Allied divisions for secondary landings in Southern France (15 August).

3. THE GOTHIC LINE

The Allies, deprived of the seaborne initiative with which to flank Kesselring, launched a series of brutal frontal attacks against the Gothic line (26 August-29 September) without adequate concentration of means. The withdrawal of additional forces to aid the Greeks and Yugoslavs and to reinforce Eisenhower (December 1944-February 1945) left Alexander even less power and fighting in Italy degenerated into a stalemate. The Higher Direction decided that no effort could be made to break through either to Vienna or Hungary via the Lublijana Gap, because the resources simply were not available.

A series of minor advances during the winter gradually forced the Germans back until on 2 April 1945, a last offensive was mounted in which a breakthrough was made by the American Fifth Army past Bologna, followed by the Eighth (now under McCreery). Both forces debouched onto the Po where German resistance crumbled and unconditional surrender was accepted on 2 May.

III. CONCLUSIONS

Strategically, the drives from El Alamein and Casablanca fulfilled their purpose in clearing the Axis from Africa. The invasion of Sicily and then of the Italian peninsula drove Italy out of the war and tied down large numbers of Germans, who refused to accept the lesser partner's withdrawal from the war. But once Rome was occupied, the Allies had to make a decision. They could continue to exploit their initiative by a leapfrog movement up the peninsula using their superior seapower to seize the vital area about Milan and secure additional political objectives for the coming peace, or they could choose to adhere to the principle of economy of force with an offensive defense which would have contained Kesselring at little cost. They did neither and suffered the consequences—a weary battle of attrition with little forward momentum.

Tactically, the later North African and Italian campaigns show that the Allied Air Forces improved their tactical cooperation with the Army. As had been true in the desert too little attention, however, was paid to the destruction of communications. Moreover, apart from the shortage of long-range air cover and of landing-craft, military tactics deteriorated partly because the Allies tried to do too much with too little. There is much to J. F. C. Fuller's comments that the fighting tended to revert to the standards of World War I, with massive bombardments preceding frontal attacks and undue reliance being placed on mass. Moreover, especially at Cassino, these preparations—as in 1915-1918—hindered rather than helped the mobility of the advance. A defensive holding operation was quite possible in Italy—as the Germans had demonstrated in 1943-1944—because of the nature of the country and because of the German lack of the seaborne or airborne means of turning the flanks. Moreover, in terms of casualties the Italian campaign became more costly than it was worth.

CHAPTER XXX

The War in Russia, 1941-1944

I. INTRODUCTION

THE GERMAN ATTACK on Russia was based on a strategy of annihilation with the intention of breaking Russian economic power by the seizure of the industrial, oil, and agricultural vitals, so that with her armies vanquished in the field she could not counter-attack, even at some future date. Until 1943 the Germans were motivated by Haushofer-inspired geopolitical considerations. Hitler's aim was to knock out Russia and establish his own ability to make war before the United States could come openly to Britain's aid. Inability to defeat the Russians caused a change to an anti-Communist crusade and a strategy of attrition.

The initial German failure to take Moscow was due partly to inadequate strategic intelligence. The Germans appear to have under rated the Russians, forgetting that the Third Five-Year Plan had been devoted to creating a heavy armaments industry, especially east of the Urals, and failing to grasp both the importance of oil to the enemy and his ability to operate successfully in winters which ran to 40 degrees below zero. The last mentioned meant that for the first two years of the Great Patriotic War—as the Soviets call it—the pattern was German offensives in summer and Russian counter-offensives in winter, separated by brief respites during the annual Spring thaw. From 1943 onwards the Russians were strong enough, thanks to both their own production and to Allied supply lines through Archangel-Murmansk and Iran, to seize the offensive at will. At the same time German commanders were hampered by Hitler's refusal to allow strategic withdrawals.

II. THE FIRST GERMAN OFFENSIVE, 1941

A. *Strategy and Forces*

The German invasion of Russia began on 22 June 1941. Strategic planning envisioned penetrations by three Army groups to take the main Russian forces massed along the frontiers in huge double envelopments. The Finns to the north and the Rumanians to the south undertook parallel actions aimed respectively at Leningrad and Odessa. The objective was first to annihilate the Russian armies by making them defend Leningrad and Moscow and then to set up a defensive line, stretching from Archangel on the White Sea to the Volga east of Moscow and thence down its course to the Caspian Sea. The Russians would thus be deprived of their economic center of gravity and would be driven so far to the East that Germany's vitals would be beyond the range of Soviet air power. In this fashion, Hitler hoped to convert Russia's space into a liability.

The German Army Group North (von Leeb) consisted of two armies and a four-division armored force; Army Group Center (von Bock) three armies and ten armored divisions; and Army Group South (von Rundstedt) two German and one Germano-Rumanian army supported by four armored divisions. They were opposed by Russian armies under Voroshilov, Timoshenko, and Budenny. In contrast to their opponents, the Russian forces suffered from lack of experience and from the presence of political commissars (a system of dual politico-military unit command abandoned in October 1942).

The Russians had large reserves and their historic strategy of bartering space for time. As the Germans thrust forward, the Russians intended to retreat—without the panic seen elsewhere in the face of blitzkrieg—scorching the earth as they went. They left behind a partisan organization to prey upon the invader's lines of communications as they and the Spanish had done against Napoleon, thus tying down defensively a large number of German support troops. This Russian effort was possible not only because of the generally agrarian nature of their society, but also because for the first time the Germans faced a well-disciplined police state with a strong ideological hold upon its people. Nazi brutality to initially-friendly civilians played into Stalin's hands as well. And though space and geography favored mobility, the near roadless nature of Russia limited German consolidating operations, leaving vast unoccupied territories. Consequently, the Germans in many ways were subtly exhausted by their lack of complete control over their occupied area.

B. *The Northern Offensive*

In the north the Finns, bent on revenge for the defeat of the previous year, advanced down the Karelian Isthmus until they were halted outside Leningrad. However, their drive north of Lake Lagoda succeeded in cutting the vital Murmansk-Leningrad railway, forcing the Russians to build a new line farther east. Von Leeb struck northward from East Prussia and reached Leningrad in mid-September. Repulsed, he took the key fortress of Schlüsselburg, 30 miles to the east, and laid siege with his left on the Baltic and his right stretching down to the source of the Volga. When winter came, the Russians were able to open a motor road over the ice of Lake Lagoda (January 1942). Von Leeb remained stalled until the Russian winter offensive of 1942 began to push him back and he was replaced by Kuechler.

C. *The Central Offensive*

In the center, the Germans were more successful in terms of ground gained, but they still failed to reach their major objective—Moscow. Von Bock advanced a column from Tilsit via Vilna and another from Warsaw via Brest-Litovsk. The two met at Minsk where they inflicted a tactically decisive defeat on the Russians by July. Von Bock then turned the so-called Stalin Line along the marshes between Lepel and Vitebesk and arrived before Smolensk on 16 July. Here the Russians bitterly contested the position with tanks until 7 August. This battle of attrition exhausted the Germans and they remained on the defensive until 2 October, while Kiev was being taken on Hitler's orders.

Heavily reinforced the Germans resumed the drive on Moscow. After another great tank battle at Trubehevsk, von Bock advanced on Orel. On 15 October, Mozhaisk, some 65 miles from Moscow, fell to the Germans. The northern wing of von Bock's armies managed to take Klin (5 December), but 35 miles from Moscow the offensive ground to a halt, victim of Clausewitzian friction. Winter came three weeks early, which was an advantage to the Russians. Their defenses were strongly reinforced by the weather with which they knew how to cope and for which the Germans were entirely unprepared. German soldiers froze without coats, while summer-weight lubricants thickened in their vehicles. On 8 December Zhukov launched the first serious Russian counter-attack.

D. *The Southern Offensive*

Meanwhile to the south progress had been made, but as elsewhere the offensive failed to achieve its strategic goal. Von Rundstedt, who later faced the Allies in France, moved out of the Carpathians, pushing Budenny eastwards until he was over the Pruth (5 July). His northern wing continued to advance now more rapidly until it was blocked at Smolensk by the end of August. Von Rundstedt's center rumbled on forward until by the beginning of September it was holding the western bank of the Dnieper with the right encircling Odessa, which fell on 31 October 1941. During the next two weeks, Kiev was isolated by Bock's armor while Guderian's struck down from the north and von Rundstedt's from the south. The two met on 14 September at Lokvitsa, 120 miles east of the beleaguered city. After Kiev fell (19 September), von Rundstedt pushed on and by the end of October was along the Kursk-Kharkov-Stalino-Taganrog line, after a thrust which encircled Stalino. Rostov was taken on 11 November. This whole Kievan operation was ordered by Hitler, but it was a mistake, since it diverted forces which should have been used either to continue the offensive to take Moscow or to capture the Caucasian oil fields. Von Rundstedt's southern armies had by this time stormed Kherson at the mouth of the Dnieper and advanced on the Isthmus of Perekop, the gateway to the Crimea. On 30 September, the German commander, von Manstein, forced the bottleneck and advanced on Sevastopol, which he besieged.

E. *Evaluation*

By the beginning of December 1941 the Germans had come to a crossroads of the war. Behind them were extraordinary victories, but also that insular aircraft carrier, Britain, and the still uncommitted arsenal of the United States. In the Middle East, Turkey had been neutralized by treaty (18 June 1941) and Rommel stood at the gates of Egypt. But on 7 December the Japanese attacked America, a stroke with enormously fatal consequences for all members of the Axis. In Russia, Hitler had failed. By having refused to let Kiev die on the vine, by failing to see both the psychological and the railway significance of Moscow, and by not destroying the Russian oil centers in the Caucasus—by strategic bombing if not by conquest—he had lost his gamble on a short war in the East. Logistically he faced a winter struggle for which his armies were unprepared. His lines of communications were menaced by partisans. The time had come for a strategic withdrawal, regrouping and resupply so that the deathblow could be delivered in the Spring. Hitler, however, had dismissed most of his best generals (von Brauchitsch, the Commander-in-Chief, Halder, his Chief of Staff, von Rundstedt, von Leeb, von Bock, List, Guderian and von Kleist) and personally assumed command in the field with Jodl and Zeitzler as aides. The reasons for this may be traced to the success of his intuition over his generals' fears starting with the Rhineland incident of 1936, but it created a crisis in the High Command which ultimately led to the 20 July 1944 plot on Hitler's life.

III. THE RUSSIAN WINTER COUNTER-OFFENSIVE, 1942

Against the advice of his generals Hitler refused to retreat, even though he saw the disaster that frozen communications might bring. He also saw the need to save the troops and their logistic system from the Russian winter so that the offensive could be resumed in the Spring. Therefore the advanced depots on the railway systems (Staraya Russa, Rzhev, Vyazama, Kaluga, Bryansk, Orel, Kusk and Kharkov) were converted into vast garrison posts into which the fighting forces were withdrawn and where

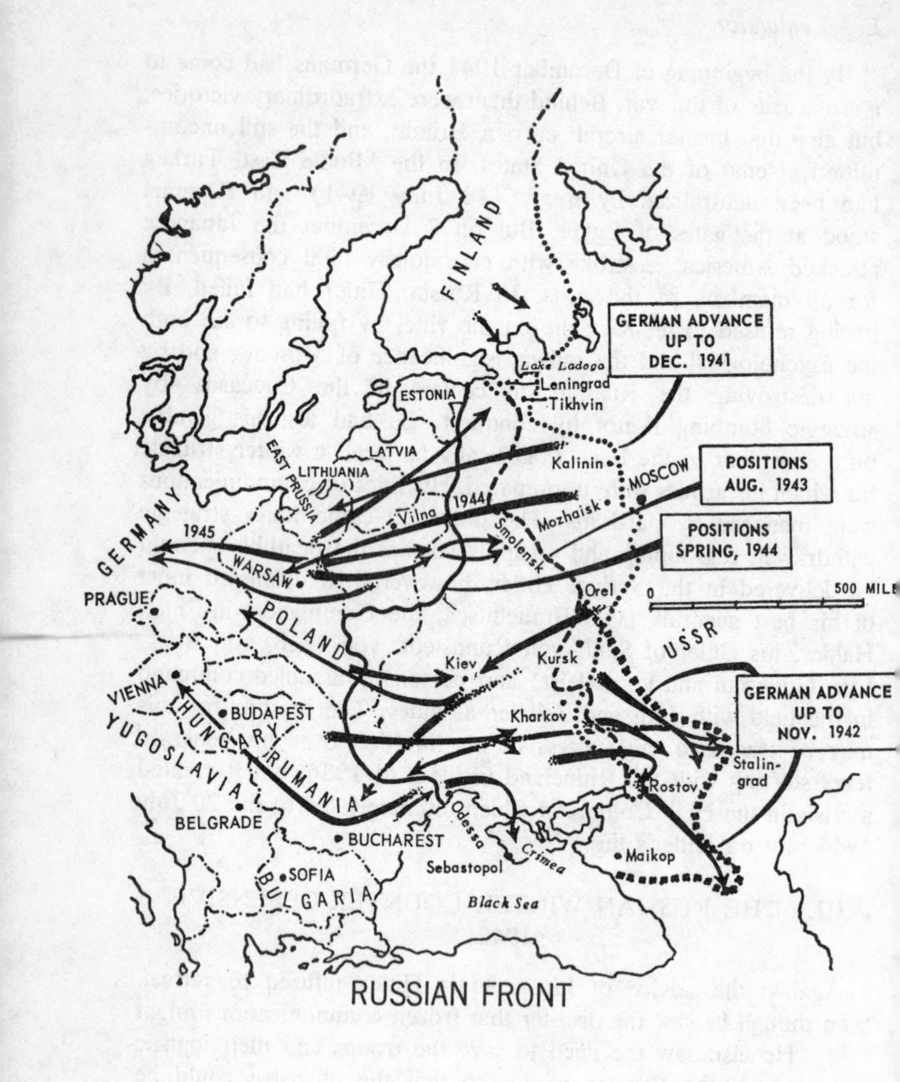

RUSSIAN FRONT

they could live off stocks until new supply lines and depots were opened. The effect was something like the "boxes" employed in the Western Desert campaigns.

The Germans, however, lacked the ability to operate mobile reserves to mop up Russian forces which infiltrated the gaps between these hedgehogs (*Igels*). The smaller posts were overrun by a combination of regulars and partisans. In the Moscow sector the Russians even thrust out and took the main Kaluga hedgehog (30 December 1941). They then drove westwards in two pincers which met some 50 miles north of Smolensk, thus pushing a large salient into the German position and leaving the Germans nearest Moscow in a long narrow salient. Its eastern tip was Rzhev in the midst of the Russian front, especially after the winter advances west and south of the capital forced the Germans back to a line just east of Orel. On the Leningrad front, the Tikhvin salient was eliminated and position warfare was established on the Schusselburg-Novgorod line. In the south the Russians bypassed a number of hedgehogs in order to retake Kharkov, but this thrust was contained as a small salient to the west of Izyum and within 30 miles of Poltava. In general the Russians continued to operate aggressively in the deep mid-winter snows until the thaw set in.

The moral effect of their resistance and counter-offensive was even greater outside the Soviet Union than within it. In addition, the German summer campaign for 1942 had to start farther back and against a seasoned enemy, while the German High Command was at last faced with the one thing for which it was not prepared, another war of attrition. This meant that just when the British air offensive was finally beginning to be effective, demands were made upon the German economy and manpower from both the Home defense and the Russian fronts, shortly to be aggravated by the Allied invasion of North Africa.

IV. THE SECOND GERMAN OFFENSIVE, 1942

A. *Introduction*

The first German summer campaign failed to annihilate the Russians or to secure their economically vital area for German exploitation. Hitler, determined to wear down the Red Army by depriving it of its arsenal area of Kharkov-Stalingrad-Baku-Batum, now adopted a new line of operations. The strategic approach was a "wedge-and-trap" movement from Kirsk and Izyum which would trap the Russians against the great bend of the Don River and be followed by the capture of Stalingrad on the Volga. The new German salient would then be organized as a defensive belt while the advance into the Caucasus captured the oil fields. The plan failed because Hitler did not concentrate on his principal objective—Moscow. He also attacked Leningrad while, at the same time, he became hypnotized by failure to take Stalingrad, and lost sight of the fundamental objective, which was to prevent the Russians from molesting the strike against the oil fields. Moreover, the failure to capture the Moscow rail hub enabled the Russians to shift troops up and down their side of the 1000-mile front. German inability to take Moscow excluded the Luftwaffe from bombing range of important supply points.

B. The Crimea

The campaign opened with von Manstein's storming of Kerch (8-13 May). Timoshenko pressed forward south of Kharkov on 12 May, but after some progress was beaten back by 28 May. A week later von Manstein advanced on Sevastopol, besieged and took it (1 July), and thus secured the whole of the Crimea in one of the few German campaigns not run by the Supreme Command. The objectives of this campaign were to impress Turkey and to eliminate Russian air bases which threatened the Rumanian oil fields.

C. The Central Front

Meanwhile the Russians had predicted the main German attack and had heavily reinforced the Voronezh-Rostov line along the Donetz River. A sudden German thrust on 22 June drove them out of Kupyansk and then von Bock, back in command, struck through the main front between Shigri and Tim. The second half of the usual double envelopment was mounted from the Byelgorod-Kharkov line on 2 July. The Germans unsuccessfully assaulted the field fortress of Voronezh three days later. To the south, however, the advance progressed and von Manstein entered Rostov on 27 July. Hitler decided to mask Voronezh, but failed to break its supply link with the North, a critical error which left his armies open to eventual encirclement in Stalingrad due to the shortage of manpower and to the strategic error of twin drives which had divergent, rather than convergent objectives. This vital flank was, moreover, manned with Italian, Hungarian, and Rumanian divisions of generally low combat capacity, although some Rumanians fought well.

Meanwhile von Hoth pressed down the Don and forced crossings on 15 and 25 August, the latter allowing the Germans on the southern part of the Don bend also to move forward. In the meantime von Kleist roared across the Caucasian plains from Rostov until he was within 100 miles of the Caspian near Russian-held Grozny. The Russian Black Sea naval base of Novorossisk fell on 10 September, virtually ending the campaign due to shortcomings of fuel, communications, terrain, exhaustion of the troops and, as usual, insufficient replacements.

D. *Stalingrad*

In the second week of September the Germans arrived at Stalingrad, a city of 500,000 inhabitants, located on a bend of the two-and-one-half-mile-wide Volga. Here the Germans committed both serious tactical and strategic mistakes. They attempted a frontal assault which was so costly by 15 October that von Hoth was ordered to reduce the city by artillery fire. As at Cassino in Italy and as in World War I—this created a highly defensible rubble-heap which could only be taken by cellar-to-cellar infantry action. The Germans, with Voronezh on their northern flank, lacked the full freedom of maneuver needed to divert the enemy while they crossed the Volga and created a bridgehead with which to isolate and neutralize Stalingrad. Instead, though the Volga as an economic artery was severed, Hitler persisted in eliminating the city by assault. The end result was another Verdun in which the Germans lost a whole army, despite attempted air resupply. The whole operation was the more senseless considering that had von Kleist been given the men and material thrown into Stalingrad, he might have been able to reach the oil fields and bring Russia, then in tenuous economic straits, to heel.

By 18 November the German advance was everywhere stalled on a line roughly Leningrad-Moscow-Stalingrad-Grozny-Novorossisk. Hitler's fortuitous success as a strategist was at an end and the deficiencies of his command system now became acute.

V. RUSSIAN OFFENSIVES

A. The Strategic Situation

Just as in the West time was on the side of the Allies in allowing them to develop their arsenals and to bring industrial production to bear on the war, so it was in Russia. The new and salvaged factories behind the Urals were moving into high gear and equipping the vast manpower reserves with weapons such as they had never had in World War I. Moreover, the Germans had failed to take or bomb into uselessness—a very difficult task—the key rail centers of Saratov to the north of the Stalingrad salient and Astrakhan to the south. The Russians were now ready to field strong mobile forces. These were able to penetrate between the German winter hedgehogs, which were no longer protected by mobile reserves because manpower was tied up in Stalingrad and the Caucasus. The Germans had reverted to early Vaubanism, when they should have been acting on his later ideas. Russian partisans grew increasingly active.

B. The Victory at Stalingrad (October 1942-February 1943)

In November von Paulus assumed command of the 22-division Sixth Army. The enemy planned to force his withdrawal, so as to automatically endanger the Germans in the Caucasus. On 19 November the thinly-spaced Italians and Rumanians to the north were scattered and the Don crossed at Kalash. Complementary to General Rokossovsky's attack was one from the south in an armored German-style double envelopment. Faced with simultaneous defeats at El Alamein and in Tunisia, Hitler ordered von Paulus to hold, although his supply line was but twenty-miles wide and had to be heavily augmented by air. This operation consumed fuel at an alarming rate and also cost some 600 scarce transport aircraft by the end of January 1943. This mistaken action was based upon more false assurances by Goering as to the Luftwaffe's capabilities.

Von Paulus could not be relieved, for the Russians on 25 November launched an offensive against the Rzhev salient, which drew in all the available German reserves. Troops, therefore, were brought from as far away as France to allow von Manstein to break through at Kotelinikovo, but the Russians countered by crushing the Italians on his left and his reserves were sent to Millerovo to block the latest Red thrust. This, in turn, led to the 27 November defeat of his right by Malinovsky, who had escaped the Purge of 1936-37, while Rokossovsky bottled up von Paulus. This, in turn, obliged von Kleist to pull out of the Caucasus in January and to retire into fortifications near Rostov and to the Taman Peninsula opposite Kerch.

Stalingrad, after a desperate defense, fell on 2 February 1943, a useless sacrifice of German manpower, but one which von Manstein, at least, considered necessary to allow the front to be stabilized. He blamed Hitler for failing to learn the lessons of the debacle brought on by his personal leadership and disregard of the professionals. Hitler did not retire from command till March; von Manstein and Halder were responsible for the Russian front in the interim.

C. The Red Advance

The Russians continued their heavy drive, completing the destruction of the Hungarians near Voronezh 22-26 January and on 14 February Rostov and Voroshilovgrad fell, together with Kursk (7th) and Kharkov (16th). In the north the Germans yielded the Rzhev salient (11 February) to shorten their lines and obtain reserves. With these von Manstein then struck into the new Kharkov salient sufficiently hard to shock the Russian command into an action (21 February-15 March) in which Kharkov was retaken. Thereupon, the annual thaw set in.

The Germans had definitively lost the initiative and their correct strategy—as had been so often demonstrated in Libya—

would have been to withdraw until the Russians were overextended. For the Allies in general, peace aims needed to be brought to the fore. Instead they called for "unconditional surrender," a now debatable aim.

VI. THE BATTLES OF ATTRITION, 1943-1944

A. *The 1943 German Offensive*

In the summer of 1943, Hitler, aware that he no longer had the strength for anything but a retrograde movement in the face of increasing Russian power and that therefore victory was no longer possible, converted the campaign into a traditional Teutonic crusade against the Asiatic hordes and called upon the *Volk* to man the Eastern Wall. The Casablanca ultimatum made a negotiated peace impossible. With some 100 divisions tied down elsewhere—some unnecessarily—he needed a great tactical victory in Russia to forestall the new enemy offensive. This complemented Russian planning.

On 5 July the Germans launched a morale-building envelopment to eliminate the Kursk salient. But von Kluge's conventional blitz tactics were now familiar to the Russians. They counterattacked at once and the consequent loss of panzer equipment seriously weakened German defenses. The Red Army then forced the Germans out of the Donetz Basin while farther south, Taganrog was recaptured (30 August) and an advance made along the north shore of the Sea of Azov. This forced the Wehrmacht to withdraw in the center, where Rokossovsky pressed westwards, cutting the north-south rail lines and taking Smolensk (23 September). Fighting was sporadic since the lines were stretched too thin for continuous contact.

B. *The Russian Offensive*

Early in October the Russians opened a renewed drive along the whole front and by 18 November had cut the Leningrad-Odessa railroad and taken Kiev. Late in November the Allied leaders met at Teheran (Iran) and gave Stalin a free hand in eastern Europe, with the result that he at once shifted his strategic objective from the mere defeat of Germany to the conquest of the Slavic countries. His winter campaign aimed, therefore, at the gates of Vienna—the strategic center of eastern Europe—and at the Rumanian oil fields. The main force of the attack fell upon von Manstein's six armies on the Ovruch-Kerson line where there were few topographical defensive positions and no man-made ones.

The Russians sought to pinch off the Dnieper salient and to split the German forces against the anvil of the Carpathians. Once again they struck at the north-south rail network so as to paralyze German defensive flexibility (13 January 1944 onwards). Four separate secondary attacks unsettled the Germans from Leningrad south. The main attack under Zhukov—who replaced Vatutin—and Koniev broke the Lvov-Odessa railway (9 March). By the end of the month they had isolated the Germans in South Russia from Poland and stood on the Pruth ready for the next offensive as soon as the thaw ended. In the meantime Malinovsky had entered undefended Odessa (10 April) and joined Koniev on the Pruth. A few days later the remnants of the isolated German armies in the Crimea surrendered (12 May).

Thus by D-Day in France, the Russians had repelled and seriously weakened the Germans, pinning them against the Carpathians so that the drive on Vienna could be pursued without enemy ability to shift his forces easily from the Polish front to hold the defenses.

VII. CONCLUSIONS

The Russian campaigns are almost textbook lessons. The German offensive attempted too much too soon. It lost sight of the objective, becoming hypnotized like the combatants in the American Civil War with the importance of cities rather than of communications. The result was that the Russians were free to move troops through the key junctions east of Moscow and to retain the necessary freedom of movement with which to conduct an active defense. The German drive—like the Allied air operations against Germany—failed to strike at the vital oil upon which Russia depended for tactical mobility.

The Germans were overoptimistic and failed to consider the

nature of the country and its people and were unprepared to meet either winter or partisans. Hitler's anti-Slavism alienated anti-Communists, especially in the Ukraine. He had a second chance in 1942 and spoiled it. Thereafter, the Allies all around the German "Fortress Europa" began to attack. Though remaining mobile, the Germans failed to develop new offensive methods, and thus facilitated correct Russian counter measures.

For their part, the Soviets made good use of their lateral railways to shift reserves, never attacked beyond their logistic means, and almost always assured themselves heavy artillery and air support. They made effective use of surprise to achieve piecemeal annihilation, while maintaining constant pressure; the Germans rarely could retire into fortified positions and became so weak in mobile forces that they could not even defend the gaps between their hedgehogs.

Lastly, on several occasions Hitler insisted on making a stand when, prudently, he should have retreated, notably at Stalingrad and in the Crimea. If the Germans had had a strategic bomber force, they might have been able to destroy the Russian oil industry, and thus bring Russia to her knees.

CHAPTER XXXI

The Battle of the Atlantic

I. INTRODUCTION

BOTH THE WAR at sea and in the air followed definable patterns in which the principles of war applied. In spaciousness, operations were similar to those in the Western Desert or in Russia, and the attacker, more than the defender, was in a position to use strategic mobility to shift operations against weak areas and away from sectors in which the initiative was being lost. The constant at sea was the North Atlantic lifeline between North America and Britain, a logistic center of gravity. In the strategic air offensive, the objective was the German industrial heartland as a whole, communications and oil in particular. Both at sea and in the air major emphasis had to be put upon tactics and the technical developments on which they depended. In neither element were the striking forces adequate or properly equipped in 1939 for the job ahead. Despite two years' warning, in 1941 the United States Navy in anti-submarine warfare and the U.S. Army Air Corps in bomber penetration were no more ready than had been the other powers in 1939.

These two vital campaigns—the one centering on the British vital area and the other upon the German—were closely related, but even some of the most brilliant military commentators have failed to grasp this, for in neither case are the struggles as clear as in land warfare. Some contend that less effort expended on the air war against Germany and more on the Battle of the Atlantic might have paid better dividends sooner. Both campaigns depended for their success on the continuous accuracy of economic intelligence, which neither side had collected in sufficient detail before the war.

British sea power, though unprepared for anti-submarine warfare, was not (as traditionally it had been and as Fuller, Liddell Hart and Richmond had urged) the basis of strategy until after the army was thrown off the Continent in 1940. And even then certain campaigns—Norway, Dakar, Greece—were undertaken in disregard of the need to husband strength until a telling offensive blow could be struck. Once freed of France, Britain adopted a traditional maritime strategy in which she fought two long defensive campaigns, using offensive means, in the Western Desert based on Cairo and in the Battle of the Atlantic. These were still in an indecisive state when the German invasion of Russia took place in June 1941.

The Germans had started building a fleet of surface ships before the war, but these were not to have been ready for war until 1943 or later. Their submarine fleet was small and largely composed of shorter-range types, but doctrine and tactics had been studied effectively. A key weakness was Hitler's lack of appreciation of sea power.

In the air the British were just building a force to defend their home base, while the aircraft which were to carry the brunt of the war into Germany were only in the prototype stage or, like the Wellington medium bomber, too small to be effective. Not until 1944 did the Allies begin to have the means to deliver crippling blows against Germany on anything but a sporadic basis. By then the U.S. Army Air Forces supplied half the strength available. British doctrine had concentrated on the knock-out blow, not on a long drawn out battle of economic and military attrition. The Germans had virtually no strategic air capability since the Luftwaffe was designed as a tactical air force. As a defensive arm it suffered from inability to attack enemy bases or supply lines, in contrast to the Royal Navy's anti-submarine campaign which included strikes against U-boat production by Bomber Command.

II. THE BATTLE OF THE ATLANTIC

At sea the basic defensive measure was the escorted convoy. Prior to September 1939 the British Admiralty's attitude was that convoy would only be adopted when the loss rate rose to an unacceptable level. Having paid almost no attention to anti-submarine warfare (ASW) since just after World War I, it was short of escorts. Moreover, ports were not prepared to handle convoys and statistics on the distribution of cargoes brought in from overseas were lacking. Basically early convoys consisted of 35 merchant ships in nine to twelve short columns with one escort at each corner of the rectangle and any additional warships ahead. U-boats could easily penetrate such a weak screen, despite the defenders' use of asdic (also called sonar, an under-water radar).

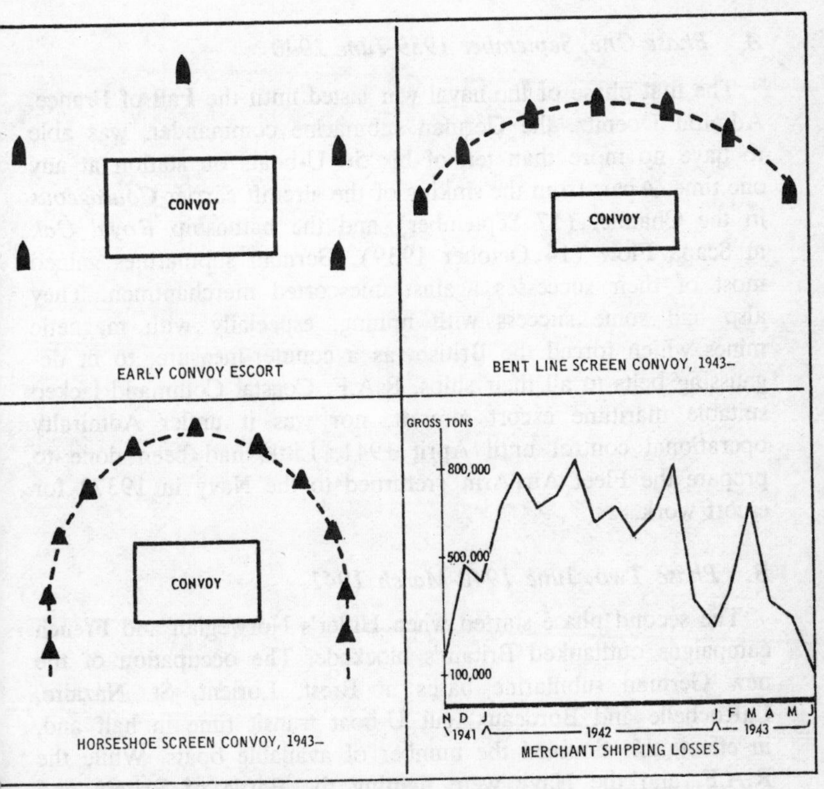

Battle of the Atlantic

Not until the catastrophic losses of March 1942 did the Admiralty accept the advice of statisticians and increase the size of convoys. This actually made both escorting and the use of shipping more efficient. By 1943 fast convoys (9-15 knots), which could outrun submarines, had a "bent-line" screen across their front, while slow ones (6-9 knots) had a horseshoe-shaped escort pattern which extended to the rear of the convoy box. The escorts thus saved were formed into independent groups which either aided convoys under attack—just as mobile forces plugged the gaps between German hedgehogs in Russia—or acted as hunter-killer forces which carried the offensive to the enemy. The essential strategy was simple: the convoy was on the defensive and drew the attackers in to be counterattacked.

A. *Phase One, September 1939-June 1940*

The first phase of the naval war lasted until the Fall of France. Admiral Doenitz, the German submarine commander, was able to have no more than ten of his 56 U-boats on station at any one time. Apart from the sinking of the aircraft carrier *Courageous* in the Channel (17 September) and the battleship *Royal Oak* at Scapa Flow (14 October 1939), German submarines gained most of their successes against unescorted merchantmen. They also had some success with mining, especially with magnetic mines which forced the British, as a counter-measure, to fit degaussing belts to all their ships. R.A.F. Coastal Command lacked suitable maritime escort aircraft, nor was it under Admiralty operational control until April 1941. Little had been done to prepare the Fleet Air Arm (returned to the Navy in 1937) for escort work.

B. *Phase Two, June 1940-March 1941*

The second phase started when Hitler's Norwegian and French campaigns outflanked Britain's blockade. The occupation of the new German submarine bases at Brest, Lorient, St. Nazaire, LaRochelle and Bordeaux, cut U-boat transit time in half and, in effect, this doubled the number of available boats. While the R.A.F. and the Navy were fighting the Battle of Britain and conducting anti-invasion patrols, the Germans without molestation built special bombproof pens at the new bases. By July 1940, when their augmented force put out through the Bay of Biscay, it had the advantage of Luftwaffe patrols from Norway to France.

Doenitz then instituted wolfpack operations against convoys and following a 500,000-ton month achieved a four-month stretch known as "the Golden Age." When contact was made with a convoy, Doenitz at Lorient homed other nearby boats in for the kill. To this campaign the Italians contributed 27 submarines, but for various reasons they were assigned a patrol area south of 45°N. The British, desperately short of escorts because of destroyer losses, fought a losing battle until corvettes—and later frigates (destroyer-escorts)—came into action. To counter the U-boats the British extended their escorts to 19°W, but basically they lacked a sufficient *number* of small warships. Air patrols, too, were strictly limited in range, the Sunderland being the only aircraft with even a 200-mile radius of action.

Consequently, out in mid-Atlantic the wolfpacks sank 217 ships, but German construction had by the end of 1940 barely made good the 31 boats lost so far. Doenitz was convinced until March 1941 that wolfpack tactics were sound. But then the attrition rate rose to 20 per cent in the Northwestern Approaches. He thereupon started "tonnage warfare" in which he shifted the attack as soon as his losses rose sharply. His move westwards coincided with Admiralty operational control of Coastal Command and with active ASW air patrols from Iceland. At the same time the commissioning of frigates enabled escorts to extend to 35°W (although the British were slow to develop refuelling at sea). On 27 May 1941, convoy HX-129 out of Halifax became the first to be protected for the entire crossing. During this period only 10 per cent of the ships lost had been in convoy, but 60 per cent of the U-boats sunk had been destroyed while in action against convoys.

C. *Phase Three, April-December 1941: The Growth of United States Participation*

The British were helped by the friendly attitude of the Roosevelt administration and of the U.S. Navy. On 3 September 1939, a U.S. Neutrality Patrol was established, followed in October by an inter-American 300-mile safety belt along the hemispheric coast. In 1940 the United States began construction of a two-ocean navy and in September negotiations were completed in which they received a 99-year lease on a string of bases from Newfoundland to Trinidad in exchange for 50 "over-age" destroyers and 10 modern ASW Coast Guard cutters.

On 6 June 1940, Hitler responded with completely unrestricted submarine warfare against British ships. In March 1941 Congress passed Lend-Lease. Exploratory talks with Britain hardened into operational agreements to be implemented if—or perhaps better, when—the United States declared war. On 1 February 1941 the Neutrality Patrol became the U.S. Atlantic Fleet. American escort was planned, Marines landed in Iceland (7 July 1941), and soon U.S. forces began operations.

In the meantime, when in May the Germans attacked liner *Zam-Zam* and the freighter *Robin Moor* and pursuit of *Bismarck* passed through his patrols, Roosevelt eagerly declared an unlimited national emergency. On 31 October, the U.S. destroyer *Reuben James* was sunk. Immediately the White House removed all restrictions from naval action in defense of convoys and it extended escorting east to within 400 miles of Ireland. This enabled Admiral Max Horton, the British commander, to shift some of his forces to combat the arrival off West Africa of new long-range U-boats. At the same time, a solution for the Greenland Air Gap and for marauding German long-range aircraft was found in catapult ships and, later, in escort-carriers, starting in December 1941. Thus the third phase ended on an optimistic note. American entry into the war, however, opened another soft, lucrative hunting ground.

D. Phase Four, January 1942-April 1943

The fourth phase of the Battle started in early 1942. The Anglo-American Combined Chiefs of Staff and the U.S. Joint Chiefs at once concentrated on the struggle at sea. The U.S. Navy was reorganized and Admiral Ernest J. King, the Chief of Naval Operations, promptly set up operational Sea Frontiers, to which the British sent experienced units. Within a month Doenitz, reckoning that a sinking rate of 700,000 tons a month would defeat the Allies, opened a stunning attack on the defenseless

American coastal shipping routes, aiming especially at tankers. In March the loss rate rose to more than 800,000 gross registered tons, but in April progress began to be made with larger trans-Atlantic convoys freeing escorts for coastal convoys. A trans-continental pipeline also eased the tanker shortage.

The Germans sailed south in May into the Gulf of Mexico and the Caribbean. The Allies countered with the air- and surface-escorted Inter-Locking Convoy System from New Orleans to New York. The U-boats now supplied by "milch cows," the new submarine tankers, then shifted still farther south. In August they entered South American waters and brought Brazil into the war. A second group of boats had slim pickings in November and December 1942. Doenitz had returned operations to the North Atlantic, but he was at once forced to divert submarines to attack the North Russian convoys, until the latter ceased after the massacre of PQ-17 (July 1942). Another followed in September, but thereafter no more sailed until air escort could be provided starting in March 1944.

E. *The Turning Point*

By mid-1942, when U-boat production reached 30 per month, most Allied escorts were radar-equipped, but the situation was still serious, as shown by a loss of over 800,000 tons again in November ("Operation Torch" month). The Allies adopted still larger convoys and established the secret U.S. Tenth Fleet, an ASW research organization. Though the Germans succeeded in sinking nearly 700,000 tons in March 1943, the turning point came on 28 April when westbound convoy ONS-5 ran into 51 U-boats but with the aid of two additional escort groups destroyed 6 submarines against a total loss of 12 merchantmen. After this battle off Newfoundland, the Germans were never the same. In July Allied ship construction surpassed world-wide losses, and was 40 per cent more than the Germans estimated.

F. *Phase Five, May 1943-May 1945*

In May, Doenitz shifted pack operations to the Azores to attack Mediterranean-bound convoys, only to play into the hands of the new American escort-carrier, hunter-killer groups. These sank 15 in three months at a loss of four aircraft, despite submarines staying on the surface to fight.

Meanwhile R.A.F. Coastal Command had started, in Spring 1942, a radar offensive against U-boats in transit in the Bay of Biscay. The Germans countered with a radar detector (*Metox*); the British changed wave-lengths (to 10 cm.), added Leigh lights and attacked at night; U-boats secured anti-aircraft guns. In July 1943 British aircraft sank 6 submarines in 21 days and 9 in the next seven with surface help. The Germans then stopped all boats sailing until September when Doenitz sent them out via the Spanish coast to use acoustic torpedoes against the main convoys.

What ultimately defeated the U-boats was close air cover all the way across the Atlantic and plenty of escorts both for convoys and for hunter-killer groups. Bombing of German submarine production delayed the introduction of the high-underwater-speed Walther Type XXI until too late. The morale of the German crews declined despite the use of schnorkels (a U-boat breathing apparatus) and Allied convoys eventually sailed unmolested. An attempt to operate in mid-1944 in the Indian Ocean cost Doenitz 34 of 45 boats.

The Germans lost 781 U-boats, the Italians 85, in addition to a large proportion of their surface warships. The Royal Navy lost 729 warships of all classes of which only 77 were submarines, but 171 were destroyers and escort vessels. The defeat of the German submarine in the Battle of the Atlantic was an Allied effort in which the British played the primary fighting role for six years, supported by the Canadians, the Allies and ultimately by the U.S. Navy. The New World's greatest contribution was in matériel.

There remained the problem of German surface ships. These made some sorties from Norwegian waters after the notable Channel Dash (11-13 February 1942). *Scharnhorst* attempted an attack on a Russian convoy on 26 December and was sunk by the British support force in the Battle of the North Cape. *Bismarck's* sistership *Tirpitz* was constantly kept under air watch and attacked by the British, who capsized her with special bombs at Trömso (12 November 1944). The others were either damaged in air attacks or captured by the Russian Army in its final advances.

III. CONCLUSIONS ON THE WAR AT SEA

The Battle of the Atlantic was a fluid operation. It was a matter of detection and penetration. For the Germans the problem was to find a convoy and slip through or swamp its defenses; for the Allies to locate U-boats and destroy them. If either side had started the conflict with enough ships the war might have been shortened. Both the Royal Navy and the United States Navy, however, had neglected anti-submarine warfare in peacetime, while Doenitz had not expected to have to fight so soon. This was a technological battle in which mastery passed back and forth as scientific advances, gadgets, and experienced leadership gave one side or the other an advantage. But in the end—just as on land—it was a combination of industrial power with the principles of war which gave the Allies victory through logistical strength, adequate numbers of ships and aircraft, and concentration of effort.

IV. INDUSTRIAL PRODUCTION

If World War I had seen mass production create stalemate in limited geographical areas, the period 1939-1945 saw it make possible a truly global conflict. In Germany, Britain, the United States and Russia war production reached its peak in 1944. In the first two nations the means were then stretched to their maximum, while in the two super powers there was still capacity to spare. In the United States war production absorbed only one-third of the nation's industrial potential. In all countries there was from the very beginning a much more systematic allocation of manpower and resources. The United States, of the major powers, was the only one whose production was not disrupted by enemy attacks, thus making it even more potent as the arsenal of democracy.

One indication of the changed nature of supply is the fact that during the Civil War the U.S. Military Railroad Service employed 24,964 ex-railwaymen behind the Union lines. In World

War I the figure was 83,000, when railways were the principal means of supply, but in World War II, when the motor truck and some airborne supply had come into direct competition, only 43,500. Nevertheless, on the move into Germany in 1945 a typical U.S. Army needed eighteen trains a day and on a normal post-victory day in Europe (7 June 1945) the MRS operated 1219 military trains carrying 529,274 tons of supplies, much of it moved by the 1,300 locomotives and 20,000 loaded cars shipped to France in converted LST's between June and October 1944.

As early as the Munich crisis in September 1938 Franklin Roosevelt ordered the armed forces to modernize their production plans. In 1939 a War Resources Board was established which endorsed the Industrial Mobilization Plan. The latter, while a good analysis of World War I's problems, was a poor prognosis for World War II. Various civilian agencies were organized to control the economy, but not until the War Production Board of early 1942 and the Office of Economic Stabilization (later of War Mobilization) in October was order at last established. Meanwhile companies had been reluctant to return to armaments manufacture because of their stigmatization by the 1935 Nye Committee as "merchants of death." In addition they worried about overcapitalization and overproduction, adequate profit margins, and rapid tax write-offs.

In the latter part of 1940 major defense spending began, though 75 per cent of all contracts went to only 56 corporations, leaving some 45,000 small metal-working firms without even raw materials. They were not brought in to manufacture components until 1942. Pre-war stockpiling suffered from a cautious approach and the United States was woefully short of rubber when Japan attacked. But by emergency action synthetic plants more than made up the need by 1943. By Pearl Harbor the United States was already producing more war materials than Germany and Japan combined and had an annual production rate of 25,000 aircraft. An immediate consequence of the declaration of war was a chaotic overordering of all sorts of equipment completely beyond the nation's industrial capacity resulting in the collision of various programs thus destroying with great waste what little planned balance there had been. The first step was to cut back the overexpansion of defense plants, the second the implementation of a Controlled Materials Plan and of a Components Scheduling Program. The first regulated the flow of raw materials, the second of finished parts. This new system enabled industry to be used so efficiently that the construction time of Liberty ships, the standard wartime cargo vessels, dropped from 355 days to 56.

United States war production ultimately supplied 86,330 tanks, 296,400 airplanes, 2,681,000 machine guns, 64,500 landing craft, 6,500 naval vessels, 5,400 merchant ships, and ammunition and fuel for all of them. In addition to 15,000,000 men and women in the armed forces, the civilian work force absorbed the 7,000,000 unemployed, and finally solved the problem of the Depression. Universities kept functioning through military research projects and training programs. The war also saw some $187 billion raised in bonds and loans.

In Britain the story was much the same on a smaller scale. The wartime Ministry of Supply employed 68,000 non-industrial staff while its sister Ministry of Aircraft Production had 21,000 and bossed an industry employing 1,700,000. The railways of Britain ran 258,624 passenger and 279,935 freight trains for the Government, a feat made possible in part by curtailment of civilian services. Between September 1938 and September 1945, 560 airfields were built in Britain at an average cost of over £500,000 apiece, each one involving moving some 30,000 tons of raw materials for the runways alone. During the war manpower in the 18-39 age bracket in the United Kingdom was divided in approximately equal parts between the military forces and industry. Only 16 per cent of all men and only 10 per cent of all women were found to be unfit for service. At the peak of activity in mid-1943 there were over 5,000,000 men and 650,000 women in the armed forces and 5,350,000 in the munitions labor force.

In Germany, despite a reputation for orderliness, production suffered from many of the same political and planning ills as in Allied countries. While the Germans had been farsighted in terms of being able to modify their tanks to carry heavier armor and guns, because they only expected a short war, aircraft types were frozen in production too soon, contributing to a gradual deterioration in fighting strength. The latter was, however, accentuated by a shortage of fuel which curtailed training.

In Russia industrial production was hampered at first by the long withdrawal, though much machinery was moved east of the Urals, where new plants were built. But this meant both a strain on the Allies to supply the Soviet Union through Persia, and via Murmansk and Archangel, and a longer haul when the Russian armies started once more to move westwards. Here, as elsewhere, the reliability and availability of motor transport removed a large burden from the railroads.

CHAPTER XXXII

The Strategic Air Offensive Against Germany, 1939-1945

I. THE STRATEGIC AIR OFFENSIVE

A. Background

IN THE INTERWAR years theorists had advertised airpower as the great offensive weapon, but they had failed to obtain the equipment to translate their ideas into technical reality, itself much under-estimated. In September 1938 the R.A.F. had found it could not strike at the will of the German people because it could scarcely reach the Reich, let alone Berlin. Initially, therefore, Bomber Command was limited to leaflet raids. Moreover, apart from the surprise token raid on Wilhelmshaven on 4 September 1939, two daylight sorties soon proved that, despite their four-gun power turrets, British bombers were no match for cannon-armed German fighters.

The next two years revealed many other serious weaknesses: poor night navigation and target finding, inaccurate bombing and inefficient bombs, expectations that peacetime professional standards could be achieved by hastily trained "hostilities only" airmen. Not until 1942 was the careful evidence, accumulated by photo-intelligence (PRU), accepted and remedial action taken.

B. British Tactics

In the early days of the war the R.A.F. was limited to strictly military targets for fear of a massive retaliatory German raid if civilians were attacked. Because for many months the claims of pilots rather than photographic evidence were accepted, the slight damage done to Germany was over-estimated. There was also a consistent belief in certain circles—as in World War I—that German morale could be cracked by bombing, in part because the people were presumed to be restless under Hitler. These two factors led to the adoption of the attack on workers' homes in August 1941, when the British Cabinet at last realized the inaccuracy of night bombing. By 1942 the heavy bombers (Stirling, Halifax, and Lancaster) designed in 1936 were becoming operational as were bombs heavier than the standard 500-pounder. At the same time radar-equipped Pathfinder aircraft, generally Mosquitoes, began to mark targets visually so that mass bombing could be accurate. The scattered all night procession of British raiders was reorganized into a compact stream which could deliver a potent weight of attack in a matter of minutes, with the average bombing error reduced from 5 miles to under 500 yards. Nevertheless, as a war-winning weapon Bomber Command's capabilities remained limited until 1944. Then at last it had the power to deliver the kind of city-devastating blows British statesmen and airmen had talked about in 1939.

C. *American Tactics*

United States airmen had been trained since World War I to deliver daylight precision attacks. But the success of these maneuvers at home had obscured two essential European combat facts —weather and enemy fighter opposition. The Eighth Air Force made a few sample attacks in 1942. When at last in 1943 it undertook serious operations, it was rocked back on its heels by German fighter attacks. Its work was, therefore, restricted for some time to those missions on which it could have continuous fighter escort. The American answer was similar to that of the Royal Navy in the Atlantic; it did not give up the Battle of Germany. It pressed for the solution which both its own generals and R.A.F. air marshals had thought impossible, the development of a long-range fighter. The result was that during 1943, the escort range rose from the 175 miles of a Spitfire or early P-47 Thunderbolt to 340 by July 1943 and finally to over 850 for the P-51 Mustang, which entered operations in January 1944.

In mid-1943, casualties were so heavy in raids on Schweinfurt and Regensburg that many thought night raiding the only reasonable answer. The precision Norden bombsight with which the U.S.A.A.F. was equipped, however, would have been wasted at night. The decision to develop the long-range fighter went hand-in-hand with that to fight an aerial battle of attrition over Germany in which Luftwaffe fighter strength was destroyed as part of the preparations for D-Day. Whereas the R.A.F. flew in a loose stream in which—towards the end of the war—its own night-fighters patrolled, the U.S.A.A.F. adopted the tight box formation (a flying hedgehog) but one which, as naval men knew, played into German hands. Like the unescorted convoy at sea, it was vulnerable once located for its own defensive firepower could be penetrated.

The solution, as at sea, was the development of powerful escort fighter groups both for close defense and for hunter-killer attacks against the Luftwaffe on its own airfields. Just as in the maritime war, so the proper application of the technological-logistical might of America—coupled with the principles of concentration and economy of force—produced ultimate victory in conjunction with surface forces. But if there had been a proper appreciation of aerial warfare before the war, casualties might have been much lighter because the Battle of Germany might have been fought before the Germans had perfected their defenses.

II. THE STRATEGIC BOMBER CAMPAIGN

A. The Early Ineffective Years, 1939-1943

After a few attempts at daylight raiding, the R.A.F. contented itself with night leaflet raids over Germany. With the invasion of France, the air force was switched to transportation targets, but these were too far from the front to have any effect on a blitzkrieg; a good example of the failure of generalship to see the most urgent target. On 25 August 1940 Berlin was bombed in retaliation for a raid the previous day on London. This led Goering—whose pride had been hurt—to order attacks on various British cities. At the same time the British were undertaking a dual campaign which was a compromise between the Air Staff's desire for precision bombing of the oil industry and the Cabinet's wish for retaliation. Sir Charles Portal, Chief of the Air Staff from October 1940, had already suggested in May, limiting operations to special targets in heavily populated areas so as not to waste bombs. After the German attack on Coventry (14 November 1940) this proposal was adopted. But this twin attack on oil and morale was commonly only 100 tons a raid. Fire became the principal destructive weapon to be used against 41 selected cities. The plan to destroy Hitler's oil industry foundered on the rock of inaccurate bombing, at last revealed by PRU aircraft in November 1940. The small force available was further weakened by participation in the Battle of the Atlantic. Early in 1941, Bomber Command proposed reviving the transportation plan, since this was more within its powers. The new July 1941 directive coupled the attack on transportation with that on morale. The next month the Butt Report to the Cabinet supported the PRU reports on aiming accuracy. The immediate effect was the adoption of area bombing. The search for a technical-tactical formula to make the Command effective led eventually—after considerable resistance—to the creation a year later of the Pathfinders who, by means of new airborne radar sets, pinpointed targets with visible markers at which the less experienced crews aimed. The Butt Report also caused Air Marshal Sir Arthur Harris' appointment as the tough and beloved leader of Bomber Command, which he saw grow from 500 medium bombers available daily in 1942 to an effective force of 1000 heavies by May 1945.

The R.A.F.'s reputation as an offensive striking force began to recover with a series of successes against the Renault Plant, near Paris, in March and upon Lübeck and Rostock in April, culminating in the 1,000-plane attack on Cologne (30 May 1942). At the same time Harris established a close personal relationship with the Prime Minister, while his staff did likewise with the experts on the German economy.

B. The U.S.A.A.F. Joins the Struggle

Advanced elements of the U.S. Army's Eighth Air Force arrived in England early in 1942 and on 17 August made their first precision attack with 12 aircraft against Rouen. The necessity of forming the Twelfth Air Force for the North African operation delayed the build-up of the Eighth to such an extent that in April 1943 its strength was still but a daily average of 100 aircraft. Until 12 December, American operations were limited to the coast of France; then Bremen and Kiel came within escort range. In July 1943, the Eighth struck Rostock and, on 17 August, the ball-bearing plant at Schweinfurt and the Messerschmitt works at Regensburg, the latter on a "shuttle" flight to North Africa.

Casualties on these partially-escorted raids led directly to the rapid development of the Mustang as a practicable alternative to night attacks. The British pushed American daylight raids as the means of making a significant contribution to winning the war by wearing down German fighter strength. Efforts of airmen to get maximum priority for their attack were invariably defeated by the Battle of the Atlantic. The need to form an army to exploit the disruption created by a successful air assault also complicated the situation. An effort to strike a balance was made at Casablanca and subsequent conferences.

C. *The Years of Achievement, 1943-1945*

1. "OPERATION POINTBLANK"

The Casablanca Directive became "Operation Pointblank" into which the Eighth Air Force was worked gradually to develop a round-the-clock assault on Germany itself. This was a mixture of massive night area assaults by the newly re-equipped R.A.F. and of selective daylight raids by the U.S.A.A.F. The failure—or inability—of the Eighth to win air superiority brought on a crisis. The solution was better co-ordination of the night and day attacks together with resting the Eighth until the Mustang appeared. The weight and precision of the new night assault—when coupled with full escort by day—brought from February 1944 onwards the desired decimation of the German fighter force before "Overlord" (6 June 1944).

As part of the long battle of the Ruhr came the raid on the Mohne and Eder Dams (16/17 May 1943); the round-the-clock assault on Hamburg (24 July-2 August) in which German radar was foiled with "Window" ("chaff"), while 9,000 tons of bombs were dropped in 3,095 sorties, with casualty rates reduced from the 19.9 per cent of the Ruhr raids to 8.4. On 7 August the first "Master Bomber" raid, on the experimental rocket station at Peenemunde, was followed by the Battle of Berlin (23 August, 18 November 1943-24 March 1944) during which German night fighters began to have considerable success.

Claimed to be the battle to end the war, the Battle of Berlin was lost because—after the costly Schweinfurt raid of Black Thursday, 14 October 1943—the Eighth had to retire to regroup. It returned to Schweinfurt on 20 February 1944—the opening day of the "Big Week" in which it struck on five out of six days—and in one of the decisive battles of the war American escort fighters sent the Luftwaffe into decline. It could only fight in the air, or be destroyed on the ground.

The new Battle of Germany saw the Eighth Air Force tactics changed from evasion to provocation, despite the fact that much of its effort was devoted to preparations for D-Day and to the newly-located, flying-bomb (V-1) sites. The one special raid of the period was that of 177 B-24's against Ploesti on 1 August 1943. A brilliant attack delivered from Italian airfields, it nevertheless failed to prevent an increase in Germano-Rumanian oil production. Later in April-August 1944 another 5,287 sorties were flown against this target system. Raids on Germany were more successful and by 22 June 1944 Speer, the German economic czar, was forced to report to Hitler that 90 per cent of the capacity to produce aviation petrol had been lost; and that repairs would take six to eight weeks.

2. "OVERLORD"

The "Overlord" planners demanded that in addition to the "Pointblank" campaign, massive attacks on specific targets closer to the beaches should be undertaken. As a result, "Pointblank" virtually halted General Spaatz's Eighth, which did not return to targets in Germany until 16 July, when its new Mustang-equipped Combat Air Scouts flew ahead to spy out the weather, etc. The new attack heralded the beginning of the final offensive against oil, communications, and morale, in which the advance on the ground helped the greater effort in the air.

The communications plan was the work of Eisenhower's deputy, Tedder of the R.A.F. It was designed to co-ordinate the efforts of Bomber Command, the Eighth and the Allied Expeditionary Air Forces. The bomber forces were placed under the Supreme Commander in March, and Eisenhower's April 1944 directive allocated destruction of the German Air Force to the Eighth, while Bomber Command was to continue its attacks on cities.

In the meantime the latter—much to Harris' surprise—had become a precision force and was in fact able to make a considerable contribution to the destruction of the French railway system prior to D-Day. The air weapon was now used independently—as had been intended in 1918—as a supplement to the tactical air force when conditions so required.

From March to September the bomber forces were directly under Eisenhower's command. By the latter date a joint Anglo-American oil-targets committee had been established to study and determine priorities. But after arguments over both oil and "morale-busting Berlin," partly to aid the Russians and partly to rub into the German people the lesson of defeat, the blow fell upon Dresden (13-14 February 1945). Though the attack on oil and communications called for dispersion of forces, it could be justified as concentration of effort and economy of operations.

3. THE FINAL OFFENSIVE

The new campaign was complicated by the fact that command arrangements made General H. H. Arnold in Washington and Sir Charles Portal in London the responsible Commanders-in-Chief. They had to deal with an increasing number of offices interested in Germany. In addition, the armies had become accustomed to call for massive bombing to solve minor tactical problems. Tedder wanted a co-ordinated effort to help the land forces achieve a quick victory, but this was never attained because the air staffs saw oil and communications as competing target systems. At the same time the Admiralty showed justifiable concern over the new high-speed U-boats. In the British High Command the matter reached a crisis in which only Harris' great reputation saved him from removal (January 1945).

Despite Harris' objections, Bomber Command attacked oil targets after September 1944, when German aircraft production at last began to decline. In addition canals were regularly breached and on 12 November 1944, Billy Mitchell was again vindicated when the R.A.F., using 22,000 pound "Tallboy" bombs, sank the German battleship *Tirpitz* in Norway. German commerce and naval operations were continually hampered by Allied mine-laying which accounted for between 60 and 70 per cent of all German and Italian merchant ship losses as well as helping to employ some 3000 minesweepers and escort vessels. Attacks on naval installations kept all but one of the 119 Type XXI U-boats—delivered to the German Navy in 1944-45—from becoming operational.

By the end of the war, Bomber Command was capable of dropping 67,000 tons a month with 98 per cent falling within three miles of the aiming point. The Eighth almost reached the same tonnage figure. Thus the 1941 goal of 4,000 aircraft with 25 per cent of their bombs on target was surpassed. During the war, Bomber Command despatched 364,514 sorties; of these 8,325 aircraft were lost and 47,000 aircrew killed. In its much shorter operational life of 995 days, the Eighth sent out 332,645 bomber sorties from which 31,934,952 bombs weighing 701,300 tons were dropped. These together with 294,255 fighter sorties consumed 869,821,058 gallons of fuel. The cost to the U.S.A.A.F. was 43,742 killed or missing and 1,923 wounded. But the Eighth destroyed 15,439 enemy fighters. And how many aircraft the Allied strategic air offensive denied the Germans is a matter of dispute, the figures ranging from 5,000 to 15,000 depending upon interpretations of production and destruction statistics.

III. CONCLUSION AND EVALUATION

The strategic air offensive against Germany was not only a controversial operation during the war itself, but since 1945, historical and moral arguments have added to the confusion. Neither the R.A.F. nor the U.S.A.A.F. were—until the last year or so of the war—in a position to deliver blows of sufficient strength to destroy the Luftwaffe, or the industries, fuel and transportation systems upon which the German armed forces depended. Even then, assured single-strike annihilation remained a technical impossibility. This has left the field open for discussion of the moot question whether air power alone could have won the war or whether the D-Day invasion—as well as the Russian land attack—was essential.

The long, slow build-up of Allied air power gave the Germans the opportunity to learn how to meet the threat posed, which they did by dispersion, concealment of factories, and ability to effect rapid repairs. At the same time it took the Allied airmen many months to realize that their claims far exceeded the actual damage, to undertake remedial action, and to win the fight among their own strategists for the most desirable program. The real breakthrough came with the development of airborne radar for position-finding and bomb-aiming and with the development of efficient long-range fighters, especially the Mustang by day and the Mosquito by night. But even after the major onslaught began early in 1944, it took approximately nine months before German war production reached its peak and began to decline to the final point where it was brought to a standstill by a combination of invasion and paralyzation from the air.

The Mustang showed that defending fighters could be overcome if sufficient effort was put into producing the right aircraft, while Mosquito operations indicated that small versatile machines were far more economical and flexible than larger, more expensive and more vulnerable conventional types of aircraft. Finally, civilian morale proved far tougher than most experts believed; Churchill was right when in 1917 he warned against strengthening the enemy's will to resist by attacks on the civilian population.

The frustration of British daylight attacks in 1939 and of American raids in 1942 and 1943 showed that Mahan's principles still held good: unless a *guerre de course* was undertaken, the enemy's main forces had to be defeated before a major attack upon his homeland could be undertaken. Evasion and surprise might be used, but ultimately air superiority had to be won or losses would climb above acceptable levels.

After the war both German field marshals Kesselring and von

Rundstedt believed Germany had been defeated by strategic bombing behind the fronts, by incessant low-level attacks by fighter aircraft, and by the systematic destruction of German war industry by bombing.

The lessons to be drawn from the campaign are that there must be adequate technological and doctrinal preparation for the type of war that is to be fought and that the one must be adjusted to the other. Furthermore, thorough intelligence of the enemy's economy must be acquired before war starts and must be kept current during the struggle. Targets must be carefully selected whose destruction will both paralyze enemy operations as quickly as possible and be within the tactical and technical competence of the attackers; these targets must be attacked rapidly and repeatedly to ensure a decisive effect. With the coming of the atomic bomb, airpower finally obtained the destructive force to destroy major targets with a single blow.

CHAPTER XXXIII

Finishing Off Germany, 1944 – 1945

I. INTRODUCTION

ON D-DAY, 6 June 1944, the Allies opened the final stage of the war against Germany with a successful cross-Channel amphibious assault. On that day the Germans had 212 divisions on the Russian front, twenty-five in Italy, twenty-five in the Balkans, nine in Germany and sixty-one in France, nominally of 12,800 officers and men apiece, but on the Russian front the divisions were at half that strength. The initial Allied assault was made by eight divisions gradually increased by 1945 to fifty of more than 14,000 men each. The Russian and Italian fronts served as secondary holding actions where the Normandy landings were concerned.

With the directive issued to Eisenhower in December 1943—after the Cairo-Teheran talks—the grand strategic objective became not a local victory but "operations aimed at the heart of Germany and the destruction of her armed forces." The goal was primarily political; the means traditional. The long-awaited "second front" relieved some of the pressure on the Russians, but by mid-1944 they stood at the gates of Warsaw well on their own way to smashing the Germans in the East. Germany was squeezed in an inexorable vise while her life-blood was sapped by loss of motive power through the Russian seizure of the Rumanian oil fields, Allied bombing of the synthetic oil industry, and air interdiction of her railways, which paralyzed coal shipment. In part, because of "unconditional surrender," Hitler's personal views, German fears of the Russians, and Allied suspicions, there could be no negotiated peace—only the complete annihilation of the Third Reich. Churchill's plea for an attack on the "soft underbelly of the Axis" to bring in Turkey and to deny the Russians the Balkans and Vienna was rejected by Roosevelt who, since early 1942, had had his eye on an early defeat of Germany through an invasion of France.

II. THE D-DAY INVASION

A. Planning

Planning for "Overlord"—as the D-Day operation was called—began after the Casablanca Conference when, in January 1943, General Frederick Morgan was appointed Chief of Staff to the Supreme Allied Commander. All landing beaches from Portugal to Norway were surveyed and the fundamental outline developed which led to success. At Teheran (November 1943) Roosevelt, Churchill and Stalin agreed that the invasion would take place about 1 May 1944. The next month Eisenhower was appointed to command, and in 1944 the plans strengthened. The planners, after balancing the strategically desirable and logistically possible, settled on the Normandy beaches. The Pas de Calais was ruled out as too obvious, although the German Army insisted, to its own misfortune, that the main landings would be there; the Navy did better in guessing Normandy. With good beaches protected from the prevailing westerly weather by the Contentin Peninsula, it was within range of fighter cover from England, it had adequate sally ports on both flanks, and it contained two major ports (Le Havre and Cherbourg). A diversionary attack (first called "Anvil," then "Dragoon") was to be carried out on Southern France, but the shortage of landing craft—caused by the insistence of both Eisenhower and Montgomery that the initial landing be with five rather than three divisions, as well as strategic arguments—resulted in its postponement until 15 August. The Allied plan was to land simultaneously on five beaches ("Utah" and "Omaha" in the American sector; "Juno," "Gold" and "Sword" in the British) after paratroopers secured the flanks, to amass supplies and troops and, as soon as possible, to break out.

B. *German Defensive Thinking*

The Germans hoped to counter the invasion with their defensive Atlantic Wall, but the defense of France was secondary to the defensive fighting against Russia. Accordingly, von Rundstedt, who was placed in command, was denied the men and material with which to fashion a new German "Maginot Line." Moreover, he did not trust the concept of static defense and, when early in 1944 Hitler placed Rommel in subordinate command of defenses from the Loire to the Scheldt, a conflict of defensive ideas developed which ultimately aided the Allies.

Von Rundstedt wished to keep his mobile reserves well back from the beachhead areas until he was sure which was the main landing. Rommel, more familiar with Allied operations from bitter experience, wanted them far forward so that Allied air power could not isolate them from the battlefield. Hitler gave Rommel part of the armor, but left most of the reserves in von Rundstedt's hands. Unwilling to try a mobile defense in these circumstances, Rommel went to static defense—all too reminiscent of World War I command techniques—but only received four per cent of the 100,000,000 mines he asked for and insufficient beach obstacles. He was also short of the necessary transport by means of which the defenders of the beach fortifications and the secondary line of flooded works could be reinforced.

Moonlight and tidal conditions impelled Eisenhower to select 5 June as D-Day. The weather, however, deteriorated and a 24-hour postponement occurred. Then—unknown to the Germans—the weather began to clear to the west and the "go-ahead" was given for 6 June. Thus a tactical surprise was achieved while, in addition, the Germans were induced by radar tricks to believe that the landings would be in the Pas de Calais, where their V-1 rocket sites had been discovered and from which launchings started on 12/13 June.

C. *Air Preparations*

Observing the principles of war, the Allies prepared after considerable arguments between Harris of Bomber Command, and Tedder and Leigh-Mallory of SHAEF (Supreme Headquarters,

Allied Expeditionary Force) backed by Eisenhower, to isolate the battleground by using the strategic bomber force in a tactical role. Despite the fears of the British High Command that too many French civilians would become casualties, French and Belgian saboteurs and others loyally joined the fray. The "transportation plan" went into effect in mid-April and by D-Day German rail traffic was down 50 per cent. The second stroke was the demolition of the bridges across the Seine and the Loire so as to isolate the battlefield, and the third was the mauling of enemy airfields within 130 miles of the 70-mile-long landing beaches.

D. *The Amphibious Landing*

The actual Allied assault was opened with airborne landings from 2,395 aircraft and 867 gliders with a supporting bomber force of 2,219 aircraft. This was followed by a preliminary bombardment at dawn with the first wave of the assault hitting the beaches from the 4,266-vessel force (ranging from battleships to landing-craft) at 0630. Success was achieved with the aid of amphibious tanks, surprise, weather, courage, and especially naval interdiction gunfire and overwhelming air superiority provided by 171 fighter squadrons. The most hotly contested beach was Omaha, but nevertheless 34,000 troops were landed with only 2,000 casualties. By the tenth, the first Continental airfield was in operation and Montgomery's 21st Army Group (U.S. First Army, British Second) was established ashore against the German Seventh Army, while the German Fifteenth was near Calais.

The Germans were, in fact, taken completely by surprise; Rommel was away and von Rundstedt, convinced that the main landing would come farther east, held back his reserves. When Hitler finally realized what was happening, he ordered these forces thrust into the Caen area where, according to British plans, they were held down while the Americans pushed west to the Gulf of St. Malo and then north to assault Cherbourg (25 June).

E. *The Normandy Campaign*

By 6 July the Allies had, with the aid of "Mulberry" harbors, "Gooseberry" breakwaters, and "Pluto" pipelines—in addition to landing craft—put 929,000 men, 586,000 tons of supplies, and

177,000 vehicles ashore. This gave the invaders a two-to-one margin in men and a three-to-one advantage in tanks and artillery. After delay by Allied bombing, which made the streets impassable, Caen was taken on the eighth. Ten days later the Americans took St. Lo. While the British faced the German Seventh Army, the U.S. First broke out on 26 July and the recently-formed U.S. Third, under Patton, promptly drove south to Avranches, then fanned out in all directions to take the U-boat bases at Brest and St. Nazaire from the rear, while the main U.S. mass pressed eastward along the open flank of the Germans. To meet them, Canadians moved south from Caen and helped complete the Falaise gap envelopment on 19 August.

Meanwhile Hitler again played into Allied hands by replacing von Rundstedt with von Kluge and by ordering the Seventh Army to strike westwards, thus sending it deeper into the trap. Some 40,000 Germans managed to escape, but 60 per cent of the Seventh were killed or captured and most of their weapons lost. At the same time (20 July 1944) a small group of German generals, realizing their fight was hopeless, brought to the boil a long-standing plot and unsuccessfully attempted to assassinate Hitler. Von Kluge and Rommel, who was recuperating from injuries received in an air attack, committed suicide. The Allies proceeded apace and liberated Paris (25 August) while the British Second Army pushed up the coast to take the V-weapon launching sites, fearing the Germans would equip the V-2 rocket with a crude atomic warhead. On 1 September, Eisenhower, who had already landed in France, personally took overall field command from Montgomery.

III. OPERATION DRAGOON

As soon as they could be spared from the Normandy landings, landing-craft were shifted to the Mediterranean, followed a little later by the faster support ships. A landing force under the overall command of Vice-Admiral Kent Hewitt, who had handled various invasions since 1942, succeeded on 15 August in putting ashore three American and then two French divisions between Toulon and Cannes. Air support was provided by nine escort carriers.

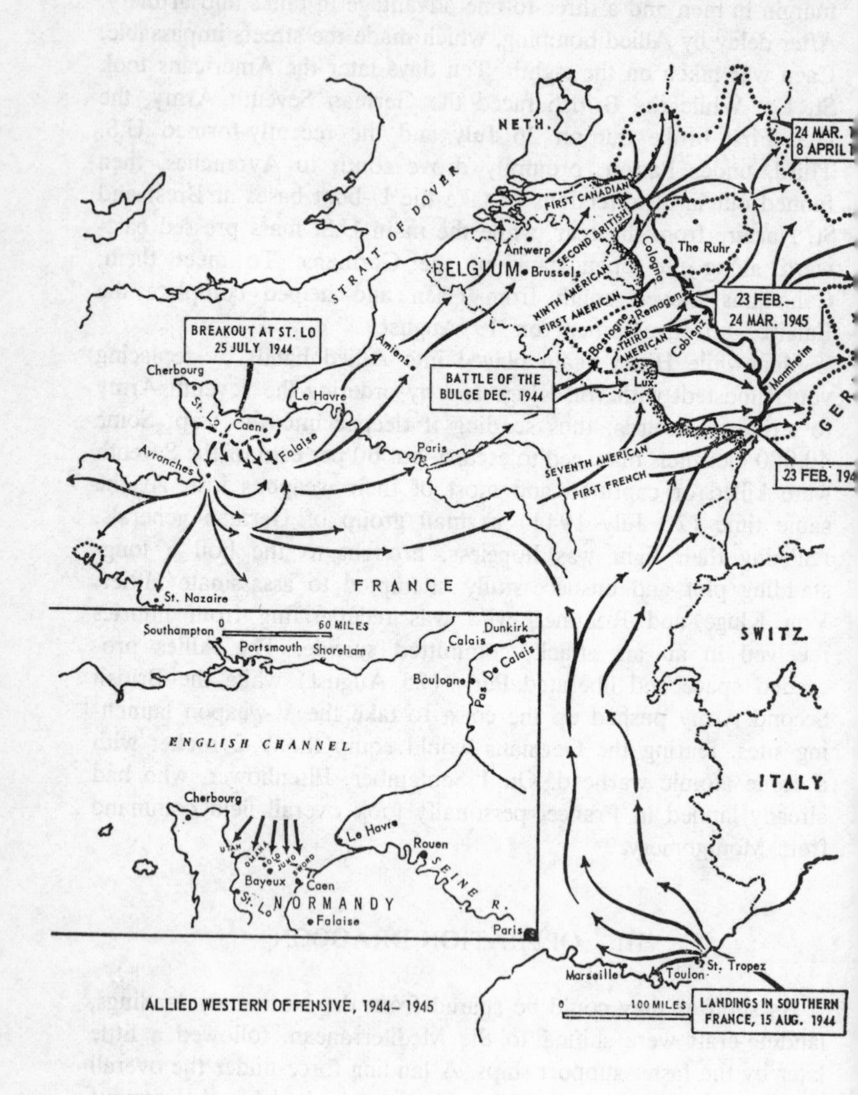

ALLIED WESTERN OFFENSIVE, 1944–1945

The French quickly advanced west from Toulon and cleared the major port of Marseilles (28 August), while the Americans—ultimately built up to 19 divisions—accompanied by the new seven-division French First Army, pushed rapidly up the Rhone Valley. On 11 September U.S. General Jacob Dever's 6th Army Group made contact with Patton's right wing near Dijon, wheeled right and raced for the Rhine and the Swiss frontier. This isolated the Germans in southwest France.

IV. PUSHING HOME THE ATTACK

The Seine was reached (25 August) and at once crossed on new bridges. Due to smoothly functioning supply organizations, the Allies pressed eastward straight across the 1914-1918 battlegrounds. By 14 September, the Canadian First Army had the Germans in the north penned into four coastal areas; the British Second had taken Antwerp, a major supply port; the U.S. First was holding the Aachen-Luxembourg line; and the U.S. Third controlled the front south to the Swiss frontier. There had been no major fighting during the German retreat.

The Allies now launched a series of attacks aimed at clearing the Scheldt-Antwerp area, turning the West Wall north of Aachen and penetrating through Aachen itself. They hoped to force a bridgehead at Metz for future use. These operations met with limited success. The Canadians cleared the mouths of the Scheldt after considerable difficulties on Walcheren Island (6 October-8 November). Montgomery attempted a rapid advance to seize the bridges across the Rhine. Airborne troops were landed on 17 September. The Americans at Nijmegen succeeded in holding out until the van of the British Eighth Army relieved them. But the British at Arnheim landed on top of a panzer division in rest and suffered from bad weather which hampered resupply and tactical air support. The morale failure was much greater than the casualties.

On 2 October the U.S. First Army struck in a double envelopment at Aachen, finally seized it 21 October and thus penetrated the West Wall, exposing the road to the Ruhr industrial area some 50 miles to the northeast. The Allies, unfortunately, were then obliged to pause to build up supplies. Their advance had been hampered by the German tactic of holding and destroying major ports and by their own over-enthusiastic destruction of railways and bridges, as well as of occupied villages ahead of their advance, and by a shortage of gasoline. Engineers had, therefore, constantly to clear the roads so that both fighting and supply elements could move ahead.

The Allied armies spent November and early December threatening the Germans with a breakthrough on a broad front in order to make them commit their reserves. The British attacked in a southeastward direction from north of Aachen and the Americans aimed due eastwards (17 November and 15 December) in a costly campaign pushing the line to the Roer River and threatening Cologne. Much farther south, the U.S. Third Army took Metz and then, with the Seventh on its right, bridged the Saar River (15 December); on the extreme right the French pushed through the Belfort Gap, by-passed Colmar, and reached the Rhine just north of the Swiss frontier.

V. THE RUSSIAN CAMPAIGN, SUMMER AND WINTER, 1944-1945

In the East, the Germans increasingly found themselves facing Russian thrusts without secure bases, good lateral communications, or adequate reserves. Moreover, the quality of reinforcements for their units—which were already well under strength—was physically low. Lack of fuel had forced abbreviated training of air and armored forces. The Russians, however, were now in full flow and were aiming to win the political peace. The Germans, who expected the main offensive to be directed at the oil fields, assembled their remaining strength between the Pripet Marshes and the Carpathians. On the other hand, the enemy—despite three-to-one superiority—aimed at attrition unless annihilation was cheap, and moved to free the northern front. Early in June, the Russians drove the Finns out of the war. Then on 23 June, 100 divisions hit the hedgehog system defended by Busch's Fourth and Ninth German Armies, took the four vital works of Vitebsk, Orsha, Mogilev and Zhlobin in quick succession, and pushed on almost to Minsk, which fell on 3 July. The next day, the 1939 Polish frontier was crossed. No sooner had the Germans shifted their reserves to stem this tide than the enemy drove towards Riga, forcing their withdrawal from Latvia and Estonia in August.

Meanwhile a double envelopment began on 16 July which took Lvov and brought the replacement of Busch with Field Marshal Walter Model, a Hitlerian. Other Russian forces took Brest-Litovsk and swept past Warsaw, where the Polish underground arose, but was allowed to die. Model fought a delaying action until Rokossovsky reached Praga on 15 September and the advance stopped. The Russians once again shifted the offensive to reduce von Kleist's 25 divisions and open the road to Vienna. The first attack (20 August) scattered the Rumanians and a coup d'état in Bucharest ended their resistance. Bulgaria deserted Germany on 26 August and the bulk of the new German Sixth Army was trapped. The Russians sped on to the Danube, Ploesti and Bucharest. A three-stage conquest of the Danube Basin followed which cleared Bulgaria and Hungary and linked up with Marshal Tito's Yugoslav partisans, taking Belgrade on 19 October. On 3 December the Russians from the Galician front joined hands with their Danubian cohorts in eastern Slovakia.

Meanwhile, on 15 September the Russians had opened a drive to clear the road to East Prussia by taking Riga and Libau. This isolated some 20 German divisions in Courland and Memel and only a few of them were rescued by the German Baltic fleet.

VI. THE BATTLE OF THE BULGE

The day after the Allied offensives halted near the Rhine, von Rundstedt delivered the second German surprise through the Ardennes—a drive for which the Allies were no more disposed than in 1940, but for which they enjoyed better air cover. Compared with operations on the Russian front, it was but a counter-attack. Its importance lies in the fact that von Rundstedt nearly managed to roll up the Allied left, his ultimate objective being the destruction of Antwerp, a strategically justifiable gamble. On 16 December the Germans struck from the area of St. Vith past the American 101st Airborne division in Bastogne and drove westward south of the American First, which held the vital north shoulder of the German salient. By 24 December they had almost reached Dinant on the Meuse, when they ran out of luck, fuel, and bad weather. At once Allied airpower, which low ceilings had kept on the ground, coupled with infantry blows on the flanks of the salient, eliminated the Bulge (31 January 1945). Again a cordon defense had failed.

Hitler refused to surrender, so the Germans had to reorganize again. Eisenhower, obeying his political master, Roosevelt, considered the invasion of Germany only from a strategic rather than from a grand strategic standpoint. In keeping with his orders, he was only concerned with defeating the enemy armies. Berlin as the political focus of northern Europe and an undivided Germany as a bulwark against historical Communist aggression, were ignored. The task was still seen as the simple Clausewitzian destruction of the German armed forces. So for the second time an advance on a broad front was selected, in part because Eisenhower did not wish to give the glory of taking Berlin to a single commander, i.e., Montgomery, Patton, or Bradley.

VII. THE INVASION OF GERMANY

A. The West

The final campaign in the West opened with a stolid advance by the Canadians through Holland (8-14 February 1945); the U.S. Ninth Army belatedly got under way clearing Wesel (10 March). In the meantime the U.S. First Army had driven to Cologne (10 February-7 March) and to the south another American group seized the bridge at Remagen and was the first to cross the Rhine to the later benefit of others. The U.S. Third cleared the Remagen-Mannheim sector and on 22 February Patton made a surprise crossing of the Rhine. Further to the south, the left or western bank of the Rhine had been cleared by the 6th Army Group by 25 March. The valuable Saar coal basin was in Allied hands. The major assault over the Rhine was preceded by air interdiction starting on 21 February and was effected as an amphibious operation (23-24 March), followed by the dropping of the U.S. 17th and British 6th Airborne Divisions. It was D-Day in miniature. The main northern envelopment of the Ruhr by the U.S. First Army was underway while Patton launched a second column from the south. By 1 April the whole of the eastern bank was virtually under Allied control. The German forces now began to collapse. The Ruhr was encircled on 1 April and on the eighteenth Model, recently transferred to the West, surrendered his armies.

Eisenhower now definitely decided that Berlin was of no military importance and aimed instead at the widely separated Germans in the Danish Peninsula and at the mythical German "National Redoubt" in the mountains of southern Germany and the Austrian Tyrol, which had no vital area to support it and which a simple aerial operation would have reduced. So the U.S. Third Army raced via Jena into Pilsen in Czechoslovakia. The Ninth reached the Elbe south of Magdeburg, while the U.S. First cleared the Harz mountain area bringing the 12th Army Group to a standstill. Meanwhile to the North, Montgomery's 21st Army Group, minus the U.S. Ninth Army which had only been attached for the Ruhr operation, reached Luneburg on the day Model capitulated, crossed the Elbe and moved on Lübeck. To the south the French First Army reached Austria just east of Lake Constance, while the U.S. Seventh crossed the Upper Danube, took Munich and marched down towards Vienna (taken by the Russians on 13 April), largely supplied by air because its advance sometimes reached 100 miles a day.

B. *The East*

Meanwhile the Russians, after a lull on the Russo-Polish frontier from mid-August 1944 to mid-January 1945—during which the Danubian campaign was fought—resumed their advance with some 300 divisions and 25 tank armies. The Germans' mounting fear of the Red Army and of consequent Communist political control considerably eased resistance to the western Allied invasion. The Germans were hampered by the deteriorating condition of their men and supplies and by clouds of their own refugees who, often without warning, found the Russians literally on their doorsteps.

The Danubian campaign had re-opened on 29 November when

Malinovsky and Tolbukhin advanced to encircle Budapest. They broke down an attempted German counter-offensive and took Pest on 18 January 1945 and Buda on 13 February. The Communist road to Vienna was now clear.

On 12 January 1945, Koniev broke through the German Polish lines and forced the evacuation of Warsaw. In the South the Germans abandoned Cracow and in the center, Zhukov took Kutno and Lodz, west of the Polish capital. In the North, the attack on East Prussia opened on the fourteenth with two armies and by 26 January, East Prussia was isolated with the Russians moving up the Baltic coast. Königsberg fell on 9 April.

The Russians now had nothing to overcome but the ancient refortified German line along the Oder. Their objective was political—Berlin and a large occupation zone. Koniev crossed the German frontier north and south of Breslau on 20 January and then swept Upper Silesia to within 70 miles of Dresden, destroying the eastern German coal and iron area. Meanwhile Zhukov took Posen after which he clove Pomerania in two, by advancing to Kolberg on the Baltic. Concurrently Rokossovsky cleared Danzig (30 March) and ended the Baltic campaign.

In the Danube yet another desperate German offensive (3-15 March) failed—as in the Ardennes—for lack of fuel. The Russians struck back, turned the German-Hungarian position on the Drava Lake-Belaton line, and crossed into Austria. Malinovsky advanced north of the Danube and Tolbukhin south of it, reaching Vienna on 7 April and subduing it six days later. Another political objective had been obtained, but there still remained Berlin and the commercially valuable Elbe.

On 17 April the last great Soviet drive of the war started. Zhukov advanced from the Oder due west and Koniev north from the Niesse. On 22 April, Zhukov had reached the autobahn encircling the capital and Koniev struck Berlin from the south. In three days it was surrounded and the Russian van joined hands with the U.S. First Army at Torgau on the Elbe. Hitler shot himself on the last day of the month and on 2 May Berlin surrendered. The next day German generals offered to surrender to the western Allies. Diplomatic and military negotiations delayed the actual conclusion of the war until 8 May 1945 (VE-Day).

VIII. CONCLUSIONS ON THE WAR IN EUROPE

By an expert policy of the indirect approach—in which he constantly caught his opponents off balance both before and after the declaration of war in 1939—Hitler gave Germany *lebensraum.* But he made two fatal mistakes. He thrust Britain off the Continent without defeating her and finally forced her to revert to a traditionally successful maritime policy. Then with an enemy remaining at his back, he invaded Russia where he failed rapidly to achieve his objectives before the Russians brought their full resources to bear. Not only did he underestimate British sea power and the new mood in the United States, but he forgot the vital importance of railways and oil in modern wars, becoming fascinated instead with places like Stalingrad rather than with the Suez Canal, the railways near Moscow, or the oil wells of the Caucasus.

The Allies, however, were little better. They neglected to concentrate the strategic air offensive against German oil and transportation industries—a task which proper targeting could have accomplished, as isolated raids proved. Even more importantly, Roosevelt and his grand strategists failed to understand the political nature of war and the need to aim for the pivots of post-war power—Vienna and Berlin. Clausewitz and Jomini went unread and the end result was the Cold War. Churchill, not necessarily a good strategist although a great wartime leader, at least had a clearer vision of grand strategy based upon long experience of European affairs, and a wholesome distrust of Russians.

Tactically the war quickly revealed the failures of both sides. The Germans were expert at the lightning war, a mailed diplomatic fist, but they had not thought out—let alone planned or prepared for—a long war of attrition. Ultimately, as in World War I, they were ground down by superior Allied industrial power. They had neither the navy or the long-range airpower to strike Britain, nor did they have the means to wage a successful two-year campaign in Russia. Yet they came so close to success at sea with their U-boats, in the Battle of Britain with the Luftwaffe and in Russia with their armored thrusts that their gamble was perhaps justifiable. The Russians proved to have learned the lessons of history well and to have studied the principles of war. Their defensive and offensive tactics were effective. Moreover, they never lost sight of their political objective.

On the Allied side, the British recovered from their usual slow start and, by a massive effort which badly strained the economy, disciplined their whole society to win. After fumbling, they moved successfully ahead with a maritime strategy from 1941 onwards, while by 1943—with American tanks and slow co-operation with the R.A.F.—a mobile army was created, just when its command went to Montgomery, a man with 1919 ideas. The strategic air offensive against Germany by both the R.A.F. and the U.S.A.A.F. suffered from the fact that no long-range fighter was available until 1944 and from the failures of intelligence, command, and target selection. As a holding operation until the coming of the second front it was justifiable; after that it should have played a tactical-strategic role. The destruction of German cities did bring the war home to the people, but it also led to a most remarkable economic resurgence after the war. Tactical bombing also was often overdone, creating more trouble for the Allies than for the Germans. The campaign in Northwest Europe showed that an efficient tactical air force could be used to guard a flank and that, more importantly, air resupply on a large enough scale could help intelligently-directed armies achieve political objectives before a retreating enemy could rally.

The war in Europe could not have been won without American aid to Britain from 1940 onwards, the United States' industrial might, nor without the co-operation of the U.S. Navy in the Battle of the Atlantic and in amphibious operations, not to mention the direct participation of American troops and of the U.S.A.A.F.

Above all else, perhaps, the war in Europe confirmed what Fuller, Liddell Hart and others had preached since World War I. The problem in any war is to isolate the political objective and to discern the means which will best bring the enemy to terms.

CHAPTER XXXIV

The Japanese Gamble in the Pacific, 1941-1942

I. INTRODUCTION

THE PACIFIC IS a gigantic theater spreading 8,500 miles from Anchorage, Alaska, to Sydney, Australia, and 10,000 from San Francisco to Singapore. Dotted across its vast open spaces are clusters of volcanic islands and tropical paradises with steaming jungles. Its very vastness—despite air reconnaissance—made the Pacific a fluid battlefield with naval and amphibious tactics having much more resemblance to those of the Battles of the Atlantic, of Germany, and of Russia than to ordinary, conventional warfare. The Japanese supposed that space would be a barrier; it turned instead into a trap. The attacker had the advantage of surprise and concentration. The Japanese failed to deprive the United States either at Pearl Harbor or at Midway of the Hawaiian Islands staging post, whose importance diminished as complete mobility at sea was achieved by self-contained U.S. forces. Nor did the Japanese exploit their submarines to harass U.S. shipping and supply routes. Throughout the war the key factor was air bases, either mobile on carriers or fixed upon islands. Strategy and tactics were dictated by the operational radii of fighters. The Japanese, as in the earlier conflict with Russia, were prepared only for a short war. Their inner and outer island defense system crumbled when America developed new strength and new skills.

II. THE ROAD TO WAR

After Japan joined the anti-Comintern Pact (November 1936), thus securing her Russian flank, the Army proceeded—in the summer of 1937—to invade China proper. Close American ties with China impelled Roosevelt to abstain from invoking the Neutrality Act. But this also allowed war materials to flow to Japan and led to diplomatic difficulties. The 1911 commercial treaty with Japan was ended in January 1940. Licensing of exports, which followed in July, stopped the sale of aircraft and aviation fuel to Japan, although oil continued to be shipped there until July 1941. Then the United States froze all Japanese assets as a counter to Tokyo's domination of French Indo-China. This precipitated the fall of the civilian government and the rise to power of an army junta under General Tojo.

The Japanese strategy was simple, military, and economic. The problem stemmed from failure to bring the Chinese war to a conclusion. The conflict in Europe distracted Britain and France and in the summer of 1940 also reduced Holland to impotence. Thus for Japan the way was open to the rice, coal, and zinc of French Indo-China, rubber, oil, and tin of the Dutch East Indies and rubber and tin of Malaya, which after mid-1940 were being withheld by an Allied embargo. The Japanese at once began preparing for war. Elaborate studies were made—including a model of Pearl Harbor—and the fleet prepared for a blow which would eliminate the United States while the Japanese seized the vital raw materials of the Southern Resources Area and fashioned a Maginot Line of island fortresses from the Aleutians to New Guinea.

Japanese intentions to spread southwards were clear enough and America prepared for war accordingly, but without public opinion backing executive action. Though in 1940 a large increase in the U.S. Navy had been sanctioned, most of the new ships—including 19 carriers—were still on the ways. Thus even before Pearl Harbor the U.S. Navy was inferior to the Japanese Imperial Navy, especially in carriers (3:10). It was only in July 1941 that a real attempt was made to create a state of readiness. In general American officials were convinced that the Japanese would continue their drive southward into Southeast Asia and neglected the lesson of the Russo-Japanese War. And this despite the fact that the Japanese diplomatic code had been broken, so that the dishonesty of the then-current Washington negotiations was patently obvious. On 27 November a "war warning" was sent to both Pearl Harbor and the Philippines. Early on 7 December, when the last vital message was decoded, Washington knew that war was imminent.

III. THE ATTACK ON PEARL HARBOR

The operational plan for annihilating the U.S. Pacific Fleet had its genesis early in 1941 in the suggestion of Admiral Yamamoto, Commander-in-Chief of the Combined Japanese Fleet. The plan was designed to secure the strategic flank against the principal enemy while the Southern Resources Area was being conquered. The final decision was taken on 1 December 1941. The task force had sailed on 10-18 November for a secret rendezvous in the Kuriles. It was composed of six carriers and escorting vessels and stayed north of the shipping lanes to avoid U.S. air patrols. It was preceded by 27 submarines, some carrying aircraft or midget subs.

At 0630 on Sunday the seventh, Rear Admiral Nagumo launched the first striking force of 183 planes. Though on Hawaii General Short and Admiral Kimmel, the Army and Navy Commanders, had been warned by Roosevelt that Japan might start a war in Southeast Asia, precautions had been taken only against sabotage. Although a midget submarine was sunk off the entrance to Pearl Harbor at 0645, no alert resulted. The first Japanese bombs were dropped at 0755. The battleships at anchor were attacked with torpedoes; two capsized and three either sank at their moorings or were beached. Attacks on airfields cost the U.S. 80 Navy and 152 Army aircraft while the Japanese lost only 29 airplanes in action.

Although they achieved strategic and tactical surprise, the Japanese failed. Because of a shortage of shipping, owing to the move into Southeast Asia, the Japanese could not occupy the Hawaiian Islands and thus achieve a conquest of the Pacific the United States would not challenge. Instead, their strategy united the American people for war as nothing else had and forced the U.S. Navy to abandon its obsolescent battleships and to concentrate on carriers.

IV. SECURING THE SOUTHERN RESOURCES AREA

A. Introduction

With magnificent speed, small forces, and an excellent understanding of geography and transportation as well as of the divided nature of the Allied positions, the Japanese proceeded to establish themselves—six months ahead of their own schedule—from China to New Guinea to India by mid-1942. They operated on interior lines making many new conquests which they used as stepping stones, particularly for providing air cover, for each new invasion. The Allies suffered from the fact that they were fully engaged elsewhere, had very long supply lines, and had only recently begun to study and strengthen the defenses of their Far Eastern possessions. The Philippines were 4,500 miles from Hawaii and the Japanese took the intermediate bases—then in the process of fortification—of Guam (10 December) and stoutly defended Wake Island (23 December) together with the British Crown Colony of Hong Kong (25 December).

B. Malaya

The Japanese Army undertook the invasions of Siam, Malaya, Burma, Sumatra, and Luzon in the Philippines, while the Navy assaulted the other islands. Each controlled its own air arm. Having already established advanced bases in Indo-China, the Army occupied Siam, and started down the Malay Peninsula 10 December 1941, thus cutting the British air-support route from India, the railway and road. Air attacks paralyzed the northern British airfields and the Singapore docks. On 2 December the capital ships *Repulse* and *Prince of Wales* arrived without their escorting carrier and were despatched against Japanese transports landing troops at Khota Baru. Both were sunk eight days later by Japanese aircraft. British morale fell. The Japanese worked their way through the nearly impenetrable jungle, to take Penang

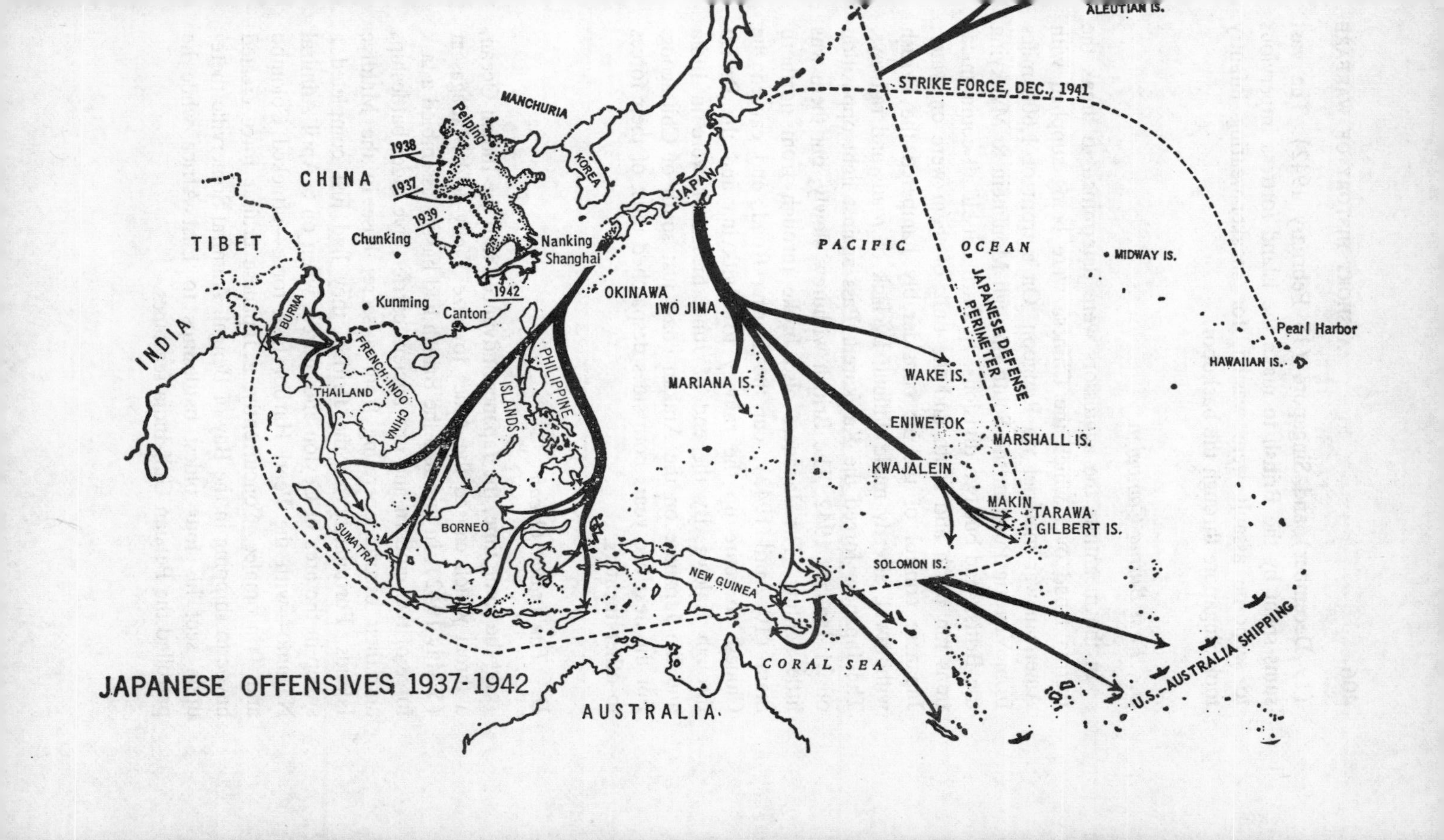

JAPANESE OFFENSIVES 1937-1942

(19 December) and Singapore (15 February 1942). The vast sums spent by the British to make the island fortress impervious to seaborne assault were wasted, for sneaker-wearing infantry took Singapore through the backdoor.

C. *First Burma Campaign*

In the meantime the aggressors were determined to break the Burma Road over which the Chinese were being supplied with American war matériel via Rangoon. On a front of 1,600 miles from Victoria Point in the South through Moulmein to Myitkyina the British had but two divisions. In Burma itself all communications ran north and south and the bulk of them were on water. Japanese control of the air considerably hampered the British withdrawal, already made difficult by lack of roads and railways. The Japanese forced the Kawkareik Pass against light opposition on 21 January 1942. The British withdrew slowly, but there was little fighting. The Japanese also broke through from northern Siam (10 April 1942), cut the Burma Road, and caused the Chinese to retire up the railway to Myitkyina and the British through Kalewa. By the end of June, the latter were in India and the Japanese on the Arakan coast just south of Chittagong. For the next two years both sides despatched most of their forces to other theaters.

D. *The Indian Ocean*

At the same time, the Japanese advanced into the Indian Ocean, a threat which caused the Allies to seize Vichy-held Madagascar (5 May 1942). In this area the British had hastily assembled a task force of two modern and one ancient carrier, five older battleships and their escorts operating from a secret base in the Maldive Islands. Fortunately for the British, they had just completed a sweep in the area of Ceylon and retired, when on 5 April Admiral Nagumo—with the Pearl Harbor task force—attacked Colombo and Trincomalee. Concurrently, a Japanese cruiser force created havoc to shipping in the Bay of Bengal. Admiral Somerville thereupon sent his four oldest battleships to East Africa while he patrolled the Persian Gulf-India sea lanes.

Concurrently Churchill asked Roosevelt for an American diversion in the Pacific. This request coincided with the launching on 18 April of 16 U.S. Army B-25's under Colonel James H. Doolittle from the carrier *Enterprise* for a strike against Japanese cities. The physical damage done to Tokyo, Nagoya, Osaka, and Kobe was negligible, but the morale effect was notable and the Japanese High Command reacted at once by recalling two carriers from the Southwest Pacific. This action allowed the Americans to win the Battle of the Coral Sea.

E. The Philippines

In the meantime the Japanese landed small forces on Luzon, the northernmost island of the Philippines, on 10 December 1941. Their air attacks, delivered some hours after Pearl Harbor, caught the U.S. Army's planes on the fields. The surface part of the U.S. Asiatic Fleet had been withdrawn and the submarines left behind were ineffective. Their base at Cavite was one of the earliest targets of Japanese aircraft, owing to the lack of modern fighters and bombers to match the then excellent Japanese Zero. For these reasons the invasion was successfully established. The main landing came at Lingayen Gulf on 21 December. After seven additional landings the enemy drove towards Manila.

General Douglas MacArthur, the former Chief of Staff of the American Army who had become Field Marshal of the Filipino forces, was upset by the strength of enemy action. Manila was declared an open city, but was nevertheless assaulted on 2 January 1942 and devastated by Japanese bombers. MacArthur then ordered his 19,000 Americans and 71,000 Filipinos to retreat to the Bataan Peninsula in the hope that they could withstand a siege until help could arrive. Japanese General Homma's forces attacked continuously in the rugged country. Rations became scarce as American supply ships failed to get through. MacArthur was ordered out of the Philippines, repeatedly delayed departure, but on presidential orders early in March, he handed over command to General Jonathan Wainwright. On 1 April the Japanese launched an all-out assault and in eight days subdued the exhausted Bataan garrison. Corregidor, the long-isolated island base off Bataan, held out until 5 May, doing much to raise U.S. morale.

F. The East Indies

On 17 December 1941 the Japanese landed in Borneo to secure its oil and quickly added Davao on Mindanao in the southern Philippines as an advanced naval base. Control of the sea and air was vital since most islands had no internal communications. The Japanese thus took key points with light forces. The U.S. Asiatic Fleet under Admiral Hart fell back on the Dutch East Indies. On 10 January, Sir Archibald Wavell arrived in Java to take command of American, British, Dutch and Australian (the ABDA) forces, but he dissolved this combined command on 25 February when the situation became hopeless, partly as a result of conflicting national interests.

V. NAVAL ACTION

A. Early Developments

The only successful Allied naval surface engagement occurred on 23/24 January 1942, when four American destroyers attacked a convoy in Makassar Strait. Otherwise naval war was hampered by Japanese air superiority and excellent anti-shipping air strikes as well as superiority of numbers and unity of command. Using carriers, battleships, and cruisers, the Japanese seized Amboina (31 January 1942), the Dutch east flank anchor, then Palembang in eastern Sumatra (16 February). A series of frustrating naval actions followed in which the Allied forces were whittled down while the Japanese seized the air-staging post of Timor Island (24 February), cutting the link between Australia and Java. On 19 February the Japanese flattened defenseless Port Darwin, the northern Australian base, by a carrier-launched air attack. They then sent down two invasion forces, which reached Java after beating the Dutch-led ABDA navy in the battle of the Java Sea (27 February). Only four American destroyers escaped, but the delay saved the Southwest Pacific lifeline.

B. Coral Sea (7-8 May 1942)

In the meantime MacArthur had arrived in Australia, charged with three objectives: establish a base for future operations there, stop the Japanese southwestward thrust, and maintain communications with the U.S.

Australian communications with Britain and the Middle East were apparently destroyed by the Japanese foray into the Indian Ocean. Therefore it was vital that communications to the United States be kept open, a task of which the U.S. Navy was already well aware. The Japanese, who had in the East Indian and other campaigns succeeded despite dividing their forces, did so once again, aiming both to neutralize Australia and Midway. This ultimately allowed the U.S. Navy to defeat the superior enemy in detail.

The appearance of American carrier task forces in the Southwest Pacific in March 1942, after a series of raids on enemy-held Central Pacific atolls, caused postponement of Japanese plans to take Port Moresby, New Guinea, a vital Australian beachhead outpost. The Japanese were concerned with holding Rabaul on the New Britain coast, both to neutralize Australian airfields and to guard their flank while they drove on Samoa to break the Australian-American lines of communication.

On 28 March 1942 U.S. Seabees (Naval Construction Battalions) started building a base at Espiritu Santo at the northern tip of the New Hebrides. On 3 May the Japanese invaded Tulagi in the Solomons and were attacked next day by Admiral Fletcher's *Lexington-Yorktown* group. On the sixth a superior Japanese carrier task force came within 70 miles of Fletcher's group, but bad weather saved him.

Meanwhile the main Port Moresby invasion fleet had been sighted and Fletcher sent his cruisers to the attack. On the morning of 7 May almost simultaneously aircraft from each fleet sighted its opponent. An American strike sank the carrier *Shoho*. The next day *Shokaku* was bombed out of action. The Japanese caused *Lexington* to be abandoned, their evasive attacks having split her defensive screen. They then withdrew with only nine planes remaining.

The Port Moresby invasion was called off, an effective result of the first naval action in which the offensive was entirely carried out by aircraft, neither surface fleet sighting the other. Tactically an enemy victory, it became strategically an American one since the damaged hostile carriers were unable to be present at Midway, the climax of the Japanese grand offensive.

C. *Midway* (*3-4 June 1942*)

The Japanese objective was to complete the destruction of the United States fleet, begun on 7 December 1941. The Japanese High Command believed that Nimitz, the Central Pacific commander, would either have to defend Midway or attempt to retake it. In either event he would hazard his forces and the Japanese could spring their trap. They also wanted to plug the hole through which the Doolittle raiders had come.

On 5 May Imperial Japanese Headquarters ordered the Midway operation for early June. Admiral Yamamoto's staff reckoned that three American carriers might be present, but assumed that none would be. The strategic conception was based on a naval version of Cannae. Its more recent precedent was Jutland. As in the 1916 German plan, so in the Japanese one of 1942, two lines of submarines were to be used both as an early warning device and as a trap. Japanese carriers would then maneuver to cut American forces off from their Pearl Harbor base, whereupon the Main Body with its battleships would steam in for the kill. This would eliminate the United States fleet before it could be reinforced by the 1940-program ships, then nearing completion. Japan would be safe behind her defense in depth and a negotiated peace could be obtained.

Additionally, the plan called for the occupation of Midway as a patrol plane base and for a diversionary attack on the Aleutians. It failed because Nimitz, who had access to superior cryptographic intelligence—which had broken the Japanese naval code—had detailed prior knowledge of the enemy plan. Moreover, since the Japanese fleet operated in ten scattered groups, it had neither surprise, concentration nor mutual support.

The Japanese submarine line took station on 1 June, but by then three U.S. carriers (*Yorktown, Enterprise* and *Hornet*) had already passed to the west of it. Only *Saratoga* was on her way from the West Coast.

Nimitz was faced with the choice of leaving the Aleutians to their fate or despatching inadequate forces to their aid. He chose to send five cruisers and assorted vessels under Theobald, who thought the whole Japanese operation a hoax. However, on 3 June a strike against Dutch Harbor—repeated the next day—was followed by the landing of Japanese troops on Kiska and on Attu (6/7 June). These were not discovered by American patrol planes until the tenth.

American forces at Midway meanwhile had been strengthened by a variety of aircraft, mines, anti-aircraft guns, and men. In arcs, ranging out from 50 to 700 miles, were 19 submarines as additional lookouts. Nimitz retained overall command, but the admirals on the spot were Raymond A. Spruance and Fletcher, who took command when the two U.S. carrier groups rendezvoused on 2 June and steamed north of Midway. Nimitz' instructions were to take a calculated risk—not to attack unless quite sure of inflicting severe damage on the enemy. The admirals understood that air power was the key, and consequently made the Japanese carriers top priority targets.

Early on 3 June a patrol plane from Midway spotted the enemy invasion force some 700 miles west-southwest. Correctly perceiving its nature, the United States commanders waited. The next morning Nagumo, approaching from the northwest, launched a strike against Midway. Shortly thereafter, his ships were spotted by a patrol plane; within minutes another discovered the Japanese carriers, but made a 40-mile error in its position report. The air attack on Midway and the B-17 counter-strike from the island exhausted the defenders' planes. The unco-ordinated land-based attacks on the carriers did, however, prevent their launching another strike.

The American carriers by this time had drawn within their 175-mile striking radius and set out in hopes of catching Nagumo with his planes on deck. Nagumo had elected to rearm and refuel that half of his force which had been standing by to attack American carriers, although none had been reported by either his scouts or by the submarine line. When the sighting report came in, he desperately attempted to launch, albeit under attack from the U.S. submarine *Nautilus*. When U.S. carrier aircraft arrived, the Zeros effectively disposed of the torpedo planes, but not the U.S. dive-bombers which hit three of Nagumo's four carriers (*Akagi, Kaga,* and *Soryu*) while they were refuelling aircraft. The fourth carrier, *Hiryu,* countered with a strike which partially disabled *Yorktown.* A second strike put her out of action. Fletcher handed over command to Spruance, who at once launched a strike which destroyed *Hiryu.*

Yamamoto was learning meanwhile that there were more American carriers present than intelligence had suspected and that his forces were too widely dispersed for mutual support. *Enterprise* and *Hornet,* though weary, now had won control of the air. Yamamoto did not realize this, nor did the U.S. command suspect that the crisis was past. That it was was largely due to Spruance's excellent sense in steaming eastwards during the night to avoid being surprised by Japanese surface ships, now being vectored onto the remains of Nagumo's retreating force. By midnight on 4 June, Yamamoto knew that the initiative had passed to Spruance and that the latter's air strikes might bring disaster by dawn. Consequently Yamamoto ordered cancellation of the Midway operation.

The U.S. command still believed a landing imminent. But searches on the fifth revealed nothing. Once again on the night of the sixth, Spruance cruised eastwards and thus avoided a last Japanese attempt to smash him with surface forces. Next day, however, *Yorktown* was torpedoed and sank.

D. *Summary*

Thus ended one of the most decisive naval battles of history. It was a victory for the American command, which correctly conceived the situation and applied the appropriate means to profit from Japanese mistakes. Moreover, naval intelligence provided priceless foreknowledge of the enemy's strategic intentions. For the Japanese, Midway was the first serious defeat in three centuries. It frustrated their plans for a quick victory, cost them the initiative at sea in a naval-amphibious war, and marked the turning point of the Pacific conflict.

By the end of 1942, however, the Japanese had attained their basic war objectives at a cost of 15,000 men, 386 aircraft, five aircraft carriers and a few other warships. They suffered severely thereafter from a shortage of the carriers and trained aircrews upon which successful defense of the Pacific perimeter depended.

The U.S. Navy, on the other hand, went from strength to strength. Its torpedoes were rectified, its aircraft were replaced with higher performance models, and it was expanded by new carriers and fast battleships which slid down the ways in increasing numbers. The U.S. Navy moreover, changed rapidly from a battleship to a carrier fleet with vastly increased mobility and striking range. The war in the Pacific demonstrated that naval actions might be short in time, but were—especially in the vastness of the Pacific—more vital than actions upon land. Swiftly fought over increasing ranges as carriers became the principal capital ships, the tactics of these conflicts had much in common with those on land and similarly reflected the principles of war.

CHAPTER XXXV

The Allied Offensive Against Japan, 1942 – 1945

I. INTRODUCTION

AFTER MIDWAY THE initiative passed into Allied hands. Despite agreement that the European war came first, theater commanders were able to launch counter-offensives which stopped further Japanese expansion. MacArthur from Australia and Nimitz from Hawaii drove to the Philippines where they linked up for the assault—which never came—on the Japanese home islands. In addition U.S. submarines strangled Nipponese maritime power. Ultimately Japan was defeated by the resolute application of power such as the Germans had failed to exercise against Britain.

The war was notable because it was always conducted under fighter cover, provided either from islands taken for the purpose or from carriers. This enabled amphibious forces to leapfrog through the defenses leaving important enemy garrisons isolated and impotent. The whole was made possible by a remarkable mobile logistics organization.

Concurrently a minor campaign cleared the Japanese from the Burma Road and from Burma itself, enabling the Chinese with American aid to threaten Japanese land communications to Southeast Asia.

II. THE AUSTRALIAN LIFELINE AND THE SOUTHWESTERN PACIFIC OFFENSIVE, 1942-1944

The Japanese by mid-1942 had developed outer and inner defensive belts and the problem for the Allies was both to prevent their enlarging this perimeter and to break through it to the vital insular, homeland industrial area. The Japanese position was approximately a pair of triangles with a common base—Singapore-Sakhalin—with one apex resting in northern Burma and the other on the Ellice Islands. Japan could not hold both flanks of the South Pacific salient with enough force to prevent an Allied penetration. The situation was much like that the Germans faced in Russia and the answers and results were much the same also. Islands were fortified, but the Japanese lacked the mobile forces to prevent their enemy from penetrating between the natural boxes. The center of gravity in the Southwest was Rabaul in New Britain; against this pivotal position MacArthur launched an offensive which aimed at its neutralization, not its capture.

A. Guadalcanal

Allied planning—initiated by Admiral Ernest J. King, then about to become Chief of Naval Operations—was in full swing on 18 February 1942, when intelligence indicated that in June the Japanese planned to attack Port Moresby on the southern side of New Guinea and to establish an air base in the Solomons to threaten the U.S. supply line to Australia. The immediate United States response was an assault on the incomplete airfield on Guadalcanal, which was occupied on 7 August. There followed seven major naval engagements: Savo Island (9 August), Eastern Solomons (23-25 August), Cape Esperance (11-12 October), the Japanese reinforcement of Guadalcanal (16 October), Santa Cruz Islands (26 October), and Guadalcanal (13-14 November 1942).

In most of these actions the United States Navy held its own and usually inflicted significant damage on the Japanese, but on 30 November off Tassafaronga a radar-equipped patrol of U.S. cruisers blundered into a Japanese force and was badly beaten. The disaster was hushed up, a succeeding Japanese force failed to get back, and as a result their High Command decided to withdraw from Guadalcanal in order to reinforce the New Guinea campaign (7-8 February 1943). The Imperial Army had suffered its first major defeat, a tribute to the hard fighting of the U.S. Marines and Army.

B. *Port Moresby*

Meanwhile, on 21 July 1942, the Japanese launched the first part of a three-pronged drive on Port Moresby with a landing at Gona. From there they pushed south through the jungles and mountains. On 26 August a second landing unsuccessfully attempted to take the Milne Bay airfield. The seaborne assault on Port Moresby was frustrated by the Allied landing at Guadalcanal. The overland column was repulsed only 30 miles from Port Moresby and driven back to its base at Kokoda (3 November) by air-supplied Australians.

MacArthur, now ready for a second offensive, struck with the airborne behind the Japanese at Buna. Owing to the impenetrability of the jungle, they could not concentrate sufficient forces to frustrate his purpose. By the end of January 1943, they had lost their coastal bases and were forced to abandon their counteroffensive. The Japanese surprise attack on Wau was foiled by airborne support and on 3/4 March 1943, their last major attempt to reinforce the area was sunk by Allied bombers of General George C. Kenney's Fifth Air Force at the Battle of the Bismarck Sea.

C. *New Guinea*

It was six months before the United States could again take the initiative, but during this period occurred a notable coup: the shooting down of Admiral Yamamoto, Commander of the Combined Fleet. MacArthur started an advance in late June which was based upon the radius of action of his fighter aircraft. Islands were seized which first provided a link between Guadalcanal and New Guinea and closed the northern gate to the Coral Sea. Next a series of jumping amphibious assaults, supported by Admiral Halsey's fast-carrier South Pacific Fleet, seized a ring of posts which isolated the main enemy base at Rabaul and left it impotent through air attack. These operations included the seizure of Rendova (30 June), Munda on New Georgia (5 August), Vella Lavella (9 October); at the same time other forces captured Salamaua on the eastern end of New Guinea (30 June) and the Australians took Lae in September. Bougainville and other islands in the Solomons were neutralized from nearby airfields and Bougainville itself successfully assaulted on 1 November.

MacArthur then proceeded to leap up the coast of New Guinea with the most brilliant indirect approach of the war. Large enemy forces were left isolated by geography as he successfully advanced his scanty supply of men and matériel past the major Japanese concentrations, avoiding costly frontal attacks. The Admirality Islands were seized on 29 February 1944 and the main enemy base at Truk, already bombarded by the Navy, brought within bombing range. The Japanese thereupon decided to move their headquarters from Rabaul to Hollandia, but were forestalled by MacArthur's leap of 600 miles to take this town and its three airfields (22 April). On 27 May he made another jump of 350 miles to capture Biak and on 30 July Sansapor, New Guinea, fell into Allied hands, providing an air base within 600 miles of the Philippines. On 15 September MacArthur reached Morotai and halved that distance.

III. THE CENTRAL PACIFIC CAMPAIGN, 1942-1944

Both the Southwestern and the Central Pacific theatres were dependent, in varying degree, upon the new seaborne airpower. U.S. industry made possible increasing the Navy—despite losses—from 383 to 613 warships, from 1,076 ships of all classes to 4,167, and from 1,744 planes to 18,269. Landing-craft production also rose, so that by the end of the war some 80,000 had been constructed. Though some of this new power, particularly landing ships, was deployed in the European theater, the bulk was available for operations in the Pacific, where nearly 100 carriers were employed by the time the Philippines were invaded in October 1944.

A. *Tarawa*

Admiral Chester Nimitz at Pearl Harbor was the overall commander of American naval forces and directed the Central Pacific offensive. The first of a succession of pulverizing blows was aimed at the Gilberts, one of the many strings of coral islands which the Japanese had occupied in their expansion or over which they had

had a League of Nations mandate. The initial objective in the Gilberts—some 2,500 miles from Hawaii—were the atolls of Makin and Tarawa. Makin was taken on 20 November 1943, after a short preliminary bombardment, but Tarawa proved to be much tougher. Despite a heavy, but short preliminary bombardment, the Japanese garrison of 3,000 élite marines fought tenaciously. U.S. Marine casualties in a bloody frontal assault—for on a small island there are no flanks—were the same as the strength of the garrison. Admiral Kelly Turner, the American commander, at once noted that several serious errors had been committed: the naval bombardment was not long or heavy enough, the air strike ill-timed and insufficient, and much of the matériel employed was useless, amtracs (amphibious personnel carriers) were too few and unreliable, and communications equipment poor. Amphibious operations were therefore reorganized and technical improvements made. Tarawa, despite the journalistic storm over the casualties, was at once converted into a major advance base by Seabees.

B. *The Marshalls*

Nimitz then surprised the Japanese by not striking towards the Ellice Islands. Instead, he turned the vast spaces of the Pacific into a liability for them, obliging them to spread thinly their defensive forces, uncertain of where the next blow would fall. He selected Majuro and Kwajalein in the Marshalls, some 500 miles north of the Gilberts. Majuro fell shortly after a two-day bombardment which ended on 1 January 1944, but the larger Kwajalein was not taken until 8 February; Namu, Roi and Eniwetok were subdued later in the month. Once again the technique was to capture the island airfields and to neutralize the rest of the atoll and surrounding areas. Despite *banzai* suicidal charges and bitter foxhole-to-foxhole resistance, the lessons of Tarawa had been learned and American casualties were 356 men against 8,122 enemy dead.

This left Truk—the last major bastion connecting the inner and outer perimeters—to be taken. Nimitz decided against an assault. Instead, Truk was pulverized by a task force led into the Carolines on 16 February 1944 by Admiral Raymond A. Spruance.

After devastating carrier air attacks, the 50,000-man enemy garrison was by-passed and left impotent. By this time MacArthur had isolated 135,000 Japanese in the Southwestern Pacific to be mopped up by the Australians by VJ-Day 1945.

C. *The Marianas*

Nimitz next turned to the Marianas. Following bombardment of the Palaus in March, United States forces landed on Saipan (15 June), for the first time penetrating Japan's inner ring with the intention of stepping on to the Bonins, from which air raids could be launched upon insular Japan itself. Naturally, the enemy reacted to this threat, sending a major naval force to disrupt the invader's plans. Spruance with his vast armada—so different from Fletcher's position at Midway—was ready. The action, formally called the Battle of the Philippine Sea, quickly turned into what airmen called the great "Marianas Turkey Shoot" in which 315 enemy planes were destroyed by naval airmen from the 15 carriers in Admiral Marc Mitscher's Task Force 58. Three Japanese carriers, were sunk, two of them by U.S. submarines. The Japanese fleet was mortally wounded, for most of its skilled pilots were now lost, training programs were grossly inadequate, and it was falling behind in aircraft quality. The Hellcat, which by 1944 was the mainstay of U.S. carrier air wings, was superior to enemy planes.

The battle of Saipan was not so easy a victory. Some 30,000 of the enemy were skillfully dug in and they inflicted 16,500 casualties on their attackers. Yet, although losses in atoll fighting in the Pacific were heavy, they were infinitesimal compared to similar assaults on entrenched opponents in World War I. The loss of Saipan (9 July) caused the resignation of Premier Hideki Tojo's Cabinet. Tinian was taken on 23 July with a loss of only 195 men, while on Guam (assaulted on 20 July 1944) United States dead were only a tenth of the 10,693 enemy killed.

During early 1944 Roosevelt had the timetable in the Pacific under consideration. Admirals King and Nimitz wanted to bypass the Philippines, but MacArthur persuaded Roosevelt (26 July 1944) to honor his pledge to liberate the Filipinos. MacArthur was now ready for the liberation, an operation whose timetable was advanced by the successes of both Allied drives in isolating Truk, reaching Morotai, and by the development of self-contained naval and amphibious forces which could operate thousands of miles from fixed bases. In the meantime, on 24 November 1944, Twentieth Air Force B-29's from airfields in the Marianas opened a strategic bombing campaign against the Japanese home islands, a solid follow-up to the symbolic Doolittle raid of 1942.

IV. THE LIBERATION OF THE PHILIPPINES AND THE BATTLE OF LEYTE GULF

A. *Invasion Preparations*

The liberation of the Philippines was a bold tactical stroke based upon the ability of carrier airpower to provide fighter cover during the initial phase until airfields could be seized or constructed and made operational. MacArthur realized that by striking at Leyte in the Central Philippines, he could not only split the Japanese defenders on Luzon from those on Mindanao, but also make use of his proven tactic of leaving large garrisons helplessly isolated behind his advancing front. Halsey had already demonstrated that his carrier task forces could operate as far as Formosa with impunity. This meant that if the Philippines were freed, there would be an even better chance of splitting the entire Japanese Empire by severing the sea routes through the South China Sea, the vital artery between the homeland and the Dutch East Indies resources area, a line already dangerously weakened by American submarines.

The campaign opened with the securing of MacArthur's flank by the seizure of Peleliu (15 September). This was followed by roaming attacks by American carrier-borne aircraft on Japanese fields both in the Philippines and on Formosa. Then on 20 October, in a typical MacArthur operation, American troops made a surprise landing on Leyte rather than on Mindanao. The Sixth Army under General Walter Krueger made rapid progress ashore, but before it had really made more than the initial assault, its whole future was placed in doubt by a major naval battle.

B. *Leyte Gulf (24-25 October 1944)*

The Battle of Leyte Gulf was brought on by the Japanese reaction to the invasion. The *Sho* plan aimed, as in the Battle of the Philippine Sea, to fight a showdown action. Japanese forces, as usual violating the principle of concentration, were ordered up from four areas. The Southern Force consisted of battleships and cruisers under Nishimura from Singapore and cruisers under Shima from the Pescadores; the Central, of a major battleship-cruiser force under Kurita from Singapore; and the Northern, of ships from the home islands including Japan's few remaining carriers. Both sides were operating under divided command with separated forces, for in addition to the enemy's having three separate groups, Halsey's Third Fleet was controlled by Nimitz at Pearl Harbor while Thomas C. Kinkaid's Seventh Fleet was under MacArthur. Yet both were supposedly defending the Leyte beachhead.

The first Japanese force to be reported was Kurita, whose approach was signalled by submarine patrols. To counter it Halsey, while detaching one task force to Ulithi to reprovision, headed with the other three to block San Bernardino Strait. On 24 October, he launched a violent strike against Kurita, already chastened by the loss of three cruisers—including the flagship—the day before to submarines. Believing his airmen's reports that they had disposed of Kurita, Halsey was convinced that he should turn against the Northern Force with its carriers when—later in the day—they were located off Cape Engano to the north of Luzon. Halsey had, in the meantime, sent out preparatory orders for the formation of battleship Task Force 34 to remain behind to block San Bernardino Strait, but he never detached it.

Kinkaid, however, believed Halsey had done so and was concentrating on the Southern Force, the first part of which—under Nishimura—sailed up Surigao Strait at dawn on 25 October into a perfect trap, allowing its "T" to be crossed by Admiral Oldendorff's fire-support battleships. After this disaster, Shima's division turned about and sailed away.

Meanwhile, during the night, Kurita again reversed course and continued eastward, emerging from San Bernardino Strait shortly

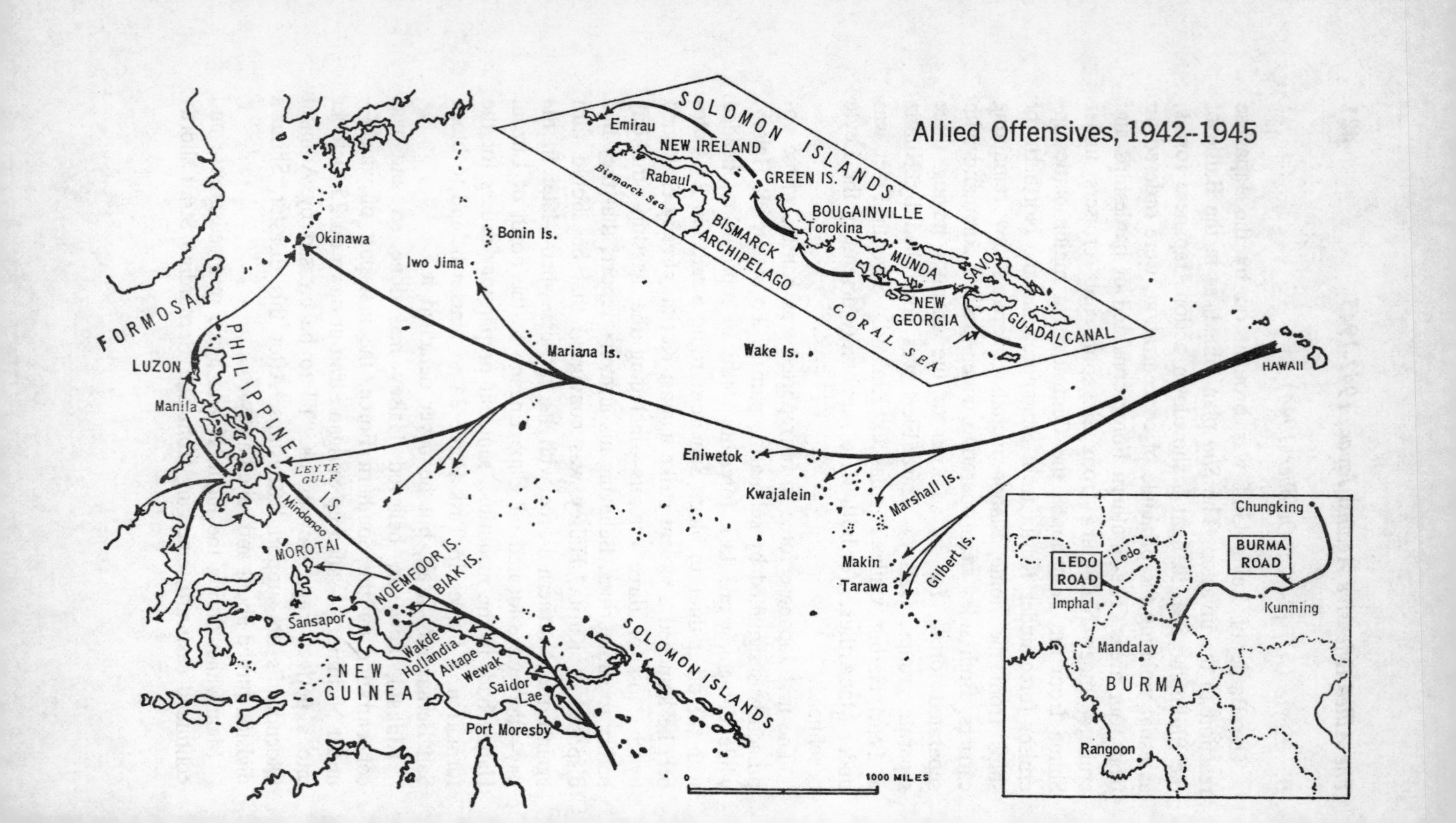
Allied Offensives, 1942--1945
SOLOMON ISLANDS
Emirau
NEW IRELAND
Rabaul
Bismarck Sea
GREEN IS.
BOUGAINVILLE
Torokina
BISMARCK ARCHIPELAGO
MUNDA
SAVO
NEW GEORGIA
GUADALCANAL
CORAL SEA
Okinawa
Bonin Is.
Iwo Jima
FORMOSA
LUZON
Manila
PHILIPPINE IS.
LEYTE GULF
Mindanao
MOROTAI
Mariana Is.
Wake Is.
HAWAII
Eniwetok
Kwajalein
Marshall Is.
Makin
Tarawa
Gilbert Is.
NOEMFOOR IS.
BIAK IS.
Sansapor
Wakde
Hollandia
Aitape
Wewak
Saidor
Lae
Port Moresby
NEW GUINEA
SOLOMON ISLANDS
0
1000 MILES
Chungking
BURMA ROAD
LEDO ROAD
Ledo
Imphal
Kunming
Mandalay
BURMA
Rangoon

after dawn. He surprised C. A. F. Sprague, whose thin-skinned escort carriers and destroyers were no match for battleships. News of this attack thoroughly alarmed Kinkaid, who had assumed that Halsey was watching Kurita. Then began the "battle of Bull's Run." Halsey, almost in sight of the Northern Force, which actually had pilots incapable of carrier landings, was recalled by Nimitz' famous message, "The whole world wants to know where is Task Force 34?" Fuming, Halsey returned south. By the time he reached the battle area again, Kurita had long since unexpectedly departed.

Both sides had lost their chance—Halsey of annihilating the Japanese carriers, Kurita of disrupting the amphibious forces at their most vulnerable stage. Thereafter, for lack of trained pilots, the Japanese Navy was largely limited to *Kamikaze* suicide-plane attacks on American shipping.

C. *The Philippine Campaigns*

Krueger had in the meantime begun to break out of the beachhead and, by the end of the month, had cleared a large part of Leyte. With the aid of Filipino guerrillas, Krueger took Ormoc (16 December 1944) on the west coast through which Japanese reinforcements were streaming.

Meanwhile MacArthur captured Mindoro and established airstrips for the assault on Luzon. This convinced the enemy that the invasion of Luzon would come from the South. Instead, after giving them time to shift forces to that area, MacArthur landed in the north at the base of Lingayen Gulf—as had the Japanese in 1941—on 9 January 1945. With additional landings, MacArthur's troops soon freed devastated Manila and proceeded to Corregidor, which was taken by a Far East Air Force (Fifth and Thirteenth Air Forces) airborne assault by 22 February. Mindanao was invaded on 10 march, and by 5 July MacArthur could announce the liberation of the Philippines by his 17 divisions of the Sixth and Eighth Armies whose superior equipment, command, strategy, and training had enabled them to defeat 23 enemy divisions comprising about 400,000 men.

The stage was set for the final actions of the war, but in the meantime two other campaigns had been going against the Japanese.

V. THE ALEUTIANS, 1943-1945

After a year of unnoticed planning, U.S. forces suddenly glided out of the Alaskan fog and landed on Attu (11 May 1943). This action by-passed Kiska, the main Japanese base, which was soon subjected to the usual neutralization by air. As the Japanese could no longer spare forces to counter these attacks, they achieved a tactical surprise of sorts by evacuating their forces (28 July). It was not until 15 August that Canadian-American forces making the assault discovered it! From then on, Eleventh Air Force bombers raided the Kuriles and threatened Tokyo.

VI. THE CHINA-BURMA-INDIA THEATRE, 1942-1945

A. The Roads to China and Malaya

Allied leadership was forced to relegate the China-Burma-India theatre to the lowest priority, for it was both difficult to supply and the least-threatened important area. Thus it was two years before much could be done other than to maintain a defensive position. Moreover, from May to October, ground operations and even those in the air were largely brought to a halt by monsoon conditions. The first offensive operations were conducted by Orde Wingate's British Chindits, who were supplied by air while they disrupted enemy communications in the Upper Irrawaddy Valley. The American Merrill's Marauders performed a similar function along General "Vinegar Joe" Stilwell's Chinese army front in the north. These actions kept the Japanese unbalanced and unable to threaten India.

In the meantime, the problem of supplying Chiang Kai-shek's forces was solved with the Tenth Air Force airlift over the Hump and by the building of the 478-mile Ledo Road (December 1942-January 1945). Exactly what operations should be undertaken with the limited forces available was complicated by the presence of command difficulties. British Admiral Lord Louis Mountbatten was the overall Southeast Asia Commander, but Stilwell was his deputy. Mountbatten wanted to head for Singapore via Rangoon; Stilwell fought for his Road. Eventually Mountbatten gave in after being instructed to do so at the Quebec Conference. In early 1944, Stilwell advanced towards Myitkyina, which had three airfields useful for the Hump route. Wingate moved into the interior and a thrust by the Fourteenth Army was aimed at Akyab to provide a base for continued air supply of columns working down the Irrawaddy Valley. As these started the Japanese themselves launched an assault which, though held by "boxes" supplied from the air, frustrated the Allied offensive until after the monsoon ended in August. The Japanese also countered with an attack (15 March) towards Imphal, which was besieged until 7 June when they suddenly departed.

B. Burma

During the 1944 monsoon, Mountbatten made new plans. First, Stilwell and the Chinese armies would continue to move south into Burma; second, Sir William Slim's Fourteenth British Army would thrust eastward from India to take Mandalay; third, an amphibious force would outflank the Arakan coastal mountains, land in the Rangoon area and drive the Japanese north against the other two armies. The failure to defeat Germany in the Fall of 1944 caused the abandonment of the third element. The general aim was to clear Burma and push the Japanese back east of the Salween.

By 3 December 1944, the Fourteenth Army had reached Kalewa on the Chindwin while a steady advance south from Bengal was clearing the way to Akyab. Air supply for 356,000 men was built to a peak rate of 94,300 tons a month in March 1945. Slim crossed the wide Irrawaddy by feinting with a small bridgehead against which the Japanese concentrated, while he himself—using motorized troops and tanks—switched his main force south, crossed near Meiktila, and took eight airfields and Mandalay (20 March 1945). In the meantime the Arakan coast to Cheduba Island had been cleared (February 1945) and the main air supply base moved 500 miles south from Assam. One British column then swept through Toungoo while the other trudged down the Irrawaddy. Doing 300 miles in 16 days the eastern force reached Pegu (1 May) while the western cleared Prome. Meanwhile an amphibious force from Akyab entered Rangoon on 3 May 1945 despite the monsoon's starting two weeks early.

The campaign in Burma was virtually over. By the time the monsoon ceased, the Japanese had surrendered. The offensive was medically as well as militarily a remarkable feat. Casualties from disease in 1943 were 120 for every battle casualty; by the end of the campaign they were reduced to six.

C. *China*

China, though a large theater of war, was merely secondary for both sides. This was because of geography and in part because of the dissensions between the Nationalist and Communist Chinese which, after January 1941, broke into open hostility. The result was that the Japanese had almost a free hand to carve out an inland road for the movement of supplies from Shanghai to Singapore. In early 1944 they launched their last major offensive in China which sealed off the coastal ports and forced Chennault to withdraw the advanced elements of the U.S. Fourteenth Air Force. An emergency airlift of two Chinese divisions from Burma enabled the Chinese to counter-attack and once more allowed Chennault to move forward. Stilwell was contemptuous of Chiang Kai-shek, his chief, and in October 1944 was replaced by General Albert Wedemeyer. Eventually the Japanese were forced to withdraw in Southeast Asia. But here as in Burma, the surrender of Japan itself precluded final local offensives.

VII. THE DEFEAT OF JAPAN

By early 1945 Japan had lost in action or in isolation some 750,000 men. Her navy had sacrificed 12 battleships, 19 aircraft carriers, 34 cruisers, and 125 submarines, while the merchant marine which had started the war at 10,000,000 tons was now reduced to one-tenth that size—some 2,000,000 tons below the minimum needed to sustain life in the home islands. And worse was to come from both American naval and B-29 raids culminating in the atomic bombs.

A. *Iwo Jima*

The Allied plan was to advance close to the home islands to obtain bases for tactical air forces and then to launch an all-out invasion. The first step was Iwo Jima, a volcanic ash island on which Tokyo's early-warning radar was located. With its three airfields it was desirable for a B-29 recovery base—since the Marianas were at the limit of endurance for these aircraft when they attacked Tokyo—but even more it was needed as a fighter base. Iwo itself was to suffer the fate of many other islands in the Pacific war. Intensively fortified by an expert, it was given a massive bombardment, seared with flame-throwers, and taken in bloody hand-to-hand, foot-by-foot fighting. After a pre-invasion bombardment of seventy-four days by the Seventh Air Force, followed by a three-days' pounding from naval fire-support groups, the island was assaulted on 9 February 1945. The battle was bloody; casualties were high and pillboxes thick, but the Marines persevered and on 15 March the island was taken. The Marines suffered approximately one casualty for every enemy soldier killed, and few surrendered.

A few days later the Japanese fleet made its last sortie and was soundly thrashed for its pains by carrier aircraft.

B. *Okinawa*

The next Allied operation was against Okinawa in the Ryukyus. Twenty miles wide and nearly seventy long, it commanded Japan's ocean communications. During the softening up process, the British Pacific Fleet arrived to join the Americans, undertook attacks on southern Japan, and guarded the flank towards Formosa. On 1 April the assault was launched, met the usual last-ditch resistance from 70,000 troops in the garrison, and fought a yard-by-yard action which continued until 22 June. Japanese casualties mounted in all to 109,000 killed and 7,800 prisoners, by far the largest number yet taken. American killed and wounded came to almost 50,000. At the same time U.S. ships had to deal with the banzai charge of the Japanese air forces in kamikaze attacks, especially against radar-picket ships. If these attacks had been kept up, some have concluded, the invasion of Japan might have been seriously delayed.

Okinawa was the last of the major assaults in the Pacific. In each case the Japanese suffered from a dearth of tactical air power and inferior weapons. Despite superb discipline and courage, they simply could not cope with the enormous firepower which United States forces could bring to bear.

C. *Air Attacks Upon the Japanese Home Islands*

When the B-29 went into production in 1943, it became possible to think of a world-wide striking force. Initial planning envisaged employing them for attacks on Japanese steel plants from bases in India with refuelling in China, but logistical considerations forced the planes to spend more time ferrying their own supplies than bombing. They struck Bangkok (27 May 1944), Yawata, Japan (15 June), and Singapore (30 March 1945) before they were moved to the Pacific. There General Millard F. Harmon had created five great bases on Guam (2), Tinian (2), and Saipan (1), upon each of which were 180 B-29's and 12,000 men. After training attacks against Truk, they opened the air offensive on the Japanese homeland on 24 November 1944. These daylight precision raids were also supported by attacks from the Fast Carrier Task Force under Admirals Raymond A. Spruance and Marc Mitscher, which struck Tokyo on 16 and 17 February 1945. A week later Task Force 58 co-ordinated an attack with 200 B-29's, which shortly thereafter were based on Iwo Jima and then upon Okinawa.

By 1945 Air Force planners, backed by General Curtis LeMay in the field, had decided that fire raids would do more damage in Japan than high explosives. The first large attack by 344 B-29's was on Tokyo on 9 March and killed 80,000, burning out one-fourth the city. Nagoya, Osaka, and Kobe were then hit in rapid succession, maxim loads of incendiaries being carried since the Japanese had no defenses against night attacks and the aircraft did not need their defensive armament. When P-51's became available, their services were unneeded.

What had been attempted in Europe from 1939 onwards was achieved in the campaign against Japan because the experience, matériel and lack of opposition were all in favor of maximum destruction by a precision force. At the same time Twentieth Air Force planted some 12,000 mines about Japan to aid the efforts of U.S. submarines. By mid-summer the maritime and air campaigns had Japan on her knees.

D. The Triumph of U.S. Navy Submarines

Both sides were saved the ultimate test, a military conquest of Japan, which in itself might have been disastrous. Two things prevented such a contest—the growing Japanese realization that they were beaten, and the dropping of the atomic bombs.

Despite their natural affinity for the sea, the Japanese failed to learn from their British mentors the importance of the manifold ramifications of sea power. Much as the British had in World War I, they concentrated on the fleet, while leaving shipping to sail independently. The U.S. at once adopted unrestricted submarine warfare. The result was that after the fall of the eastern archipelagoes, U.S. Navy submarines operating from their base at Pearl Harbor roamed the Japanese sea-lanes. At first they operated singly against both independents and small convoys, usually with but a single Japanese patrol vessel as escort. In November 1943 the Japanese finally established the Grand Escort Command Headquarters and started proper convoys. The U.S. Navy countered with three-submarine wolfpacks with a flexible on-the-spot command system. The value of convoy was proved once again for not only did the Japanese lose two-and-a-half times fewer escorted ships than of those which sailed independently, but United States submarine losses were heaviest against convoys. American boats accounted for 1,113 merchant ships totalling over 5,000,000 gross registered tons and in addition disposed of over 200 Japanese warships totalling 577,600 displacement tons for a loss in action of 45 submarines plus seven from other causes. So effective was their attack that after 1 April 1945 the enemy could only attempt to keep open the route to South China, while U.S. Navy boats invaded the Sea of Japan itself thanks to minefield detection gear. By the end of the war Japanese shipping was unable to bring into the Home Islands the necessary supplies. A modern sea and air blockade had been established in contrast to the German failure against Britain. In addition, there were enough submarines to spare to allow fourteen to be used for air-sea rescue work in connection with air attacks on Japan itself.

E. The Advent of the Atomic Age

The Anglo-American scientific race for the atomic bomb, based upon suspected German developments, was the best kept secret of the war. It was only revealed to President Truman after he took office. Yet probably 180,000 persons had helped prepare this technological triumph. The first actual test took place at Alamogordo, New Mexico, on 16 July 1945. By then only four major Japanese cities remained undamaged by the great fire raids carried out by B-29's. With Churchill's, later Attlee's, consent, Truman ordered atom bombs to be used if the Japanese did not heed a surrender ultimatum sent from the Potsdam Conference on 26 July, for the alternative was believed to be the loss of 500,000 men in the invasion of Japan itself. Unfortunately the Japanese had attempted to seek peace through Russia, which preferred that the war continue until she could reap a profit in eastern Asia by her belated entry (8 August 1945). Therefore, since no answer came to Truman's demand, a bomb was dropped on Hiroshima (6 August). The resulting conflagration killed 88,000 and injured 37,000. Three days later another bomb exploded above Nagasaki. The enemy capitulated and General MacArthur ended the costliest war in history by accepting the unconditional surrender of the Japanese armed forces aboard the USS *Missouri* in Tokyo Bay on 2 September 1945.

VIII. THE WAR IN THE PACIFIC—CONCLUSIONS

The conflict in the Far East was an extraordinarily mobile war in its offensive stages. Both sides—when on the offensive—showed great ability in moving so fast as constantly to keep the opponent off balance and in such a way as to make the maximum use of space, too much of which, as Mahan had suggested, is not always an advantage to the defender. Geography played an important part in that islands became boxes which were fortresses if mobile forces could hold the gaps between them and liabilities if they were insufficiently strong, as the Germans had found in Russia with their hedgehogs. Moreover, the jungle was neutral. Either side could use it. The Japanese infiltrated through it, but MacArthur turned it against them by depriving them of their sea communications and leaving them in the islands to rot.

More than anything else, the Far Eastern conflict was an air war. At first the Japanese with their Zeros had the advantage afloat and ashore. Their anti-shipping tactics were expert. When they lost the initiative, however, they did not have the defensive airpower to prevent the Allies from gaining air superiority and often supremacy, thus forcing their enemy underground. The mobility of airpower enabled the British in Burma and the Americans in the Pacific to employ mobility to the full. In Burma this meant transports, in the Central Pacific carrier-bases which moved along with amphibious forces so as to provide air cover where there were no airfields. Both sides used the technique of the indirect approach advocated by Liddell Hart and went further by not even bothering to mop up strongpoints left in useless isolation.

The fast pace of the war in the Pacific was only made possible by the combination of the American genius for improvisation and the enormous industrial capacity to mass-produce such innovations.

CHAPTER XXXVI

Armed Forces in a Transitional Age

I. INTRODUCTION

THE TWENTY YEARS from 1945 to 1965 have seen far-reaching changes in the range and destructive capabilities of military forces. Ironically, the spread of nationalistic, communist-led brushfire wars has increasingly necessitated guerrilla-fighting infantry and simple weapons which can be maintained by less advanced peoples, even under extreme operational conditions. The interrelationship of military and civil affairs has become much more pronounced and in many newly independent countries, the pattern foreseen by Edmund Burke at the time of the French Revolution has become reality, with military leaders—the men on horseback—taking up the reins of government when inept civilians have been unable to control the horse.

The sheer enormity of the atomic bomb had an early influence out of proportion to its real place in the armory. In the United States and in Britain this led to effective reliance on "massive retaliation" in the 'fifties to the neglect of conventional warfare. Atomic weapons were, however, refined for limited battlefield use, but thus far they have not been employed. At the other end of the firepower spectrum, the bulk of nuclear devices was assigned to strategic air forces until—with the advent of missiles—the navy also was admitted to this role.

Though the missile and space age can be said to have been inaugurated with 1944 German V-2 operations, relatively little was done until the Soviets launched their earth satellite, Sputnik I, into orbit in October 1957. This served to accelerate the arms race, this time in a partially new dimension: aerospace.

Primarily this contest has been between the two super-powers which emerged from World War II—Russia and the United States. The British had cooperated in the development of the original American atomic bomb and first exploded their own weapon on 3 October 1952; the Russians detonated theirs on 22 September 1949. The French under de Gaulle followed with their own atomic bomb a few years later, while the Chinese Communists exploded their first atomic device in October 1964. Developments on the space front have largely been conditioned by national budgets and the willingness of governments to devote vast sums to spatial developments.

In a majority of countries, but perhaps most notably in Britain, the rising cost of defense in an age of rapid technological advance has resulted in a regular paring away of military manpower. Responsible for this have been not only the costs of major weapons, but those of the electronic systems upon which they depend.

II. MILITARY DEVELOPMENTS IN THE UNITED STATES, 1945-1950

The massive expansion of the air forces in World War II, the sudden appearance of the atomic bomb, and the inter-service co-operation achieved in three dimensional warfare, demanded revision of the direction of military affairs in the United States, for which airmen had been calling since the days of Mitchell. A battle within the Pentagon and in Congress was waged all through 1946. The Navy felt its political position endangered because the Army and Air Force was being stationed among more voters. In part the Navy attributed the struggle to the fact that Army and Air Force commanders had spent World War II in the land-bound European theater and the admirals in mobile war in the vast Pacific. But this was not entirely true since the airmen also had run the B-29 campaign against Japan. To calm the Navy's fears, Congress limited the powers of the Secretary of Defense and clearly defined the roles of naval and marine aviation, whose loss the Navy had expected. President Truman signed the National Security Act on 26 July 1947, setting up the Defense Department and a separate Air Force, issued Executive Orders defining the roles and missions of the three services, and nominated James V. Forrestal as first Secretary of Defense.

Once more the three services fought over appropriations, the conflict this time centering on the U.S.A.F.'s claims that the B-36 super-bomber was *the* principal strategic weapon, while the Navy argued for super-carriers. Forrestal called conferences at Key West and at Newport, R. I., from which emerged agreement that the primary roles of one service—the responsibility for planning, selection of weapons, and the overall direction of functions of the mission assigned it—were the secondary roles of the other. The resolution of these difficulties was accelerated by the Berlin Air Lift (1948) and the creation of the North Atlantic Treaty Organization (NATO), both of which emphasized the need to meet Russian force with force. Within the defense establishment itself were created a War Council (composed of the Service Secretaries and their Chiefs of Staff), the Joint Chiefs of Staff, the Munitions Board (to handle industrial mobilization), and the Research and Developments Board.

With its customary haste the United States dismantled its military machine, 1945-1947. Aircraft were mothballed, ships cocooned, tanks scrapped, and men released. A new Secretary of Defense, Louis A. Johnson, attempted to cut the fat out of military appropriations in the normal peacetime political manner. The result was that all the armed forces were in a severely reduced state when, in June 1950, the Korean War broke out. This called for a massive rearmament which once again disrupted the economy.

III. THE KOREAN WAR

A. Background

The Soviet Union declared war on Japan two days after the atomic age was born at Hiroshima. The Red Army advanced rapidly through Manchuria, a province garrisoned throughout the war by a large, élite Japanese army which now had been ordered not to fight since peace was being sought. In a few days, the Russians avenged their 1905 defeat, regained their sphere of influence in Manchuria, and expelled the Japanese from Korea.

The oriental balance of power was overthrown and the pre-Russo-Japanese War status quo of 1904 essentially restored—except that the United States reluctantly replaced Japan in the vacuum left in Korea south of the 38th parallel, an artificial demarcation between the U.S.S.R. and the U.S. for accepting Japanese surrender.

As an aspect of the Soviet policy of consolidating politically all areas which had fallen to the Red Army, a Communist regime developed in North Korea, and U.S. efforts to achieve a free and unified Korea failed. Washington turned the problem over to a Commission of the fledgling United Nations, which proceeded in 1948 to form a republic "in such parts of Korea as are accessible." Thereupon, the Joint Chiefs of Staff, while advising that military withdrawal could produce dangerous politico-military effects in the Orient, stated that Korea lacked strategic importance to the U.S. In 1949, in response to a U.N. request, all U.S. forces were removed except for a Military Assistance Group (K.M.A.G.) under State Department control. The Russians then established the Democratic People's Republic, a puppet-state that immediately began preparations for the conquest of the south.

B. *The North Korean Invasion, 1950*

K.M.A.G. advised the Republic of Korea (R.O.K.) Army, which was built up to an eight-division constabulary of about 100,000 men. Four divisions were deployed in a position defense along the 38th parallel.

Warnings from MacArthur's headquarters in Tokyo—which actually had no jurisdiction over Korea—went unheeded in Washington. Early on 25 June, the North Korean People's Army (N.K.P.A.)—spearheaded by about 100 Russian T-34 tanks and covered by tactical air—drove across the frontier toward Seoul, the R.O.K. capital. As the R.O.K. Army collapsed, the U.S. ordered air and naval support to slow the N.K.P.A. blitzkrieg. The U.N. called upon its members to come to the aid of the Republic of Korea, thus bringing on the first "U.N. police action," actually, a full-scale bloody war. Washington then authorized MacArthur, who had been busy in Japan carrying on the most exemplary military government in modern times, to send in ground

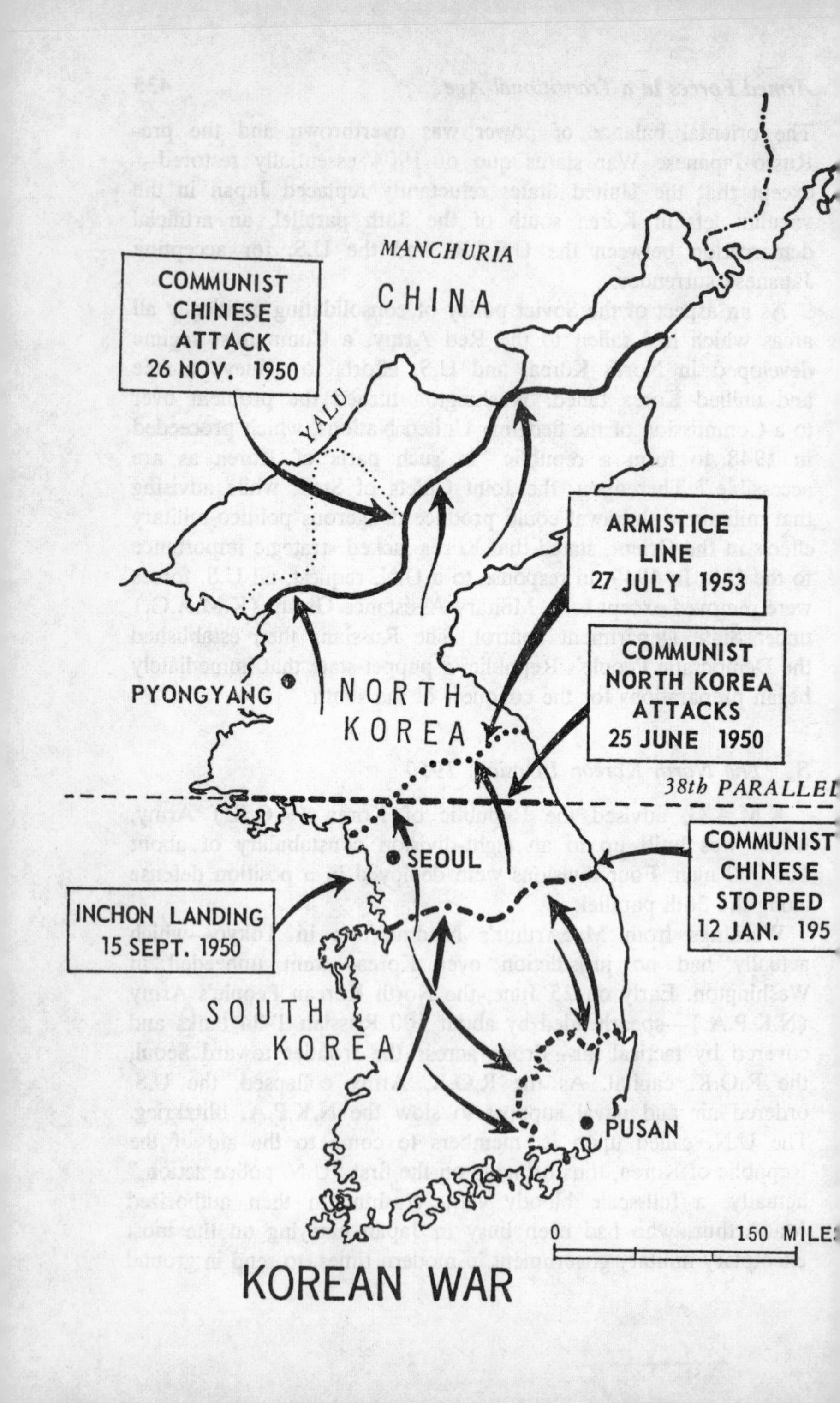
MANCHURIA
CHINA
COMMUNIST CHINESE ATTACK 26 NOV. 1950
YALU
ARMISTICE LINE 27 JULY 1953
PYONGYANG
NORTH KOREA
COMMUNIST NORTH KOREA ATTACKS 25 JUNE 1950
38th PARALLEL
SEOUL
COMMUNIST CHINESE STOPPED 12 JAN. 195
INCHON LANDING 15 SEPT. 1950
SOUTH KOREA
PUSAN
0
150 MILES
KOREAN WAR

forces. With little infantry available, he committed the 24th Division piecemeal in an effort to slow the enemy advance, gain time to cover defensive preparations, and shore up the R.O.K. Army. A U.S. naval blockade was placed around the Korean Peninsula and the Navy began improving docking facilities at Pusan. On 7 July, nominally as United Nations Commander-in-Chief, MacArthur took supreme command in his third major war.

As the U.S. Eighth Army (Lt. Gen. Walton Walker) was ordered to Korea, the 25th Division joined the 24th and the R.O.K. Army. By 31 July, the defenders were behind a sixty by ninety-mile perimeter, where Walker used a mobile reserve—operating on interior lines—to meet major threats. Air interdiction largely prevented the N.K.P.A. from mounting a coordinated offensive, although August fighting was desperate.

C. *Inchon (15 September 1950)*

MacArthur, meanwhile, had been planning and at Inchon he achieved the most brilliant strategic envelopment in military history by landing the X Corps. Surprise was complete. Kimpo airfield was quickly secured, permitting air resupply. N.K.P.A. communications lines were seized, the Far East Air Force (F.E.A.F.) punished enemy transportation and on the twentieth, Walker (with the Twenty-seventh Commonwealth Brigade joining the Eighth Army) snapped the N.K.P.A. line in front of the Pusan perimeter. Inchon thus was the key that unlocked an offensive which, by November, reduced Communist Korea to a kind of narrow "Yalu perimeter" and an area bordering on the Soviet Union.

Small units from several U.S. Allies—Philippines, Thailand, Australia, Canada, France, the Netherlands, and later Colombia and Ethiopia—and an excellent Turkish brigade had joined the British to make the war nominally a U.N. affair, although in reality more than 90 per cent of the men were American and South Korean, and the matériel was virtually all American.

D. *The Chinese Invasion*

Chinese foot soldiers and Russian jet fighters began to appear in early November, but F.E.A.F. had been hamstrung by a controversial political decision: there could be no violation of Manchurian airspace and no hot pursuit. Consequently, the enemy enjoyed a privileged base-area directly across the Yalu from which he could resupply and mount air operations. However, MacArthur opened an offensive on 24 November, aimed at clearing all of North Korea with a U.S.-R.O.K.-Allied combat force of less than 200,000.

MacArthur had had three choices: to withdraw to the waist of North Korea and establish a Wonsan-Pyongyang defense line; to remain where he was while evidence indicated possible Communist intervention; or to retain the initiative with a limited advance. The first alternative, which would have been militarily weak given available manpower, would have permitted the People's Republic of Korea to re-establish itself in opposition to U.N. war aims. It would have left the original Korean problem unresolved and would have meant full loss of the strategic initiative. The second possibility would have left the U.N. forces in an indefensible position. The last alternative carried the risk of broadening the war by bringing in the Communist Chinese. MacArthur believed, however, that if that possibility occurred, restrictions on his air power would be lifted and he would be able to cripple enemy supply lines.

The Chinese Communists, who had been fighting a civil war with the Nationalist government since the twenties, received Manchuria as a strategic base-area from the Russians in 1946, contrary to promises made by Roosevelt to Chiang Kai-shek at Cairo in 1943, when the situation was different. Perhaps aided by a series of still controversial political decisions, the Communists conquered all of the Chinese mainland by December 1949, confining the regular government to Formosa and a few lesser islands. Aggressive and eager to extend their dominance in Asia, the Communists poured eighteen divisions across the Yalu bridges and struck the Eighth Army on 26 November 1950. A new war thus was opened just as the U.N. war against the N.K.P.A. was drawing to a close.

Covered by a desperate defense by the U.S. 2nd Division and the Turks, the Eighth Army fell back to a line near the 38th parallel. East of the rugged mountains, the X Corps—which had been independent of the Eighth Army—was evacuated by sea after some of the hardest fighting of the war. By 31 December the Communists had more than 800,000 Chinese and 150,000 North Koreans available for a mass offensive which frontally pressed the badly outnumbered U.N. forces back without regard for casualties. By late January, however, MacArthur stabilized a new line south of Osan and thence across the Peninsula.

E. *Stalemate and Truce*

From there, General Matthew Ridgway, who took over the Eighth Army when Walker was killed, launched a winter offensive which liberated most of South Korea by late April. A Communist Spring offensive with about 700,000 men forced Ridgway's smaller army back below the parallel and a U.N. counteroffensive (22 May to 8 July) placed the Communists on a line running northeastward across Korea from the Han River. The enemy had lost 250,000 and gained nothing; for the first year of the war, he lost more than 1,100,000 against 79,000 American, 170,000 South Koreans and some Allied casualties.

The Soviet Union, apparently convinced that the war begun by her North Korean puppet could not be won, proposed peace talks and U.N. war aims were changed from the destruction of the North Korean aggressor to a negotiated withdrawal. The talks dragged on for two years, while men fought and died all the while along the stalemated front. By 27 July 1953, when the frustrating, unwon war ended in a troubled truce, the United States had suffered 142,000 casualties in the third bloodiest war in their history; South Korea at least 275,000; and the Allies 17,000. Total Communist losses probably ran to 2,000,000.

The Korean War was historically the most violent phase of the politico-military consolidation of the world into two armed camps. It was a conflict fought with World War II equipment, tactics, and—largely—officers. American military men generally believe that it could have been won but, with expanding global political implications, the diplomats and politicians who controlled grand strategy opted for a lesser objective.

IV. THE GENERALSHIP OF DOUGLAS MACARTHUR

MacArthur was summarily removed from all commands by President Truman on 11 April 1951, an unfortunate casualty of the politico-military controversy over the objectives and conduct of the Korean War. He had been (at his death in 1964) a general officer for longer than any other American save Winfield Scott; the only one to serve as Field Marshal as well as General of the Army; a front line commander of high personal courage; and possessor of a superior mind.

MacArthur was possibly the wisest employer of the strategy of the indirect approach, using frontal means only when imperative. An exceptionally skillful user of combined land, air, and sea, he generally relied upon sweeping strategic envelopments. He was a master at retaining the initiative and luring the enemy to self-destruction. Limited means obliged him to be frugal. In the Pacific, MacArthur had had 2 per cent of the total U.S. forces and only 10 per cent of available supplies. In Korea, the Eighth Army was outnumbered except possibly in October 1950. Economy of force was of necessity MacArthur's standing principle; he was noted for his light casualties.

MacArthur's strategic conceptions—from the beginning of his leap-frogging up New Guinea to the amphibious landing at Inchon—reflect probably the greatest genius of any theatre commander since Bonaparte. Like Lee, MacArthur accomplished much with little; like Grant, he understood the interrelationship of technology and tactics; like Alexander, he operated over exceptionally vast distances; like Napoleon, he possessed great talent for governing, as confirmed by his statesmanly proconsulship of occupied Japan. MacArthur was probably the last Great Captain of Military History to have the opportunity to exercise so expansive a politico-military role.

V. UNITED STATES MILITARY DEVELOPMENTS, 1953-1965

On a wave of discontent with the conduct of the Korean War, General Eisenhower became President and in 1954 instituted a military policy styled the "New Look." The United States Air Force, which expanded with the Korean War from 48 to 143 wings was reduced to 137, but its Strategic, Tactical, Air Defense, and Air Research and Development Commands were strengthened. The Air Force budget became the largest of the military appropriations and primary reliance was placed upon "massive retaliation." In November 1956 a further inter-service squabble was settled when Secretary Charles Wilson limited Army missile development and the size of planes in the Army's new light air force. The "New Look" for the Navy meant new aircraft-carriers to help counter Russian submarine threats and to share in the strategic bombing capability. The flexibility and immunity of the carriers off Korea helped gain them this new role, which was vastly expanded as the emergence of new states with shaky governments often called for a show of force to maintain peace.

With the rapid acceleration of technology and the missile race, further developments in the Department of Defense were bound to come. When President Kennedy assumed office, he appointed Robert MacNamara Secretary of Defense. Once again a bitter controversy broke out between the military and civilian directors of American policy. The military did not believe that civilians should make decisions about equipment which, in turn, would shape operations; the politicians countered that they were responsible for the expenditure of funds. With the high cost of modern defense, the Secretary—a cost-conscious businessman—attempted once more to rationalize the needs of the services in terms of functions, roles, and missions of each piece of hardware demanded. Faced with an increase in the threat of Communist guerrilla warfare, MacNamara carried out a major build up of conventional land forces at the partial expense of the Eisenhower strategic air emphasis.

VI. RUSSIAN MILITARY ORGANIZATIONAL CHANGES

A. Air Power

If changes towards an independent strategic air force loomed large in post-World War II American thinking, the impact of the nuclear age was even greater in Russia, which had no strategic air force worth the name. Air power became linked, of course, to foreign policy and with the United States as the natural enemy, the Russians developed their defenses against air attack.

In 1946 unified command of the armed forces was established, but in 1950 separate War and Navy Ministries appeared once again only to be unified once more in 1953. By then, through the use of German technicians and imported British jet engines, the Soviets had gained technical independence. The Korean War was a testing ground for men and machines and although loss of Russian MIG 15's to U.S. F-86's was on the ratio of 10:1, rotation of pilots was continued to blood as many as possible. From 1953 to 1955, jet bombers and nuclear weapons entered service and in 1960 a Rocket Force was commissioned. As in Washington, so in Moscow the question of the composition of the armed forces swung from reliance on the Army, to nuclear deterrents, to a balance including increased support for guerrillas.

B. *The Red Army and Navy*

The Russian Army at the end of World War II comprised some 7,000,000 men out of the 11,000,000 in the Soviet armed forces. It was reduced to about two-thirds this size by 1948, but has generally remained strong. Well supplied with tanks, it has emphasized mechanized forces while extensively training people for guerrilla warfare. Much Russian equipment—notably T-34 tanks—was used in Korea. While the Russian Army has always been evident in May Day parades and at the barricades between East and West Germany, its one big peace-time operation was the suppression of the Hungarian revolt of late 1956. Russian military advisers and technicians have spent a great deal of time showing other countries, such as Egypt and Indonesia, how to use their equipment.

The Soviet Navy has long been noted for the high speed of its cruisers, the size of its destroyers, and the quantity of its submarines. Apart from the development of nuclear and conventionally-powered ice-breakers, the Soviet Union has expended much time and money upon oceanographic research.

VII. BRITISH AND FRENCH ORGANIZATIONAL CHANGES

A. British Military Policy

The high cost of armaments has caused Great Britain—as its Commonwealth shrinks—to retrench. The last battleship, *Vanguard,* completed in 1945, was "mothballed" in 1950 and later scrapped. The R.A.F. was dismantled so rapidly in the post-war world that during the Korean War it had to be supplied with American F-86 jets and B-50 bombers until rearmament—hastily undertaken in 1950—could be effective. The Army continued to run a poor third for appropriations and new equipment. As the strategic V-bombers entered service in the mid-fifties—and aided by the pen of Sir John Slessor—the Government decided to go all out for the nuclear deterrent, a policy crystallized in the famous 1957 White Paper, *Cmnd. 124,* in which all planning was predicated upon a three-day war.

By the early 1960's this policy was becoming bankrupt and in 1964 Admiral Lord Louis Mountbatten succeeded in getting a more rational, conventional organization established, based upon aircraft-carriers. In the meantime the vast cutback in defense orders was having serious consequences economically, notably in the aircraft industry and in shipbuilding, despite orders for five nuclear submarines, starting with H.M.S. *Dreadnought.*

Meanwhile, the post of Minister of Defence, held by Churchill during the war, was made permanent in 1946, but it was not until April 1964 that the Service Secretaries were abolished and all was consolidated into a single service ministry.

B. Post-war French Developments

Across the Channel the other traditionally formidable Western European Army, that of France, brought up in a spirit of risk and adventure by its Free French days, seemed unable to settle down. It fought hard, only to meet defeat in Indo-China and Algeria. As a result of the first of these struggles, it formulated a new doctrine of revolutionary warfare based on the idea that the Russians would never drop an atomic bomb in anger, but would instead aim to disrupt NATO by an indirect approach through Asia and Africa, where French and British colonial outposts would be attacked. In this move they would be helped by the Americans because, said French military theorists, the United States was always anti-colonial and pro-revolutionary. Since the problem facing the French forces under this doctrine was a politico-military one, members of the French Army officer corps regarded participation in politics as their duty. The new French theory laid the emphasis upon the psychological factors which an inferior enemy could exploit to defeat a much better equipped regular force, and the need, therefore, of the latter to undertake political and economic action in order to convince the populace that the government rather than the rebels were its friends. Thus in Algeria the French attempted to destroy the insurgents by offensive action, to seal off their sources of supply, and to teach the inhabitants that not only could they defend themselves by creating armed hamlets, but also that the French would and could help them with schools, medical centers, and economic aid. By 1956 this doctrine for war waged within a state was accepted by the Army's *Ecole de Guerre*. However, as Peter Paret has pointed out, its weakness lay in its failure to relate its action to outside events and to its misestimation of Russian intentions in the post-Stalin era.

After the defeats in Indo-China in 1954 it seemed to the Army that a new day had dawned when General Charles de Gaulle, the great modern man on horseback, became President in 1958. Denied a free hand in Algeria, however, in 1960 the Army attemped a coup and lost, but thereafter it returned to its normal place in the State. The French Navy and Air Force, meanwhile, remained loyal and concentrated on creating a modern force in support of NATO. But de Gaulle, seeking *la gloire,* withdrew from NATO in 1966 upon the development of French nuclear capability (*Force de Frappe*). The intent appeared to be to create a balance-of-power role for France.

The French Navy and Air Force, meanwhile, went quietly about their own business, took little interest in the Army's political views, and concentrated instead on creating a modern force in support of NATO.

France has been by no means the only country in which the military have felt a responsibility for the internal security and safety of the State. In Turkey also, for example, the Army has undertaken a great deal of economic work in order to create the political stability which will provide the stable background needed to protect the country against internal as well as external aggression.

C. West Germany

As in the case of Japan, rapidly changing diplomatic positions caused the revival of the German armed forces. On 5 May 1955 West Germany joined NATO and a few months later uniformed men again appeared under the German flag. In the new German armed forces, however, the principle of civilian control has been powerfully established through both a civilian Commander-in-Chief and through a Bundestag Defense Committee. Compulsory military training was re-introduced—as it has been in Australia to meet the Malaysian crisis—and by 1963 the strength of the Army was 245,000 men, of whom about half were conscripts. The ultimate goal is 12 divisions fully integrated into NATO. In this respect, much work has been done to develop common equipment which all the Allies use, there being 450 such standardized items by 1960. The Navy has also been revived and had by 1963 reached its full strength of 28,000 men (five per cent conscripts), but was still short of many of its ships, all of which are to be destroyers or smaller craft. The Air Force, largely equipped with American aircraft, has a strength of 93,000 men of whom 20 per cent are draftees.

D. The Canadian Approach

Canada became integrated into the United States defensive system in 1940, a commitment which was made more formal with the establishment in 1958 of the North American Air Defense Command (NORAD) system. Canada had recognized in 1945 that she could not afford to become a nuclear power, nor to join SEATO. Instead she took much more interest in the integrated forces proposed by NATO in 1951. Faced with the problem of improving her mobilizational base and of shortening her moblizational period, she concentrated on naval and air forces due to her advanced technological status, to objections to conscription which had arisen in 1939-1945, and to her distance from likely conflicts. Great emphasis was placed upon research and development. But in 1959 the mobilizational base was abandoned and the Army assigned instead a role simply in national survival. At the same time it became obvious that the administrative side of the services was becoming too large. A rationalization, therefore, took place which in 1964 resulted in the creation of a single armed force, thus abolishing some 200 tri-service committees. The Royal Military College of Canada has long been the only tri-service academy; in recent years the emphasis has been upon training officer-candidates to expect to command not great field armies but UN peace-keeping forces, a role in which officers from India, Pakistan, and the other smaller states can increasingly expect to perform.

VIII. MINOR WARS AND QUASI-MILITARY ACTIONS

In all nations the military are increasingly concerned with anti-guerilla and civic-action problems, especially in the less developed areas of the world. This has meant that the nature of the armed forces has changed and in some cases conscription has been reintroduced to provide a new kind of fire-brigade to put down inflammatory outbreaks in neighboring areas. The United Nations has been engaged in a number of such peacekeeping operations, of which the militarily most extensive, apart from Korea, has been that in the Congo (1960-1964). This nearly bankrupted the organization and placed in question the ability of the U.N. to mount and finance large-scale operations in the future, thus casting doubt on its future policing ability without direct U.S. aid.

A. *Arab-Israeli Tension**

No sooner was World War II over than the British had to take police action in mandated Palestine. On 29 November 1947 the United Nations passed the partition resolution and at once an Arab-Israeli War erupted. This was a battle of highways and

* See Note, p. 452.

byways. The Jews took the initiative early in 1948, but were countered by an Arab invasion. A truce was arranged in June; it was broken by the Israeli offensive to recover the Negev. Finally hostilities were brought to a halt in 1949 by agreements with Egypt, Syria, Lebanon, and Jordan although border incidents have continued despite the presence of U.N. observers. Apart from border incidents, things smoldered until in 1956 the Suez crisis brought Israel into conflict with Egypt.

B. *Berlin Blockade*

It was also during the Arab-Israeli War that the Russians chose to blockade West Berlin (25 June 1948-12 May 1949). The Allies undertook an airlift—which overcame the weather and the Russians—with 276,926 sorties in which 2,323,067 tons of food and coal were delivered to keep the city alive. Berlin has remained intermittently threatened by the U.S.S.R.

C. *Suez*

In 1955 the new nationalist government of Egypt under General Nasser purchased arms from Czechoslovakia and—when the United States and Britain withdrew economic support—seized the Suez Canal in which the British and French had a considerable investment and through which their oil supplies were shipped. At the same time, Israel determined to break the ring of Arab encirclement and Egyptian provocation.

On 29 October 1956, the Israelis launched a surprise offensive across the Sinai Peninsula. Three lightning mobile thrusts humiliated the Egyptian forces by taking them off balance and pursuing them back to the Suez Canal, thus freeing the port of Aqaba, the only Israeli outlet to the Red Sea and important in trade with the East. The next day Britain and France, having concentrated troops in strife-torn Cyprus, sent Nasser an ultimatum over the Canal. (But indecision then prevailed in London and surprise was lost.) Not till 5 November was an airborne and amphibious attack delivered on the Canal, which merely succeeded in provoking Egypt to block the waterway. Although hopelessly defeated,

Nasser was saved by U.S. and U.S.S.R. pressure in the U.N. Suez coincided with a revolt in Hungary against Russian domination, distracted western attention from trouble in the Communist camp, weakened the cooperation of the major western powers in NATO, and underlay de Gaulle's decision to construct a national nuclear force and to withdraw militarily from NATO, whose headquarters was in 1966 shifted to Belgium.

D. Peacekeeping by the U.S.

In the summer of 1958 the U.S. Sixth Fleet—maintained in the Mediterranean since 1946 as a replacement for the dwindling Royal Navy—demonstrated its usefulness by stabilizing the government in Lebanon during a political crisis by landing Marines (15 July-September 1948).

When a coup in the Dominican Republic threatened to place that country under Communist control in May 1965, the United States joined by Brazil and several other members of the Organization of American States, committed troops to maintain order. Although assailed in some quarters as unjustified intervention, the action was in keeping with the trend toward international collective security and peacekeeping and it strengthened the credibility of U.S. determination to resist Communist subversive designs.

IX. COMMUNIST GUERRILLA WARFARE

A. Theory

Although not generally so considered, Lenin was a notable military theorist. Building on Marx and misunderstandings of Clausewitz, Lenin laid down a system of revolutionary warfare. He asserted that war is always a part of a whole, which is politics; therefore, war is always a political instrument. Since war, according to Lenin, is inevitable until the global triumph of socialism, the Communist saw all facets of life as parts of a military struggle. Within the limitations of Leninist semantics, a war of conquest can only be waged by the "capitalist-imperialist" camp, while a just war can only be a struggle for the liberation of peoples from colonialism or capitalism.

Several characteristics to achieve this liberation are clear in Lenin's writings. He conceived war as a unified struggle, under a single direction, on a spectrum so broad as to include interchangeable military and political means ranging from total armed struggle to ostensible "peace." This multi-dimensional conflict aims for the destruction of capitalism by the exploitation of, among other things, anti-colonial movements and popular economic and social aspirations.

Mao Tse-tung propounded practical methods for applying these general concepts and in turn his ideas were copied and modified to fit local conditions by the Viet Minh Marshal Giap and the naturalized Cuban "Che" Guevara. These theorists advised the acceptance of long, protracted conflict expanding eventually from small harassing actions to a final stage in which the guerrillas employ regular forces in open actions. They emphasized the development of a sympathetic attitude on the part of the rural people—who must shelter and help the guerrillas—by means of full exploitation of their aspirations, particularly for agrarian reform. Where they are present, the expulsion of foreign influences is recommended to draw the support of local nationalists and to achieve a rallying purpose for all elements.

B. *Operations*

The staunchness of the U.N. action in Korea caused a shift in the Cold War to a balance of deterrents. This, while leaving the Russian High Command still determined to surpass the United States in nuclear weapons, also led slowly to a reappraisal of the military situation and resulted in greater Soviet support of guerrilla-type rebellions in various parts of the world, in which local nationalism and economic feudalism played a considerable part.

1. MALAYA, KENYA, AND ADEN

In both Malaya and the Philippines, the nucleus for Communist-led rebellions came from some of the guerrillas who had fought the Japanese to 1945. In 1948 the Communist success in China led to the outbreak of terrorism in Malaya. In 1951 General Sir Gerald Templer, as High Commissioner, instituted a tight security operation including the use of helicopters and bush patrols. This was combined with strict controls on food and the declaration of a state of emergency. By 1954 the combination of political, economic, and military action was proving effective. In 1956 Malaya assumed responsibility for its own internal security, but British troops and airmen remained into the 'sixties to help eradicate terrorists and, starting in 1964, Indonesian commandos. The latter were sent by President Sukarno to harass newly-independent Malaysia.

In Kenya a similar use of joint patrols of British regulars and local militia eventually brought the Mau Mau to heel. In Aden, however, a long running battle with the local Arabs dragged on from the interwar years with the tribesmen aided by Egypt.

2. THE PHILIPPINES

In the Philippines as in Malaya certain anti-Japanese forces became the nucleus of a politically-oriented guerrilla movement. Again the settlement of the problem came from a combination of military force and economic enticements. In 1949 the Hukbalahap (Huks) turned on the landowners of Panay and Luzon provinces. Communist-led into terrorist activities, they were seriously weakened by the program of Secretary of Defense Ramón Magsaysay, which combined (1951) military pressure and the granting of homesteads. When in February 1954 the Huks refused to renounce allegiance to Moscow, he instituted an all-out offensive both to exterminate terrorists and to build settlements for those who would change their allegiance. By December 1955 the struggle was over because Magsaysay had struck at the heart of the matter.

3. HOLDING OPERATIONS

After the French retreated from Indo-China, the Chinese Communists looked to Formosa, the seat of Chinese Nationalist Chiang Kai-shek. The United States interposed the Seventh Fleet in early 1955 and the President was authorized by Congress to use force at his own discretion. The U.S. Navy posted regular patrols from South Vietnam to Korea, and from October 1964 these acted against aggressive North Vietnamese boats and their bases.

4. INDO-CHINA (VIETNAM)

Upon French recognition of an anti-Communist government in Indo-China in 1948, the Communist Vietnamese forces of devious Ho Chi Minh increased their efforts to fill the position vacated by the Japanese. A civil war broke out and until 11 August 1954, the French poured wealth and military power into the rice paddies and jungles. But, despite American aid, results were negligible owing to strong anti-French feeling amongst the anti-Communists. The French never came to grips with the real problems of guerrilla warfare and allowed a force to be trapped in the spring of 1954 in the fortress of Dienbienphu. After a gallant, but hopeless, defense in which air supply failed to prevent disaster, the French abandoned Dienbienphu and withdrew from Indo-China. Though the U.N. attempted boundary settlements, Ho Chi Minh infiltrated further and in 1961 American military advisers and equipment entered the struggle in South Vietnam. For several years attempts were made to train and equip local forces to defend the area. But by 1965 it was obvious that more drastic action had to be taken and U.S. forces equipped with helicopters, jet aircraft, and napalm assumed a far more active part. Moreover, unlike in Korea where the Yalu marked the division between outside support and the theater of war, in Vietnam U.S. and South Vietnamese aircraft began to strike across the border into North Vietnam to break up supply lines and to strike in 1966 at oil and port facilities. By the end of 1966 each side had more than a quarter of a million troops engaged, not counting the U.S. Seventh Fleet cruising offshore from which strikes were also being flown. Escalation of the war on the ground and in the air constantly raised the question of full-scale Chinese participation, as in Korea. But, although the Soviet Union provided North Vietnam with antiaircraft missiles and other equipment and China has attempted to keep expendable supplies flowing south, co-operation between the two major Communist powers has faded. The ideological dispute over the role of international communism together with Chinese accusations that the Russians were inadequately supporting the Vietnamese, constricted Soviet freedom of action on the international stage. Within the U.S. and the free world President Johnson disarmed his critics by both firmness in support of military action in the war and by constantly seeking a peaceful solution.

X. CONCLUSION

Unlike the interwar years, the post-1945 period has, due to the Cold War and the magnitude of weapon power, seen a growing interest in and awareness of military affairs. Politico-military relations have become increasingly important, continuing a trend begun in Bismarck's Europe. The military implications of space, while not yet fully determined, will be governed, nevertheless, by the same general principles which have held in the past although the instruments and equipment will be vastly more expensive and much more sophisticated. Yet, the outcome will always depend upon men and they are much the same as they have been since Alexander's time.

The long history of warfare time and again teaches that weapons and formations are important, but that given reasonable odds, the most vital factor is leadership, the ability to employ the principles of war—from this is derived the unity of the history of war.

NOTE: In the late Spring of 1967 the Arab states, with Soviet backing, formed a provocative alliance against Israel. In a perfect example of preemptive war the Israelis struck on 5 June. Making maximum use of tactical airpower and eschewing strategic bombing of cities, the Israelis effectively knocked out the opposing Arab air forces. At the same time, Israeli armor struck south into the Sinai peninsula, fanning out to reach the Suez Canal in the north and the Strait of Tiran at the mouth of the Gulf of Aqaba in the south. Jerusalem was also captured and the Syrians beaten back into their own land in the north. In a six-day repetition of the 1956 campaign, General Dayan gave another exhibition of his perfect grasp of modern air-and-armor tactics.

Suggested Additional Reading

The suggestions which follow are not intended to be either definitive or even necessarily the classic works in the field. Availability has been the criterion. Therefore, books likely to be out of print have generally, especially in the modern period, been avoided. Since memoirs are primary sources, these have been omitted. Students wishing to pursue the subject further will find in each of these books a bibliography which will act as a further guide. The order is strictly alphabetical by author and not a value judgment of contents.

I. GENERAL MILITARY HISTORIES

Brodie, Bernard and Fawn. *X-Bow to H-Bomb*. New York: Dell Publishing Co., Inc., 1962. A useful introduction to weapons development.

Dupuy, Colonel R. Ernest and Colonel Trevor N. Dupuy. *Military Heritage of America*. New York: McGraw-Hill Book Co., 1956. United States wars, broadly interpreted. Civil War and World Wars I and II predominate, although the book contains a brief reference to pre-United States warfare and runs through the Korean War. Closely follows United States Military Academy course materials. Contains extensive military history bibliography.

Earle, E. M. *The Makers of Modern Strategy*. Princeton, N.J.: Princeton University Press, 1952. Military thought from Machiavelli to Hitler. Standard work now dated and subject to revision.

Falls, Cyril. *The Art of War*. London: Oxford University Press, 1961. A good, concise study.

Fuller, Major General J. F. C. *A Military History of the Western World*. 3 vols. New York: Funk and Wagnalls Co., 1954-

1956. One of the greatest military histories, employs a decisive battle approach with summary connecting narratives. Rich from standpoint of strategy and interrelationship of war with other societal factors. Spans from ancient times through World War II.

Liddell Hart, Captain Basil H. *Strategy*. New York: Frederick A. Praeger, 1954. Brief analytical history, ancient times through World War II, focusing upon military strategy. Advances provocative thesis of the indirect approach. Excellent. By a most influential pundit.

Montross, Lynn. *War Through the Ages*. New York: Harper and Bros., 1960. A well-written layman's account from earliest times through Korea. Considerable detail on medieval and early modern periods. Tends to inaccuracy and erroneous judgment, especially in twentieth century. Maps. Illustrations.

Potter, E. B., and Admiral Chester W. Nimitiz (eds.). *Sea Power, A Naval History*. Englewood Cliffs, N.J.: Prentice-Hall, Inc., 1960, and later editions. Standard general work covering world naval history from ancient times through the Korean War. Chapters have been written by professors at the United States Naval Academy. Maps. Illustrations.

Preston, Richard A., Sydney F. Wise, and Herman O. Werner. *Men in Arms*. London: Thames, 1963. A military-affairs type history from ancient warfare to the Cold War. Provides the societal context of wars. Selected bibliography. Illustrations.

Ropp, Theodore. *War in the Modern World*. New York: Collier Books, 1962. A more detailed and analytic military affairs history. Greater attention to doctrine and organization. Begins about 1500 and comes through Korea. Outstanding bibliographic notes throughout. Excellent, especially the latest edition from Duke University Press.

Vagts, Alfred. *A History of Militarism*. New York: Meridian Books, 1959. The classic in its field.

II. ANCIENT WARFARE

Adcock, Sir Frank E. *The Greek and Macedonian Art of War*. Berkeley: University of California Press, 1962. A highly regarded series of lectures.

Boak, Arthur E. R. *Manpower Shortage and the Fall of the Roman Empire in the West*. Ann Arbor: University of Michigan Press, 1955. Challenges the Gibbon thesis.

Fuller, Major General J. F. C. *The Generalship of Alexander the Great.* New Brunswick, N.J.: Rutgers University Press, 1960. A professional's analytic account of Alexander's times and campaigns.

Mellersh, Harold L. *Soldiers of Rome.* London: Hale, 1964. A new study.

Tarn, Sir William. *Alexander the Great.* Boston: Beacon Press, 1956. Abridgment of a best seller and still a standard work.

Thucydides. *The Peloponnesian War.* Oldest western politico-military history. Available in many editions.

Vegetius. *The Military Institutions of the Romans.* Harrisburg: The Military Service Publishing Co., 1944. Convenient edition of one of the oldest works of western military thought.

Warrington, John (ed. & tr.). *Caesar's War Commentaries.* New York: E. P. Dutton and Co., 1958. Standard translation of Caesar's autobiography, but see 1965 study by Fuller.

Xenophon. *Anabasis.* A fighting retreat from ancient Persia. Interesting leadership study in many editions.

III. MEDIEVAL AND EARLY MODERN WARFARE

Hollister, C. Warren. *Anglo-Saxon Military Institutions.* New York: Oxford University Press, 1962.

———. *The Military Organization of Norman England.* Oxford: The Clarendon Press, 1965.

Fresh interpretations of the military establishment in England before and after Hastings.

Keevil, J. J. *Medicine and the Navy,* 1200-1900. London: Livingstone, 1957-1958. The first large study of a vital subject.

Lamb, Harold. *Genghis Khan.* New York: McBride, 1927. Acceptably accurate, well narrated, if low-level account.

Marcus, G. J. *A Naval History of England.* Vol. I: *The Formative Centuries.* Boston: Little, Brown and Co., 1961. A comprehensive new account which supersedes Michael Lewis, *The Navy of Britain* (1948). Other volumes are forthcoming.

Mattingly, Garrett. *The Armada.* Boston: Houghton Mifflin Co., 1959. Best selling history of the first important modern naval campaign.

Oman, Sir Charles. *The Art of War in the Middle Ages, A.D. 378-1515.* Ithaca: Cornell University Press, 1953. A series of brief essays which are covered in more detail in Oman's major work.

———. *A History of the Art of War in the Middle Ages, A.D. 378-1485*. 2 vols. New York: Burt Franklin [1959]. Older (reprinted) standard work, partially outdated by more recent scholarship. The fall of Rome through the fifteenth century with a broad examination of military developments and political history, as well as campaigns and battles.

———. *A History of the Art of War in the XVIth Century*. London: Methuen and Co., 1937. An additional century treated in the same fashion.

Parry, J. H. *The Age of Reconnaissance*. New York: Mentor Press, 1963. The best account of the men, materials, and methods in the expansion of Europe.

Prawdin, Michael. *The Mongol Empire*. London: Allen and Unwin, 1952. More authoritative history.

Smail, R. C. *Crusading Warfare (1097-1193)*. Cambridge: Cambridge University Press, 1956. A major contribution to medieval military history.

Taylor, F. L. *The Art of War in Italy, 1494-1529*. Cambridge: Cambridge University Press, 1921. A standard work on Italian wars.

Thompson, James Westfall. *The Wars of Religion in France, 1559-1576*. New York: Frederick Ungar Publishing Co., 1964. The internecine struggle in France by a distinguished historian.

Treece, Henry. *The Crusades*. New York: Mentor Press, 1962. A broad military, social, political, economic treatment.

IV. SEVENTEENTH AND EIGHTEENTH-CENTURY WARFARE

Churchill, Sir Winston. *Marlborough*. 4 vols. London: Harrap, 1933-1938. A descendant's agile-penned view of a great general and his times.

Corbett, Sir Julian. *England in the Seven Years War*. 2 vols. London: Longmans Green, 1907.

———. *Fighting Instructions, 1530-1816*. London: Navy Records Society, 1905.

Dodge, Colonel Theodore A. *Gustavus Adolphus*. Boston: Houghton Mifflin Co., 1895. Old, but still an excellent study of Gustavus.

Dorn, Walter. *Competition for Empire*. New York: Harper and

Bros., 1940. Not intended as a military history, but contains some splendid chapters on the Seven Years War.

Firth, Sir Charles H. *Cromwell's Army*. London: Methuen and Co., 1902. Standard work on the English Civil War.

Fortescue, Sir John. *History of the British Army*. 13 vols. New York: St. Martin's Press, 1899-1930. A monumental, classic work. Narrative from Roman Britain through World War I. Excellent treatment of seventeenth and eighteenth-century conflicts.

Frederick the Great. *Instructions for His Generals*. Harrisburg: The Military Service Publishing Co., 1951. Thought of another eighteenth-century great.

Mahan, Alfred Thayer. *The Influence of Seapower upon History, 1660-1783*. 2 vols. Boston: Little, Brown and Co., 1893. (Sycamore Press, 1957.) Standard work reflecting the military thought of A. T. Mahan; an excellent analytic naval history of the period.

Marcus, G. J. *A Naval History of England*. Vol. I: *The Formative Centuries*. Boston: Little, Brown and Co., 1961. A comprehensive new account which supersedes Michael Lewis, *The Navy of Britain* (1948).

Richmond, Sir Herbert. *Statesmen and Sea Power*. London: Oxford University Press, 1946. A classic study of the use of sea power in the Corbett tradition.

Roberts, Michael. *The Military Revolution*. London: Longmans Green, 1956. An important new book on the period.

Saxe, Maurice de. *My Reveries on the Art of War*. Harrisburg: The Military Service Publishing Co., 1953. Military thought of one of the greater eighteenth-century soldiers.

Turner, Gordon B. *A History of Military Affairs in Western Society Since the Eighteenth Century*. New York: Harcourt, Brace and Co., 1956. Collection of readings edited by Turner, beginning with eighteenth century.

Wedgwood, C. V. *The Thirty Years War*. Harmondsworth: Middlesex, 1961. The best modern account of that vast, dismal conflict.

V. EARLY AMERICAN WARS

Alden, John R. *The American Revolution, 1775-1783*. New York: Harper and Bros., 1954.

Bernardo, C. Joseph, and Eugene H. Bacon. *American Military Policy*. Harrisburg: The Military Service Publishing Co., 1957. Sometimes overly-detailed examination of the evolution of U.S. military policy. Wealth of material.

Billias, George Athan. *George Washington's Generals*. New York: Wm. Morrow and Co., 1964. The basic work is, of course, Douglas Southall Freeman's *George Washington*. New York: Scribner, 1948-1955.

Bird, Harrison. *March to Saratoga: General Burgoyne and the American Campaign, 1777*. New York: Oxford University Press, 1963. One of a number of new books on the subject.

———. *Battle for a Continent*. New York: Oxford University Press, 1965.

Chapelle, Howard I. *The History of the American Sailing Navy*. New York: W. W. Norton and Co., Inc., 1949. A classic on the development of naval vessels.

Downey, Fairfax. *Indian Wars of the U. S. Army, 1776-1865*. New York: Doubleday and Co., Inc., 1963.

———. *Indian-Fighting Army*. New York: Charles Scribner's Sons, 1941. These two volumes cover the frontier life of the U. S. Army in the nineteenth century.

Dupuy, R. E. *Compact History of the Revolution*. New York: Hawthorne, 1960.

Fuller, Major General J. F. C. *Decisive Battles of the U.S.A.* New York: Thomas Yoseloff, 1942. A master military historian's not-always accurate, campaign-style military history of the United States from the Revolution through World War I.

Ganoe, Colonel William Addleman. *The History of the United States Army*. New York: Appleton-Century-Crofts, 1942. Authoritative history with much useful detail which has not carried into later books. Revolution through World War I.

Macksey, Piers. *The War for America, 1775-1783*. Cambridge: Harvard University Press, 1964. A widely hailed modern version of the Revolutionary War.

Mahan, Alfred Thayer. *The Major Operations of the Navies in the War of American Independence*. Boston: Little, Brown and Co., 1912.

———. *Sea Power in Its Relations to the War of 1812*. 2 vols. London: Sampson, Low, Marston and Co., 1905. These continue the Mahanic tradition of the influence of sea power.

Malone, Joseph J. *Pine Trees and Politics: Naval Stores and Forest Policy in Colonial New England*. Seattle: University of Washington Press, 1964. In the Albion tradition. (See VI below).

Millis, Walter. *Arms and Men.* New York: G. P. Putnam's Sons, 1956. A military affairs history critical of the evolution of U.S. military policy in many eras.

Singletary, Otis A. *The Mexican War.* Chicago: University of Chicago Press, 1960. Short, well-written work rapidly becoming the standard for schools.

Smith, Justin H. *The War with Mexico.* 2 vols. New York: Macmillan Co., 1919. The classic history of the Mexican War.

Steele, Matthew F. X. *American Campaigns.* 2 vols. Washington: Combat Forces Press, 1951. Older summary U.S. history but still useful. Covers the Revolution through the Spanish-American Wars.

Upton, Major General Emory. *The Military Policy of the United States.* Washington: Government Printing Office, 1912. The original, provocative and now-classic examination of the subject. Amounts to a military history from the Revolution through the Civil War.

Weigley, Russell F. *Towards an American Army: Military Thought from Washington to Marshall.* New York: Columbia University Press, 1962. A useful modern approach.

VI. NAPOLEON

Albion, Robert G. *Forests and Sea Power.* Cambridge: Harvard University Press, 1924. The original classic study of the influence of timber problems on tactics and strategy.

Bamford, Paul W. *Forests and French Sea Power, 1660-1789.* Toronto: University of Toronto Press, 1956.

Davies, Godfrey. *Wellington and His Army.* Oxford: Blackwell's, 1954.

Esposito, Vincent J., and John Robert Elting. *A Military History and Atlas of the Napoleonic Wars.* New York: Frederick A. Praeger, 1964. An integrated history and battle-maps approach. The West Point guide to Napoleon.

Geyl, P. *Napoleon For and Against.* London: Cape, 1964. A revised edition by the controversial Dutch historian.

Glover, Richard. *Peninsular Preparation: the Reform of the British Army, 1795-1809.* Cambridge: Cambridge University Press, 1963. Both these books give essential background on the development of the Army which eventually won at Waterloo.

Goodspeed, Captain D. J. *The British Campaigns in the Peninsula, 1808-1814*. Ottawa: The Queen's Printer, 1958. A brief, readable and accurate account of the Peninsular War.

Herold, Christopher J. *The Age of Napoleon*. London: Weidenfeld and Nicolson, 1963. Gives the feel of the period.

The Horizon Book of the Age of Napoleon. (This is the American edition of the above item.)

Hunter, T. M. *Napoleon in Victory and Defeat*. Ottawa: Army Headquarters, 1964. The official Canadian version.

Hutt, Maurice. *Napoleon*. New York: Oxford University Press, 1965.

Lewis, Michael. *A Social History of the Navy, 1793-1815*. London: Allen and Unwin, 1960. By the Professor of Naval History at the Royal Naval College and Greenwich. Good.

Mahan, Alfred Thayer. *The Influence of Sea Power upon the French Revolution and Empire, 1793-1812*. 2 vols. London: Sampson, Low, Marston and Co., 1892. One of Mahan's key works, and an excellent account of the naval phase of the long struggle against revolutionary France.

Yorck von Wartenberg, Count. *Napoleon as a General*. 2 vols. USMA. [n.d.] A standard professional's analytic history of Bonaparte.

VII. NINETEENTH CENTURY

Baclagon, Colonel Uldarico S. *Philippine Campaigns*. Manila: Graphic House, 1952. A Filipino officer's narrative of the U. S. struggle against Spain, and the later pacification operations as the U. S. took Spain's empire.

Clausewitz, Karl von. *On War*. Washington: Combat Forces Press, 1950. Jolles edition, widely used in the U. S. Armed Forces, of this classic of military thought. Possibly the most influential military book since Napoleon.

Collins, Colonel Edward M. (ed.) *Clausewitz. War, Politics, and Power*. Chicago: Henry Regnery, 1962. An excellent abridgement of *On War*.

Craig, Gordon A. *The Politics of the Prussian Army*. New York: Oxford University Press, 1956. Historian's learned study of the evolution of the Prussian state and its military system. Excellent on the nineteenth-century developments.

DuPicq, Colonel Ardant. *Battle Studies*. Harrisburg: The Military Service Publishing Co., 1947. A work with tremendous influence on French military thought in World War I and after.

Earle, Edward Meade (ed.). *Makers of Modern Strategy*. Princeton: Princeton University Press, 1952. Standard work, military-affairs oriented, from Machiavelli to the eve of World War II. Nineteenth-century sections strong.

Falls, Cyril. *A Hundred Years of War*. London: Gerald Duckworth and Co., 1953. Probably the best general military history of the nineteenth century. Perhaps overemphasizes European and especially British activities.

Freidel, Frank. *The Splendid Little War*. Boston: Little, Brown and Co., 1958. The best account of the Spanish-American War.

Fuller, Major General J. F. C. *The Conduct of War, 1789-1961*. New Brunswick: Rutgers University Press, 1961. Fuller's synthesis of the historical sweep of military development in this crucial era.

Furneaux, Rupert. *The Zulu War*. Philadelphia: J. B. Lippincott Co., 1963.

de la Gorce, Paul-Marie. *The French Army*. Toronto: Ambassador, 1963.

Halasz, Nicholas. *Captain Dreyfus; the Story of a Mass Hysteria*. New York: Simon and Schuster, Inc., 1955. The French army in political trouble.

Hargreaves, Reginald. *Red Sun Rising: the Siege of Port Arthur*. Philadelphia: J. B. Lippincott Co., 1962. A concise account.

Hibbert, Christopher. *The Destruction of Lord Raglan*. Harmondsworth: Middlesex, 1961. Four classic tales of one of the most misconducted campaigns in history.

Holt, Edgar. *The Boer War*. London: McClelland, 1958. A decent one-volume account.

Hough, Richard. *The Fleet That Had to Die*. London: Chatto, 1963. The course to Tsushima. Deals with Russian fleet.

Howard, Michael. *The Franco-Prussian War*. London: Hart Davis, 1959.The best one-volume coverage of a decisive campaign.

Jomini, General Henri. *The Art of War*. Harrisburg: The Military Service Publishing Co., 1947. Next to Clausewitz, probably this book had more impact on military thought than any other in the last two centuries.

Luvaas, Jay. *The Military Legacy of the Civil War: the European Inheritance*. Chicago: University of Chicago Press, 1959.

———. *The Education of an Army: British military thought, 1815-1940*. Chicago, University of Chicago Press, 1964.

Two excellent books by one of the new American scholars.

Marder, Arthur. *The Anatomy of British Sea Power.* (Reissued by Archon Books, Hamden, Conn., 1964.) This is the classic study of seapower and politics.

Pemberton, W. Baring. *The Battles of the Crimean War.* New York: Macmillan Co., 1962.

Purcell, Victor. *The Boxer Uprising.* Cambridge: Harvard University Press, 1963. Deals with colonial conflicts late in the century.

Woodham-Smith, Cecil. *The Reason Why.* New York: McGraw-Hill Book Co., 1953. The Crimean War.

———. *Florence Nightingale.* New York: McGraw-Hill, 1951.

Worcester, Donald E. *Sea Power and Chilean Independence.* Gainesville: University of Florida Press, 1962. Brief account of important Latin-American naval campaigns.

VIII. THE AMERICAN CIVIL WAR

The American Heritage Picture History of the Civil War. (Ed. in charge: Richard M. Ketchum.) New York: Doubleday and Co., Inc., 1960.

Anderson, Bern. *By Sea and By River: the Naval History of the Civil War.* New York: Alfred A. Knopf, Inc., 1962. The best one-volume work so far; by an ex-admiral.

Andreana, Ralph. *The Economic Impact of the American Civil War.* Cambridge, Mass.: Schenkman Publishing Co., Inc., 1962. An edited collection of essays on a new aspect.

Black, Robert C. III. *The Railroads of the Confederacy.* Chapel Hill: University of North Carolina Press, 1952.

Catton, Bruce. *Mr. Lincoln's Army.* New York: Doubleday and Co., Inc., 1954.

———. *A Stillness at Appomattox.* New York: Doubleday and Co., Inc., 1954.

Catton is the best writer on the Civil War and has numerous titles to his credit, of which these are but two. See also his *Centennial History of the Civil War.*

Fite, E. D. *Social and Industrial Conditions in the North During the Civil War.* New York: Frederick Ungar Publishing Co., 1964.

Fuller, J. F. C. *Grant and Lee.* London: Eyre and Spottiswoode, 1959. A study in personality and generalship.

Gosnell, H. Allen. *Guns on Western Waters; the Story of River Gunboats in the Civil War.* Baton Rouge: Louisiana State University Press, 1949.

Henderson, G. F. R. *Stonewall Jackson.* New York: Longmans Green and Co., 1932. A classic.

Liddell Hart, B. H. *Sherman.* New York: Frederick A. Praeger, 1958. A standard biography.

Nevins, Allan. *The War for the Union.* New York: Charles Scribner's Sons, 1959. Another powerful series.

Randall, J. G., and David Donald. *The Civil War and Reconstruction.* New York: D. C. Heath and Co., 1961. It has a dated approach, but remains one of the best one volume studies complete with a mammoth bibliography.

Wood, W. B., and J. S. Edmonds. *The Military History of the Civil War.* (Reissue.) New York: Capricorn Books, 1960. A classic in its day and still useful.

IX. THE FIRST WORLD WAR

The 1914-18 War is now undergoing a re-evaluation and a whole torrent of new books on the subject in general and in particular are now becoming available. These are of varying scholarliness and usefulness, but nearly all have bibliographies. For extensive research see Jacques de Launay, *The Two World Wars; A Selective Bibliography* (1965), and the reviews in the current issues of the United States Naval Institute *Proceedings, Military Affairs, The Airpower Historian,* the *Journal of the Royal United Service Institution,* and the *Monthly Accession Lists* of the Ministry of Defence Library (London).

Albrecht-Carrié, René. *The Meaning of the First World War.* Englewood Cliffs, N.J.: Prentice-Hall, Inc., 1965.

Barnett, Correlli. *The Swordbearers.* London: Eyre and Spottiswoode, 1964. A provocative reappraisal of the leadership.

Churchill, Winston. *The World Crisis.* New York: Charles Scribner's Sons, 1923-1931. Various editions, including a paperback in 1960 in one volume. This is the classic inside description by "the man of the first half of the twentieth century" (TIME).

Falls, Cyril. *The First World War.* London: Longmans, 1960. A reasonable one volume treatment by a former official historian.

Graves, Robert. *Goodbye to All That.* (Reissue.) New York: Alfred A. Knopf, Inc., 1957.

Remarque, Erich Maria. *All Quiet on the Western Front.* (Many editions.) Boston: Little, Brown and Co., 1929. Two 1929 pacifist classics of life in the trenches.

Lawrence, T. E. *The Seven Pillars of Wisdom.* (Reissue.) New York: Dell Publishing Co., Inc., 1962. The story by their leader of the Anglo-Arab guerrillas against the Turks. A classic.

Liddell Hart, B. H. *The Real War.* Boston: Little, Brown and Co., 1964. By the doyen of twentieth-century military critics.

———. *The Tanks.* 2 vols. London: Cassell, 1959. A history of the trench-breaking weapon by one of its early adherents.

Marder, Arthur. *From the Dreadnought to Scapa Flow.* New York: Oxford University Press, 1961-. The history of the Royal Navy from 1904 to 1919.

Moorehead, Alan. *Gallipoli.* London: Hamish Hamilton, 1956. The epic how-not-to-do-it campaign told by a first-class war correspondent of the Second World War.

Mosley, Leonard. *The Duel for Kilimanjaro.* New York: Ballantine Books, Inc., 1963. The little known East African campaign —a limited war.

Reynolds, Quentin. *They Fought for the Sky.* New York: Rinehart and Co., Inc., 1957. This glamorizes the fighter pilots. There is no good balanced air history for this war. The official histories are biased and unreliable.

Robinson, Douglas H. *The Zeppelin in Combat.* London: Foulis, 1961.

Higham, Robin. *The British Rigid Airship, 1908-1931.* London: Foulis, 1961.

Robinson's is a fine study of combat operations; the other volume follows an unsuccessful weapons program.

Stallings, Laurence. *The Doughboys.* New York: Harper and Bros., 1963. The best account of the American Expeditionary Force.

Taylor, A. J. P. *Illustrated History of the First World War.* London: Hamish Hamilton, 1963. The pictures are unusual; the text inaccurate.

Tuchman, Barbara. *The Guns of August.* New York: Macmillan Co., 1962. The best description of the opening of the war in 1914.

Wolff, Leon. *In Flanders Fields.* New York: The Viking Press, 1958. The classic exposé of the battle of Passchendaele which revived interest in the First World War.

X. THE INTER-WAR YEARS

Relatively little has been written on the period between the World Wars. Some of the best work is in the introductory volumes to the various official history series, such as those produced by the Office of the Chief of Military History in Washington and the Cabinet Historical Office in London, to mention but two. Many more studies are needed, however.

Churchill, Winston. *The Second World War.* Vol. I: *The Gathering Storm.* Boston: Houghton Mifflin Co., 1948. By a World War II leader of stature.

de la Gorce, Paul-Marie. *The French Army in Politics.* New York: George Braziller, Inc., 1963. Most apropos in view of the military revolt against de Gaulle.

Goerlitz, Walter. *History of the German General Staff.* New York: Frederick A. Praeger, 1953. The basic study; but see also Gordon Craig.

Goldberg, Alfred. *A History of the U. S. Air Force.* Princeton: D. van Nostrand Co., Inc., 1957. An illustrated work.

Higham, Robin. *Armed Forces in Peacetime: Britain, 1918-1940.* Hamden, Conn.: Archon Books, 1963. The first detailed study of a much-neglected subject.

Kilmarx, Richard. *A History of Soviet Air Power.* New York: Frederick A. Praeger, 1962. A fine one-volume treatment.

Liddell Hart, B. H. *The Tanks.* 2 vols. London: Cassell, 1959. See previous comment.

Luvaas, Jay. *The Military Legacy of the Civil War; the European Inheritance.* Chicago: University of Chicago Press, 1959, and *The Education of an Army.* Chicago: University of Chicago Press, 1964.

Good studies of intellectual influence and lack of it.

Masters, John. *Bugles and a Tiger.* London: Michael Joseph, 1956. The British Indian Army by one of its officers.

Millis, Walter. *Arms and Men.* New York: G. P. Putnam's Sons, 1956. The development of the U. S. Armed forces.

Morison, Elting E. *Turmoil and Tradition.* Boston: Houghton Mifflin Co., 1960. An able life of U. S. Secretary of War Stimson.

O'Ballance, Edgar. *The Red Army.* New York: Frederick A. Praeger, 1964. A useful short history.

Pogue, Forrest. *George C. Marshall, Education of a General.* New

York: The Viking Press, 1963-. A most able life of a Chief of Staff.

Potter, E. B., and Chester Nimitz. *Sea Power*. Englewood Cliffs, N.J.: Prentice-Hall, Inc., 1960 and later editions. The Naval Academy text, and a good basic history of naval developments.

Snow, C. P. *Science and Government*. New York: Mentor Press, 1963. The controversial book on the origins of radar.

Stewart, George. *The White Armies of Russia*. New York: Macmillan Co., 1933. A pioneer work in Russian military history.

Thomas, Hugh. *The Spanish Civil War*. New York: Harper and Bros., 1961. The classic study of internecine strife.

Zook, David H., Jr. *The Conduct of the Chaco War*. New York: Twayne Publishers, Inc., 1960. One of the best accounts of a Latin American War.

XI. THE SECOND WORLD WAR

The 1939-45 conflict has seen one of the largest collections of literature of any war so far, perhaps because it was fought by men more literate and more conscious of history and of people than ever before. More than 200 volumes of official histories of a high caliber have already appeared. These are supplemented by a large number of memoirs, by autobiographical novels, and by secondary studies. More come off the presses every day. For biographical information, see the comment in the introduction to the 1914-18 literature.

Auphan, Paul. *The French Navy in World War II*. Annapolis: U. S. Naval Institute, 1959. One of a series on the various navies in the Second World War published by the U.S.N.I.; see *The Proceedings* for others.

Babington-Smith, Constance. *Air Spy*. New York: Ballantine Books, Inc., 1959. On the photo aspect of the air war by a person with a professional interest in it.

The Bantam Eyewitness History of World War II. New York: Bantam Books, 1962.

Barnett, Correlli. *The Desert Generals*. London: Kimber, 1960. One of the first serious debunking books on Montgomery.

Beach, Edward L. *Submarine*. New York: Holt, Rinehart and Winston, 1952. The American classic on Pacific operations.

Brickhill, Paul. *The Dam Busters*. New York: Ballantine Books, Inc., 1955. The story of a precision bombing squadron.

Churchill, Winston. *The Second World War*. 6 vols. Boston: Houghton Mifflin Co., 1948-1953. The classic history of the British participation in the war as seen by the Prime Minister.

Crisp, Robert. *Brazen Chariots*. New York: W. W. Norton and Co., Inc., 1960. A tank commander in the deserts of North Africa.

de Launay, Jacques. *European Resistance Movements, 1960-1963*. 2 vols. New York: Pergamon, 1965.

Dodson, Kenneth. *Away All Boats!* Boston: Little, Brown and Co., 1954. The classic novel of amphibious warfare transports.

Flower, Desmond. *The Taste of Courage*. New York: Harper and Bros., 1960. A large and well-done compendium of first-hand accounts by participants in the war.

Frankland, Noble. *The Bombing Offensive Against Germany*. London: Faber, 1965. Book on aspect of the air war by person with a professional interest in it as a flyer and as scholar.

Fuchida, Mitsuo and Masatake Okumiya. *Midway*. Annapolis: U. S. Naval Institute, 1955. The Japanese side of the battle that doomed Japan.

Fuller, J. F. C. *The Second World War*. London: Eyre and Spottiswoode, 1948. A valuable one-volume account with some controversial views by one of the great modern pundits.

Galland, Adolf. *The First and the Last*. New York: Ballantine Books, Inc., 1957. Autobiography of a leading German airman.

Hill, Jim Dan. *The Minute Man in Peace and War*. Harrisburg: The Stackpole Co., 1964. A history of the U. S. National Guard.

Hyde, H. Montgomery. *Room 3603*. New York: Farrar, Strauss and Co., 1962. British Counter-Intelligence in New York.

Isely, Jeter A., and Philip Crowl. *U. S. Marines and Amphibious Warfare*. Princeton: Princeton University Press, 1951. The classic study.

Lord, Walter. *Day of Infamy*. New York: Holt, Rinehart and Winston, 1957. Pearl Harbor by a journalist.

Lott, Arnold S. *The Most Dangerous Sea*. Annapolis: U. S. Naval Institute, 1959. The history of sea-mine warfare.

MacArthur, Douglas. *Reminiscences*. New York: McGraw-Hill Book Co., 1964. The great soldier's own story.

Masters, John. *The Road Past Mandalay*. New York: Harper and Bros., 1961.

Slim, William. *Defeat into Victory*. London: Cassell, 1956. Two accounts by commanding officers of the Burma campaign.

Monsarrat, Nicholas. *The Cruel Sea*. New York: Alfred A. Knopf, Inc., 1951. The best anti-submarine warfare tale of the period.

Morison, Samuel Eliot. *The Two-Ocean War*. Boston: Little, Brown and Co., 1964. A one-volume condensation of the 15-volume set on USN operations.

Plievier, Theodore. *Stalingrad*. New York: Berkley Books, 1948. A good German account.

Roskill, S. W. *White Ensign*. Annapolis: U. S. Naval Institute, 1960. Like the Morison above, only on the Royal Navy.

Ruge, Friedrich. *Der Seekrieg*. Annapolis: U. S. Naval Institute, 1957. The German side by the later head of the West German Navy.

Smith, Gaddis. *American Diplomacy During the Second World War, 1941-1945*. New York: John Wiley and Sons, Inc., 1965.

Snell, John L. *Illusion and Necessity: the Diplomacy of Global War*. Boston: Houghton Mifflin Co., 1963. Useful short summaries.

Snyder, Louis L. *The War; a Concise History, 1939-1945*. New York: Dell Publishing Co., Inc., 1964. A useful, detailed one-volume account.

Warlimont, Walter. *Inside Hitler's Headquarters, 1939-1945*. New York: Frederick A. Praeger, 1964.

Werth, Alexander. *Russia at War, 1939-1945*. New York: E. P. Dutton and Co., 1964. The first of several new books on the epic conflict in the East. Werth was there.

Wood, Derek, and Derek Dempster. *The Narrow Margin*. London: Hutchinson, 1961. The best recent history of the Battle of Britain.

XII. SINCE 1945

The postwar world has been filled with the Cold War, great deterrents and little guerrillas, and the space race. For the first time people in the West have taken a national interest in national security problems. The result is an ever-increasing number of experts and works on all aspects of modern war.

Cagle, Malcolm, and Frank Manson. *The Sea War in Korea*. Annapolis: United States Naval Institute, 1957. The semi-official USN account.

Clarke, Arthur C. *The Exploration of Space*. New York: Harper and Bros., 1952.
The Astronauts. *We Seven*. New York: Bantam Books, 1963. Clarke predicted the space race; the astronauts participated in it.
Coffin, Tristram. *The Armed Society; Militarism in Modern America*. Baltimore: Penguin Books, Inc., 1965.
de Gramont, Sanche. *The Secret War*. New York: G. P. Putnam's Sons, 1962. The story of international espionage.
Dulles, Alan. *The Craft of Intelligence*. New York: Harper and Bros., 1963. By the former Director of the Central Intelligence Agency.
Eccles, Henry C. *Military Concepts and Philosophy*. New Brunswick, N.J.: Rutgers University Press, 1965. A new American analysis.
Finer, S. E. *The Man on Horseback*. London: Pall Mall, 1962. A provocative study of military leadership in politics.
Huntington, Samuel P. *The Soldier and the State*. Cambridge: Harvard University Press, 1957. A pioneer study in the theory and politics of civil-military relations.
Janowitz, Morris. *The Military in the Political Development of New Nations*. Chicago: University of Chicago Press, 1964. Another pioneer sociological study.
———. *The Professional Soldier*. Glencoe, Ill.: Free Press of Glencoe, Ill., 1960. A sociological study of the American officer.
Knebel, Fletcher and Charles W. Bailey II. *No High Ground*. New York: Harper and Bros., 1960. Two reporters' account of the American development of atomic bombs.
Leckie, Robert. *Conflict: the History of the Korean War*. New York: G. P. Putnam's Sons, 1962. One of several good one-volume accounts.
Lyons, Gene M., and Louis Morton. *Schools for Strategy*. New York: Frederick A. Praeger, 1965. A Dartmouth study of education and research in national security in the United States.
Paret, Peter. *French Revolutionary Warfare from Indo-China to Algeria*. Princeton, N.J.: Princeton University Press, 1964. Explains how the French army got into politics in the 1950's.
Roskill, S. W. *The Art of Leadership*. London: Collins, 1964.
———. *The Strategy of Sea Power*. London: Collins, 1962. The distilled wisdom of the British official naval historian.
Snow, C. P. *The New Men*. Harmondsworth: Middlesex, 1959.

A British insider's novel of the creation of the atomic bomb.
Snyder, William P. *The Politics of British Defence Policy, 1945-1962*. Columbus, Ohio: Ohio State University Press, 1965. A West Pointer's acute observations.
Sokolovskii, V. D. *Soviet Military Strategy*. Englewood Cliffs, N.J.: Prentice-Hall, Inc., 1963.
Thayer, Charles W. *Guerrilla*. New York: Mentor Press, 1963. A useful short history of modern guerrilla actions.

XIII. TECHNOLOGY AND WAR

This is a relatively new field and the number of books of breadth available in it is still limited. Many good accounts can be found in the official histories of the last two World Wars, especially in volumes on logistics, ordnance, factories, manpower, and health problems. Books on older subjects tend to veer into the realm of guides for collectors of artifacts rather than into the broader area of political, economic, and social history. For more special guidance see the bibliographies used in Kansas State's Technology and War courses.

Abell, Westcott. *The Shipwright's Trade*. Cambridge: Cambridge University Press, 1948. A short, illustrated history of ship building. Useful.
Barrie, Alexander. *War Underground*. New York: Ballantine Books, Inc., 1961. Mining and counter-mining in the First World War.
Bishop, Edward. *The Guinea Pig Club*. London: Macmillan Co., 1963. The development of plastic surgery for aircrew.
Bruce, Robert V. *Lincoln and the Tools of War*. Indianapolis: Bobbs-Merrill Co., Inc., 1956. Useful for the Civil War in America.
Chapelle, H. I. *The History of the American Sailing Navy*. New York: W. W. Norton and Co., Inc., 1949. With detailed drawings it describes the evolution of American sailing warships.
Crowell, Benedict. *America's Munitions, 1917-1918*. Washington: U. S. Government Printing Office, 1919. The Report of the Under-Secretary for War; it covers all manufactured items.
Dornberger, Walter. *V-2*. New York: The Viking Press, 1954. The autobiography of the German rocket development commandant.

Higham, Robin. *The British Rigid Airship, 1908-1931*. London: Foulis, 1961.

Hogg, O. F. G. *The Royal Arsenal*. 2 vols. London: Oxford University Press, 1963. Describes from medieval times the principal British gun-making and explosives works.

Holley, I. B., Jr. *Buying Aircraft*. Washington: U. S. Government Printing Office, 1965.

———. *Ideas and Arms*. New Haven: Yale University Press, 1953. These two studies cover aeronautical procurement in the First and Second World Wars. Good.

Knebel, Fletcher, and Charles W. Bailey II. *No High Ground*. New York: Harper and Bros., 1960. On the atomic bomb.

Liddell Hart, B. H. *The Tanks*. London: Cassell, 1959.

Manucy, Albert. *Artillery Through the Ages*. Washington: U. S. Government Printing Office, 1949.

Parkes, Oscar. *The British Battleship, 1860-1950*. London: Seelye Service [c. 1958]. With illustrations, drawings and detailed text, the whole development of the metal warship is described. Similar volumes for other types are almost non-existent.

Parkinson, C. Northcote. *Portsmouth Point*. Cambridge: Harvard University Press, 1950. A useful little work on Nelson's time, with diagrams.

Pawle, Gerald. *The Secret War*. London: Harrap, 1956. Miscellaneous weapons development and its hazards.

Schlaifer, Robert, and S. D. Heron. *The Development of Aircraft Engines and Fuels*. Boston: Graduate School of Business Administration, Harvard University, 1950. A valuable study.

Scott, J. D. *Vickers: a History*. London: Weidenfeld and Nicolson, 1962. Tells the story of Britain's big private manufacturer.

Underhill, Harold. *Sailing Ship Rigs and Rigging*. Glasgow: Brown, Son, and Ferguson, 1938.

Villiers, Alan. *The Way of a Ship*. New York: Charles Scribner's Sons, 1952. On how to sail a square-rigger.

Whittle, Frank. *Jet*. London: Muller, 1953. The autobiography of the engine pioneer.

Wilson, A. W. *The Story of the Gun*. Woolwich: Royal Artillery Institution, 1944.

At present these two books represent the only convenient and available histories of artillery.

Wise, David, and Thomas B. Ross. *The U-2 Affair*. New York: Random House, Inc., 1962. On the hazards of modern technical snooping.

(keyed to previous sections).

III. Webb, Henry J. *Elizabethan Military Science: the books and the practice*. Madison: University of Wisconsin Press, 1966.

V. Coles, Harry. *The War of 1812*. Chicago: University of Chicago Press, 1966. A short modern history written with the undergraduate in mind.

VII. Heinl, Colonel Robert D., Jr. *Soldiers of the Sea. The United States Marine Corps, 1775-1962*. Annapolis: United States Naval Institute, 1963. Selected in 1963 for the official White House Library.

VII. Schurman, D. M. *The Education of a Navy: the development of British Naval Strategic Thought, 1867-1914*. London: Cassell, 1965.

IX. Fredette, Raymond H. *The Sky on Fire: the first Battle of Britain*. New York: Holt, Rinehart & Winston, 1966. The Gothas over London in World War I.

X. Higham, Robin. *The Military Intellectuals in Britain, 1918-1939*. New Brunswick, N. J.: Rutgers University Press, 1966.

X. Hurley, Alfred. *Billy Mitchell: crusade for Airpower*. New York: Watts, 1964. A sound modern biography.

XI. Armstrong, Anne. *Unconditional Surrender: the impact of the Casablanca Policy on World War II*. New Brunswick, N. J.: Rutgers University Press, 1961.

XI. Bragadin, Marc' A. *The Italian Navy in World War II*. Annapolis, Md.: United States Naval Institute, 1957.

XI. Clark, Alan. *Barbarossa: the Russian-German Conflict, 1941-45*. New York: New American Library, 1965. An excellent new account.

XII. Huntington, Samuel P. *Changing Patterns of Military Politics*. New York: Free Press (Macmillan), 1962.

XIII. Williams, Francis Leigh, *Matthew Fontaine Maury, Scientist of the Sea*. New Brunswick, N. J.: Rutgers University Press, 1963.

XIII. Zuckermann, Sir Solly. *Scientists and War*. London: Hamish Hamilton, 1966. The author has been a very influential scientific advisor in Britain since World War II.

Index

Other Important Titles from Twayne Publishers

GREAT HISTORIES SERIES

The Great Histories Series introduces to the modern reader works of most important historical writers from the time of Herodotus to the present day. Each volume is given over to the significant works of a single author and probes the scope of his contribution to the study of history and the development of historical writing. Intelligently written for enjoyable reading by layman or student, each contains a critical introduction by a distinguished scholar.

bbon	THE DECLINE AND FALL OF THE ROMAN EMPIRE *and Other Selected Writings* Edited by Hugh Trevor-Roper, Oriel College, Oxford	$6.50
hucydides	THE PELOPONNESIAN WARS Edited by P. A. Brunt, Oriel College, Oxford	$6.50
erodotus	HISTORY OF THE GREEK AND PERSIAN WAR Edited by W. G. Forrest, Wadham College, Oxford	$6.50
acitus	THE HISTORIES AND ANNALS Edited by Hugh Lloyd-Jones, Christ Church, Oxford	$6.50
oltaire	THE AGE OF LOUIS XIV *and Other Selected Writings* Edited by J. H. Brumfitt, St. Andrews University	$6.50
enry Adams	THE EDUCATION OF HENRY ADAMS *and Other Selected Writings* Edited by E. N. Saveth, New School for Social Research	$6.50
osephus	THE JEWISH WARS *and Other Selected Writings* Edited by M. I. Finley, Jesus College, Cambridge	$6.50
uicciardini	THE HISTORY OF ITALY *and Other Selected Writings* Edited by J. R. Hale, Jesus College, Oxford	$6.50
rescott	THE CONQUEST OF MEXICO THE CONQUEST OF PERU *and Other Selected Writings* Edited by Roger Howell, Bowdoin College	$6.50
Polybius	SELECTED HISTORICAL WRITINGS Edited by E. Badian, Durham University	$6.50

THE ANCIENT FLEETS

John Van Duyn Southworth

THE ANCIENT FLEETS is the story of naval warfare "under oars," beginning about 2600 B.C. and ending in 1597 A.D., when the last important galley action was fought. The navies of ancient Egypt, Phoenicia, Crete, Greece, Persia, Macedonia, Rome, Byzantium, the Saracens, the Norsemen, the Mediterranean peoples of the Middle Ages, and the peoples of the Far East all come within the purview of this volume. Types of ships, weapons, and naval procedures are presented as background for the story itself in this carefully researched, well-documented history, unprecedented in publishing annals. The author is long-time associate member of the United States Naval Institute, first President of the Syracuse Council of the Navy League of America, possessor of a unique personal library on naval and military history, and a widely published author.

November 384 pp. Illustrated Bibliography $7.50

Library of Congress Catalog Card Number: 67-16200

VARIORUM CIVIL DISOBEDIENCE

Annotated and with an Introduction by Walter Harding

This timely reissuance of Henry David Thoreau's principles of civil disobedience is accompanied by an informative and graceful introduction, which traces the world-wide influence exerted by Thoreau's words in Gandhi's movement to free India in the 1940's, in the Danish resistance against the Nazis, and in the civil disobedience movements in the United States. Walter Harding is Professor of English at State University College, Geneseo, New York, and Secretary of the Thoreau Society.

October $3.50

Library of Congress Catalog Card Number: 66-28155

THE NEW AMERICANS

Cecyle S. Neidle

A fascinating account of famous and unknown immigrants who have contributed to the cultural heritage of the United States, founded upon their own writings describing their reaction to the American challenge. Included are biographical summaries for each of the personalities, as well as discussions on the history of immigration for each period presented—from 1620 through the 1930's. Oscar Cargill, in his Foreword to the book, says of *THE NEW AMERICANS,* "I would make it . . . 'required reading' in any course that dared to prefix the word 'American' to its content." Dr. Neidle is a teacher and writer.

October 342 pp. Bibliography $6.00

Library of Congress Catalog Card Number: 67-25187

ZION RECONSIDERED Jakob J. Petuchowski $4.50

In this important book by Jakob J. Petuchowski, Professor of Rabbinics and Jewish Theology at Hebrew Union College, Zionism as a total philosophy of Jewish existence is examined and the role of Israel as the fulfillment of the Zionist dream is carefully questioned. Professor Petuchowski maintains throughout the book an attitude of reason and objectivity.

THE NEW SOVIET MAN $6.00

by Herschel and Edith Alt

The authors of RUSSIA'S CHILDREN, the first study of child welfare in the Soviet Union, now examine the status and condition of the contemporary Russian reared and educated since the revolution. The Soviet educational system has as one of its principal objectives the development of character traits which are identified with the "new" Soviet man, and this study was prompted by the following questions: How far has the Soviet Union achieved a new balance in motivation between egotism and altruism, between self-interest and the common welfare? What evidence is there of lessening competitive spirit among those brought up since the revolution? Have Soviet methods of child rearing and social control achieved a new type of motivation or merely more repression and harnessing of individual impulse?

... also available

ADMIRAL AND THE EMPRESS, THE • Lincoln Lorenz • $3.50
ASPECTS OF NEAR EAST SOCIETY • Moshe Zeitzer • $6.00*
ASPECTS OF REVOLT • Max Nomad • $5.00
BATTLE OF ATLANTA AND GEORGIA CAMPAIGN • William Key • $3.00
BELGIAN FOREIGN POLICY • Jane K. Miller • $5.00*
BEN BUTLER: THE SOUTH CALLED HIM "BEAST!" • Hans L. Trefousse • $5.00
BENJAMIN FRANKLIN WADE: RADICAL REPUBLICAN FROM OHIO • Hans L. Trefousse • $6.50
BIRTH OF THE ERIE CANAL, THE • Harvey Chalmers, II • $3.50
BLACK ROBE AND BUCKSKIN • John Perry Pritchett • $3.00
CAPTIVE NATIONS, THE • Roman Smal-Stocki • $3.50
CASE OF THE ABBE DE MONCRIF • Edward P. Shaw • $2.50*
CENTURY BOOK, THE, of the Long Island Historical Society • Walton H. Rawls, Ed. • $7.50
CIVIL WAR AND RECONSTRUCTION • Gideon Welles • $4.50
COLONIAL FREDERICKSBURG • Oscar H. Darter • $5.00
CONDUCT OF THE CHACO WAR • David H. Zook, Jr. • $6.00
CONGRESS AND THE CHALLENGE OF BIG GOVERNMENT • Oscar Kraines • $3.00*

CONVENTION PARLIAMENT, 1689, THE: A BIOGRAPHICAL STUDY OF ITS MEMBERS . George L. Cherry . $6.00*
COTTON REGENCY, THE . George R. Woolfolk . $5.00*
DETROIT: A STUDY IN URBAN DEVELOPMENT . Sidney Glazer . $3.50
EARLY ENGLISH LIBERALISM . George L. Cherry . $6.00*
ESTONIA: NATION ON THE ANVIL . Emanuel Nodel . $5.00*
EXPLORATIONS IN AMERICA BEFORE COLUMBUS . Hjalmar R. Holand . $6.95
FATEFUL VOYAGE OF CAPTAIN WILLIAM KIDD . Dunbar M. Hinrichs . $3.50
FEDERAL STREET PASTOR: LIFE OF WILLIAM ELLERY CHANNING . Madeleine Hooke Rice . $6.00
FRANCOIS-AUGUSTIN PARADIS DE MONCRIF . Edward P. Shaw . $3.50
FUNDAMENTAL LAWS OF THE STATE OF ISRAEL . Joseph Badi, Ed. . $15.00*
GERMANIC PEOPLE, THE . Francis Owen . $6.00*
GODKIN, E. L., AND AMERICAN FOREIGN POLICY . William Armstrong . $5.00
GOVERNMENT LAWYER . Malcolm A. Hoffman . $4.00
GOVERNMENT OF THE STATE OF ISRAEL, THE . Joseph Badi . $5.00*
GUATEMALA . Mario Rosenthal . $6.00
HETMAN OF THE UKRAINE . Clarence A. Manning . $3.50
HISTORIC FREDERICKSBURG . Oscar H. Darter . $1.00
HISTORY OF EFFICIENCY RATINGS IN THE FEDERAL GOVERNMENT . Mary S. Schinagl . $5.00*
IMPROPER BOSTONIAN: EMILY GREENE BALCH . Mercedes M. Randall . $6.00
ISLAM AND THE MODERN AGE . Ilse Lichtenstadter . $5.00
JOHN PURROY MITCHEL, BOY MAYOR OF NEW YORK . Edwin R. Lewinson . $6.50
JOHN QUINCY ADAMS: THE CRITICAL YEARS . Robert A. East . $5.00
LABOR AND POLITICS IN LIBYA AND ARAB AFRICA . John Norman . $4.50
LAST STAND OF THE NEZ PERCE, THE . Harvey Chalmers, II . $5.00
LENIN ON THE QUESTION OF NATIONALITY . Alfred D. Low . $4.00*
LETTERS OF OGIER GHISLAIN DE BUSBECQ TO THE HOLY ROMAN EMPEROR MAXIMILIAN II . Robert E. Jones and Bernerd C. Weber, Eds. . $5.00*
LINCOLN'S ADMINISTRATION . Gideon Welles . $4.50
MADAME DE STAEL AND THE ENGLISH . Roberta J. Forsberg . $5.95
MADAME DE STAEL AND FREEDOM TODAY . Roberta J. Forsberg and H. C. Nixon . $4.00
MARXISM AND FREEDOM . Raya Dunayevskaya . (2nd ed.—with a NEW CHAPTER on Mao Tse-Tung) $6.00 cloth; $1.98 paper
MIDDLE WEST, THE . Sidney Glazer . $3.50
MIND AND THE SWORD . Jay W. Stein . $4.50
MOSCOW AND THE UKRAINE . Basil Dmytryshyn . $5.00
NATHANAEL GREENE, STRATEGIST OF THE AMERICAN REVOLUTION . Theodore Thayer . $6.95
NEUTRALISM AND NATIONALISM IN FRANCE . John T. Marcus . $4.50
NEW SOVIET MAN, THE: HIS UPBRINGING AND CHARACTER DEVELOPMENT . Herschel and Edith Alt . $6.00
NORTH CAROLINA IN 1861 . James H. Boykin . $5.00*

OLD PENINSULA DAYS . Hjalmar R. Holand . $4.00
ORIGINS OF INTERVENTIONISM . Robert Sobel . $4.50
POLISH CHAPTER IN CIVIL WAR AMERICA, A . Joseph W. Wieczerzak . $6.00
PROPHET OF LIBERTY: WENDELL PHILLIPS . Oscar Sherwin . $10.00
PSYCHOLOGICAL STUDIES OF FAMOUS AMERICANS: THE CIVIL WAR ERA . Norman Kiell, Ed. . $6.00
RACE AND REICH . Joseph Tenenbaum . $7.50
RESTORATION EPISCOPATE, THE . Walter G. Simon . $5.00*
RISE AND FALL OF THE PATRIOT HUNTERS . Oscar Kinchen . $3.25
RUMANIA AT THE PARIS PEACE CONFERENCE: A STUDY OF THE DIPLOMACY OF IOAN I. C. BRATIANU . Sherman David Spector . $5.00*
SHORT HISTORY OF WARFARE, A . David H. Zook, Jr., and Robin Higham . $7.50
SOVIET RUSSIA AND INDIAN COMMUNISM . David N. Druhe . $8.50*
SOVIET RUSSIA IN WORLD POLITICS . Robert D. Warth . $7.50
STATES IN WEST GERMAN FEDERALISM, THE . Roger Hewes Wells . $4.00*
STRESEMANN AND THE GREATER GERMANY . Marvin L. Edwards . $5.00*
STUDIES IN MODERN EUROPEAN HISTORY . Frederick Cox, *et al.*, Ed. . $6.00
TEMPERAMENT AND CHARACTER OF THE ARABS . Sania Hamady . $5.00
TIBET: TODAY AND YESTERDAY . Tieh-tseng Li . $6.00*
TOWNSEND MOVEMENT, THE . Abraham Holtzman . $5.00
UNCIVIL WAR, THE . James Whyte . $5.00
UNITED STATES AND CUBA . Robert F. Smith . $5.00
UNITED STATES AND FRENCH SECURITY 1917-1921 . Louis A. R. Yates . $4.00
VALLEY FORGE UNITED STATES HISTORY SYLLABUS . David F. Gardiner . $1.95*
WHAT HAPPENED AT PEARL HARBOR? . Hans L. Trefousse . $6.00* cloth; $2.45 paper
WHAT HAPPENED IN CUBA? . Robert F. Smith . $6.00*
WOMAN SUFFRAGE MOVEMENT IN TENNESSEE, THE . A. Elizabeth Taylor . $3.50
ZARUMILLA-MARANON: THE ECUADOR-PERU DISPUTE . David H. Zook, Jr. . $6.00*